£2.-

D0996581

The Theatres of London

BY THE SAME AUTHORS

HAMLET THROUGH THE AGES
(Second revised edition)

THEATRICAL COMPANION TO SHAW

THEATRICAL COMPANION TO MAUGHAM

THEATRICAL COMPANION TO COWARD

THE ARTIST AND THE THEATRE
(The Story of the W. Somerset Maugham Theatrical Pictures)

A PICTURE HISTORY OF THE BRITISH THEATRE

A PICTURE HISTORY OF OPERA
(In collaboration with Philip Hope-Wallace)

THE GAY TWENTIES
(In collaboration with J. C. Trewin)

THE TURBULENT THIRTIES
(In collaboration with J. C. Trewin)

A PICTURE HISTORY OF GILBERT AND SULLIVAN

BRITISH MUSIC HALL. A STORY IN PICTURES
(Second revised edition)

THE LOST THEATRES OF LONDON

MUSICAL COMEDY. A STORY IN PICTURES

REVUE. A STORY IN PICTURES

PANTOMIME. A STORY IN PICTURES

A new edition revised and enlarged of

THE THEATRES OF LONDON

by

RAYMOND MANDER

and

JOE MITCHENSON

FOREWORD by IAN ALBERY

*Wherever there is a playhouse
the world will not go on amiss.*   *HAZLITT*

NEW ENGLISH LIBRARY
TIMES MIRROR

155444

Copyright © Raymond Mander and Joe Mitchenson 1961, 1975

First published 1961 by Rupert Hart-Davis Ltd
Second edition revised 1963

This new, revised and enlarged edition first
published by New English Library, Barnard's
Inn, Holborn, London, EC1 in 1975

All rights reserved. No part of this publication
may be reproduced or transmitted, in any form or
by any means, without permission of the publishers

Printed and bound in Great Britain by Pitman Press, Bath

0 45002123 8

FOR
SIR JOHN GIELGUD
in sincere admiration
and because there cannot be a theatre in
London in which at least one of his family,
the Terrys, has not at some time acted.

Come through one of the doors and sniff
the perfume from our altars—the dust
of our divine stage—and you then shall be
happy and be our real servant.

ELLEN TERRY

Contents

Contents vii

26	The Piccadilly Theatre	151
27	The Prince of Wales' Theatre (The Prince's Theatre)	155
28	The Queen's Theatre	162
29	The Regent Theatre (The Polytechnic Great Hall, The Polytechnic Theatre, The Cameo-Poly Cinema)	167
30	The Royal Court Theatre	170
31	The Royalty Theatre (The London Opera House, The Stoll Theatre)	179
32	The St Martin's Theatre	186
33	The Savoy Theatre	192
34	The Shaftesbury Theatre	199
35	The Strand Theatre (The Waldorf Theatre, The Whitney Theatre)	204
36	The Vaudeville Theatre	210
37	The Victoria Palace (The Royal Standard Music Hall)	219
38	The Westminster Theatre	224
39	The Whitehall Theatre	228
40	The Windmill Theatre	231
41	Wyndham's Theatre	234

Part II

The Outer Ring

	Introduction	243
1	The Greenwich Theatre (Crowder's Music Hall, The Parthenon, Barnard's, The Greenwich Hippodrome), Greenwich, S.E.10	246
2	Lyric Theatre (The Lyric Opera House, The New Lyric), Hammersmith, W.6	249
3	The Mermaid Theatre, Blackfriars, E.C.4	256
4	The Old Vic (The Royal Coburg Theatre, The Royal Victoria Theatre), Lambeth, S.E.1	260
5	The Open Air Theatre, Regent's Park, N.W.1	267
6	The Round House, Chalk Farm, N.W.1	269
7	Sadler's Wells Theatre, Finsbury, E.C.1	273
8	The Shaw Theatre, Euston Road, N.W.1	280
9	The Theatre Royal, Stratford, E.15	283
10	Wimbledon Theatre, S.W.19	288
11	The Young Vic, The Cut, S.E.1	291

Part III

Club Theatres

	Introduction	295
1	The Arts Theatre	297
2	The Players' Theatre (The Arches Music Hall, The Hungerford, Gatti's, Charing Cross Music Hall)	299

Part IV
Otherwise Engaged

APPENDICES

Foreword

'THERE ARE TWO WAYS FOR A CITY TO DIE. IT CAN FAIL TO PROVIDE SHELTER AND THE DIGNITY OF A LIVELIHOOD, AND IT CAN LOSE THE CREATIVE FORCE THAT MAKES IT CENTRAL TO MEN'S EXISTENCE. WITHOUT THE FIRST, NO CITY CAN SURVIVE, WITHOUT THE SECOND NO CITY IS GREAT.'

New York Times Editorial of January 15th 1972.

After an absence of several years, this timely re-appearance of a revised, up-dated version of Mander and Mitchenson's fascinating record of the surviving London theatres, with their triumphs and disasters, is most welcome. This is a vital document—a must for every theatregoer's bookshelf, which, unfortunately, in succeeding reprints may well suffer casualties, as developers with office blocks and Local Authorities with road schemes rub out some well-loved theatres.

To proclaim that the British and West End Theatre is dying, or on its last legs, has been fashionable over the past fifty years and, indeed, Theatre has had to survive the onslaughts of Talkies, Technicolor and Television, which have not only provided alternative forms of entertainment for the public but also siphoned off artists and technicians. However, as long as the theatres themselves have survived, youth and talent have been drawn in, and West End theatres now have more paying customers throughout the year than ever before, even though the majority of these for many months of the year may be visitors to London.

Our present London theatres range from Victorian to the present day, but a characteristic common to many is that the freeholds are owned by ground landlords eagerly awaiting the termination of existing Leases, so that in conjunction with grandiose Local Authority comprehensive development and road schemes they can throw up 1984 office blocks.

As a sop to public opinion and the arts, Local
Authorities often express concern about the future of
theatres, but practical action is usually limited to insisting
on an ersatz replacement theatre in the basement of the
new office tower. This approach is analogous to tearing
down a cathedral and replacing it with a chapel next to
the boilerhouse, as a theatre should not only make an
architectural statement but be a focal point for the
neighbourhood.

In Piccadilly Circus, Covent Garden and elsewhere,
theatres have become rallying points for embattled community and amenity groups, threatened jointly by the
property developers and the very Local Authorities that
should be protecting them. I would prophesy that future
editions of *The Theatres of London* will list several battle
honours for theatres that, in fighting for their survival,
have helped save the heart of the West End from being
comprehensively developed out of all recognition.

Ian B. Albery
1974

Introduction

To chronicle the theatres of London has tended, over the
years, to become a melancholy task. The Arts Council
thought fit to commission a report in 1973 by Sir James
Richards on 'Planning and redevelopment in London's
entertainment area with special reference to the theatre',
and many theatres have been placed on the Statutory List
of Buildings of Architectural or Historical Importance
issued by the Department of the Environment. Nevertheless, the threatened destruction and closure of numerous
theatres has to be recorded since the time of the first two
editions of our book, in 1961 and 1963, and now, in 1974,
the situation is anything but stable.

Since our last revision, the long reign of the Lord
Chamberlain as Censor of plays and Licenser of theatres,
which commenced in 1737, ended on 26 September 1968.
The following night *Hair* was produced, complete with
nudity and four letter words, but little in the ensuing years
can have shocked or startled anyone in a permissive age
except the Aunt Ednas or the Mrs Whitehouses. The
former, Terence Rattigan's creation, has probably 'got with
it' or vanished altogether from her stall, and the latter, it
would seem, is not a dedicated theatre-goer, being concerned with the more fugitive dramatic arts.

The last full history of the West End and Suburban Music
Halls was covered by Charles Douglas Stuart and A. J.
Park in *The Variety Stage* (1895) and much useful infor-
mation on Sadler's Wells, the Lyceum and some lost
theatres is to be found in *Some London Theatres Past and
Present* by Michael Williams (1883), Erroll Sherson's
London's Lost Theatres of the Nineteenth Century (1925)
and our own *Lost Theatres of London* (1968).

In 1970 the Library Association published *London
Theatres and Music Halls 1850–1950*, which had originally
been a thesis, by Diana Howard. A valuable book, though
it lacked imagination, and must be used with extreme
caution both pictorially and factually.

New Theatres in Britain, by Frederick Bentham (a Tabs,

Rank-Strand Electric publication, 1970) covers buildings from 1957.

Between those books and these present pages lies over half a century of more or less unrecorded history. Many new theatres have come and many more, alas, have gone. The Second World War put an end to the Shaftesbury Theatre (in Shaftesbury Avenue), the Kingsway Theatre and the Little Theatre (in the Adelphi). The Gaiety Theatre and the Royalty Theatre (in Dean Street), both of which were derelict before the war, later vanished. It was not until the St James's Theatre slipped through the net of town planning and was demolished in 1957, amid much public discussion, that the authorities demonstrated that they would do their best to make it impossible for London to completely lose any of its theatres. It is now stipulated that in any redevelopment of the site of an existing theatre, a new place of entertainment must be included in the plans. Under these conditions came the building of the first new West End theatres, the Royalty in 1960 and the New London in 1973. The Royalty arose on part of the site of the Stoll Theatre in Kingsway and was the first new theatre to be built since the Saville in 1931 which is now, alas, converted into two cinemas, ABC 1 and 2. The New London was built on the site of the Winter Garden.

Nevertheless the threat of demolition still hangs over many London theatres, particularly those covering land in valuable central positions which offer great possibilities to the highly commercially-minded property developer.

The listing of and Preservation Orders on many buildings, achieved by placing them on the Statutory List of Buildings of Special Architectural or Historic Importance by the Department of the Environment, may help to ease the strain. During this century in the West End the cinema has claimed both theatres and music halls: the Empire, the Alhambra (now the Odeon, Leicester Square), and Daly's (now the Warner Theatre) were all completely rebuilt as cinemas between the wars. Other West End music halls vanished altogether. The Tivoli, closed in 1914, was rebuilt after the First War as a cinema, which in turn was completely swept away for commercial purposes. The Holborn Empire was a Second World War casualty and the Oxford, after conversion to a theatre, completely vanished to give way to a Corner House in the mid-twenties. To this picture of the more recent diminution of London's places of live entertainment must be added the Saville, the Prince Charles (built in 1962 but now a cinema) and the large number of club and experimental theatres which came and went between the wars. These were an economic casualty rather than one which could be blamed on the coming of television, and their revival in the last few years in basements, attics and pubs must be the subject for another book.

In compiling this book we have tried, wherever possible, to go back to contemporary accounts of the building of the theatres, mostly from the files of *The Era* and *The Stage*, accounts which have not so far been reprinted and will, we hope, be of interest. The modern seating capacities are those given by the theatres themselves in 1974. The form of the work and its divisions are self-explanatory. We have made use of an unpublished manuscript, *London Playhouses*, by Arthur F. M. Beales, which was uncompleted at the time of his death in 1949 when his manuscript and notes passed into our care. We would like to pay tribute to the pioneer work of our old friend 'Peter' Beales, which has been of inestimable value to us.

We would also like to thank the following who have been particularly helpful in answering awkward questions with which we have inundated them: the Greater London Council, Historic Buildings Department (Anne Riches); the Middlesex County Record Office; the Enthoven Collection at the Victoria and Albert Museum (Anthony Latham) and the Librarians of the outer London districts. We would also like to thank Dr Richard Southern for casting his expert eye over the chronology in the appendix; Dr Francis Sheppard for his assistance, Mrs Constance Göhns, who untiringly coped with the transcription of our illegible manuscript when it was first written in 1961 and to Mary Quinnell who has coped with its revision. We would also like to thank Reginald Cornish of the Society of West End Theatre Managers, and last, but not least, Ian Albery for his foreword. It was after the first edition of the book was published that Ian asked us to tea in the Royal Retiring Room at Wyndham's, then used as his office. He expressed interest in our work and has done so ever since, for which we are deeply grateful, and we are only too pleased to include him between the covers of our book.

It was sad that in June 1963 Timothy Birdsall died at the early age of twenty-seven, but we are proud to have given him one of his first commissions—to draw the theatres of London. These were exhibited at Foyle's Art Gallery in May 1961 on the first publication of the book. The originals are now scattered in collections or in the theatres themselves. Whenever possible we have retained his impression of a theatre even when, as in the case of the New becoming the Albery, there has been a change of name. The new drawings of recent theatres have been added by Ellie Willats and Sidney Ferris (Wimbledon Theatre).

Theatres come and go, but the only continuity in the London theatre scene, in spite of all the re-planners, is *The Mousetrap* which, during its twenty-second year, moved, under Peter Saunders' management, from the Ambassadors to the St Martin's Theatre next door.

WEST END
THEATRES
OF LONDON

1. Adelphi
2. Albery
3. Aldwych
4. Ambassadors
5. Apollo
6. Cambridge
7. Coliseum
8. Comedy
9. Royal Opera House
10. Criterion
11. The Theatre Royal Drury Lane
12. Duchess
13. Duke of York's
14. Fortune
15. Garrick
16. Globe
17. Haymarket
18. Her Majesty's
19. London Casino
20. London Palladium
21. Lyric
22. May Fair
23. New London
24. Palace
25. Phoenix
26. Piccadilly
27. Prince of Wales'
28. Queen's
29. Regent
30. Royal Court
31. Royalty
32. St. Martin's
33. Savoy
34. Shaftesbury
35. Strand
36. Vaudeville
37. Victoria Palace
38. Westminster
39. Whitehall
40. Windmill
41. Wyndham's

PART 1

The West End

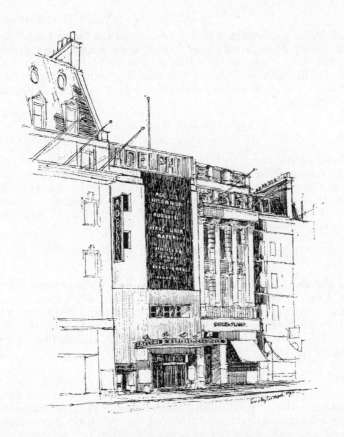

1 · The Adelphi Theatre

(The Sans Pareil, The Theatre Royal, Adelphi, The Century Theatre)

Strand, W.C.2

THE FIRST THEATRE

Opened as the Sans Pareil 27 November 1806, with *Miss Scott's Entertainment.* Became the Adelphi Theatre 18 October 1819 and the Theatre Royal, Adelphi, October 1829.

THE SECOND THEATRE

Capacity: 1500

Opened as the Theatre Royal, New Adelphi, 27 December 1858, with *Mr Webster's Company is requested at a Photographic Soirée,* an introductory apropos sketch, by Edmund Yates and H. Harrington, followed by an occasional address written by Shirley Brooks and spoken by

Sarah Woolgar. After which a revival of the farce *Good for
Nothing* by J. B. Buckstone, concluding with a pantomime
*Mother Red Cap; or Harlequin and Johnny Gilpin; His
Ride to Edmonton.* Under the management of Benjamin
Webster. After 1867 the name the Royal Adelphi Theatre
was adopted.

THE THIRD THEATRE
Capacity: 1297

Opened as the Century Theatre 11 September 1901 with *The
Whirl of the Town*, a musical absurdity by Hugh Morton,
music by Gustave Kerker. Produced by George B.
McLellan and Frank de Jong, under the management of
Tom B. Davis. The name reverted to the Royal Adelphi
Theatre in February 1902.

THE FOURTH THEATRE
Capacity: 1481

Opened as the Royal Adelphi Theatre, 3 December 1930
with *Ever Green*, a musical show by Benn W. Levy, lyrics
by Lorenz Hart, music by Richard Rodgers. Produced by
Frank Collins under the management of Charles B.
Cochran. The 'Royal' has been dropped from the name
since 1940.

*

The present Adelphi Theatre is virtually the fourth new
theatre on the site, though the earlier theatres underwent
many reconstructions, and parts of the buildings have over-
lapped and remained incorporated in their successors.

At the beginning of the nineteenth century some very
dilapidated dwellings stood in the Strand; these dated back
to the time of Charles II and were traditionally said to have
been part of a farm and dairy supplying cream and butter to
the Royal household. They were situated next to the shop
of John Scott, a colour maker, who had accumulated a large
fortune by the invention of a particular kind of washing blue
called 'True Blue'. In 1802 he acquired the leases of these
properties, numbers 411 and 412, at a cost of £10,000, pulled
down the old buildings and built a theatre in order to exhibit
the histrionic talent of his daughter. The theatre opened on
27 November 1806 as The Sans Pareil Theatre. The opening
programme consisted of songs, recitations and imitations,
all given by Jane Scott, and called *Miss Scott's Entertainment*. The programme finished with a display of fireworks.
The talented Miss Scott also acted as manager. The theatre
became very popular, Scott obtained a licence, and the
Entertainment eventually gave way to performances of
melodrama in which Miss Scott usually took the leading
role (she was later to create Susan in *Black-Eyed Susan* at

the Surrey in 1829). As 'Adelphi Drama' was to become
almost a byword in future years, it is interesting to note
this early beginning.

In 1814 John Scott spent £5000 on redecorating the
theatre and building a new front. During this period the
theatre was often billed as the Strand Theatre—the Sans
Pareil. In 1819 he sold it for £25,000 to Messrs Jones and
Rodwell, who again reconstructed it and opened it as the
Adelphi Theatre on 18 October 1819. At this reopening the
public were informed that 'the brilliant effect of the gas
chandelier suspended from the dome is the subject of universal admiration'. An opening address written by William
Moncrieff was delivered by Mrs Chatterley, and the entertainment commenced with a *burletta* entitled *The Green
Dragon; or, I've Quite Forgot*. Planché described the legal
definition of a *burletta* as follows: 'The Adelphi . . . had
the Lord Chamberlain's licence for the performance of
burlettas only, which description caused much controversy
in and out of court, we were desired to understand dramas
containing not less than five pieces of vocal music in each
act.' As a means of circumventing the existing legal restric-
tions on dramatic performance the introduction of 'vocal
music' into otherwise 'straight plays' was adopted, thus
turning them into *burlettas*. It is recorded that even *Othello*
was once presented as a *burletta* by 'having a low pianoforte
accompaniment, the musician striking a chord once in five
minutes, but always so as to be totally inaudible'. This state
of affairs remained in force until the monopoly of the Patent
Theatres was broken in 1843.

Later on Jones and Rodwell established a reputation for
staging dramatic versions of the novels of Walter Scott.

By 1821 the Adelphi had become one of the most popular
houses of entertainment in London, and in that year it underwent further alterations and improvements. Theatrical
history was made when *Tom and Jerry*, by William
Moncrieff (from Pierce Egan's book), secured the honour
of being the first play to run a hundred consecutive
performances—from 26 November 1821 to 30 March
1822.

In 1825 the theatre again changed hands and was taken
over by Daniel Terry and Frederick Yates who bought it
for £25,000. It reopened under their management on 10
October of that year. A drama by Edward Fitzball, *The
Pilot*, adapted from the romance of Fenimore Cooper with
T. P. Cooke, beat the record of *Tom and Jerry*, and ran for
two hundred nights from 31 October 1825. In 1828 Terry's
financial position became considerably embarrassed, and
the partnership changed the following season to Yates and
Charles Mathews. Both Yates and Mathews were 'one-man
entertainers' before they joined forces (Mathews paid
£17,000 for his partnership).

The English Opera Company, burned out of their own theatre, the Lyceum, gave a summer season here in June 1831. Dramatic versions of the novels of Charles Dickens were seen. *The Pickwick Papers* appeared in 1837 and was followed by *Nicholas Nickleby* (1838), *Oliver Twist* (1839), *The Old Curiosity Shop* (1840), *Barnaby Rudge* (1841), *A Christmas Carol* and *The Chimes* (1844), and *The Cricket on the Hearth* (1845).

Meanwhile, in 1833, Madame Céleste made her first appearance in a speaking part at this theatre, and in 1834 the mechanical device of 'the Sinking Stage' was first exhibited in this country. The next year we find the theatre described by a contemporary writer as 'by far the most fashionably attended theatre in London'. In this year Charles Mathews died and was succeeded by his son, Charles James. But the younger Mathews retired after the end of his first season and was succeeded by a man named Gladstone, whom Yates took into partnership.

A new 'composition' façade to the theatre, designed by Samuel Beazley, was added in 1840. Yates died in 1842 and Gladstone was joined by Mrs Yates in management.

In October 1844 Madame Céleste and Benjamin Webster became joint managers, and in September 1848 some reconstruction and new interior decorations were carried out by Digby Wyatt, the style being suggested by his collection of Louis XIV engravings. In 1853 Webster became sole manager. On 2 June 1858 the theatre, having fallen into 'incurable disrepair', was closed for demolition. The last performance was the occasion of a benefit for Webster, who received a testimonial and a gold watch.

A new theatre was built to the designs of T. H. Wyatt, the work being done by J. Willson. It was larger than the old building and was much wider. It had an act-drop by Clarkson Stanfield. This building opened on 27 December 1858, with a pantomime and other attractions.

In 1859 *The Dead Heart* was produced and on 10 September 1860 Dion Boucicault's play *The Colleen Bawn* began a successful run of 231 performances, which counted as a very long run in those days. It was followed by *The Octoroon*. Other successes were *Leah* with Kate Bateman (1863) and *Rip Van Winkle* with Joseph Jefferson (1865). On 31 August 1867 was Kate Terry's farewell benefit, and in December of that year *No Thoroughfare* by Charles Dickens and Wilkie Collins had a successful presentation with Charles Fechter, who also produced a series of melodramatic romances.

From 1870 to 1872 the management was shared by Webster and F. B. Chatterton, the latter taking sole charge in 1872. In 1873 there was a short season of opera by the Carl Rosa Company, and *The Shaughraun* by

Boucicault (after a production at Drury Lane in 1875) was revived here with great success in 1876.

The Gattis took over the theatre in 1879; it was renovated and redecorated, and they presented many successes. *The Harbour Lights*, a drama by George R. Sims and Henry Pettitt, ran for 510 performances from 23 December 1885. This was the period at which G. R. Sims, Henry Pettitt and Sydney Grundy collaborated in producing 'Adelphi dramas': *Michael Strogoff* (1881) and *In the Ranks* (1883) preceded *The Harbour Lights*; and *The Bells of Haslemere* (1887), *The Union Jack* (1888) and *London Day by Day* (1889) were subsequent successes.

In 1887 the Gattis again reconstructed the theatre and carried out extensive redecorations. They bought a public house known as the Hampshire Hog, 410 Strand, and the next house, number 409, together with the Nell Gwynne Tavern in Bull Inn Court, in order to enlarge the theatre. They built a new enlarged façade, part of which still remains above the Crystal Room. The architect was Spencer Chadwick.

The reopening play was *The Bells of Haslemere*. From 1890 there was presented a series of popular melodramas which were the work of G. R. Sims and Robert Buchanan, including *The English Rose*, *The Trumpet Call*, and *The Lights of Home*. On 16 December 1897 there occurred one of the tragedies in the history of the stage when the popular actor and leading man of so many melodramas, William Terriss, was assassinated by a madman as he was entering the theatre by the Royal Entrance in Maiden Lane, which he used as his private door (the stage door of the theatre was then in Bull Inn Court). The play in which he was appearing was William Gillette's *Secret Service*. Melodramas continued to be played until 1900.

The theatre was almost completely reconstructed in March 1901, with an extended frontage, this time westward (the Queensland Government coming into possession of the other part), and the stage door moved to Maiden Lane. The remodelling was the work of Ernest Runtz. It was reopened on September 11 by Tom B. Davis with an American musical comedy called *The Whirl of the Town*. The name of the theatre was changed at this time, becoming the Century Theatre. Popular indignation at this was so strong, however, that the original name was reinstated in 1902.

Though the Gattis remained the owners, the theatre was let to various managers in the years to come.

In 1904 the Adelphi came under the management of Otho Stuart, and became noted for productions of poetic dramas by modern authors and for Shakespearean revivals. Among the plays which he presented were *The Prayer of the Sword* by J. B. Fagan, *Tristram and Iseult* by J. Comyns Carr, *Dr. Wake's Patient* by N. Gayer Mackay and 'Robert Ord'

(Edith Ostlere), and *The Virgin Goddess* by Rudolf Besier.
Stuart's Shakespearean revivals included *The Taming of the
Shrew* (Oscar Asche and Lily Brayton), *A Midsummer
Night's Dream* (also with Oscar Asche and Lily Brayton),
Hamlet (with H. B. Irving), and *Measure for Measure* (with
Walter Hampden, Oscar Asche and Lily Brayton). We read
that 'his management was distinguished for its judgement,
enterprise and liberality'.

In 1908 the Adelphi became the home of musical
comedy under George Edwardes and from November 5 of
that year *The Quaker Girl* ran for 536 performances;
subsequent successes were *The Girl in the Taxi* and *The
Dancing Mistress* (1912), *The Girl from Utah* (1913), *Tina*
(1915), *High Jinks* (1916). Alfred Butt then took over and
presented *The Boy*, which was a musical adaptation of
Pinero's *The Magistrate* and this ran for 810 performances
(1917), *The Naughty Princess* (1920), *The Golden Moth*
(1921), *The Island King* (1922) and *Head Over Heels*
(1923).

The run of musical comedies was broken in June 1922
by a production of *The Way of an Eagle*, a dramatisation of
the popular novel by Ethel M. Dell.

Peter Pan at Christmas 1923 brought Gladys Cooper to
the Adelphi and she remained there in management, reviving
Diplomacy and Pinero's *Iris*. The next years are filled by
The Green Hat, Tallulah Bankhead in a stage version of
Michael Arlen's novel, *Betty in Mayfair*, a musical
comedy version of John Hastings Turner's play *Lilies of
the Field*, with Evelyn Laye, both in 1925, and *Aloma*, a
sultry South Sea Island drama, in 1926.

The outstanding productions of the last three years of this
building's life were *Mr Cinders* with Binnie Hale and
Bobby Howes (1929), which came in between two
Jack Hulbert and Cicely Courtneidge revues, *Clowns in
Clover* (1927), and *The House that Jack Built* (1929).
After the latter's run of 270 performances the theatre
closed.

In 1930 the theatre was again reconstructed, the architect
being Ernest Schaufelberg. As a result of this rebuilding
nothing remained of the old theatres except the outer walls
and the Royal Entrance beside the stage door in Maiden
Lane. (The part of the 1887 frontage, now an amusement arcade (or the Crystal Room) also remains.) The
vestibule and main staircase were carried out in black
marble, relieved by deep rose-coloured doors, chromium-
plated grilles, and Lalique fountain lights and Sunray
trough-lighting. The house was also refronted in imitation
black and grey marble.

A review of this work in the *Architects' Journal* of 3
December 1930 is headed 'Trigonometry in the Theatre'
and says:

The reconstructed Adelphi Theatre is designed with a complete absence of curves. Externally and internally the entire conception is carried out in straight lines and angles, the angle of thirty-two degrees being used as the master note. Considerable public attention was rivetted on the work during its final stages, owing to the big hustle performed by the builders to keep to the schedule. It is understood that the theatre was to open on November 24, and that the owners were to pay Mr Cochran a penalty of £450 for every day they were late in handing over the theatre . . . The lower half of the walls and fronts of the two circles has been panelled in wood of a deep orange colour, perfectly plain, polished and with no decorative motif whatsoever. This, with the general colour scheme of orange, green, and gold, with bronze insets on the underside of the circles, gives a most bizarre and opulent atmosphere.

The general contractors for this work were the Pitcher Construction Company. The central black triangular panel in the façade was removed in 1937, the space flattened and a pediment carried across the top bearing the name Adelphi.

The Gatti family still remained owners of the theatre with Musical Plays Ltd as lessees.

The theatre reopened on December 3 with *Ever Green*, under the management of Charles B. Cochran. This was the first of a series of successes to be produced here by Cochran, and there followed *Grand Hotel* by Vicki Baum in 1931; *Helen!* an *opéra bouffe* based on *La Belle Hélène*, written, with additions, by A. P. Herbert, to Offenbach's music (1932); *Words and Music*, the revue in which Noël Coward was responsible for all the lyrics and music (1932); *Nymph Errant*, a play with music by Cole Porter, adapted by Romney Brent from James Laver's novel (1933); *Magnolia Street*, a play by Louis Golding and A. R. Rawlinson (1934); *Stop Press*, a revue presented by Clifford Whitley (1935). Cochran returned with *Follow the Sun*, another revue on a lavish and spectacular scale (1936); and *Home and Beauty*, A. P. Herbert's Coronation revue (1937).

Balalaika, a musical play produced in December 1936, left the Adelphi to continue its run elsewhere, but returned to its first home in February 1938 to complete its 570 performances. The next years are not outstanding, and include a mixture of revues, musicals and plays. A revival of *Dear Octopus* in 1940 gave London playgoers their last glimpse of the great Marie Tempest. Opera and ballet were staged in the early war years until, in 1942, a revival of Ivor Novello's *The Dancing Years* opened and ran 969 performances (its original production at Drury Lane was broken by the outbreak of war in 1939).

After this there is nothing of importance to recall until Cochran returned to the theatre presenting A. P. Herbert's *Big Ben*, in 1946, followed by *Bless the Bride* in 1947 and *Tough at the Top* in 1949.

In 1950 Jack Hylton, who had become lessee of the theatre during the run of *The Dancing Years*, began a series of revues, featuring broadcasting stars, which were to be the main attractions for the next six years.

In 1955 the Gattis sold their interest in the theatre to Woolworth's, but in November 1960 it was announced that, as permission to turn the premises into a store had been refused, a development corporation was preparing plans for an office block, including a theatre, to replace the Adelphi at the end of the present lease.

Auntie Mame (1958) with Beatrice Lillie, and *Blitz!*, which opened in April 1962, proved to be spectacular successes.

They were to be followed by Dora Bryan's revue, *Six of One*, in September 1963 which ran for 306 performances. The next successful musical production was *Maggie May* running for 499 performances, then came the return of Anna Neagle, under the management of Harold Fielding, in *Charlie Girl* in December 1965 which continued until 1971 with well over 2000 performances, followed by *Meet Me in London* starring Tommy Steele. A very successful revival of *Show Boat* in July 1971 and of *The King and I* in October 1973 kept the theatre busy well into the following year.

2 · The Albery Theatre

(The New Theatre)

St Martin's Lane, W.C.2

Capacity: 877

Opened as the New Theatre on 12 March 1903 with a revival of *Rosemary*, a play by Louis N. Parker and Murray Carson. Produced by and under the management of Charles Wyndham.

THE BUILDING

The New was the second theatre to be erected in St Martin's Lane. The Trafalgar Square (Duke of York's) opened in 1892 and the London Coliseum, though in preparation since 1902, did not eventually open its doors until 1904.

Charles Wyndham, when he left the Criterion in 1899 after managing there for twenty-three years, moved to the theatre he had built in Charing Cross Road, and to which he had given his name (see No. 41). In 1901 overtures were made to Wyndham to sell the rest of the land he had been obliged to acquire when he built Wyndham's Theatre, but, the negotiations falling through, he decided to build another theatre on the vacant site.

This plot fronting on St Martin's Lane is bounded on one side by St Martin's Court, which also runs behind the theatre.

A name for the theatre was undecided and tentatively it was referred to while building as the 'new' theatre and this eventually was adopted as its name; it is also opposite New Street (now New Row).

The opening night souvenir says:

The front elevation is of the free classic order, and is at once dignified and effective. The Theatre is approached by a roomy Vestibule leading to one of the most picturesque Crush Rooms to be found in any theatre in London. Mr W. G. R. Sprague, the Architect, has excelled himself, in this, his thirtieth theatre, and from an architectural point of view Sir Charles's New Theatre is the acme of perfection.

On entering the Auditorium one is immediately struck with the exquisite lines on which the theatre has been designed, a clear and uninterrupted view of the stage being obtained from literally every part of the Theatre, even to the extreme corner seats at the back of the gallery.

The Theatre is constructed on the modern cantilever principle, thus rendering columns of any sort unnecessary. The Theatre is equipped with all modern and scientific appliances. In short, everything that ingenuity and experience can accomplish has been done.

Perhaps the most noteworthy feature of the Theatre is the exquisite treatment of decoration, which is of the period of Louis XVI and has been adhered to, even down to the minutest details, throughout.

The prominent colours are white and gold, relieved by curtains and hangings of Rose du Barri brocade and antique velvet.

The seats in the Stalls and Dress Circle are exceptionally beautiful being upholstered in Aubusson tapestry. Over the Proscenium will be seen a perfectly modelled gilt trophy emblematic of Peace and Music, while on either side are models of Cupids, illustrating Winter and Summer, copied from bronzes in the collections of Mr Claude Ponsonby.

The panels in the Auditorium are decorated with beautiful portrait medallions of the French Kings and Queens.

Claude Ponsonby, a friend of Wyndham's, acted as artistic adviser on the decoration of the theatre; the construction was in the hands of Messrs Owen Lucas and

Pyke. A three-tier house, it still retains its elegant Edwardian atmosphere.

Its name was changed to the Albery Theatre on 1 January 1973. The original Dress Circle, Upper Circle and Gallery are now called Royal Circle, Grand Circle and Balcony.

THE PLAYS

The theatre opened with a revival of *Rosemary* on 12 March 1903, in which Wyndham and Mary Moore appeared. It was put on for only a limited number of nights, and, with a special matinée of *David Garrick* on March 25, served to launch the theatre. The following month Forbes-Robertson transferred his production of *The Light that Failed* here from the Lyric to finish its run. Mrs Patrick Campbell had a short season and on September 23, Wyndham appeared in Hubert Henry Davies' play *Mrs Gorringe's Necklace*, which he brought from Wyndham's Theatre. The next year he produced several new plays and revivals of his old and tried successes.

In August 1904, during the rebuilding of the Haymarket Theatre, Cyril Maude and his company appeared here in *Beauty and the Barge*, by W. W. Jacobs and Louis N. Parker. Fred Terry and Julia Neilson played an annual season of about six months' duration at this theatre from 1905 to 1913. Their great success, *The Scarlet Pimpernel*, was produced in January 1905 and revived in the December. Further revivals of this play were also given in January and December 1907, April 1908, March 1910, and January and June 1911. Two more outstanding productions during 1905 were C. M. S. McLellan's *Leah Kleschna* and Hubert Henry Davies' *Captain Drew on Leave*, in the first of which Lena Ashwell scored a great success.

Fred Terry and Julia Neilson's other successes included *Dorothy o' the Hall* (1906), *'Matt' of Merrymount* (1908), *Henry of Navarre* (1909 and 1910), and *The Popinjay* (1911).

Between these seasons several successful productions held the stage at the New Theatre: *Amasis*, a comic opera by Frederick Fenn and Michael Faraday (1906), with Ruth Vincent and *Count Hannibal* (1910), being among those particularly worthy of mention. In 1911 Fred Terry revived *As You Like It* and *Romeo and Juliet* to introduce his daughter Phyllis to the stage.

Allan Aynesworth entered into the management in August 1912 with *Ready Money*, a comedy by James Montgomery, which ran for 232 performances; he followed this with *Bought and Paid For*, a comedy by George Broadhurst, in 1913.

In February 1914 a musical play called *The Joy-Ride Lady*, with music by Jean Gilbert, ran for over a hundred performances, and in May of the same year *Grumpy* started a run of 151 performances, with Cyril Maude in his famous part of Andrew Bullivant, in which he had scored a great success in New York.

Dion Boucicault became manager in December 1915 and opened with a revival of *Peter Pan*, which then made its home here each Christmas until 1919. The successive Peters at the New Theatre were Unity More (1915 and 1916), Fay Compton (1917), Faith Celli (1918), and Georgette Cohen (1919). Boucicault then produced a series of successes including Somerset Maugham's *Caroline* (1916), 141 performances; A. E. Thomas's *Her Husband's Wife* (1916), a revival of Somerset Maugham's *The Land of Promise* (1917); J. M. Barrie's *The Old Lady Shows Her Medals* (1917); Pinero's *The Freaks*, which he described as 'an idyll of Suburbia' (1918); A. A. Milne's *Belinda* (1918), and the same author's *Mr Pim Passes By* (1920). Leon M. Lion had a season here, during which he produced *The Chinese Puzzle* (1918), *Jack O' Jingles* (1919), and *Little Women* (1919), in which Katharine Cornell made her one and only London appearance. In July 1920 Noël Coward's first produced play, *'I'll Leave It to You'*, was staged. He appeared in it himself, the play was presented by Mary Moore, and it ran for five weeks, an inauspicious start for one of our leading dramatists.

The name of Matheson Lang was associated with this theatre for many years; on numerous occasions he took over the management and produced a series of successes including *Carnival* (1920), during the run of which he also gave matinées of *Othello*; he revived *Carnival* here in 1923 and 1925; *The Wandering Jew* by E. Temple Thurston (1920), *Christopher Sly*, an English translation of a 'fantastic play' by Giovacchino Forzano (1921); *Blood and Sand* (1921); *The Great Well* by Sutro (1922); *The Bad Man* (1923); *The Hour and the Man* (1924); *The Tyrant* (1925).

March 1924 saw the production of Bernard Shaw's *Saint Joan*, the play in which, according to many critics, he reached the height of his powers. In the name part of this play Sybil Thorndike scored one of her greatest successes: it ran for 244 performances. She had also been here in management in *Jane Clegg*, *Scandal* and *The Cenci* in 1922, and with *Cymbeline* and *The Lie* in 1923.

In July 1925 Robert Atkins assumed management of the New, when he produced Israel Zangwill's *We Moderns*. The great success of 1926 was Margaret Kennedy and Basil Dean's dramatic version of the former's book *The Constant Nymph*. Produced in September of that year, it ran for 587 performances, during which both Noël Coward and John Gielgud played Lewis Dodd.

The Wrecker, by Arnold Ridley and Bernard Merivale, ran for 165 performances from December 1927, and two plays by P. G. Wodehouse and Ian Hay, an excellent

comedy-author partnership, *A Damsel in Distress* (1928),
and *Baa, Baa, Black Sheep* (1929) ran for 234 and 115
performances respectively.

The beginning of the thirties was uneventful though
numerous transfers, short runs and foreign seasons kept the
theatre busy. The 'black and white' production of *Twelfth
Night* left its mark on stage history in 1932, and later the
same year Barry Jackson presented Shaw's Malvern
Festival play *Too True to be Good*.

The next important chapter in the history of the New
Theatre began in February 1933 when John Gielgud became
associated with the theatre. Gordon Daviot's *Richard of
Bordeaux* was produced and began its run of 472 performances. In June 1934 came the same author's *Queen of
Scots*, with 106 performances, Gwen Ffrangcon-Davies
playing the leading part. November 1934 brought *Hamlet*,
which secured the second longest run on record for this
play, 155 performances, and this was followed by Rodney
Ackland's adaptation of Hugh Walpole's *The Old Ladies*
(1935), which Gielgud produced.

In July 1935 came André Obey's *Noah*. This play had
attracted much attention when it was played in French by
the Compagnie des Quinze under the direction of Michel
St Denis, at this theatre, in 1931. The English translation
was by Arthur Wilmurt. In October 1935 there was a
revival of *Romeo and Juliet*, which scored the longest run
on record for this play, 186 performances. This production
had an interesting cast. At the beginning of the run Laurence
Olivier played Romeo and Gielgud Mercutio, but these
parts were reversed in November; Peggy Ashcroft played
Juliet and Edith Evans was the Nurse. Chekhov's *The
Seagull* was given in May 1936 with great success.

After Gielgud left the New, *Parnell* was staged with
Margaret Rawlings and Wyndham Goldie. In 1937 there
were three Shakespearean productions: *As You Like It*
from the Old Vic with Edith Evans and Michael Redgrave;
The Taming of the Shrew with Edith Evans and Leslie
Banks; and *Macbeth*, again from the Old Vic, with
Laurence Olivier and Judith Anderson. During 1938–9
there was a mixed assortment of plays, none of which
achieved long runs, though *Mourning Becomes Electra*
(1938) and *Johnson over Jordan* by J. B. Priestley are
memorable.

The Man in Half Moon Street by Barré Lyndon had
enjoyed a run of 188 performances at the outbreak of war in
September 1939. From January 1941 the New Theatre became the London headquarters of the Old Vic and Sadler's
Wells companies in plays, operas and ballet. The opening
of the first West End season of the Vic-Wells Ballet was on
14 January 1941. During their wartime sojourn at the New
many notable productions in all three departments were

seen and particular mention must be made of *The Beggar's Opera*, *King John*, *The Cherry Orchard* and *Hamlet* (with Robert Helpmann in the name part).

In 1944 it became the home of the Old Vic Theatre Company only, to quote the official announcement: 'By arrangement with Howard Wyndham and Bronson Albery, the Governors of the Old Vic, in association with C.E.M.A. present Ralph Richardson, Laurence Olivier, Sybil Thorndike, Nicholas Hannen, and the Old Vic Theatre Company.' This repertory season included Ibsen's *Peer Gynt* in a new translation by Norman Ginsbury, Bernard Shaw's *Arms and the Man*, Shakespeare's *Richard III* and Chekhov's *Uncle Vanya*.

The 1945 season added *Henry IV*, *Parts I and II*, *Oedipus* and *The Critic*. During the summer of 1946 while the Old Vic were on tour *Our Town* and *Crime and Punishment* were produced.

The Old Vic returned in September 1946 with *King Lear*, Laurence Olivier and Ralph Richardson again leading the company. It was not until 1950 that the company returned to their old south bank home, and a full history of these years will be found in the many books on their activities.

In the summer of 1948 Aldous Huxley's *The Gioconda Smile* was a great success and was transferred to Wyndham's when the Old Vic returned. 3 May 1950 saw the first night of *The Cocktail Party* by T. S. Eliot, running for 325 performances. Notable later productions include Vivian Ellis's musical version of J. B. Fagan's *And So To Bed* (1951), *The Young Elizabeth* (1952), Katharine Hepburn in Shaw's *The Millionairess* (1952), *Dear Charles* (1952), *I am a Camera* (1954), *The Remarkable Mr Pennypacker* (1954), *Gigi* (1956), *Under Milk Wood* (1956), *Summer of the Seventeenth Doll* (1957), *The Party* (1958), *The Rose Tattoo* (1959), *The Long and the Short and the Tall* (1959), from the Royal Court, and *Make me an Offer* (1959) from the Royal Stratford. In June 1960 *Oliver!* a musical based on Dickens's *Oliver Twist*, was produced with great success and it continued to run until September 1967, adding up to 2618 performances. Short runs then became the order of the day. *Jorrocks*, a musical, ran for 181 performances; *Howards End* (137), *World War 2½* (166) while *The Constant Couple* lasted for a season preceding a transfer from the Apollo of the Mermaid success *Spring and Port Wine*. After this some more short runs included a Ballet season till another transfer, this time from the Royal Court, of *The Hotel in Amsterdam*. Then came the controversial *Soldiers* in December 1968. In April 1969 *Anne of Green Gables*, a new musical, was presented with Polly James in the lead. In January 1970 Glynis Johns returned in *Come as You Are!* by John Mortimer and in November a revival of *The Winslow Boy* by Terence

Rattigan, with Kenneth More, enjoyed a successful run. In May 1971 the National Theatre Season included *Rules of the Game*, *Amphitryon 38*, *Tyger*, *Danton's Death* and *Long Day's Journey into Night*.

On 5 April 1972 *London Assurance*, transferred from the Aldwych, opened with Judi Dench, Donald Sinden and Michael Williams, a commercial run of the Royal Shakespeare Company's production. It was during this run that the theatre changed its name from the New to the Albery. The next show, *Joseph and the Amazing Technicolour Dreamcoat*, was followed by a revival of Somerset Maugham's *The Constant Wife* with Ingrid Bergman which ran until May 1974 when a revival of Shaw's *Pygmalion* was staged.

The theatre is now controlled by Wyndham Theatres, Ltd, which also runs the Criterion and Wyndham's.

3 · The Aldwych Theatre

Aldwych, W.C.2

Capacity: 1024

Opened 23 December 1905 with *Blue Bell* (a new edition of *Bluebell in Fairyland*). A musical dream play by Seymour Hicks and Walter Slaughter, lyrics by Aubrey Hopwood and Charles H. Taylor. Produced by Seymour Hicks under the management of Charles Frohman.

THE BUILDING

London's old Theatreland which had grown up in the shadow of Drury Lane was almost wiped out in the reconstruction of the area between Wellington Street, Strand, and the beginning of Fleet Street. The whole maze of slums, stretching up towards Drury Lane on one side, and Lincoln's Inn on the other, was demolished, and the new streets, Aldwych and Kingsway, constructed. This vast operation began in the last years of the nineteenth century and was not finally completed until after the First World War, and now, today, some of the early buildings of the scheme are already giving way to modern redevelopment.

Four theatres were demolished during the early stages of the work. The Olympic Theatre in Wych Street and the Opera Comique in the Strand were closed in 1899, the Globe Theatre in Newcastle Street shut its doors in 1902 (this is no connection with the present theatre of this name, which was opened as the Hicks Theatre in 1906: see No. 16). This was followed by the closure of the Gaiety Theatre in the Strand in June of the same year. Work on reconstruction had been proceeding during this period and the second Gaiety Theatre was able to open the following October on a new site at the corner of the new Aldwych and the widened Strand (this building closed in 1939 and was finally demolished in 1957). The other theatres in this locality, the Lyceum, Terry's, and the Royal Strand, were unaffected, though the old Lyceum was pulled down and entirely rebuilt (except for the portico in Wellington Street and the rear wall) on the same site in 1904 (see part IV, No. 6).

Almost opposite what had originally been the entrance to the Lyceum Theatre before 1830, when its main façade was in the Strand, stood Terry's Theatre. This was built by Edward Terry, the comedian, in 1887 on ground once occupied by the notorious Cole Hole, famed for 'Baron' Nicholson and the Judge and Jury Club. Terry's ceased to be a theatre in 1910, becoming a cinema, and was eventually pulled down in 1923 when the Strand was widened; its site is now occupied by Woolworth's.

The Royal Strand Theatre, on the river side of the road further down towards Fleet Street, remained open until 1906, when it was demolished and Aldwych Tube Station built on the site. (Meanwhile the theatre which we now know as the Strand opened in Aldwych in 1905 as the Waldorf and was not named the Strand until 1909: see No. 35).

The Vaudeville (see No. 36), the Adelphi (see No. 1) and the Tivoli Music-Hall were too far down the Strand to be affected by these changes, though the Tivoli, closed in 1914 and demolished, was not rebuilt as a cinema until 1923. This too has now given way to modern progress, falling under the pick-axe in 1957. Peter Robinson's occupied the site until it became New South Wales House.

The new theatres built in the vast Aldwych–Kingsway reconstruction were: the London Opera House (the Stoll), Kingsway, opened in 1911 (closed 1957), a new theatre, the Royalty being incorporated in the rebuilding (see No. 31), and on the large oblong site in Aldwych, between Catherine Street and Drury Lane with Tavistock Street in the rear, were planned two theatres with identical façades

and an hotel, the Waldorf, which was not built until after
both the theatres were opened.

The Waldorf Theatre (now the Strand) on the corner of
Catherine Street was opened in May 1905, and its companion, the Aldwych Theatre, on the Drury Lane corner in
the following December.

The Aldwych Theatre was built by Seymour Hicks in
association with the American impresario Charles
Frohman. At this time they were both also concerned in
building the Hicks (the Globe) and the Queen's in Shaftesbury Avenue (see Nos. 16 and 28).

The Aldwych Theatre was designed by W. G. R. Sprague
(who was also responsible for the Waldorf Theatre and the
new block then being planned in Shaftesbury Avenue). Its
builder was Walter Wallis of Balham.

It was a two-tiered theatre. *The Era* of 30 December 1905
tells us:

> Mr Sprague has not only introduced into his archi-
> tectural scheme the latest improvements in theatre
> construction, but has also made certain departures which
> are all in the right direction. The decorations are in the
> Georgian style and the general appearance of the interior
> of the building is pleasing in the extreme. Handsome and
> ornate it certainly is, but the words that correctly
> describe the impression conveyed by a first glance
> round, are cosy and comfortable. The prevailing scheme
> in crimson, cream and gold and the contrast with Rose du
> Barri draperies and upholstery is striking and artistically
> effective. One of the innovations that will be greatly
> appreciated by the male members of the audience is
> a commodious 'smokers' gallery' above the entrance
> hall.

A Painted Act Drop remained in use into the 1930s and the
theatre still retains much of its old-world appearance
although in post-war years the lower stage boxes were
removed and the pit absorbed into the stalls seating while
the gallery was transformed into an extension of the upper
circle, by the removal of the benches and the substitution
of tip-up seats.

In 1958 a threat to the building by a redevelopment
scheme was revealed, and the L.C.C. rejected plans in
October and again in July 1959. After much speculation, it
was finally announced in July 1960, that arrangements had
been concluded for the Governors of the Shakespeare
Memorial Theatre, Stratford-upon-Avon, to take over the
Aldwych Theatre as their London Headquarters for the
next three years. When they took possession in November,
drastic alterations were commenced. An apron stage with a
new proscenium and lighting was constructed, similar to
that at Stratford, at a cost of £75,000.

The theatre was again redecorated during 1963. New Circle Boxes were made and the old ones converted to stage use. Another re-seating took place in March 1971 but the modern stage and lighting, bringing with it new sight lines for the audience, does not altogether fit happily into the essentially Edwardian atmosphere of the auditorium.

THE PLAYS

The theatre opened on 23 December 1905 with a new version called *Blue Bell* of Seymour Hicks's musical dream play *Bluebell in Fairyland*, which had previously been produced at the Vaudeville in 1901. This was followed by other musical comedies including *The Beauty of Bath* with Hicks and Ellaline Terriss (1906), *Nelly Neil* with Edna May (1907) and *The Gay Gordons* again with the Hicks (1907).

In February 1909 Marie Dressler, following a great success at the Palace, took the Aldwych to present *Philopoena* and *The Collegettes*, but the venture was not successful. In 1911 the Stage Society gave Chekhov's *The Cherry Orchard* its first performance in England at this theatre. After Hicks left the theatre in 1910 it passed through several hands; it was owned by Sir Joseph Beecham from 1912 to 1919 and then passed to a company.

During the war, J. Bannister Howard was manager, and several popular productions were staged, including revivals of *The Earl and the Girl*, *The Dairymaids* and *Pete*, which was a dramatisation of Hall Caine's *The Manxman*. Enemy aircraft bombing London caused considerable damage to the theatre, every sheet of glass was broken and the staircase rails were twisted. Later in the War it became a club for Australian soldiers.

It was in May 1920 that C. B. Cochran, who had taken the theatre the previous year, introduced the Guitrys here, playing *Nono*, with Sacha Guitry as Robert and Yvonne Printemps as Nono, and during the same month *La Prise de Berg op-Zoom*, *Jean de la Fontaine*, *L'Illusioniste*, *Pasteur*, and *Mon Père avait Raison*. Viola Tree was in management in 1920 and revivals of *Macbeth*, *The Tempest* and *Pygmalion* were staged. In January 1922 Donald Calthrop became manager and produced and appeared in *Money Doesn't Matter* and *Double or Quit*, and other uneventful productions. *Tons of Money* was transferred from the Shaftesbury Theatre in 1923 and in February 1924 there began a run of 598 performances of *It Pays to Advertise*, a farce by Roi Cooper Megrue and Walter Hackett, which was presented by Tom Walls and Leslie Henson, and from July 1925 the Aldwych became famous for the series of what came to be known as 'Aldwych Farces', by Ben Travers. These were *A Cuckoo in the Nest* (1925), *Rookery Nook* (1926), *Thark* (1927), *Plunder*

(1928), *A Cup of Kindness* (1929), *A Night Like This* (1930), *Turkey Time* (1931), *Dirty Work* (1932), and *A Bit of a Test* (1933). With this series must be mentioned two other farces which appeared between the Ben Travers successes, *Marry the Girl* (1930) and *Fifty-Fifty* (1932). Tom Walls and Ralph Lynn appeared in all of them, and other members of the excellent team were Mary Brough, Winifred Shotter and Robertson Hare.

The theatre during this period came into the hands of A. E. Abrahams, in whose family it still remains: though it was under the direction of Prince Littler until his death in 1973.

After the Lynn-Walls farces a mixed bag of productions followed which included *Indoor Fireworks* (1934) and a long series of transfers of plays which had begun in other homes. These were the days of the Privilege Ticket: 'two seats for the price of one'. Many successes extended their runs by this method. The early years of the Second War saw a quick succession of productions, and the first solid success was *Watch on the Rhine* in April 1942. This was followed by the Lunts in *There Shall be no Night* the next year. In 1946 Robert Donat presented himself in *Much Ado about Nothing*, and in 1947 Michael Redgrave was seen as *Macbeth*. From America came the two Menotti operas, *The Medium* and *The Telephone*, in 1948. After this first nights followed far too quickly until Gertrude Lawrence's success in *September Tide* in November 1948. *A Streetcar Named Desire* had its London production at this theatre in 1949 then once again it had its ups and downs, though notable plays were *Figure of Fun* (1951), *Under the Sycamore Tree* (1952), *The Dark is Light Enough* (1955), *The Bad Seed* (1955), *The Sound of Murder* (1959), and *Watch it, Sailor!* (1960), which transferred to the Apollo to make way for the Stratford-upon-Avon Company. (Their new theatre in the Barbican development, approved in 1965, is still on its way in 1974.)

The new régime opened on December 15 with Webster's *Duchess of Malfi* followed four days later by *Twelfth Night*. The two plays commenced the repertory season, with a large company interchangeable between London and Stratford, it included *Ondine* and a new play *The Devils* by John Whiting early in the following year.

Since then the success of the policy has been assured and London has seen some magnificent new productions, besides revivals and transfers, from the now renamed Royal Shakespeare Theatre, Stratford-upon-Avon. Among the plays staged by the Royal Shakespeare Company have been the London première of Anouilh's *Becket* (1961), which transferred to the Globe Theatre for a run, and, in December, a star revival of *The Cherry Orchard*. 1962 saw *The Caucasian Chalk Circle*, a double bill bringing together

Harold Pinter and Strindberg, with *The Collection*, and *Playing with Fire*, a revival of John Mortimer's *A Penny for a Song* and the long-awaited Christopher Fry play about Becket, *Curtmantle*.

The Shakespearean revivals include *The Taming of the Shrew*, *As You Like It*, *Troilus and Cressida*, *King Lear*, *A Comedy of Errors*, and the Cycles, *The Wars of the Roses* and the Roman plays, as well as the most successful productions from Stratford.

A persistent success was *The Hollow Crown*, an arrangement by John Barton of songs and poems by and about the Kings and Queens of England, which from 1961 was seldom out of the repertoire during the following years.

Nineteen-sixty-four saw the first of the World Theatre seasons, presented by the Royal Shakespeare Company and Peter Daubeny, which were presented annually until 1973. *Tartuffe* was performed by Comédie Française and companies from Berlin, Naples, Warsaw, Athens, Moscow and Dublin were included. Later visitors came from Czechoslovakia, Israel, Japan, Poland, America and South Africa with their own productions. The Royal Shakespeare Company returned in June; among their plays were *Birthday Party*, *The Marat/Sade* and *The Jew of Malta*. The next season included *Hamlet* and *The Homecoming*, as well as other productions. Stratford has presented, among other plays, *Staircase*, *Days in the Trees*, *Ghosts*, Dion Boucicault's *London Assurance*, later seen at the New Theatre (now the Albery), *Old Times*, *Enemies*, *The Man of Mode*, *Exiles*, *The Balcony*, *The Lower Depths*, *Murder in the Cathedral*, *The Island of the Mighty*, *Section Nine*, *Duck Song* and many others. In 1972 the Prospect Company gave a season with *Love's Labours Lost* and *King Lear*. March 1973 saw Eileen Atkins at the theatre for three weeks in *Suzanna Andler*, by Margaret Duras, as a fill-in between seasons. The revival of *Sherlock Holmes* at Christmas 1973 proved an unexpected hit.

4 · The Ambassadors Theatre

West Street, Shaftesbury Avenue, W.C.2

Capacity: 453

Opened 5 June 1913 with *Panthea*, a play by Monckton Hoffe. Produced by Clifford Brooke, under the management of Durrant Swan.

THE BUILDING

It was planned to build two theatres on ground lying between Cambridge Circus and Upper St Martin's Lane. The first, the Ambassadors, was built and opened before the outbreak of the First World War, while the second, the St Martin's, had to wait until 1916 before opening. The theatres are separated by Tower Court, with Tower Street running behind them, and fronting on to West Street.

Though the two theatres were entirely separate financial enterprises, they were both designed by the same architect, W. G. R. Sprague. The Ambassadors was built by Kingerlee and Sons of Oxford for a syndicate, The Ambassadors

Theatre, Limited, of which J. Herbert Jay was the managing director.

The lease of certain property on the site of the St Martin's Theatre had not been acquired at first and the Ambassadors was forced to be a low building so as not to interfere with the ancient lights of the other property. The stalls are below ground level.

The general scheme of decoration [said the *Era* of 7 June 1913] is Louis XVI and the colour scheme of Parma violet ivory, and dull gold is a refreshing change to the warm colours usually selected in decorative schemes . . . The auditorium is arranged with a commodious stalls area, behind which is a good roomy pit, and above this level is the dress circle, and forming part of the same tier is the family circle, or upper boxes, sufficiently raised to form another distinct circle.

Ambassadorial crests were also part of the original decorations. Since that time only minor alterations have been made and except for redecoration and reseating the theatre remains the same.

THE PLAYS

The opening production *Panthea* only survived for fifteen nights and the miscellaneous entertainments that followed until C. B. Cochran took a lease of the theatre in May 1914 fared little better. Cochran produced the first 'intimate' revue in this country, *Odds and Ends*, on 17 October 1914. This revue was by Harry Grattan, with music by Edward Jones. 'Intimate' revue proved a popular form of entertainment and one which was well suited to a small theatre like the Ambassadors. It was in *Odds and Ends* that Alice Delysia made her first London appearance and scored an immediate success. The actual production expenses amounted to £200, and the revue netted £30,000 during its run of 376 performances. It was followed by *More* (*Odds and Ends*) by the same author and composer in July 1915, and *Pell Mell* by Fred Thompson and Morris Harvey, with music by Nat D. Ayer, both again including Delysia, from June 1916. Subsequent outstanding productions here by Cochran included *The Man who Married a Dumb Wife*, adapted from Anatole France (1917), and *The Three Daughters of Monsieur Dupont*, translated from Brieux by St John Hankin (1917).

An interesting chapter in this theatre's history is associated with H. M. Harwood, whose tenancy began in 1919 and lasted until 1930. He presented many plays of outstanding merit including *Sylvia's Lovers* (1919), a light opera by Bernard Rolt and Cosmo Gordon-Lennox; *A Grain of Mustard Seed* (1920), one of his own plays, of which one critic has said 'never before had politics been presented with such dramatic power'; *The White Headed Boy* (1920), which established Lennox Robinson as one of the finest Irish playwrights; *Deburau* (1921), in which Ivor Novello and Jeanne de Casalis made first appearances; and Lord Dunsany's *If* (1921), a notably well-acted play with Gladys Cooper and Henry Ainley.

Then Nelson Keys, in March 1922, appeared in and presented a revue called *The Curate's Egg*, which did not succeed. Later productions of note include a dramatisation of Joseph Conrad's *The Secret Agent* (1922); *The Lilies of the Field* (1923); *Fata Morgana* (1924), adapted from the Hungarian of Ernest Vajda, one of the sex-problem plays which abounded at that time and which greatly increased the reputation of the young American actor Tom Douglas; *The Pelican* (1924), by H. M. Harwood and his wife F. Tennyson Jesse; *Any House* (1925), by F. Tennyson Jesse; Eugene O'Neill's *The Emperor Jones* (1925), with the first appearance in this country of Paul Robeson; John Galsworthy's *Escape* (1926); *The Fanatics*, by Miles Malleson, which caused a great deal of controversy; *Many Waters* (1928); *Rope* (1929); and then in October 1931 Barry Jones and Maurice Colbourne presented *The Queen's Husband*, in which they both appeared.

In September 1932 Sydney Carroll took charge, presenting among other productions, a revival of *The Streets of London* (1932), by Dion Boucicault, revised by W. A. Darlington; *Maritime* (1933); *Cabbages and Kings* (1933); revivals of *The Rivals* and *The Country Wife* (1934); *Family Affairs* (1934); *The Mask of Virtue*, translated from the German by Ashley Dukes (1935), in which Vivien Leigh made her West End debut; and Otway's *The Soldier's Fortune* (1935). Subsequent successes were scored with *Children to Bless You* and *Two Bouquets* (1936).

In 1938 J. W. Pemberton took over the theatre from Carroll on a 21-year lease. *Spring Meeting*, presented by H. M. Tennent, ran for 311 performances from May 1938.

Starting in March 1939 *The Gate Revue*, by Diana Morgan and Robert Macdermott, with music by Geoffrey Wright, originally put on as a Christmas show at the Gate Theatre in December 1938, broke the long-run record for the Ambassadors Theatre; it starred Hermione Gingold and Walter Crisham. When optimism was at a low ebb in the dark days of 1940 after the fall of France, Norman Marshall showed considerable courage in staging a sequel called *Swinging the Gate*. During the period when air raids made evening entertainment undesirable, *Lunch Ballet*, *After Lunch Ballet* and *After Tea Ballet* were given here by the *Ballet Rambert* and *The London Ballet*, under the aegis of the Arts Theatre Club, performances being given from 1 to 2 p.m., 2.15 to 3.15 p.m., and 3.30 to 4.30 p.m.

Subsequent productions have been *The New*

Ambassadors Revue (1941), an interesting and somewhat unusual revue of a very intimate kind by Herbert Farjeon called *Light and Shade* (1942), *Sweet and Low* (1943). and its successors *Sweeter and Lower* (1944) and *Sweetest and Lowest* (1946). London was brightened during the black-out by the wit of Gingold, Crisham and Henry Kendall.

J. W. Pemberton died in 1947 and the theatre was carried on by his trustees until a long lease was acquired by Peter Saunders in 1958. The years between were filled with *Little Lambs Eat Ivy* (1948), *Dark of the Moon* (1949), *Lace on her Petticoat* (1950), and several other productions of less note.

On 25 November 1952 *The Mousetrap*, by Agatha Christie, was produced. On 12 April 1958 this passed the record for a stage production set up by *Chu Chin Chow* with 2238 performances between 1916–21. It achieved its twenty-first birthday in November 1973, the longest run in stage history, and moved to the St Martin's Theatre, next door, on 25 March after Peter Saunders' lease of the Ambassadors Theatre ended on the 23rd. The theatre is now under the management of Ray Cooney on a three year licence from the owner, Herbert Jay.

The first production of the new regime on 10 April was a transfer from the Royal Court of two South African plays, *Sizwe Bansi is Dead* and *The Island*.

5 · The Apollo Theatre

Shaftesbury Avenue, W.C.1

Capacity: 796

Opened 21 February 1901 with *The Belle of Bohemia*, a musical farce by Harry B. Smith, music by Ludwig Englander. Produced by George W. Lederer, under the management of Henry Lowenfeld.

THE BUILDING

Shaftesbury Avenue, the new roadway running through the centre of Soho, was opened in 1887. Stretching from Piccadilly Circus, which had been reconstructed, to New Oxford Street, it was to become the main artery of London's Theatreland. The remodelling of Regent Circus, as it had been called until this change, caused the old Pavilion Music Hall to be pulled down and rebuilt at the Circus end of the avenue (see Part IV, No. 5).

The first theatres in the new Avenue were the Shaftesbury, opened October 1888, and the Lyric, opened in

December of the same year (see No. 21). The Shaftesbury Theatre (opposite the side of the Palace) near Cambridge Circus was completely destroyed by enemy action in 1941 and its site still remains unoccupied (see No. 34).

The next arrival in the locality was the Royal English Opera, now the Palace Theatre, opened at the junction of Shaftesbury Avenue and Cambridge Circus, which was commenced in 1888 and opened in 1891 (see No. 24).

This was followed by the Apollo in 1901. The block containing the Globe and Queen's Theatres arose in 1906–7 (see Nos. 16 and 28). The Princes Theatre at the Oxford Street end arose in 1911 and the last arrival in the Avenue did not appear until 1931 when the Saville Theatre opened its doors (see Part IV, No. 9). This was the same year as the Windmill Theatre opened (see No. 40), just off the Avenue in the side of the block of buildings which contains the Lyric and the Apollo Theatres. In the making of the Avenue, which cut Great Windmill Street in two, another place of entertainment became more prominent; this was the Trocadero Music-Hall, which stood on ground that had housed entertainment for many years.

In Great Windmill Street, at its southern end, stood Piccadilly Hall, a Restoration rendezvous described by Lord Clarendon in 1640 as 'a fair house for entertainment and gaming, with handsome gravel walks and with shade, and where are an upper and a lower bowling green, whither very many of nobility and gentry of the best quality resorted for exercise and conversation'.

Later in the adjoining grounds was built a small theatre called, originally, the Albion in 1832 and later the New Queen's Theatre. It closed in 1836. On the site and that of the tennis-court of Piccadilly Hall arose the Argyll Rooms, not to be confused with those of a similar name which were in Argyll Street near where the London Palladium now stands. Here were held promenade concerts, dances and other entertainments. Later it became a sort of casino which lost its licence in 1878 and was converted into a music-hall with the name of the Trocadero. Among its managers were Sam Adams, Hugh J. Didcott and Albert Chevalier; at times it was designated the Royal Trocadero and Eden Theatre. The rebuilding of the Pavilion and the bisecting of Great Windmill Street by Shaftesbury Avenue gave the building a new corner position, but in 1896 the Music-Hall was closed and swallowed up in a restaurant of the same name, which covered the site. In 1925 Charles B. Cochran made the grill-room famous for its cabarets. For the next ten years or so these continued to be a feature of London's night life. It now awaits redevelopment.

In the Shaftesbury Avenue block stretching from Rupert Street to Great Windmill Street, backed by Archer Street,

the Apollo Theatre was built at the Rupert Street end.
It was designed by Lewen Sharp, for Henry Lowenfeld,
its original proprietor and manager, and built by Walter
Wallis.

In 1900 when it was announced that Lowenfeld had
bought the freehold of a site adjoining the Lyric and was to
build a new theatre, speculation was rife as to the name it
would adopt: at one time he offered a prize of £100 and a
box on the opening night to the person who suggested the
name eventually used.

The façade is in the French renaissance style, and the
whole building is entirely without pillars. The orchestra,
invented by Lowenfeld, was originally intended to produce
the proper relation in the sound of the various instruments
to each other and to avoid any possible muffling or loss of
tonality. To this end the floor space of the orchestra pit
was constructed in the form of a hollow oval and the surface
was hard and highly glazed; a wooden sounding board was
placed over this hollow surface and on this stood a three-
tier rostrum on glass legs. The various instruments were
placed on the tiers. The idea was described as a 'free
adaptation of Wagner's construction of the orchestra at
Bayreuth'.

A souvenir of the opening of the theatre says:

> In the dress circle can be seen the mascot of the
> theatre, the original badge of the German tribe of
> gipsies who are connected with Mr Lowenfeld's family
> estate in Poland. It is a silver chain and buckle, on the
> buckle being a flying lizard supported dexter and sinister
> by lions rampant. This device is supposed to bring good
> luck and is reproduced in the scheme of decoration.

There was an idea at one time that the theatre should
be named the Mascot. Eventually, as musicals were to be
the principal attraction, the Apollo was decided upon as a
suitable name.

Today this theatre seems to have changed little since it
was built except for a much appreciated simplification in its
decoration. In recent years the gallery has been reseated
and rechristened the balcony.

THE PLAYS

The opening production on 21 February 1901 was an
American play called *The Belle of Bohemia*, which was not
a success; then Martin Harvey appeared in *A Cigarette-
Maker's Romance*, which he transferred from the Royal
Court Theatre, following this with a revival of *The Only
Way*.

The first real success at the new theatre was a musical
version of *Kitty Grey*, which had previously been played

as a straight comedy at the Vaudeville from April 1900 for a
run of over a hundred performances. The new version,
with music by Augustus Barrett, Howard Talbot and Lionel
Monckton, ran at the Apollo for 220 performances, and was
the first of a series of musical pieces to be presented by
George Edwardes. The succeeding productions were *The
Three Little Maids* and *The Girl from Kay's* (1902), the
first of which ran for 348 and the second for 432 performances. *The Three Little Maids* was both written and
composed by Paul Rubens.

In 1903 came *Madame Sherry*, with music by Hugo Felix
and then in 1904 *Véronique*, one of the most important
events in the history of Light Opera. The music was by
André Messager and an outstanding performance was given
by Ruth Vincent in the title role. In 1905 under Tom B.
Davis came *Mr Popple* (*of Ippleton*), another musical
comedy entirely by Paul Rubens, in 1906 Robert Courtneidge staged *The Dairymaids* with music by Rubens and
Frank Tours, which ran for over two hundred performances, and 1907 brought the original production of *Tom
Jones*, with music by Edward German, and the first London
appearance of Cicely Courtneidge.

In 1908 the Apollo became the home of *The Follies*.
H. G. Pélissier, 'that ever-to-be-lamented genius of the
grotesque', formed this company and they appeared here
until 1912 with short breaks for *Butterflies* with Ada Reeve
in 1908, and *The Islander* in 1910.

During the years 1913 to 1920, the policy of musical
comedy being discontinued, varied fare was presented here.
Among notable productions were George A. Birmingham's
General John Regan (275 performances from January 1913),
The Only Girl, a musical play by Victor Herbert (1915);
Harold Brighouse's Lancashire comedy *Hobson's Choice*,
which was a wartime success with over two hundred per-
formances; *Inside the Lines*, an Anglo-American play by
Earl Derr Biggers (1917), and *Tilly of Bloomsbury*, Ian
Hay's comedy adapted from his novel (1919), which
scored over four hundred performances.

In 1920 Tom B. Davis, who had been lessee since 1902,
retired and the ownership was vested in a company.
George Grossmith and Edward Laurillard became lessee
and manager until 1923, and F. J. Nettlefold presented
Don Q, Crooked Usage and *Thank You Phillips* in 1921.

In January 1922 Phyllis Neilson Terry presented J. B.
Fagan's *The Wheel*, a revival of *Trilby*, and in 1923 a new
play, *A Roof and Four Walls* by E. Temple Thurston.

Subsequent successes under various managements were
Lonsdale's *The Fake* (1924), a revue called *By the Way*
(1925), *Is Zat So?* (1926), *Abie's Irish Rose* (1927), Robert
Loraine's season of revivals the same year, Edgar Wallace's
The Squeaker, *The Patsy* (1928), O'Casey's *The Silver*

Tassie, Ivor Novello's *A Symphony in Two Flats* (1929),
Nine to Six, with an all-woman cast (1930), and *There's
Always Juliet* (1931), by John van Druten.

In 1932 Ronald Squire presented *Spring Time for Henry;*
in 1933 Diana Wynyard appeared as Charlotte Brontë in
Wild Decembers by Clemence Dane, and in 1933
Elizabeth Bergner burst upon London in *Escape Me Never.*

From 1934 Walter Hackett and his wife Marion Lorne
presented a series of successful productions, including
Hyde Park Corner (1934), *Espionage* (1935), *The Fugitives*
(1936), and *London After Dark* (1937), all written by himself and providing star parts for his wife. In between Ian
Hay's great hit, *Housemaster*, was produced in 1936.

Later successes were *Idiot's Delight* (1938), by Robert
Sherwood, which won the Pulitzer Prize in New York in
1936 and achieved great acclaim through being produced
during the year of the Munich crisis; also Patrick Hamilton's
psychological thriller *Gas Light* (1939). After the outbreak
of war Emlyn Williams' *The Light of Heart* (1940) and *Old
Acquaintance* by Van Druten (1941) were among the plays
produced, then Terence Rattigan's *Flare Path* (1942) had a
long and outstanding run. This was followed, among other
pieces, by a revival of *The Cradle Song*, J. B. Priestley's
How Are They at Home? which he wrote at the special
request of the serving men overseas, and a revival in 1944 of
Noël Coward's *Private Lives*, with John Clements and
Kay Hammond. The theatre came under the control of
Prince Littler during this year and is still run by A.T.P.
Theatres Ltd.

Then followed *Grand National Night* (1946), *The Blind
Goddess* (1947), *The Happiest Days of Your Life* (1948),
Treasure Hunt (1949), *Seagulls over Sorrento* (1950),
Simon and Laura (1954), *Tiger at The Gates* (1955),
Summertime (1955), a revue *For Amusement Only* (1956),
Duels of Angels (1958), *Fool's Paradise* (1959), and *Pieces
of Eight* (1959). In October 1960, Micheál MacLiammóir
presented his one-man recital, *The Importance of Being
Oscar*, followed by the transfer of *Watch it, Sailor!* from
the Aldwych Theatre which ran until August 1961. The
following months were ones of constant change until the
arrival, in February 1962, of *Boeing-Boeing*, which
eventually transferred to the Duchess in 1965. The
theatre was then completely redecorated before the opening of the revue *Nymphs and Satires* on May 25. After a few
months' run *Any Wednesday*, which followed, was
succeeded by *Spring and Port Wine* from the Mermaid. It
remained there till July 1967 when it again transferred.
Another comedy, *The Flip Side*, was equally successful
and ran for 461 performances, to be followed by John
Gielgud in *40 Years On* in October 1968, then came the last
play written by Hugh and Margaret Williams, *His, Hers and*

Theirs in December 1969. The theatre had a moderate success with *Happy Apple* which opened in March 1970 and was succeeded, at the end of July, by the English Stage Company's production of *Home*, with John Gielgud and Ralph Richardson, direct from the Royal Court Theatre. In November 1970 came the American success *Butterflies are Free* with Eileen Heckart playing her Broadway part, then early in 1971 the Nottingham Playhouse production of *Lulu*, followed later the same year by a transfer from the Greenwich Theatre of Peter Nichols' play *Forget-Me-Not-Lane*. Then at Christmas came a revival of *Charley's Aunt* in the evenings with matinées of *The Owl and the Pussycat*. In June 1972 *The Mating Game* opened and continued until June 1973. The Oxford Playhouse production of Molnar's *The Wolf* with Judi Dench, Edward Woodward and Leo McKern opened in October and transferred to the Queen's Theatre in December to make room for a new comedy by Gene Stone and Ray Cooney *Why Not Stay for Breakfast?* starring Derek Nimmo.

6 · The Cambridge Theatre

Earlham Street, Cambridge Circus, W.C.2

Capacity: 1275

Opened 4 September 1930, with *Charlot's Masquerade*, a revue by Ronald Jeans, music by Roland Leigh. Produced by André Charlot, under the management of B. A. Meyer.

THE BUILDING

In St Giles' between Cambridge Circus and Covent Garden is Seven Dials: this spot where seven streets meet has long been a famous district of London. Notorious for its slums in the nineteenth century, it had earlier been a fashionable area. John Evelyn, writing in 1694, says: 'I went to see the building beginning neere St. Giles's, where seven streets make a star for a Doric pillar placed in the middle of a circular area, said to be built by Mr Neale, introducer of the late lotteries in imitation of those at Venice.' The district at that time was known as Seven Streets, but to the column were affixed sundials, one to face every street, and from this fact the present name is derived. The column is now at Weybridge in Surrey.

34

Even today there remains a distinct old-world atmosphere in the streets around this area which modern redevelopment has not yet attacked. In 1930 when the Cambridge Theatre opened, there was great activity in theatre-building, the London Casino (then the Prince Edward, see No. 19) was opened on April 3 and in September no less than three new theatres rang up their curtains, the Cambridge on the 4th, the Phoenix (see No. 25), on the 24th and the Whitehall (see No. 40) on the 29th. To round off the year the rebuilt Adelphi Theatre (see No. 1), opened on December 3 and the Leicester Square Theatre (see Part IV, No. 3) on December 19. Though originally intended for live entertainment, it made its bow as a cinema, but was later to stage non-stop variety.

The Cambridge Theatre was built by Bertie Meyer on a plot of ground at the corner of Great Earl Street (now Earlham Street) and Mercer Street, backed by Shelton Street. It was designed by Wimperis, Simpson and Guthrie and constructed by Gee, Walker and Slater, Ltd. Its interior decoration was designed by Serge Chermayeff.

The modernity of the theatre, both externally and internally, was much commented upon, favourably for the most part, at the time of its erection. The *Architects' Journal* of 8 October 1930 says:

The site is a corner one and the new building presents a symmetrical design when looking at the corner, yet the subsidiary axis of the entrance hall is actually parallel to one of the boundary walls, a fact of which most visitors remain unconscious. The exterior is faced mostly with stone, the metal windows, the entrance canopy, and the display signs are painted Cambridge blue. Within, the shape is unusual where theatres are concerned, especially as regards the roof, since both vertical and horizontal sections describe elliptical curves. Across the ceiling is a series of transverse ribs, which advance in increasing proximity one to another up to the springing of the Dress Circle. Each contains concealed lighting playing upon the downward dropping dome that would in any case lead the eye to the proscenium. The effect is intensified by the scheme of decoration, carried out in bands of lacquered metal-leaf, diagonally sloped and graduated from deep gold brown to pale honey yellow. The two boxes give the impression of being lobes of the Dress circle and each has a semi-circular arched opening, the tympanum of which is filled in with an embossed design furnished in matt-silver.

'It is in fact a monolithic shell of concrete and steel,' said *The Times* of 29 November 1930, 'In the internal decorations a note of simplicity has been struck.' The *Stage*

of 4 September 1930 found that 'The beautiful, if somewhat
peculiar decorative scheme appears to be Teutonic, and is
strangely reminiscent of the then strange futuristic sets in
German films immediately after the war of 1914–1918.'

In 1950 the theatre was given an entirely new scheme of
interior decoration, this time in red. It was also completely
relit with large gilt candelabra and chandeliers.

THE PLAYS

The theatre opened on 4 September 1930 with Beatrice
Lillie in *Charlot's Masquerade*, presented by André
Charlot. Subsequent successes were a season of Nikita
Balieff's *Chauve Souris* in March 1931 and *Elizabeth of
England* in September 1931. In 1932 Sacha Guitry was here
for a season and in 1934 there was a season by the Comédie
Française. A Bernard Shaw repertory season was given in
1935 by the Macdona Players and for the next few years
the Cambridge mainly housed transfers from other theatres.
May 1939 saw the first appearance of Lydia Kyasht's
Ballet de la Jeunesse Anglaise; then for several years the
theatre was used mainly for film trade shows.

In June 1942 Jay Pomeroy presented a programme called
New Russian Ballet and the company had with them the
London Symphony Orchestra under the direction of
Anatole Fistoulari. The choreography was by Catherine
Devillier from the Moscow Opera House.

March 1943 saw an interesting revival of Bernard Shaw's
Heartbreak House, with a cast including Robert Donat,
Francis Lister, Edith Evans and Isabel Jeans, and at
Christmas of the same year *Peter Pan* was given with Ann
Todd as Peter.

A *Night in Venice*, an operetta by Johann Strauss, began
its run in May 1944 and lasted for 433 performances. For
some years the Cambridge had been famous for its Sunday
concerts presented by Jay Pomeroy; he eventually founded
the New London Opera Company and made the Cambridge
its headquarters from 1946, staging many successful
operatic revivals including *Don Pasquale*. He also brought
Ballet Companies to London and presented Italian and
French companies in seasons of plays, up to the end of 1948.

The theatre's next success was the Cecil Landeau revue
Sauce Tartare (1949) and its sequel *Sauce Piquante* (1950).
At this time the theatre came under the control of Tom
Arnold and Emile Littler.

During 1951 Menotti's opera *The Consul* was staged
and an ill-fated revival of *Hassan* followed. After this until
1952 Peter Daubeny presented foreign dance seasons with
great success.

The Cambridge again became a legitimate theatre with
Affairs of State in August 1952 and its biggest successes
were *Book of the Month* (1954), *The Reluctant Debutante*

(1955), *Breath of Spring* (1958), and *The Wrong Side of the Park* (1960), which transferred to the St Martin's in May, and *Billy Liar* later the same year, which ran until 1962, and was immediately followed by *Signpost to Murder* in February, which ran on successfully for 420 performances. Tommy Steele had a big hit with *Half a Sixpence* and a run of 677 performances, then came another musical *Little Me* for 334 performances. Ingrid Bergman appeared in a very successful revival of *A Month in the Country* in September 1965, brought from the Arnaud Theatre, Guildford.

The theatre was then used for limited seasons and had its due measure of flops until it became a cinema from September 1967 until February 1968 when a transfer of *The Desert Song* from the Palace and a revival of *The Student Prince*, both with John Hanson, kept the theatre busy for 236 performances. In February 1969 came a short lived revival of *The Merry Widow;* in April, *Ann Veronica*, a musical based on H. G. Wells' novel, quickly followed by *Highly Confidential*. Then a revival of *The Magistrate* with Alistair Sim, transferred from Chichester, was a big success. In June 1970 the National Theatre Company commenced a season with *Hedda Gabler*, directed by Ingmar Bergman, with Maggie Smith in the lead, followed by *Cyrano* by Rostand, adapted by Patrick Garland with Edward Woodward in the title role, and *The Beaux's Stratagem*. The Nottingham Playhouse Company with Alan Bates' *Hamlet* followed, then came Ingrid Bergman in a revival of *Captain Brassbound's Conversion*, which continued until the end of July 1971. Another revival of *Hamlet* opened in August with Ian McKellan, a Prospect production. This was followed in October by *West of Suez* by John Osborne from the Royal Court. In July 1972, after a series of flops, a transfer from the Mermaid of the 69 Theatre Company's production of *Journey's End* was staged. The end of November saw the first night of *Behind the Fridge* with Peter Cook and Dudley Moore when the theatre came under the direction of Larry Parnes. This was succeeded in August 1973 by *Two and Two Make Sex*, which has continued its successful run into 1974.

7 · The Coliseum

(The London Coliseum)

St Martin's Lane, W.C.2

Capacity: 2358

Opened 24 December 1904 as the London Coliseum with a variety programme.

THE BUILDING

Early in the new century Oswald Stoll conceived the idea of a vast variety theatre at Charing Cross; the original company for the project was in fact formed in 1902, and a large number of buildings, mainly ramshackle tenements, were bought at the southern end of St Martin's Lane, almost opposite the Duke of York's Theatre.

The freehold of an area of over three-quarters of an acre,
bounded by May's Buildings and Brydges Place with Bed-
fordbury at the rear, was gradually acquired. On this site
arose a building in terra-cotta designed by Frank Matcham.

It seems that from the start the name Coliseum had been
decided upon and this was to influence the style of architecture and interior design of the building.

In all its measurements it was to exceed the then largest
theatre in London, Drury Lane, and its revolving stage in
three sections was and still is a marvel of its kind.

The three-tier theatre consisted of stalls, dress circle,
grand tier and balcony (there was no pit or gallery from
the start).

The Era of 17 December 1904 says:

The Theatre has a frontage of 100 ft to St Martin's
Lane, the style adopted is Italian Renaissance, and at one
end the façade is carried up terminating with a warm-
coloured tiled roof, with a cupola over; from here dark
granite columns and arches form three openings, one
containing windows lighting the typist room, the other
the exits from the salon, and the other being the royal
entry. Over these openings are windows lighting the
managerial offices, and over these again are semi-headed
openings divided by columns, and having balconies
between each casement windows opening out to same.
These form the front of the large refreshment room or
roof garden, containing a domed roof formed of glass
and iron, and containing quite an unique feature, and
one that will be greatly patronised.

This roof-garden, though long disused, was not finally
pulled down until 1951. The scars are to be seen on either
side of the tower.

In the centre of the block, which contains the principal
entrances, arises a large square tower, most artistically
designed, and of noble proportions. It is carried up over
the bold archway containing the entrances in square
rusticated work, with a heavy bold cornice, which forms
a base for the more elaborate treatment over. This consists of heavy column pilasters, with bold carved figures
at the corners, representing Art, Music, Science and
Architecture. From here the tower assumes different
outlines, formed by trusses and niches, and the introduction of sculptured lions; the whole is carried up,
getting less in diameter as the top is approached, when
the eight figures in the shape of cupids support a large
iron revolving globe, to which is attached large electric
letters spelling 'Coliseum'. The globe is made to revolve,
and this artistic advertisement can be seen for many
miles. A further novelty in advertising is the electric

device along the front, which gives the nature of the performance taking place at the time during the evening. A veranda covers the pavement in front of the principal entrance, formed of glass and iron, a feature being the way in which the glass is curved in shapes, and the handsome panelled glass in the fascia, the whole when lighted up by electricity forming a very attractive feature in St Martin's Lane.

Of the interior and its amenities the original programme tells us:

The management have instituted a new order of things in more ways than one. The Coliseum is the only theatre in Europe which provides lifts to take the audience to the upper parts of the building. The lifts are intended primarily for elevation to the handsome Terrace Tea Room, which is under the management of Fuller's Ltd., of Regent Street, in whose hands has been placed the refreshment catering throughout the building. The two electric lifts identical with those supplied for the use of His Majesty the King at Epsom and Doncaster, are in the Grand Salon. From the Grand Salon, ladies pass through two draped archways into the Ladies' Boudoir, which is beautifully fitted. Through the Grand Salon is the Royal Entry. Immediately on entering the theatre, a Royal party will step into a richly furnished lounge, which at a signal will move softly along on a track formed in the floor, through the salon and into a large foyer, which contains the entrance to the Royal Box. The lounge car remains in the position at the entrance to the box and serves as an ante-room during the performance. Large handsomely draped openings divide the Grand Salon from the Grand Staircase. From the ground floor or entrance level the marble staircase is continued down to the large Baronial Smoking Hall, for the use of all parts of the house. There are spacious tea rooms in every tier—the Terrace Tea Room, Grand Tier Tea Room and Balcony Tea Room. There are also Confectionery Stalls and an American Bar. Dainty Snacks at moderate charges can be obtained all day in the theatre. Five o'clock tea between three to five and six to eight performances will be a speciality. The Terrace Tea Room (which is for the use of Private Box and all Stall patrons) can be reached by the Grand Staircase, or by lift from the Grand Entrance. The Grand Tier Tea Room (on the left of Grand Tier) is on the Grand Tier Staircase. The Balcony Tea Room on the left of the Balcony is on the Balcony Entrance Staircase. In each tea room there is a kiosk (Ticket Office and Information Bureau) where seats for the next performance and transfer tickets are to be obtained. To the left of the Grand Entrance on entering there is an information bureau. Physicians and others expecting urgent telephone calls or telegrams should leave a notification of the number of the seat they are occupying. If a message comes they will be instantly informed. Brief messages may be typed at and despatched from the Bureau. Telegrams will also be despatched and stamps sold. There is a Public Telephone, and a District Messenger Call. A Pillar Box will be found in the Grand Entrance Hall. Large cloak-rooms and retiring rooms fitted with every accommodation are provided on the latest and most improved principles. There are no fees.

All the seats are comfortable, richly upholstered, and provided with arm-rests. Every seat in the house is numbered and reserved, and can be booked in advance. There are four performances daily and each lasts two hours. The first commences at 12 o'clock noon. The second commences at 3 o'clock p.m. The third commences at 6 o'clock p.m. The fourth commences at 9 o'clock p.m. The first and third performances are alike, so are the second and fourth. During the one-hour intervals between the performances, a band will play in the Terrace Tea Room.

The revolving globe on the tower was soon to cause trouble. The Westminster City Council stepped in and took Stoll to court, after three months of argument as to whether it was a moving sky-sign and therefore contravening the London Building Act of 1844 or whether it was an intrinsic part of the design of the building. Finally it was agreed that if it became stationary all would be well. Stoll had the globe fixed and the interior fitted with electric bulbs which flashed on and off to give the effect of movement. This was a feature of the skyline for many years.

When it became a regular theatre in 1931 its name was shortened to the Coliseum. Stoll's original wish to exceed the size of Drury Lane (as it was then) was only unfulfilled as to the seating capacity, which was 47 less. In 1951 the theatre was reseated and the capacity increased. It now holds over 300 more than the present Drury Lane and thus is the largest working theatre in London.

THE PLAYS

The theatre was originally opened on 24 December 1904, as a variety theatre and it was intended by Oswald Stoll that it should be a family house. It proved a failure and was closed down in June 1906, remaining empty until December 1907, when it took on a new and successful lease of life. The financial collapse of the original company and its re-purchase by Stoll is an involved story. The Coliseum was the first theatre in this country to be fitted with a revolving stage, made up of three concentric rings capable of moving in either direction, and this innovation ran Stoll into an expenditure of £70,000.

The famous drop-curtain illustrating personalities in the history of the stage and music hall was painted by Byam Shaw.

Besides most of the great names of variety, many stars of the legitimate stage were persuaded to appear in single turns or short plays, amongst whom were Ellen Terry, who made her first appearance on the variety stage here in 1917 when she played Mistress Page in an excerpt from *The Merry Wives of Windsor*. Later, in February 1918, she also appeared here as Portia in the trial scene from *The Merchant of Venice*. On both occasions she was supported by Edith Evans, then at the start of her career. Lillie Langtry appeared in 1917 and 1918, and Nazimova packed the house twice daily for a month in a one-act play called *A Woman of the Earth* in 1927. Sarah Bernhardt paid five visits between 1910 and 1916.

Diaghileff's Russian Ballet gave seasons here in 1918, 1924 and 1925. It is also interesting to note that the first public stage demonstration of television was given at the Coliseum on 28 July 1930. Truly the writing was on the wall, Music-Hall was in its fast decline, even the 'talkies' took possession for a while.

To give a full story of these years is impossible here, but it has been recounted by Felix Barker in *The House that Stoll Built* (1957); also of interest is *Crowded Nights and Days* (1930) by Arthur Croxton, who was associated with the house for many years.

In April 1931 the Coliseum opened as a regular theatre and forsook its variety career. The production which initiated this change was *White Horse Inn*, a musical spectacular play adapted from the German by Harry Graham, with music by Ralph Benatsky and Robert Stolz. In this production Ernst Stern and Erik Charell applied the methods of Reinhardt to musical comedy and the theatre was transformed into a Tyrolean village. The cast included one hundred and sixty players, three bodies of bandsmen and innumerable chorus. £60,000 was invested in this production by Stoll and all the money came back in advance bookings. The production ran for 651 performances. In 1932 it was followed by another success in a similar vein, *Casanova*, also from the German by Harry Graham, with music by Johann Strauss, which ran for 429 performances. Lew Leslie's *Blackbirds of 1934*, *The Golden Toy* (1934) by Carl Zuckmayer, adapted from the Indian play *Vasantasena*, the English version of which was by Dion Titheradge and the music by Robert Schumann, were also produced. Other. large-scale productions followed until this style of entertainment began to pall, and was superseded by a 'real ice' spectacle, *St Moritz*, devised and produced by Stanley

Bell (1937), the first of a series of similar successes. The Coliseum was never shut; in between productions, seasons of variety and ballet were seen. At Christmas 1936 the theatre presented its first pantomime, *Cinderella*. Just before the war a season of weekly repertory occupied the stage. In 1940 a revival of *White Horse Inn* put the theatre back on its feet, then other revivals were seen including *The Maid of the Mountains, The Belle of New York, The Quaker Girl*, and annual pantomimes were staged up to 1945. In 1942 Stoll had died and the Coliseum had passed into the hands of Prince Littler. After two spectacular revues, *Annie Get Your Gun* burst upon London in 1947 and ran until 1950, a total of 1304 performances, the longest in this theatre's history. The days of the American musical continued with *Kiss Me Kate* (1951), *Guys and Dolls* (1953), *Can-Can* (1954), *Pajama Game* (1955), *Damn Yankees* (1957), but *The Bells are Ringing* (1957) tolled the knell of this era, and after a lean period, brightened only by Rodgers and Hammerstein's *Cinderella* (Christmas 1958), the experiment was made of bringing Sadler's Wells Opera Company to the West End with their production of *The Merry Widow*, but once again complete success was elusive. After another spectacular Christmas production, Cole Porter's *Aladdin*, a return to the American formula was made with *The Most Happy Fella* in 1960. At the conclusion of the run, in January 1961, several Dance seasons were staged before it was announced, in May, that M.G.M. had taken a long lease of the theatre for use as a cinema (while The Empire was in process of rebuilding). After some minor alterations the Coliseum re-opened in June with *Gone with the Wind*.

It was converted for the showing of *Cinerama* in 1963 and films remained until it was taken over as a West End home for the Sadler's Wells Opera Company. It was closed in May 1968, completely redecorated, restored both inside and out and a large orchestra pit constructed. It re-opened, under the direction of Stephen Arlen, on 21 August 1968 with *Don Giovanni*. Since then ballet companies from all over the world have had seasons between the regular Sadler's Wells operas. The highlight of this new venture, now under the direction of Lord Harwood, was the first complete production in English for many years of Wagner's *The Ring*. Since Christmas 1971 Robert Helpmann's production of *Peter Pan* has been staged annually, first with Dorothy Tutin and then in 1973 with Maggie Smith in the title role.

Early in 1974 the long expected new name for the Sadler's Wells Opera Company was announced—from August it became known as the English National Opera.

8 · The Comedy Theatre

Panton Street, Haymarket, S.W.1

Capacity: 820

Opened as the Royal Comedy Theatre, 15 October 1881, with *The Mascotte*, an *opéra comique* by Audran, English version by H. B. Farnie and R. Reece. Produced by H. B. Farnie, under the management of Alexander Henderson.

THE BUILDING

The streets between Leicester Square and the Haymarket were of dubious reputation until, as the *Daily Telegraph* of 14 October 1881 proclaimed, 'recent improvements have now removed altogether the doubtful resorts of the roisterers of other days'.

On a plot of ground in Panton Street at the corner of Oxendon Street and backed by James Street (now Orange Street), a theatre was built by J. H. Addison for Alexander Henderson, the original lessee.

The architect was Thomas Verity (Architect to the Lord Chamberlain) and the builders were Kirk and Randall of Woolwich.

A three-tier house, its exterior in the classical tradition, it remains today as originally conceived. *The Era* of 15 October 1881 comments on the interior:

The cunning artificers in luxury and ease have exerted their skill and ingenuity on the construction of the private boxes and the seats of the dress circle. These seats are neither cribbed nor cabined, abundant room being set apart for each person, while the upholstering has been done with no inconsiderable amount of taste and effect.

The pit is open and airy, the slope of the floor being so arranged here, as in every other part of the Theatre, that even when the house is crowded to its utmost capacity, everyone will have a full view of the stage.

The architectural ornamentation of the interior reflects the highest credit, as does, indeed, the projection and entire carrying out of the plans, on Mr Verity, the distinguished architect of the building. It is Renaissance style, richly moulded and finished in white and gold. The draperies of the boxes are of maroon plush, elegantly draped and embroidered in gold. The Royal box, with its elegantly appointed retiring room attached, is, in its chaste and artistic decorations, quite a sight in itself. It has a special entrance in Oxendon Street.

The original intention to light the theatre with electricity was abandoned in favour of the conventional gas, though the Savoy Theatre, which was opened five days before, had made history by installing the new electric light (see No. 33).

Alexander Henderson intended the theatre to be the home of comic opera and at one time it was to have been called the Alexandra or the Lyric (the present theatre of that name was not built until 1888); he seems to have had no warrant to call his theatre 'Royal' and this addition was dropped in 1884.

The theatre was redecorated and partially reconstructed in October 1911, the main changes being in the vestibule and bars; other minor alterations had been made in 1893 and 1903.

In 1933 a drastic redecoration scheme took place, though the auditorium remained structurally the oldest Victorian example in London, until 1954, when another major reconstruction took place under the supervision of Cecil Masey and Alester MacDonald.

New dressing-rooms were built, the stage door was moved into Oxenden Street, some extra land (a small bombed site at the corner of Oxenden and Orange Streets) was incorporated. The old gallery was reseated, and the upper circle became the Royal Circle. A complete re-organisation of entrances to the auditorium combined with modernisation took place in all parts of the house and in this refurbished state the theatre was reopened on 14 December 1955. A further redecoration took place in 1959–60.

THE PLAYS
The theatre opened on 15 October 1881 under the management of Alexander Henderson, with *The Mascotte*. This was followed by *Boccaccio*, *Rip Van Winkle* (with Fred Leslie as Rip) in 1882, and *Falka* in 1883; the adaptation of these three successes was the work of H. B. Farnie; other similar pieces followed.

In 1885 comic opera gave way to drama, under the direction of Violet Melnotte, who secured an extended lease of the theatre, producing amongst other plays *The Silver Shield* by Sydney Grundy; *Sister Mary* (1886), and a season of comic operas in which she often appeared herself. In 1887 Beerbohm Tree produced *The Red Lamp*, his first essay in management.

In 1888 Violet Melnotte let the theatre to Charles Hawtrey, who held the management until 1892 and produced *Jane* (1890) and many now-forgotten farces.

In 1893 the theatre was taken over by J. Comyns-Carr and he remained at the theatre until Hawtrey returned in 1896. During Comyns-Carr's régime was produced *Sowing the Wind* by Sydney Grundy (1893); *The Professor's Love Story* by J. M. Barrie given during E. S. Willard's season (1894); *The New Woman*, another play by Grundy (1894); *The Benefit of the Doubt* by Pinero (1895). Most of the plays at this period starred Cyril Maude and his wife Winifred Emery. On Hawtrey's return he opened with a play of his own, *Mr Martin*, which he followed with a successful season of light comedies including *One Summer's Day* by H. V. Esmond (1897), and R. C. Carton's *Lord and Lady Algy* (1898). Later the same year William Greet took over the theatre and Arthur Roberts and Ada Reeve appeared in a musical comedy *Milord Sir Smith*. Managements changed quickly at this time, and in 1899 Ada Reeve was here again as Cleopatra in *Great Caesar*.

For the next few years the theatre was often used for special seasons and matinées of the 'new drama'. Benson and his company were here in 1900–1.

The fortunes of the Comedy were at a very low ebb when on 25 October 1902 Lewis Waller took the theatre and presented *Monsieur Beaucaire* which proved a huge success and ran for over four hundred performances, doing much to restore the prestige and fortunes of the theatre of which Frank Curzon had become lessee. In 1904 Fred Terry and Julia Neilson were at the Comedy in *Sunday*.

John Barrymore made his first appearance on the London stage here in May 1905, when he played Charles Hine in *The Dictator*, which Charles Frohman presented. In 1906 John Hare had a short season, appearing in *The Alabaster Staircase*, and a revival of *A Pair of Spectacles*. Also in 1906 London saw its first 'crook' play at this theatre with the production of *Raffles* presented by Frohman under the management of Arthur Chudleigh, who now controlled the theatre.

From 1907 to 1909 Marie Tempest, under Frohman's guidance, added to her success in straight comedy by her appearance in *The Truth, The Barrier* and *Angela* (1907), *Lady Barbarity* and *Mrs Dot* (1908) and *Penelope* (1909). The last two plays were early works by Somerset Maugham.

Another 'crook' play was seen in 1910, *Alias Jimmy Valentine*, with Gerald du Maurier in the title role, and in 1911 Marie Löhr was seen in Pinero's *Preserving Mr Panmure*. In 1912 a popular success was *The Bear Leaders*, in which Muriel Martin Harvey made her first appearance on the stage. The next few years were marked by plays which, though by well-known authors and highly successful in their day, are now forgotten.

From October 1914 *Peg O' My Heart*, with Laurette Taylor, proved a great success, running for 710 performances. In 1915 the wave of revue which had welled up in wartime overtook this theatre, and Albert de Courville's *Shell Out* (1915) was followed by Cochran's *Half-past Eight*, André Charlot's *This and That* and *See-Saw* (1916), then *Bubbly* and *Tails-Up* in 1918.

In 1920 the matinée idol of the day, Owen Nares, appeared in *The Charm School*. Other notable productions were *The Romantic Age* by A. A. Milne, and *The Faithful Heart* by Monckton Hoffe (1921).

In 1922 J. E. Vedrenne became manager. Outstanding productions between 1922 and 1928 included *Secrets* with Fay Compton (1922), *The Creaking Chair* and *Just Married* (1924). Archibald Nettlefold took over in 1925 and his successes were *Lavender Ladies, 9-45* (1925), *The Silent House* (1927), *The Last Hour* (1928) and *The Infinite Shoeblack* (1929).

In 1932 the Comedy came under the direction of Charles Killick and Victor Payne Jennings; outstanding successes were scored by *Bally-hoo!* (1932), Charlot's two revues *How Do You Do?* (1933), and *Hi-Diddle-Diddle* (1934), *Busman's Honeymoon* (1936) and *Room for Two* (1938).

The theatre was in constant use during the war years. Successful productions included *New Faces* (1940), *Rise Above It* (1941), which ran into a second edition; *Murder without Crime* (1942), *This was a Woman* (1944) and *See How they Run* (1945).

Earl Beauchamp, owner of the theatre, sold it in September 1945 for upwards of £100,000 to H. H. Wingate, the owner of the Curzon Cinema, Mayfair. Wingate was reported to have said that the current lease would not expire for another two years, but that when he eventually took possession of the theatre it would be modernised and re-equipped. He had also purchased some adjoining land. (This promised renovation did not take place until 1954–5.)

The next few years saw constant change and the plays presented were mainly by Jack de Leon and had their birth at his Q Theatre.

Killick's lease ended in 1948 and until the renovation took place Bernard Goodman was lessee. The biggest successes of this period were *Slings and Arrows*, a revue directed by Charles Hickman with Hermione Gingold (1948), *On Monday Next* with Henry Kendall (1949), *For Better, For Worse . . .* (1952), and after its run of 617 performances the theatre closed. It reopened with *Mornings at Seven* in December 1955; a revue, *Fresh Airs*, followed.

In October 1956 the New Watergate Theatre Club was formed with the Comedy Theatre as its headquarters, the object being to present plays which had been refused a licence by the Lord Chamberlain. During the three years of their existence they presented *A View from the Bridge* by Arthur Miller (1956), *Tea and Sympathy* (1957), *Cat on a Hot Tin Roof* by Tennessee Williams (1958), and *Five Finger Exercise* (1959). These productions were largely instrumental in bringing about a change in the censor's outlook, and with the new freedom the necessity for the Watergate Club, as such, became obsolete. The public no longer needed to invest its five shillings in a subscription in order to enter the theatre.

At the end of the run of *Five Finger Exercise*, the English Stage Company's production of *Rosmersholm* transferred here from the Royal Court after its successful run. *Look on Tempests* in March 1960 was quickly followed by *A Passage to India* the next month; this ran until it was succeeded by *The Tinker*, a new play brought from the Bristol Old Vic in November, and which saw the new year in.

During 1961 the Comedy housed several plays including: *Fairy Tales of New York*, *The Tenth Man*, and a revue *On the Brighter Side*. It was in October that *Bonne Soupe*, with Coral Browne was produced. This was to transfer later in February 1962 to Wyndham's, but the plays that followed 'failed to attract'. It was the American revue *The Premise* which brought success again to the theatre in July 1962 and this ran for 186 performances, then a Christmas season of *Toad of Toad Hall* played matinées only. An uneventful year followed and *Toad* returned once more the following festive season. 1964 saw thirteen short runs. During this period there was one success, a transfer from the Lyric, Hammersmith of *Son of Oblomov* which ran, with a break, from December 1964 to April 1966, in all 530 performances. *The Boy Friend* was revived but only achieved 367 performances, nothing like its original run of 2084. The American play *Fortune in Men's Eyes*, from the Open Space, brought nudity to the Comedy for 149 performances in 1968. Their next success, from the Mermaid, was *Let's Get a Divorce:* 342 performances. In April 1969 came *Mixed Doubles*, a programme of eight one act plays by various authors. *Girl In My Soup* transferred from the Globe Theatre continuing its long run to over 2500 performances. In September 1972 a new Alan Ayckbourn comedy, *Time and Time Again*, started a successful run. The next play was *Small Craft Warnings* by Tennessee Williams with Elaine Stritch, which had only a short run. *Dear Love*, with Keith Michell and Geraldine McEwan, was presented but was quickly followed by Paul Scofield in *Savages*, transferred from the Royal Court, which ran until January 1974 and was succeeded by *Judies*, and in March, *Knuckle*.

9 · Covent Garden,
The Royal Opera House

(Theatre Royal, Covent Garden)

Bow Street, W.C.2

THE FIRST THEATRE
Capacity: 1897

Opened as the Theatre Royal in Covent Garden, 7 December 1732, with a revival of *The Way of the World* by William Congreve. Under the management of John Rich. From 1769 it became known as the Theatre Royal, Covent Garden.

THE SECOND THEATRE
Capacity: 3000

Opened 18 September 1809 with *Macbeth*, preceded by an occasional address spoken by John Philip Kemble, followed by *The Quaker*, a musical entertainment by Charles Dibdin. Under the management of John Philip Kemble.

NOTTINGHAM UNIVERSITY LIBRARY

Interior converted to an opera house and reopened as The Royal Italian Opera, Covent Garden, 6 April 1847, with *Semiramide* by Rossini.

THE THIRD THEATRE
Capacity: 2117

Opened as The Royal Italian Opera, Covent Garden, 15 May 1858 with *Les Huguenots* by Meyerbeer. Under the management of Frederick Gye. Variously known according to the entertainment as The Royal English Opera, The Theatre Royal, and from 1892 to 1939 The Royal Opera. Since then the official name has been The Royal Opera House.

*

The founding of Covent Garden theatre rests upon the second of the patents granted by Charles II for the opening of playhouses after the Restoration in 1660. The first patent granted to Thomas Killigrew brought the Theatre Royal (Drury Lane) into being (see No. 11) and the second, granted to Sir William Davenant, created the Duke's Theatre, firstly in Lincoln's Inn, then in Dorset Garden. This patent, after the passage of years, came into the hands of Christopher Rich, an attorney, who obtained control of Drury Lane in 1693 but when he was forced from the Theatre Royal in 1711, leaving Colley Cibber in charge with Killigrew's patent, he moved to Lincoln's Inn Fields Theatre, which he planned to rebuild; he died before the new Theatre was opened in 1714. Rich was succeeded by his son John, who remained there until 1732, making history with *The Beggar's Opera* in 1728 and with the establishment of pantomime in London with himself as Harlequin.

In 1732 he built a new theatre in Covent Garden, calling it the Theatre Royal and operating with Davenant's patent; thus began the rivalry of the two theatres and their monopoly of the legitimate drama which was not broken until 1843.

The building was commenced in March 1731, though the original prospectus was issued in December 1730. Rich obtained a lease of the land from the Duke of Bedford, whose family still own the site. The theatre was designed by James Shepherd and decorated by an Italian artist, Amiconi, who painted a magnificent ceiling. It was opened on 7 December 1732 with Congreve's *The Way of the World*. There is a print by Hogarth, entitled 'Rich's Glory', showing the Manager entering into possession of his new theatre, which had two entrances, one in Bow Street and another under the piazza in Covent Garden.

November 9 1734, saw the production of Handel's *Il Pastor Fido* and a ballet *Terpsichore*, with Mlle Sallé, Handel having taken the theatre for the production of opera and ballet. His operas alternated with plays until 1737.

James Quin was the leading actor in these early years and
Peg Woffington made her first appearance here on 8
November 1740, causing a sensation. Rich also performed
in his own pantomimes. David Garrick appeared here in
1746, having previously been seen at Drury Lane. Spranger
Barry joined the company in 1750 and the two theatres were
in great rivalry after Garrick returned to Drury Lane. In
1761 Rich died, and he was succeeded by his son-in-law,
John Beard, who mostly presented opera.

In the *Journal* of Lalande, the French astronomer, we
read that when he visited Covent Garden in 1763 he was
much impressed by the behaviour of the gallery. 'A great
deal of barking and howling and throwing of orange peel at a
man whose face displeased the gallery. The gallery controlled the acting and thanked the players.'

In 1767 a piano was heard for the first time in public. A
concert announced 'accompaniment by a new instrument
called Piano Forte'. The same year Beard sold the patent
for £60,000 to George Colman the elder, Thomas Harris,
William Powell and Rutherford. There were quarrels and
eventually Harris became sole manager in 1774.

January 1768 brought the production of Goldsmith's *The
Good Natured Man* and on 15 March 1773. *She Stoops to
Conquer* was given its first performance with Lewes as
Young Marlow, Quick as Tony Lumpkin and Mrs Bulkley
as Kate Hardcastle. On 17 January 1775 came the first
production of Sheridan's *The Rivals*.

In 1784 the theatre underwent its first major reconstruction, apart from redecoration, under the supervision
of Richards, and in 1792 so many important structural
alterations were made to the building that it may be said
to have been virtually rebuilt. These alterations were made
by Henry Holland at a cost of £25,000.

The first performance of *Aladdin* as a pantomime was
seen in 1788. In May 1789 Charles Macklin made his final
appearance, as Shylock; he was eighty-nine years of age
and was unable to carry through his part. In 1800 George
Frederick Cooke made his London debut and his short
career was associated mainly with this theatre.

On 13 November 1802 the first melodrama was given.
Called *A Tale of Mystery*, it was from the French by
Thomas Holcroft. In 1803 John Philip Kemble became
proprietor, with Harris's son Henry, having broken with
Sheridan at Drury Lane.

In 1804 it was announced that a tragedian only thirteen
years old, discovered in the provinces, would make his
debut on December 4. This was the child prodigy William
Betty, and the interest of the public was thoroughly aroused.
The youth was even exhibited in the streets in a carriage.

On 20 September 1808 the theatre was burnt down and in
this fire perished Handel's organ, as well as a quantity of

his manuscript scores. However, the foundation stone
of a new building was laid by the Prince of Wales on
December 31 of the same year. This building on the corner
of Bow Street and Hart Street (now Floral Street) was designed by Richard Smirke; it cost £150,000 but was
slightly smaller than the previous theatre. It was modelled
on the Temple of Minerva on the Acropolis at Athens.
Bas-reliefs and statues of Comedy and Tragedy by Flaxman
adorned its exterior. It opened on 18 September 1809 with a
production of *Macbeth*. Owing to the cost of the new
theatre there was an attempt to increase the prices. This
led to the famous O.P. (Old Prices) riots, which caused the
Riot Act to be read from the stage of the theatre. After
continual disturbances for sixty-one nights, Kemble had to
submit to public demand and make a formal apology.

Mrs Siddons made her farewell appearance on 29 June
1812; on 16 September 1816 Macready made his first
appearance, and on 23 June 1817 Kemble retired to be
succeeded in management by his brother Charles.

According to a playbill, the exterior of the theatre, the
Hall and the Grand Staircase were first lit by gas during the
1815–16 season, and the auditorium in 1817. The latter was
described in that year as 'being brilliantly illuminated with
a grand central chandelier which has been rendered still
more effective, and the three auxiliary lamps which were
complained of as impeding the sight and contour of the
theatre have been removed, and Grecian lamps substituted,
which range round the back of the Dress Circle and shed a
soft medium light, without obstructing the view of the
stage'.

In 1823 an event of great importance in the history of
stage costume was Charles Kemble's revival of *King John*,
for which Planché was commissioned to design a completely new set of dresses. This brought to a head the
revolt against the conventional costuming of plays,
timorously started by John Philip Kemble, which cul-
minated in the 'archaeological' revivals of Charles Kean.

In 1825 we find a dramatic critic writing of a performance:

> We are pleased to observe that this house is gradually
> adopting the French manner of arranging the stage,
> making a room appear like one by disposing about it
> articles of furniture. The bedroom scene had an excellent
> effect last night, though we have much to accomplish
> before we can hope to rival our neighbours in this
> respect. We suspect that the improvement already visible
> may be attributed to Mr Charles Kemble's visit to Paris.

In 1826 Weber's *Oberon*, commissioned by Kemble for
the theatre, was first produced, and in 1829 Fanny Kemble
as Juliet restored the failing fortunes of the Kembles and the
theatre.

There had been trouble with the lighting system. The gas was found to be so offensive that, when it caused an explosion of a gasometer on 18 November 1828, the management decided to revert partly to the use of wax and oil, and closed the theatre for the necessary alterations.

On 3 December 1828 there was an announcement on the top of the playbills which read:

> In reply to a statement in the Morning Journal yesterday I certify that no gasometer, chamber or receptacle of gas is now placed within the theatre and those parts of the theatre at present lighted with gas are supplied from the mains of The Chartered Gas Company. I beg leave to add that The King's Theatre, The Adelphi and The English Opera House are also supplied from the mains of the above company.

The statement was signed by the manager of the gas company. A bill was also issued stating that:

> The public attention is respectfully solicited to the following facts: The Gasometers and apparatus for making gas are destroyed and no more gas will be manufactured within the walls of the theatre. The circles of Boxes will be illuminated with wax; the lights in front of the stage and every internal avenue to box, pit and galleries will be produced by the agency of purest oil.

In 1832 Pierre François Laporte, the impresario, took over the management. On 25 March 1833 Kean made his last appearance: he was taken ill during the performance of *Othello* and carried from the stage by his son who was the Iago. In the same year the management passed to Alfred Bunn, who thus became lessee of both Drury Lane and Covent Garden.

The theatre was advertised 'To Let' in 1835, and Bunn's resources having ended, he was succeeded by Osbaldiston as manager in the same year. He engaged Macready and a strong company. During this era Charles Kemble made his series of farewell apperances, sharing the patent with Henry Harris.

From 1837 to 1839 the theatre was under the management of Macready himself. One interesting feature of his directorship was that no player was engaged for any particular part or line of parts, with the result that an important actor or actress might receive—and would accept—some comparatively unimportant role. An outstanding improvement in stage illumination was the introduction, by Macready, of limelight in his season of 1837–8. This is a landmark in theatrical history, though limelight, however, was not employed as a regular effect until Charles Kean's *Henry VIII* in 1858.

From 1839 to 1842 Charles Mathews and Madame Vestris

were joint managers. In 1841 *London Assurance* was produced. Dion Boucicault was paid £300 for this, one of the
most successful comedies of the early Victorian era. They
also staged a series of Shakespearean revivals. In 1842–3
Charles Kemble took over active management and
presented his daughter Adelaide as Norma in an English
version of the opera.

In 1843 the theatre building was occupied by the Anti-
Corn Law League and lean times followed. No manager
could find success. On 6 April 1847, after considerable
alterations, the theatre was reopened as The Royal Italian
Opera. These alterations and improvements cost £27,000;
the architect was Benedict Albano.

It was due to the usual managerial quarrels in the operatic
world that Michael Costa left Lumley of Her Majesty's
and joined in a scheme originated by Persiani, the composer, to make Covent Garden into an Opera House. After
many financial difficulties the final management devolved
on Frederick Beale of the firm of Cramer and Beale, the
music publishers. For the seasons of 1848–9 Frederick
Delafield became manager, calling in Frederick Gye to
assist him, and from 1850 Gye was in sole command. The
story of these and the following years of Grand Opera is
fully told in *Two Centuries of Opera at Covent Garden* by
Harold Rosenthal (1958).

On 5 March 1856, following a Bal Masqué, the theatre
was once again destroyed by fire. A third building, on the
same site, was built by Gye. It was designed by Sir Edward
M. Barry and erected in six months. The statues and reliefs
by Flaxman were preserved from the earlier building and
incorporated in the new one. Messrs Lucas Brothers were
the contractors. Gye obtained a lease from the Duke of
Bedford for an extended site. The theatre was laid out east
to west instead of north to south as in the previous theatres.
The frontage remained in Bow Street, with the stage door in
Floral Street. The theatre opened on 15 May 1858 with a
performance of Meyerbeer's *Les Huguenots*.

The new Opera House remained, except for necessary
alterations and redecorations, much the same as when it
was built. The main differences being the removal of boxes
on the amphitheatre level and the almost complete opening
up of the two tiers, originally divided up into boxes. Its
capacity was enlarged to 2190 from the original 1897. In
1933 a new block of offices, dressing and rehearsal rooms
was built, extending the rear of the building to Mart Street.

The history of the theatre is now almost that of Opera in
England. After the Gye régime, his sons succeeded,
followed at length by Augustus Harris, in 1888. Once again
both Drury Lane and Covent Garden were under the same
manager and he remained there until his death in 1896. The
control then passed to the Grand Opera Syndicate, who

continued to provide what is now called 'the Golden Age of Opera'. They also brought Russian Ballet to London in 1911, but the war put an end to International Opera and Ballet and Covent Garden became a Government store. After the war Sir Thomas Beecham became the great name at the head of the artistic affairs of the Opera, only to see the place become a dance-hall during the Second World War.

Covent Garden was reopened in February 1946 with a season of the Sadler's Wells Ballet Company; opera returned later the same year. After some preliminary skirmishes Covent Garden has now become the National Opera House, housing The Royal Opera and The Royal Ballet (Sadler's Wells Ballet Company became The Royal Ballet in 1956.)

In 1964 the Opera House was closed between May and September while the gallery and the amphitheatre were reconstructed into one, the auditorium redecorated and alterations made to the 'Front of House'. The old 'carriage way' entrance under the portico has now been incorporated into the foyer and a Box office, Archive premises and Administrative offices constructed in warehouses in Floral Street, opposite the side of the theatre. Other histories are *The Annals of Covent Garden Theatre* by Henry Saxe Wyndham, 2 vols (1906) and *Covent Garden* by Desmond Shawe-Taylor (1948). In 1970 *The Survey of London*, volume XXXV, was devoted to a detailed account of The Royal Opera House and the Theatre Royal, Drury Lane.

10 · The Criterion Theatre

Piccadilly Circus, W.1

Capacity: 645

Opened 21 March 1874 with *An American Lady*, a comedy by Henry J. Byron, followed by *Topsyturveydom*, a musical extravaganza in one act by W. S. Gilbert and Alfred Cellier. Under the management of Henry J. Byron.

THE BUILDING

In 1873 a large restaurant (The Criterion) was built by Spiers and Pond in what was then called Regent Circus, Piccadilly. The entire block costing some £100,000 occupied the site of the White Bear, an old posting inn which had stood there from at least 1685, and some other adjoining property. The ground stretching back to Jermyn Street, almost covering the whole area between the Haymarket and Lower Regent Street, was taken on lease from the Crown Commissioners.

In the middle of the building it was originally intended to build a small concert hall constructed as a square galleried room. It was not until the carcase of the building was finished that they decided to convert this part of it into a theatre. Designed by Thomas Verity, it was to be entirely

underground and even the upper circle had to be reached
by descending stairs.

Underground theatres are now prohibited by the regulations of the G.L.C., but in 1874 this idea was considered a
great novelty: 'an underground Temple of the Drama into
which it was necessary to pump air to save the audience
from being asphyxiated'.

After difficulties in obtaining a licence were fully overcome the theatre was let by the owners to a William Duck
on a long lease for £50 a week. Its original manager was
Henry J. Byron.

In March 1883 the theatre was closed by order of the
Metropolitan Board of Works. Charles Wyndham was then
the lessee and manager. It was reconstructed and reopened
in 1884. *Dramatic Notes* says: 'The Criterion Theatre,
transformed from a stuffy band-box to a convenient, handsome, and well-ventilated house, reopened on April 16.'

Amongst the improvements was the addition of electricity. The original architect, Thomas Verity, supervised
the alterations.

The Era, April 19, elaborates:

The principal improvements may be described as
follows—A large area open from the basement to the sky
has been formed on one side of the theatre by cutting off
a considerable portion of the adjoining Criterion Restaurant, thus giving direct light and air to all parts of the
house. As an instance of the efficiency of this new area
it may be mentioned that the morning sunshine streams
into the pit. Spacious new corridors have been constructed the whole length of the Piccadilly frontage on
the stalls, dress circle, and gallery levels, providing direct
light and ventilation to these parts. These corridors lead
on one side to a commodious crush room and to the new
Piccadilly exit, and on the other side to the box-office
entrance. In addition to this there are the former exits
into Jermyn Street, so that every part of the house is
abundantly provided on all sides with exits into two
distinct thoroughfares. The auditorium has been in a
great measure reconstructed. . . . The stage is entirely
refitted with all modern improvements, and the old
dressing rooms have been demolished and new ones
built in Jermyn Street. The tile work and wall decorations
by Simpson and Sons, and the structural work has been
most admirably carried out by the well known contractor
Mr Wm Webster, of Trafalgar Square.

A further remodelling and redecoration took place in
1902–3, when the theatre was closed for some seven months.
Happily this little theatre, consisting of only Stalls, Dress
Circle and Upper Circle, still manages today to retain much

of its 1884 atmosphere and tile decoration. Only its main entrance and vestibule are on ground level in Piccadilly Circus. The frontage is the façade of the Criterion block.

THE PLAYS

The theatre was opened on 21 March 1874 with *An American Lady*, a comedy written by the manager, H. J. Byron, in which he also acted, and a musical extravaganza by W. S. Gilbert and Alfred Cellier, as an afterpiece. This opening play had a run of a hundred performances, but the success of the theatre was far from being assured until *opéra bouffe* was produced under the management of Alexander Henderson in 1875 and 1876. Charles Wyndham came to the theatre with his own company in December 1875 with *Brighton*. This was followed by *On Bail* (1877), a farcical comedy by W. S. Gilbert from the French, and *The Pink Dominos*, a farcical comedy by James Albery, also from the French. This latter ran for 555 performances and was the first real success of its kind. It shocked the critics, but that merely proved good advertisement.

Later in 1879 Charles Wyndham became lessee as well as manager. *Truth* by Bronson Howard (1879), *Betsy* (1879) by F. C. Burnand, and other plays of a similar kind followed, including *Little Miss Muffet* by James Albery (1882).

In March 1883 the theatre was closed for reconstruction and it reopened in April 1884 with a revival of *Brighton* (first seen at the Court in 1874). A long run was scored with *The Candidate* from November 1884 to January 1886.

In the March of 1886 Mary Moore began her long association with this theatre. Her first part was in a play called *The Man with Three Wives*, but her first notable success was in her first leading part, that of Lady Amaranthe in a revival of John O'Keefe's play, *Wild Oats*. This was followed by her interpretation in November of Ada Ingot in *David Garrick*, a revival which proved a great success and was seen for 224 performances. She remained Wyndham's leading lady till the end of his career, eventually marrying him in 1916.

The next years are mainly occupied by the revival of past successes of Wyndham's management until he put on *She Stoops to Conquer* in 1890 and *The School for Scandal* in 1891.

The Criterion, having achieved a brilliant reputation as a home of light comedy, in 1893 began to present more serious work. Henry Arthur Jones' plays were produced, notably *The Bauble Shop* (1893), *The Case of Rebellious Susan* (1894), *The Physician* (1897), *The Liars* (1897); also R. C. Carton's *The Home Secretary* and *The Squire of Dames* (1895) and *Rosemary* (1896) by Louis N. Parker and Murray Carson.

A break was made when a musical farce *All Abroad* was produced with Ada Reeve in 1895, and *Bilberry of Tilbury; or, The Lady's Decline* in 1897, both needless to say by visiting managements.

In 1899 Wyndham left the theatre to go to the new Wyndham's in Charing Cross Road, but retained the lesseeship. From February 1900 to May 1901 the theatre was under the joint management of Wyndham and Arthur Bourchier, who shared the successful productions of *His Excellency the Governor*, *Lady Huntworth's Experiment*, *The Noble Lord* and *Mama*.

In 1902 the theatre was again remodelled, when Frank Curzon became manager and reopened after a closure of seven months on 10 February 1903 with *A Clean Slate*. Later successes included *The Duke of Killiecrankie* (1904), *White Chrysanthemum* (1905), *The Little Stranger* (1906). Wyndham returned to management here with *The Mollusc* (1907), which he followed with *Lady Epping's Lawsuit*, both by Hubert Henry Davies.

For the next few years several managements used the theatre. Evelyn Millard presented some plays, as did Weedon Grossmith. *Baby Mine* was his big success in 1911. In 1913 H. V. Esmond presented his wife Eva Moore in his own play *Eliza Comes to Stay*. This was followed by a French farce *Oh I Say!!* which ran for 288 performances.

In 1914 the management was taken over by Bronson Albery and Allan Aynesworth, who in February of that year presented *A Pair of Silk Stockings*. In the following year the management passed to J. Herbert Jay and A. L. Ellis. They were responsible for the production of *A Little Bit of Fluff*, the farce by Walter Ellis, which was produced in October 1915 and ran for 1241 performances; it was one of the outstanding successes of the Great War. Sir Charles Wyndham died in January 1919 and the theatre was carried on by Mary Moore, and after her death in 1931, by her son Sir Bronson Albery.

In November 1919 *Lord Richard in the Pantry* brought Cyril Maude back to the West End stage after a long absence in America and Australia. It ran for over five hundred performances and was followed in 1921 by a revival of *Grumpy*. From July 1921 *Ambrose Applejohn's Adventure* ran for 455 performances. Charles Hawtrey was the star in this play, which was written by Walter Hackett. Subsequent successes included *The Dippers* (1922), a farcical comedy by Ben Travers; *Advertising April; or, The Girl who made the Sunshine Jealous* (1923), a farcical comedy by Herbert Farjeon and Horace Horsnell, in which Sybil Thorndike played the title role, and *Mixed Doubles* (1925), a farcical comedy by Frank Stayton.

Marie Tempest became closely associated with the Criterion Theatre between 1926 and 1929, appearing in

The Cat's Cradle (1926), *The Scarlet Lady* (1926), *The Marquise* (1927), *Passing Brompton Road* (1929), and *Her Shop* (1929). In 1931 Sydney Carroll assumed the management for a time and produced van Druten's *After All* in March of that year.

Other successful productions have included *Flat to Let* (1931), *Musical Chairs* (1932); the first play of that promisingly brilliant dramatist Ronald Mackenzie whose career was tragically cut short, in which John Gielgud and Frank Vosper appeared; Ivor Novello's *Fresh Fields* (1933); *Sixteen* (1934); *Nina* (1935), which introduced Lucie Mannheim to the London stage in a dual role; and *After October* (1936) by Rodney Ackland. Also in 1936 came *French Without Tears*, which ran for 1039 performances and is said to have brought its author, Terence Rattigan, who was only twenty-four years of age at the time, a profit of £23,000. *Tony Draws a Horse* began its successful run at the Criterion in January 1939 and in December *French for Love*, with Alice Delysia in the cast, was staged. After two intimate revues the theatre was taken over by the B.B.C. and used as a studio for recordings and light entertainment broadcasts. Music Hall programmes were staged here. The theatre was handed back to Wyndham Theatres, Ltd., in September 1945. It reopened with Sheridan's *The Rivals*, with Edith Evans as Mrs Malaprop.

From then on the big successes included *The Guinea Pig* (1946), *The Indifferent Shepherd* (1948), *Traveller's Joy* (1948), *Who is Sylvia?* (1950), *Birthday Honours* (1953), *Intimacy at 8–30*, a revue which ran from April 1954 for 551 performances.

Waiting for Godot came here from the Arts Theatre in September 1955, to be followed, also from the Arts, by *The Waltz of the Toreadors* in 1956. This had a long and successful run. Then came *Not in the Book* (1958), *A Clean Kill* and *One Way Pendulum* from the Royal Court and a revue, *The Art of Living*, all in 1960. The big success of April 1961 was *The Irregular Verb to Love* which ran on until 1962, to be followed in February by *Four to the Bar*, a clever entertainment for four artists. After this came, eventually, *Miss Pell is Missing*, a typical Criterion success.

A Severed Head, from the Bristol Old Vic, opened in June 1963 and ran for 1043 performances. This was followed by two short runs, then, for a limited season, Max Adrian in *An Evening with G.B.S.* in October 1966. *Loot* by Joe Orton transferred in November from the Jeannetta Cochrane and ran for 379 performances. *Mrs Wilson's Diary* opened in October 1967 and ran 175 performances. Next *The Real Inspector Hound* and *The Audition* totalled 200 performances. Then came *Brief Lives*, a play for one player, adapted by Patrick Garland from the writings of John Aubrey, starring Roy Dotrice. After this the theatre had several short runs until *Flint* by David Mercer. In December 1970 came *The High Bid* with Eartha Kitt and early in 1971 *After Haggerty*, already seen the previous year at the Aldwych, presented by the Royal Shakespeare Company. In July *Butley* was the next play to have a very long run, right into 1972. A revue, *Hulla Baloo*, for a few nights, appeared to turn the theatre into an extension of the Piccadilly Circus 'Loo'! Eartha Kitt returned to this theatre in a new play, *Bunny*, in December; this was followed by a memorable revival of *A Doll's House* with Claire Bloom. In July 1973 *Absurd Person Singular*, by Alan Ayckbourn, started its successful run.

Over the past few years, without interrupting the use of the theatre, important structural and decorative work has been carried out and the theatre has become a centre of the controversy for the redevelopment of Piccadilly Circus. If plans go ahead as proposed the theatre will have to close for at least a year.

The theatre is controlled by Wyndham Theatres, Ltd, of which Mary Moore's grandson, Donald Albery, and great-grandson, Ian, are the directors. The company also runs the Albery and Wyndham's Theatres.

11 · Drury Lane,
The Theatre Royal

Catherine Street, W.C.2

THE FIRST THEATRE
Capacity: about 700

Opened as the Theatre Royal in Bridges Street, 7 May 1663 with *The Humorous Lieutenant* by Beaumont and Fletcher. Under the management of Thomas Killigrew.

THE SECOND THEATRE
Capacity: 2000

Opened as the Theatre Royal in Drury Lane, 26 March 1674, with *The Beggar's Bush* by Beaumont and Fletcher. Under the management of Thomas Killigrew. From 1783 it became known as the Theatre Royal, Drury Lane.

THE THIRD THEATRE
Capacity: 3611

Opened 12 March 1794 with a Concert of Sacred Music. Under the management of Richard Brinsley Sheridan.

THE FOURTH THEATRE
Capacity on Opening: 3060
Present Capacity: 2283

Opened 10 October 1812 with an address by Lord Byron,

delivered by R. W. Elliston, followed by *Hamlet* and a
musical farce *The Devil to Pay*. Under the management
of Samuel Arnold.

The portico was added 1820 and the colonnade 1831. The
present auditorium was constructed 1922.

*

The history of the Theatre Royal, Drury Lane, is, in
fact, almost the history of the English Theatre from the
Restoration until nearly the turn of the eighteenth century,
which it shares only with Covent Garden Theatre from 1732
(see No. 9) and the Haymarket, unofficially from 1720 and
officially in the summer months from 1760 (see No. 17).

To compress this into a short space is virtually impossible. There is room only to give landmarks and events
of importance in the story of what happened to the two
patents given by Charles II for theatrical companies.

Thomas Killigrew and Sir William Davenant were granted
the monopoly of theatrical affairs when the King returned
from exile in 1660. This, after some difficulties, resolved
itself into the issuing of two patents, ratified in 1662, for
companies to be called 'The King's Servants' and 'The
Duke of York's Servants'. Killigrew, in charge of the
King's Company, established himself at the Theatre Royal,
which he built on the site of a riding yard between Drury
Lane and Bridges Street (now Catherine Street). Davenant,
with the other company, converted Lisle's Tennis Court, in
Lincoln's Inn, into the first Duke's Theatre. The further
story of this charter lies with Covent Garden Theatre,
where it later came to rest.

The first Theatre Royal in Bridges Street was erected
at a cost of £2400 and opened on 7 May 1663 with Beaumont
and Fletcher's *The Humorous Lieutenant*.

Killigrew's company were technically part of the Royal
Household, taking an oath of loyalty at the Lord Chamberlain's office. They were entitled to wear His Majesty's
livery and ranked as 'Gentlemen of the Chamber', they
had an annual allowance of 'ten yards of scarlet cloth
and a suitable quantity of lace'. The annual rent of the
theatre, which was £50, was paid by Killigrew to the Earl
of Bedford, who owned the land. Samuel Pepys' description of the first theatre, which he visited with his wife the
day after it had been opened, is of interest. He says: 'The
house is made with extraordinary good convenience and
yet hath some faults, as the narrowness of the passage
in and out of the Pit, and the distance from the Stage to
the Boxes.'

The popularity of this theatre was very great, with Charles
Hart and Michael Mohun, John Lacy and Anne Marshall
among the company. It was a small theatre, approximately
the size of the present stage.

In 1665 Nell Gwynne made her first appearance here in Dryden's *The Indian Queen*. After a closure of eighteen months because of the Great Fire and the Plague, the theatre was reopened in November 1666.

On 25 January 1672 the theatre was destroyed by fire, but was replaced by a second building designed by Sir Christopher Wren at a cost of £4000. The new theatre was opened on 26 March 1674 as the Theatre Royal in Drury Lane. The foundations of this building can still be seen under the present stage. Dryden described this second house as 'plain built—a bare convenience only'.

The theatre did not succeed in its early years owing to quarrels with the rival company, but in November 1682 'The King's Servants' were joined by 'The Duke's Servants' with Betterton the leading actor in charge. Two years later Killigrew died; there were continual disagreements between the actors and Christopher Rich, the new owner of both the patents, and a rival company was set up at Lincoln's Inn Fields Theatre and later at the new Queen's Theatre in the Haymarket in 1705.

In 1711 Robert Wilkes, Thomas Dogget and Colley Cibber came into joint control, and a period of success began at last.

On 5 May 1737 a riot was caused by the abolition of the custom of allowing free admission to the gallery for the footmen of the gentlemen in the house. The offended flunkeys, notwithstanding the presence of the King, stormed the theatre and threatened to set fire to it.

In 1742 David Garrick made his first appearance at the theatre and five years later, in 1747, he entered into a partnership with James Lacey and acquired the patent. There followed one of the great eras in the history of the theatre.

Extensive alterations to the interior and exterior of the theatre were carried out by the Adam brothers during 1775, and on December 29 of that year Mrs Siddons made her debut. She was engaged by Garrick at £5 per week to play Portia to the Shylock of Thomas King and was announced as 'a young lady, her first appearance'. She was a failure and retired to the provinces until 1782.

In June 1776 Garrick retired and the management was taken over by Richard Brinsley Sheridan, who in some way found the means to pay £10,000 for two-fourteenths of the whole share. Thomas Linley paid a similar sum for another two-fourteenths, and a Dr Ford invested £15,000.

On 8 May 1777 *The School for Scandal* was first produced with great success. In 1778 Sheridan joined with his father-in-law and Dr Ford in buying the other half of the share from Garrick a year before he died.

In the Gordon Riots of 1780 the theatre was damaged, and from that time onwards a company of Guards was always kept posted at the theatre until this custom was abolished in 1896.

John Philip Kemble made his first appearance as Hamlet on 30 September 1783; and another important event in theatrical history took place in February 1785 when the theatre was first lighted with what were called 'Patent Lamps'. In 1788, at which time he was making regular appearances with his sister, Mrs Siddons, Kemble took over the active management.

By 1791 the theatre had so fallen into decay that it was found necessary to demolish it. It was therefore closed on 4 June 1791 and the company migrated to the King's Theatre, Haymarket. Designs for the new theatre were prepared by Henry Holland; Sheridan had the work put in hand, and the theatre opened on 12 March 1794. The first programme (as it was Lent) consisted of Sacred Music by Handel, and the dramatic season began on April 21 with *Macbeth*, in which production Kemble and Mrs Siddons took part. In 1800 an attempt was made on the life of George III whilst he was in the theatre.

On 24 February 1809 the theatre was once again destroyed by fire; £300,000 was raised and a Committee of Management formed to replace Sheridan. The first stone was set in place on 29 October 1811. This building, designed by Benjamin Wyatt, was planned on the model of the great theatre at Bordeaux and erected at a cost of £151,672. It opened on 10 October 1812 under the management of Samuel Arnold. The prologue was specially written by Byron, and Elliston played Hamlet. Edmund Kean made his sensational appearance here on 21 January 1814 and another chapter in its history began. In 1817 gas lighting was first introduced: this innovation followed the installation of gas at the rival theatre—Covent Garden. We read that 'the lights are enclosed in glasses and blinded from the audience by side screens and reflectors'.

Grimaldi's farewell benefit took place on 27 June 1818, raising £600.

In 1820 the portico was added, and in 1822 the interior was remodelled by Samuel Beazley at a cost of £22,000. This work was undertaken by Elliston, who also tried to improve the acoustics of the building by having the ceilings lowered and the boxes and the galleries advanced.

In 1826 Stephen Price was lessee, and on 1 October 1827 Charles Keen made his first appearance. In 1831, when Alfred Bunn was lessee, the colonnade was added to the design of Samuel Beazley.

Douglas Jerrold's *The Rent Day* and *The Factory Girl* in 1832 were early examples of 'missionary drama'—an attempt to use the stage to show the need for certain reforms.

There followed a period of chequered history for the

theatre, during which many forms of entertainment were given including opera, circus performances, melodrama and acrobatic displays.

In December 1841 Macready took over the management, an event which was hailed with enthusiasm in theatrical circles. The season began on 27 December 1841 with *The Merchant of Venice*. The interior of the house had undergone a thorough renovation, again under the direction of Beazley. An account of the various improvements made is interesting in that it shows how many things which we now take for granted were then complete innovations.

> The pit seats were covered with handsome red cloth, with backs stuffed and covered with crimson; each person sitting in a separate stall, in the centre of which was an opening, enabling the spectator to quit and return to his or her seat without inconvenience, a coffee room was exclusively appropriated for the reception of that class of visitors hitherto permitted to lounge in the principal saloon, but who were now very properly excluded . . . The crying evil, the long inflicted disgrace, that the eyes and ears of innocence were insulted and the minds of youth corrupted by the shameless scenes within its walls, was abolished. A noble example in managerial reform.

The new curtain, containing 1000 yards of crimson velvet, with gold fringes, lace, etc., opened in the centre.

On 12 June 1843 the Queen and Prince Albert visited the theatre in state. Macready's period of management undoubtedly did much to restore the prestige of Drury Lane. 'His policy was characterised by a scrupulous adherence to the best interests of the drama'. His farewell performance as *Macbeth* was a 'brilliant ceremony'. But his actual loss, financially, was about £20,000. He terminated his lesseeship in 1843.

Alfred Bunn returned and *The Bohemian Girl* was produced. In 1850 James Anderson was manager; in 1852 three managers tried their luck between July and October, and at the end of the year E. T. Smith took over. In 1863 there was a joint management of Edmund Falconer and F. B. Chatterton, the latter's management lasting, after Falconer left, until 1879.

That there were still abuses to be combated is indicated by the following letter, dated 2 January 1864:

> Sir, It is time Mr Falconer were informed of the opinion entertained out of doors of some of his box keepers. They are little better than harpies. A female servant of mine took two youths to the Upper Boxes on Monday night and having paid her money was refused admittance by the box keeper until she gave him sixpence.

In her flurry with her purse she also gave him half a
crown which he refused to refund. To make the case
worse one of the lads was left in the lobby and this
respectable person to whom the public in that part of
the house are entrusted, would not open the door for
him without sixpence more. My servant went down
to a policeman afterwards, but could get no redress.

                                                   A Father.

In 1867 a drama by Andrew Halliday called *The Great
City* contained a real horse and cab. However, this piece
of realism was eclipsed as a spectacle by a representation
of the Boat Race in *Formosa* (1869), which caused great
excitement and enthusiasm amongst the audience.

Repairs and renovations were undertaken in 1871, and
again in 1873, on both occasions under the supervision
of Marsh Nelson as architect. In April 1875 the great
Tommaso Salvini appeared as Othello.

After this somewhat changeable period and its many
vicissitudes there followed in 1879 the famous management of Augustus Harris, sometimes known as 'Dru. rio-
lanus'. The theatre now began to be renowned for its
spectacular dramas and for many years its annual Christmas
pantomimes, with Dan Leno and Herbert Campbell, all
of which were on a scale of unexampled splendour. Their
popularity 'raised Drury Lane to the highest point of
prosperity'.

In *The World* (1880) there was an explosion of a ship as
well as a scene depicting Piccadilly Circus at the hour of
midnight in a snowstorm. *Youth* (1881) showed the relief
of Rorke's Drift in the Zulu War; *A Life of Pleasure*
(1893), a representation of the Promenade at the Empire,
and *Cheer Boys, Cheer* (1895) the sinking of the *Birkenhead*.
Arthur Collins, who succeeded in 1897, continued the
same policy of spectacular melodrama, and the following
were some of the most famous spectacles: divers under
the sea and Boulter's Lock with steam yachts passing
through in *White Heather* (1897); Hampstead Heath Bank
Holiday in *The Great Ruby* (1898); a chariot race in
Ben-Hur (1902); an avalanche which hurled the villain to
destruction in *The Sins of Society* (1907); a horse-race
in *The Whip* (1909), and an earthquake in *The Hope* (1911).
It was for *The Whip* that much of the elaborate stage
machinery, still usable, was installed.

At the north-west corner of the theatre there is a drinking-
fountain of marble, terra-cotta and red granite. A taber-
nacle supported by pillars with Corinthian capitals and
bronze enrichments contains a bronze bust of Harris.
Below are seated two cherubs holding a scroll on which
are the words 'Erected by public subscription'.

Arthur Collins, who might well be called 'Druriolanus
II', well maintained the Harris tradition of drama and

pantomime. During these years the interior of the theatre was reconditioned on several occasions: in 1894 and again in 1901 when the sum of £25,000 was spent. On 25 March 1908 the stage was partially burnt out and another piece of rebuilding was necessary; it was under the supervision of Philip E. Pilditch who was also responsible for the 1901 drastic reconstruction.

Sir Henry Irving gave what proved to be his last London season here in the spring of 1905 and on 12 June 1905 Ellen Terry's stage Jubilee was celebrated.

Forbes Robertson gave a farewell season in 1913, and in 1913 and 1914 Diaghileff gave seasons of Russian Ballet and Opera.

Two new chapters in the history of Drury Lane were opened during the years of the Great War. In 1915 the cinema took possession and D. W. Griffiths' great American films *The Birth of a Nation* and *Intolerance* were shown. In 1916 a spectacular revue, an entirely new genre for this theatre, was presented; it was called *Razzle Dazzle* and was produced by Albert de Courville.

On 2 May 1916, the occasion of the Shakespeare Tercentenary Performance, Frank Benson appeared in the title-role of *Julius Caesar*, and at the conclusion was knighted in the Royal Box by King George V.

Arthur Collins directed the Drury Lane productions until he retired in 1924, continuing with the now traditional 'Autumn Drama' and Pantomime; they include *The Best of Luck* (1916), *Shanghai* (described as 'a Spectacular Operette') in 1918, *The Great Day* (1919) and in 1920 *The Garden of Allah*, a dramatisation of Robert Hichens' famous book, which contained a real sandstorm. This production proved so popular that it caused the first break in the pantomime sequence. As there was no pantomime at Drury Lane an 'emergency production', a revival of the previous year's pantomime, was put on at Covent Garden instead. This was the first time that Drury Lane had been without its annual pantomime for nearly seventy years, and it was the beginning, as things turned out, of a long break in the tradition. In 1921 there was again no pantomime, as the theatre was being reconstructed internally at a cost of £150,000 to plans of J. Emblin-Walker, assisted by F. Edward Jones. The outer walls, the famous portico, the colonnade, the rotunda and the Royal Staircases remained untouched.

The reconstructed theatre opened on 20 April 1922 with *Decameron Nights*, a romantic play by Robert McLaughlin, adapted with lyrics by Boyle Lawrence, which ran for 371 performances. This was followed by *Angelo* (1923) and *Ned Kean of Old Drury* (1923). In September 1923 *Good Luck*, a 'sporting' drama by Seymour Hicks and Ian Hay, was put on.

Alfred Butt, who with Collins had become joint
Managing Director of the company controlling the theatre
in 1919, took over in 1924 on Collins's retirement with
Basil Dean as joint Managing Director, but Dean resigned
in January 1925. Alfred Butt continued until April 1931 and
during this régime the following outstanding productions
were seen: *London Life* (1924), a play by Arnold Bennett
and Edward Knoblock; *A Midsummer Night's Dream*
(1924), with Athene Seyler and Edith Evans as Hermia
and Helena and Gwen Ffrangcon-Davies as Titania;
Rose Marie, which ran for 851 performances from March
1925; *The Desert Song* (1927), *Show Boat* (1928), *The
New Moon* (1929), a musical version of *The Three
Musketeers* (1930) and *The Song of the Drum* (1931).
The last six mentioned were all American products and
pointed the way in which things were going.

George Grossmith then succeeded Alfred Butt. May
1931 saw Franz Lehar's *Land of Smiles*, and in October
Noël Coward's *Cavalcade* was produced and ran for 405
performances. After this the theatre could not find a success
except for a pantomime *Cinderella* in 1934. From 1932 to
1939 H. M. Tennent was Managing Director.

On 28 May 1935 a Testimonial Matinée was given in
honour of Marie Tempest's Golden Jubilee. King George
V and Queen Mary were present and over £5000 was
raised, which Marie Tempest handed over for the endow-
ment of a ward bearing her name in St George's Hospital.

From 1935 onwards Ivor Novello scored a series of
successes which retrieved the luck of the 'Lane', with
his spectacular musical romances *Glamorous Night* (1935),
Careless Rapture (1936), *Crest of the Wave* (1937), and
The Dancing Years (1939).

At the outbreak of war in September 1939 the theatre
became the headquarters of E.N.S.A. and remained in
this use despite the attentions of enemy aircraft during
the Battle of Britain in 1940. Considerable damage to the
rear of the circles, through to the pit, was sustained.

The theatre was restored after the War and reopened
with Prince Littler as Managing Director on 19 December
1946. The first production was Noël Coward's *Pacific
1860*. Since then the series of American musicals which
commenced with *Oklahoma!* on 30 April 1947 have
brought thousands flocking to this historic theatre. Best
remembered from those years are *Carousel* (1950), *South
Pacific* (1951), and *The King and I* (1953).

Shakespeare was once again heard within these walls
when the Stratford-upon-Avon production of *The Tempest*,
with John Gielgud, was brought here in 1957.

From 30 April 1958 *My Fair Lady* ran for 2281 performances, breaking all the existing records for the
theatre. This success was followed by *The Boys from*

Syracuse in November 1963, which ran for only 100 performances. After various dance companies *Camelot*, from August 1964, ran for 518 performances. This was succeeded by *Hello Dolly!* running for 794 performances. After *Dolly*, for a short while Harry Secombe starred in *The Four Musketeers*. Then, in February 1969, came *Mame* with Ginger Rogers. Another visitor from the United States followed in April 1970, *Carol Channing with Her Ten Stout-hearted Men*, then in July 1970 *The Great Waltz* opened and continued until March 1972. On 3 May *Gone With The Wind* arrived, finishing its run on 7 April 1973. In May came a revival of *No, No, Nanette*, with Anna Neagle, a step back into nostalgia. Unfortunately it did not have a long run and the Lane went 'dark' but for intermittent transitory visitors, with a stage version of *Monty Python's Flying Circus* proving an unexpected attraction. A musical version of *Billy Liar* called *Billy* opened in May.

The romantic history of the theatre has been told by W. Macqueen-Pope in *Theatre Royal, Drury Lane* (1945) and *Drury Lane* by Brian Dobbs (1972), but a definitive history of the building and its management has been included in *The Survey of London* Vol. XXXV (1970), edited by Francis Sheppard.

12 · The Duchess Theatre

Catherine Street, Strand, W.C.2

Capacity: 474

Opened 25 November 1929 with *Tunnel Trench*, a war play by Hubert Griffith. Produced by Reginald Denham, under the management of J. and D. de Leon.

THE BUILDING

Arthur Gibbons promoted the scheme for a theatre on a vacant site at the Strand end of Catherine Street, opposite the side of the Strand Theatre, which had been part of the rear of 4 York Street, where De Quincey wrote his *Confessions of an English Opium-Eater*.

The problem of ancient lights and other local difficulties had defeated the plans for building a theatre on this site which had been vacant for some years. These were eventually overcome by the ingenuity of the architect, Ewen Barr. He designed the theatre on two different levels and made the circle narrower than the stalls, supporting it with steel hangers from girders at the roof-level. The theatre was built by F. G. Minter Ltd. The exterior has been described as 'modern Tudor Gothic' and has three projecting bays with enamelled panels under the windows and a canopy of blue and silver of a delicate design. There is also sculpture work by Arnold Auerbach. The original scheme of interior decoration was the work of Marc Henri and Laverdet. It was the aim of the architect to avoid the glare of visible lamps wherever possible, and hidden lighting was therefore made a special and effective feature of the scheme.

The original owners, West End and Country Theatres Ltd, held a 99-year lease of the ground. In 1934, when J. B. Priestley became associated with the management of the theatre, his wife, Mary Wyndham Lewis, revised the scheme of interior decoration.

A manifesto of that date tells us:

Mr Maurice Lambert, the brilliant young sculptor, was commissioned to design and execute two great panels, in low bas-relief, for the niches between the proscenium and the dress circle. He had a most difficult task in working out his bas-relief with less than three inches of depth in which to work. Patrons can see for themselves how well he triumphed and universal admiration has been expressed for his designs of figures holding conventional masks above applauding hands. In the corridors and staircases are various illuminated glass cases, and arrangements have been made with various galleries to keep them replenished with works of art. We feel that these objects of art will add interest and pleasure to a visit to this theatre.

Except for minor redecoration and maintenance the theatre is still fundamentally the same.

THE PLAYS

The opening took place on 25 November 1929 under the joint management of J. and D. de Leon (Jack de Leon and his sister Delia Dellvina). The play was *Tunnel Trench* and subsequent productions were a revival of *Typhoon* (1929), the Japanese play adapted by Laurence Irving from the Hungarian, and *The Man at Six* (1930) by J. de Leon and Jack Celestin, both with Dennis Neilson-Terry and Mary Grew. Unfortunately the new theatre could not find its feet and in June 1930 the property was sold privately to J. P. Mitchelhill. This was Mitchelhill's first entry into management and his opening production was *An Object of Virtue*

by Edward Percy in November 1930. In the following
month Eden Phillpotts' *Jane's Legacy* began a run of 106
performances.

From December 1931 to the middle of 1932 Nancy Price
was associated with Mitchelhill, and some interesting productions were given by the People's National Theatre.
First was a Christmas revival of *The Merry Wives of
Windsor* with Baliol Holloway as Falstaff and Miriam
Lewes and Nancy Price as the Wives. This was followed
in 1932 by Susan Glaspell's *Trifles*, *The Rose Without a
Thorn*, by Clifford Bax, in which Frank Vosper gave an
outstanding performance as Henry VIII and which ran for
113 performances from the February; and by *The Secret
Woman* by Eden Phillpotts.

In October 1932 came a play which has been described
as 'a triumph of feminine stagecraft'. This was *Children
in Uniform*, the play which told the story of life in a
German girls' boarding school. Translated by Barbara
Burnham from *Mädchen in Uniform*, by Christa Winsloe
and produced by Leontine Sagan, it had an all-woman cast
in which particularly outstanding performances were given
by Jessica Tandy and Joyce Bland. It ran for 265 performances.

Two prominent productions in 1933 were *Eight Bells* by
Percy G. Mandley (190 performances), and J. B. Priestley's
Laburnum Grove, which ran for 335 performances from
November of that year.

During 1934 J. B. Priestley became associated in the
management of the Duchess Theatre and two of his plays
were produced, *Eden End* and *Cornelius*, the former in
September 1934 and the latter in March 1935. The first
play ran for 162 performances but the second did not enjoy
a long run and was followed in May 1935 by Emlyn
Williams's psychological thriller, *Night Must Fall*, in which
the author played a leading part. This was not Emlyn
Williams's first play, but it was the one in which he came,
to quote one critic, 'to full accomplishment'. It ran for 435
performances, over a year. It is interesting to remember
that Emlyn Williams had appeared as Captain Sandys in
Tunnel Trench, the first play to be produced at the Duchess
Theatre.

In July 1936 *Springtide*, by George Billam and Peter
Goldsmith (the latter a pseudonym for J. B. Priestley) ran
for 116 performances after which Priestley retired from his
partnership in the theatre. T. S. Eliot's *Murder in the
Cathedral* was staged in October 1936, this had previously
been produced at the Mercury Theatre in November 1935
and revived in September 1936, but it was at the Duchess
Theatre that it was first played in the West End. *Mile Away
Murder* (1937), by Anthony Armstrong, was followed in
the same year by Priestley's interesting time-problem play,

Time and the Conways, which ran for 225 performances from August 1937.

Glorious Morning, by Norman Macowan, was produced in May 1938, and began a run here of 324 performances. It transferred to the Whitehall after the theatre was sold to Michael Hillman in August 1938. It made way for Emlyn Williams's *The Corn is Green,* which had occupied the stage of the Duchess for 395 performances at the time of the compulsory closure in September 1939, on the outbreak of war. The theatre reopened with Katina Paxinou in *Ghosts* and several short-lived productions followed. After the blitz the Duchess reopened in March 1942 with *Skylark,* Norman Armstrong's *Lifeline* (July 1942) and the transferred production on 6 October 1942 of Noël Coward's *Blithe Spirit,* originally produced at the Piccadilly Theatre the previous year. In all it ran for 1997 performances, the longest straight play run until *The Mousetrap.*

In May 1945 the theatre was sold by the executors of Michael Hillman, who had died in 1941, and was bought by Sir John Leigh; on his death in 1959 the family trust, which also owned the Duke of York's, controlled the theatre. Among the successes of this régime were *Message for Margaret* (1946), *The White Devil,* with Margaret Rawlings and Robert Helpmann, *The Linden Tree* by J. B. Priestley (1947), *Miss Mabel* (1948), *The Foolish Gentlewoman* (1949), *The Holly and the Ivy* (1950), *The Deep Blue Sea* (1952), *Mr Kettle and Mrs Moon* (1955), *The Bride and the Bachelor* (1956), *The Unexpected Guest* (1958), all of which had considerable runs. *The Caretaker* by Harold Pinter, transferred from the Arts Theatre, commenced its run here in May 1960 and ran for a year.

In September 1961 it was announced that Peter Saunders had purchased the freehold of the theatre, but he sold this in 1968 to Peter Abrahams of the family which also owns the Aldwych, the Garrick and the Fortune theatres. At this time *Goodnight Mrs Puffin* had transferred here from the Strand and was to remain until it left for the Duke of York's in December 1962 to make way for the new Agatha Christie, *Rule of Three.*

The next success came from the Mermaid, a transfer of *Alfie,* with John Neville, which ran for 192 performances. In January 1965 Douglas Home's *The Reluctant Peer* was a big hit, running for 475 performances. After some short runs came the transfer from the Strand of *Wait Until Dark,* which continued its successful run reaching, in all, 682 performances. Then from Hampstead Theatre Club came *Little Boxes* for 137 performances. Some more short runs followed including *Dames At Sea* by George Haimsohn, Robin Miller and Jim Wise, and in March 1970, from the

Court, *Three Months Gone*, followed in September by two
Pinter plays, *The Basement* and *The Party*. *The Dirtiest
Show in Town* which opened in 1971 ran for well over 700
performances, but in April 1973 John Mortimer's play,
Collaborators, and in September Terence Rattigan's double
bill, *In Praise of Love*, were not as successful as had been
hoped. In January 1974 *Oh! Calcutta*, by this time in its
fourth year, transferred from the Royalty, and once again
nudity was featured at the Duchess!

This theatre holds the record for the shortest run of any
production. *The Intimate Revue*, produced in 1930, did not
even see the end of its first night, the curtain being rung
down and the audience dismissed before its conclusion.

13 · The Duke of York's Theatre

(The Trafalgar Square Theatre, The Trafalgar Theatre)

St Martin's Lane, W.C.2

Capacity: 700

Opened, as the Trafalgar Square Theatre, 10 September 1892 with *The Wedding Eve*, a comic opera by F. Toulmouche, adapted from the French of Bisson and Bureau-Jattiot by C. W. Yardley; lyrics by Frank Latimer. Produced by Thomas W. Charles under the management of Michael Levenston.

THE BUILDING

The Trafalgar Square Theatre was built on a site at the south end of St Martin's Lane backing on to the Garrick Theatre (opened 1889; see No. 15) and was the first to be built in this street.

It was designed by Walter Emden for Frank Wyatt and

his wife Violet Melnotte, and the builder was Frank Kirk.
The Era of 3 September 1892 says:

> The new Theatre is pretty and unpretentious, the
> general effect being created by the judicious use of cream
> and gold and yellow tints, the back of the boxes being
> of a warm russet hue. The corridors are ornamented with
> coloured portraits of well-known actresses, and the
> decorations generally are remarkably chaste and re-
> fined . . .
>
> The stalls and dress-circle will be entered from St
> Martin's Lane. On the upper-circle tier are a large and
> ornamental vestibule and a pleasant saloon, with a
> balcony facing the roadway. The pit entrance is on the
> north side, and the entrance to the large gallery on the
> south side. The theatre is completely isolated, and from
> each of its four sections an extra exit has been made. It
> will be lighted by electricity, but in case of need gas will
> be available. The dressing rooms are in a detached build-
> ing, connected to the theatre by a short, covered iron
> bridge; and a broad stone staircase leads from the stage
> to the open air.

The new three-tier theatre was the only one in London at
that date with real fires in the auditorium.

In 1894 the theatre became known as the Trafalgar, then
in September 1895 the name was changed to the Duke of
York's.

In the Second World War it was closed from 1940 to 1943
owing to blitz damage. Taken over by the present management in 1950 the theatre was completely reconditioned, and
given an entirely new scheme of decoration, designed by
Cecil Beaton and carried out under the supervision of
W. Wylton Todd. It is one of the few London theatres still
to retain its unreserved gallery. Another redecoration took
place in May 1960. The theatre belongs to the Sir John
Leigh family trust.

THE PLAYS

The Trafalgar Square Theatre opened on 10 September
1892 under the management of Michael Levenston with an
adaption from the French, *The Wedding Eve*. This opening
piece was not a success and was followed by a revival of
Dorothy in November of the same year. In January 1893
the theatre was closed owing to a disagreement between
Levenston and the Wyatts, but it reopened in February
with *The County Councillor*. During its run matinées were
given of Ibsen's *The Master Builder* with Elizabeth Robins.
Later the same year Frank Wyatt produced *Mam'zelle
Nitouche*, then he and his wife let the theatre on a
lengthened lease to Charles Cartwright and Henry Dana
in July 1895.

In September 1895 the name of the theatre was changed
to the Duke of York's and in April 1896 Louie Freear made
her début here in *The Gay Parisienne*, with Ada Reeve,
which scored 369 performances.

A most important chapter in the theatre's history began
in 1897 when Charles Frohman, the American theatrical
manager, took a long lease. Frohman made a point of encouraging the interchange of artistes between this country
and the States, introducing many American players of dis-
tinction to London. For two or three years Evelyn Millard
was his main attraction, creating the parts of Lady Ursula
in Anthony Hope's comedy, *The Adventure of Lady Ursula*
(1898), Glory Quayle in *The Christian* (1899), and the title
role in Jerome K. Jerome's *Miss Hobbs* (1899); Belasco's
one-act play *Madame Butterfly* was the curtain raiser. Also
in 1899 Frohman introduced Maxine Elliott and her husband
Nat Goodwin in *The Cowboy and the Lady* and *An American Citizen*, and in 1901 Pauline Chase and Joseph Coyne,
both of whom were afterwards to become popular stars,
were seen with Edna May in *The Girl from Up There*,
written by the same team as *The Belle of New York*, but
which did not achieve the same success.

In 1902 Marie Tempest appeared in *The Marriage of
Kitty*, and the same year saw the first production of Barrie's
The Admirable Crichton. A sensation was caused on the
first night of this play because the scene-shifters went on
strike after the second act and the members of the cast had
to shift the scenery themselves. Many of Barrie's plays
first appeared here: 27 December 1904 saw the first production of *Peter Pan*, which was revived annually each
Christmas until 1914 at this theatre. The Peters were Nina
Boucicault (1904), Cissie Loftus (1905), Pauline Chase
(1906 to 1913) and Madge Titheradge (1914). It is also
interesting to note that Charles Chaplin played Billy in
Sherlock Holmes, a revival with William Gillette in 1905
at this theatre.

Other notable productions were Barrie's *Pantaloon*,
with *Alice Sit by the Fire* (1905), plays with Marie Tempest,
Pauline Chase, Gerald du Maurier, Cyril Maude, John
Hare, Irene Vanbrugh and many other stars follow and in
1908 *What Every Woman Knows* was first produced with
Hilda Trevelyan.

In 1910 Frohman started a repertory season, presenting
plays by George Meredith, Pinero, Shaw, John Galsworthy, Barrie, Granville Barker and others. It commenced
on 21 February 1910 and lasted until June 17 of the same
year, during which eight new plays were staged and two old
ones revived. They were produced under the direction of
Dion Boucicault, Granville Barker and Bernard Shaw. The
new plays were Galsworthy's *Justice*, Shaw's *Misalliance*,
Barrie's *Old Friends* and *The Twelve Pound Look*,

Granville Barker's *The Madras House*, Elizabeth Baker's
Chains, Meredith's *The Sentimentalists*, Anthony Hope
and Cosmo Gordon Lennox's *Helena's Path*; the revivals
were Pinero's *Trelawny of the 'Wells'* and Granville
Barker's *Prunella*. Yet this feast for playgoers was not a
success and only ran for seventeen weeks, the biggest
box-office draw being the revival of *Trelawny*.

Pinero's *The 'Mind the Paint' Girl* with Marie Löhr was
a success of 1912. Barrie's plays continued to appear and
included *Rosalind* (1912) in a programme with Shaw's *Over-
ruled* and Pinero's *The Widow of Wasdale Head*, and *The
Will* and *The Adored One* (1913), in a double bill. Somerset
Maugham's *The Land of Promise* (1914) was one of the
last new plays put on here by Frohman before he lost his
life in the *Lusitania* disaster in 1915.

Edward Sheldon's play *Romance* opened here in October
1915 and transferred to the Lyric the following
month, and scored a run of 1049 performances. It brought
to London Doris Keane in the part which had made her a
star in America. The theatre was then taken by Miss
Horniman from the Gaiety, Manchester, for a season.
Subsequent noteworthy productions were Jean Webster's
Daddy Long-Legs (514 performances from May 1916) and
The Thirteenth Chair, in which Mrs Patrick Campbell
appeared in 1917.

In July 1920 Leon M. Lion presented *Brown Sugar*,
which ran for 276 performances. Later in the year Philip
Michael Faraday became lessee and *Priscilla and the Profligate* and *The Wrong Number* (1921) were produced. In
1921 Dion Boucicault produced *Miss Nell o' New Orleans*
with Irene Vanbrugh, and the next year *The Enchanted
Cottage*, a late Pinero, was seen. In 1923 Violet Melnotte
assumed more active control and this year also saw the
production of a Charlot revue entitled *London Calling!*
most of which was by Noël Coward and which ran for
316 performances. Coward's connection with this theatre
was to continue with the production of his play *Easy
Virtue* in 1926. In between came the success of another
revue, *The Punch Bowl*, and some other productions of
less note.

Frank Wyatt died in 1926 and control passed to his widow,
Violet Melnotte, who sold the theatre two years later to
William Hunter.

In 1928 and 1929 Matheson Lang appeared in Ashley
Dukes's adapation of Alfred Neumann's *Such Men are
Dangerous*, *The Chinese Bungalow*, and Ashley Dukes's
adaptation of Feuchtwanger's *Jew Süss*, in which Peggy
Ashcroft made an early success.

In 1930 Walter Hackett produced his own play, *The Way
to Treat a Woman*, and in 1931 Van Druten's *London Wall*
was given. In 1932 the non-stop craze even reached *Grand*

Guignol, and three programmes were presented in this way. In 1933 the theatre was redecorated, when it passed again into the hands of Violet Melnotte. Between 1933 and the outbreak of war in 1939 a good many productions came and went, few of them scoring any great number of performances. Nancy Price's People's National Theatre was here in November 1933 and remained on and off for three years. In September 1935 Violet Melnotte died leaving the theatre in control of Melnotte Ltd. A season of ballet by the Markova–Dolin Company, which began on Boxing Day 1936, lasted for three months.

As a result of enemy action the Duke of York's Theatre was closed at the end of 1940 and remained so, because it was thought necessary to spend more than the legal £100 in order to put it to rights. It eventually reopened in May 1943 with *Shadow and Substance*. The following month brought a revival of Ibsen's *Ghosts* with Beatrix Lehmann and John Carol. This was succeeded in September by Roland Pertwee's *Pink String and Sealing Wax* and *Is Your Honeymoon Really Necessary?* in August 1944, which brought the return of Ralph Lynn for 980 performances. During this run the theatre was bought by the Glover Trust. For some time it seemed difficult to find an established success until the revue *One, Two, Three*, with Binnie and Sonnie Hale in September 1947. This ran into a second edition, *Four, Five, Six*, in March 1948.

In May 1950 the present management assumed control and the newly decorated theatre was seen on the first night in November of *Return to Tyassi* by Benn Levy. Successes which followed included *The Happy Marriage* with John Clements and Kay Hammond (1952), *All for Mary* (1954), *The House by the Lake* (1956), *And Suddenly It's Spring*, which had its 'first night' on the *afternoon* of the 4 November 1959, an innovation introduced by Peter Saunders who presented the play. This was not in fact the innovation, as George Alexander had opened his revival of *Much Ado About Nothing* at the St James's on a Wednesday matinée in 1898! Two transfers from other theatres, *Roots* and *Tomorrow—with Pictures!* followed in 1960; and Coward's *Waiting in the Wings* commenced its run in September. After its conclusion in February 1961, the Duke of York's found a lasting success, a revue, *One Over the Eight*, which ran from April 1961 for over a year. The other plays had made it seem like a repertory theatre. *Goodnight Mrs Puffin* ran here after its initial start at the Strand and its run at the Duchess.

Those years saw two remarkably short runs: *All the Year Round*, three nights in October 1951, and *Thirteen for Dinner*, which opened and closed the same night, 17 December 1953.

A revival in July 1963 of Noël Coward's *Private Lives*,

from the Hampstead Theatre Club, ran for 212 performances, then *Poor Bitos* ran for 245 performances, to be
followed by *A Scent of Flowers* for only 77 performances.
The next big success, from June 1965, was *The Killing of
Sister George* (620) followed by several short runs, till a
smash hit, *Relatively Speaking*, by Alan Ayckbourn (March
1967) totalled 396 performances. This was followed by six
short runs and one transfer, *The Hotel in Amsterdam* by
John Osborne. A big success arrived on 4 March 1969. *The
Price*, by Arthur Miller, but 1970 proved a year of several
short runs and on 21 December *Toad of Toad Hall* was
presented for a Christmas season, matinées only, while
Lady Frederick, from the Vaudeville, was playing in the
evenings. Another transfer from the Vaudeville, *The
Jockey Club Stakes*, and two short runs followed. The
return of *The Man Most Likely To . . .* in December 1971,
which had been on tour since it finished its run at the Vaudeville, held the stage in most recent years until *Life Class*,
from the Royal Court opened on 4 June 1974.

14 · The Fortune Theatre

Russell Street, Covent Garden, W.C.2

Capacity: 440

Opened 8 November 1924 with *Sinners*, a play by Laurence Cowen. Produced by the author under the management of Ida Molesworth and Templer Powell.

THE BUILDING

The first theatre to be built in London after the First World War, the Fortune, is situated in Russell Street, which runs along the side of the Theatre Royal, from Drury Lane to Catherine Street. It faces the stage-door and the famous colonnade of the Theatre Royal. The name perpetuates that of the seventeenth-century playhouse which had stood in Golden Lane, Cripplegate, and was burnt down in 1613.

The site on which the new theatre was built, at the corner

of Crown Court, had been that of the Albion Tavern, the haunt of actors and literati in the Georgian and Victorian eras. Construction was begun in December 1922 and under post-war conditions it took nearly two years and three times the estimated cost to build. Originally it was to be called the Crown, after its location, for it not only adjoins the Scottish National Church in Crown Court, but actually embraces it, the entrance to the church in Russell Street has the theatre built over it and under it, a remarkable piece of designing and engineering; though this passage-way traverses its entire length, stage included, on one of its sides, it is not discernible from within; a most complete example of the union of the Church and Stage.

The theatre was built for Laurence Cowen and was designed by Ernest Schaufelberg; its construction was in the hands of Bovis, Ltd.

The Era of October 30 says:

> The theatre will certainly be one of the most beautiful in London. The façade alone with its strange medieval art, is already one of the features of metropolitan architecture, and the interior decorations follow the same fresh and original note. The colour scheme of blue greys, creams, browns, red and old gold is supplemented by an almost lavish use of marble, onyx, copper and wrought iron, and the curtain is a gorgeously rich and satisfying piece of colour. Every seat has a full view of the stage, and they are all of mahogany, upholstered tastefully in dark blue leather.

> The famous Schwabe-Hazait lighting system has been installed, not only for its stage purposes, but throughout the theatre, and one of its features is that the lighting in the front of the house is by reflection; not a single lamp being visible to the eye. The entrance hall is an exceedingly handsome affair of marble and copper, and the first thing to meet the eye is the challenging inscription, 'There is a tide in the affairs of men which, taken at the flood, leads on to fortune.'

The critics were not all so favourably impressed.

> Only the life-size nude figure of Terpsichore, pendant from the walls, is a mistake. The eye travels to it from the word 'Holy' and the Cross over the Church door, and the incongruity is obvious. The figure does not even faintly suggest the dance.

After describing the interior this discriminating critic goes on:

> The whole effect is extremely satisfactory with one glaring exception. I cannot imagine how the atrocious

mural painting over the proscenium arch can have been passed by an architect of such otherwise perfect taste. It is pretty, meaningless and totally unsympathetic to the rest of the building. It is little better than the traditional modest nudes who, in older theatres, write each other letters and dab at easels among the clouds. This mural painting should be painted out.

It was; a later redecoration completely changed the bright colour-scheme to a subdued green, which remained until 1960, when the theatre, both inside and out, was renovated and redecorated.

THE PLAYS

The theatre opened on 8 November 1924 under the joint management of Ida Molesworth and Templer Powell, with a play by Laurence Cowen called *Sinners*. This was followed in the December by a revival of *When Knights were Bold*, which had Christmas productions here again from 1932 to 1937.

Are You A Mason? was revived here in February 1925 and a revue called *L. S. D.* appeared in March of the same year. In 1926 J. B. Fagan became manager and presented *Juno and the Paycock* and *The Plough and the Stars*. In April 1927 Cowen sold the theatre to a company and the management was taken over by Tom Walls. A notable success was scored with Frederick Lonsdale's *On Approval*, which ran for 469 performances. This was followed by *Mischief* (July 1928), a revival of Lonsdale's *Aren't We All?* (March 1929), *The Last Enemy* (1929), and *Cape Forlorn* (1930).

From October 1930 until August 1931 Nancy Price used the Fortune as the headquarters of her People's National Theatre, starting with a revival of *The Man from Blankley's*, and giving productions of Galsworthy's *The Silver Box* (January 1931), *Bush Fire* (April 1931), *The Ship* (June 1931), and other plays.

In 1932 Sybil Thorndike appeared in two plays, *Dark Saint* and *Fire*. The following year the theatre passed into the hands of D. A. Abrahams, and apart from Christmas seasons it was mostly used for Sunday Club performances and productions by amateur societies. During the war it was occupied by E.N.S.A.

The theatre returned to professional use with *Fools Rush In* (1946) and it joined the Prince Littler Group. The following year *Power Without Glory* by Michael Clayton Hutton brought Dirk Bogarde and Kenneth More to the West End. In 1948 *The Hidden Years* had its run in this theatre after a try-out at the Boltons. *The Paragon* produced later the same year was withdrawn to allow the theatre to return to amateur productions, only housing professional

productions occasionally during the summer months and
sometimes a Christmas entertainment. Under these conditions were presented Agatha Christie's *The Hollow*
(1951), *Joyce Grenfell Requests the Pleasure* (1954), and
several transfers. Since 1956 the theatre has completely
returned to the fold and its greatest successes have been
Michael Flanders and Donald Swann in their after-dinner
farrago *At the Drop of a Hat*, which ran from January
1957 for 733 performances. Much discussed plays of recent
years have been *The Ginger Man* and *Aunt Edwina*, with
Henry Kendall, both in 1959. The revue *Look Who's
Here* started its successful run in January 1960 and ran until
May, when R. C. Sherriff's *A Shred of Evidence* transferred from the Duchess Theatre. After its closure for
redecoration, another revue under the management of Anna
Deere Wiman, *And Another Thing . . .*, was produced in
October and continued until *Beyond the Fringe* was produced in May 1961. This revue continued for 1184 performances and then went to the Mayfair and added
another 1016. *Wait a Minim!* a South African Revue,
followed in April 1965 for 655 performances. Then came
three flops till the arrival in January 1967 of *The Promise*
with Judi Dench, Ian McKellan and Ian McShane for 290
performances. At Christmas came a revival of *Toad of
Toad Hall*. Of the next five plays four achieved runs of
only just over 20 performances each. The fifth, *Close the
Coal House Door*, had a little better luck. 1969 brought
similar short runs of plays, also a one man show and a
Revue. In January 1970 came *Three*, a revival of three of
Bernard Shaw's one act plays: *How He Lied to Her
Husband; Village Wooing* and *Press Cuttings*. In April a
success from the Royal Court Theatre, *The Contractor* by
David Storey, was presented. In January 1971 came a
revival of three Noël Coward one act plays, *We Were
Dancing; Red Peppers* and *Family Album* under the title of
Tonight at 8 and a new play from the Theatre Upstairs at
the Royal Court, *The Foursome* by E. A. Whitehead,
winner of the 1970 George Devine award, had a short run,
then in September a thriller, *Suddenly at Home*, proved a
big success for the theatre and continued until June 1973.
October 1973 saw a transfer of *Sleuth* from the Garrick
Theatre, following an earlier transfer from the St Martin's
Theatre.

15 · The Garrick Theatre

Charing Cross Road, W.C.2

Capacity: 800

Opened 24 April 1889 with *The Profligate*, a play by A. W. Pinero, produced by the author. Under the management of John Hare.

THE BUILDING

The idea for a theatre almost at the end of Charing Cross Road, where it enters St Martin's Place, owed itself to W. S. Gilbert. He financed the building of the theatre for the actor-manager John Hare, on a plot of ground for which he obtained a long lease.

The theatre was designed by Walter Emden in association with C. J. Phipps and constructed by Messrs Peto. When the building was half completed it was thought that the

work might have to be abandoned. The theatre was
planned to be built partially below ground (the back of the
dress circle at street level): deep excavations were necessary
and water was discovered. This proved to be an old river
known to the Romans, which made its way through the
foundations. W. S. Gilbert is said to have remarked that
he did not know 'whether to go on with the building or let
the fishing'. Eventually the difficulty was overcome.

The Stage for April 26 said:

> The style of Mr Hare's new theatre is classic. The
> whole of the Charing Cross Road front is executed in
> Portland Stone and Bath Stone and has a long frontage of
> 140 feet. The theatre is entered on the dress circle level,
> which is reached after passing through the outer vestibule
> by a large inner vestibule. A striking object in this is a
> handsome oil painting copy of the celebrated portrait of
> Garrick. From this, by a staircase on either side, the
> stalls are entered; and from it, by a staircase, the foyer
> level, with its refreshment saloon and smoke room, is
> approached. The saloon on the foyer opens on to a broad
> balcony facing on to Charing Cross Road, the balcony
> being covered with an arcade. The floor of the vestibule
> is laid with mosaic and that of the entrance hall and
> saloons in marquetry, and they are surrounded by dados
> of polished walnut in panels, the upper part of the walls
> being divided by marble pilasters, the panels thus formed
> being filled with mirrors and decorations in relief. The
> ceilings are of a highly ornamental character, the whole
> of these decorations being in the Italian Renaissance
> style. To every part of the house there are two separate
> means of exit, ten in all.

The Era stated on April 17:

> The house consists of four tiers, pit, stalls, dress circle,
> upper circle and gallery, and will hold about 1500
> persons. The auditorium is decorated in Italian Renais-
> sance style, the ornamental work being in high bold relief.
> The proscenium opening is formed by groups of columns
> on either side of the first proscenium box, the general
> form of the theatre being after that of Covent Garden,
> with four openings forming a square, supporting in their
> centre a circular dome. The box front of the dress circle
> tier is divided by groups of cupids supporting shields
> crowned with laurels, each shield bearing the name of a
> celebrated author.

It was not until 1892 that the Duke of York's Theatre
on which it backs was built (see No. 13).

In July 1934 it was announced that plans were being
prepared for the rebuilding of the Garrick as a super-cinema,
an architect was named and the following May the work

was said to be commencing shortly. This scheme never materialised. Today the theatre still retains its original gallery and though the theatre has been redecorated on numerous occasions it has undergone little change since it was opened, and remains essentially a Victorian playhouse. The copy of the lost Gainsborough portrait of Garrick still adorns the foyer.

The seating capacity of 1500 given by the *Era* in 1889 seems an exaggeration, as in 1912 the figure was only 1250. Shortly after this two boxes were removed on circle level, and in recent years the pit has been replaced by stalls, and the gallery considerably reduced in size by partitions, lessening the capacity of the theatre.

THE PLAYS

The theatre opened on 24 April 1889 with John Hare in Pinero's play *The Profligate*. Forbes-Robertson and Lewis Waller were also in the cast. It was a great success and ran for 129 performances. This play was a landmark in theatrical history, as it threw emphasis on the playwright rather than on the actors and heralded a new tendency for the author to have more importance than the players.

Hare remained in charge at the Garrick until 1896. *The Profligate* was followed by *La Tosca* (1889), an English version of Sardou's play, with Mrs Bernard Beere; Sydney Grundy's *A Pair of Spectacles* (1890), Pinero's *Lady Bountiful* (1891), and a revival of Grundy's *A Fool's Paradise* (1892). In 1893 a revival of *Diplomacy* contained a magnificent cast including Hare, the Bancrofts, Forbes-Robertson, Arthur Cecil, Kate Rorke and Olga Nethersole.

In 1895 *The Notorious Mrs Ebbsmith* was produced. This play, by Pinero, caused a flutter in the dovecotes of puritanism. It was written to consolidate the success won by Mrs Patrick Campbell in *The Second Mrs Tanqueray*. One strange occurrence in connection with this production was the discovery in the river of a woman whose name was Ebbsmith, and on whose person were found two used halves of tickets for the play at the Garrick Theatre.

E. S. Willard had seasons in 1895 and 1896 and the Kendals followed him in management in the latter year, for a season. After Hare's retirement from the control of the theatre it became very largely used for comic opera and musical plays, under the management of H. T. Brickwell, and for visits from overseas companies. In 1900 a long lease was taken by Arthur Bourchier and his wife Violet Vanbrugh, and much was done by them to restore the prestige of the theatre. It was in 1903 that something of a sensation was caused by Bourchier refusing admission to A. B. Walkley, the dramatic critic of *The Times*; this was the first instance of an actor-manager standing up to dramatic criticism. His régime included productions of J. M. Barrie's

The Wedding Guest (1900), Pinero's *Iris* (1901), Anthony
Hope's *Pilkerton's Peerage* and *The Bishop's Move* (1902),
Henry Arthur Jones's *Whitewashing Julia* (1903), *The
Arm of the Law*, Bourchier's own translation of Brieux's
La Robe Rouge, W. S. Gilbert's *The Fairies' Dilemma*,
Henry Arthur Jones's *The Chevaleer*, Alfred Sutro's *The
Walls of Jericho* (all in 1904), *The Merchant of Venice*
(1905), *The Duel* (1907), *Samson* (1909). In 1910 Herbert
Sleath joined Bourchier in management and later *The
Unwritten Law*, a stage version of Dostoevsky's *Crime
and Punishment*, was produced in 1911. Oscar Asche and
Lily Brayton had a season during which *Kismet* ran for 328
performances. The next few years were uneventful except
for a farce, *Who's the Lady?* (1913).

Arthur Bourchier left the theatre in 1915, then Thomas
Dott became lessee and José Levy presented a number of
now-forgotten plays. Other managements followed in quick
succession, presenting *By Pigeon Post* (1918), *Cyrano de
Bergerac* (1919), *The Edge o' Beyond* (1921), *The Man in
Dress Clothes* (1922), *Partners Again* (1923), *Outward
Bound* (1923). From 1918 to 1924 Cochran was the lessee;
A. E. Abrahams then took the theatre and among the
plays seen were *Rain* (1925), *Scaramouche* (1927), *The
Lady with a Lamp* (1929), *Almost a Honeymoon* (1930),
My Wife's Family (1931), *The Life Machine* (1931). The
theatre was not a financially successful house during the
years that followed. In 1932 and 1933 Leon M. Lion was
manager, appearing in *Man Overboard* (1932), a revival of
Galsworthy's *Escape* (1932), a revival of *Justice* (1932), and
Beggars in Hell (1933) among other plays, in rapid
succession.

In 1934 an attempt was made by John Southern to reconstruct the Old-Time Music Hall here, complete with
Chairman; and many retired veterans of variety appeared.
He also revived some old musical comedies with little
success.

After the scheme to rebuild the theatre as a cinema had
come to nothing, *Love on the Dole* was presented in January
1935. This play, which ran for 391 performances, brought
theatre audiences into contact with the tragedy of the
industrial north in the years of the economic crisis. It also
introduced Wendy Hiller, who made an immediate success.
The Garrick had at last found a winner and later some
successful productions were transferred here. *Sarah
Simple*, by A. A. Milne, was produced in 1937 and in 1939
Maurice Schwartz and his Yiddish Art Theatre of New
York gave a season.

The Garrick was closed for a considerable time after the
outbreak of war after a scheme to make it a Forces Theatre
failed and weeds were soon growing freely from the top
of the verandah.

The theatre reopened in September 1941 with a play called *Room V*, by an author calling himself 'Peter Wendy.' It then housed a good many different productions including a season of *Russian Ballet de la Jeunesse Anglaise* by Lydia Kyasht, Vernon Sylvaine's farce *Warn That Man*; a revival of the same author's *Aren't Men Beasts!*; a dramatisation of Graham Greene's *Brighton Rock*; Esther McCracken's *Living Room*; Ben Travers's *She Follows Me About*; Thomas Job's *Uncle Harry*, which was adjudged one of the best pieces of theatre during the war; and *Madame Louise*, another Sylvaine farce for Robertson Hare and Alfred Drayton, who had become associated with this theatre.

Beatrice Lillie in a revue *Better Late* (1946) was followed again by a lean period. Jack Buchanan assumed the direction of the theatre and retained it until his death in 1957. The theatre is now controlled by its owners, the Abrahams family. In 1947 Laurence Olivier produced *Born Yesterday*, which introduced Yolande Donlan to London. Buchanan appeared with Coral Browne in a revival of *Canaries Sometimes Sing* at the end of the same year. *One Wild Oat* in 1948 brought back the Sylvaine, Hare, Drayton team to the theatre. The next big success was a transfer from the Savoy of *To Dorothy a Son*, which ran during 1951–2.

Jack Buchanan was back again in *As Long as They're Happy* in 1953. More successes were *Serious Charge* (1955), the revue *La Plume de ma Tante*, which ran for 994 performances from November 1955; *Living for Pleasure*, a revue with Dora Bryan (1958); *Farewell, Farewell, Eugene* (1959). The Theatre Workshop's production of *Fings Ain't Wot They Used T' Be* kept the theatre filled from February 1960 until February 1962. After a short-lived revue, *Not to Worry*, another hit was found with *Two Stars for Comfort* by John Mortimer. When this finished in September, *Rattle of a Simple Man* commenced its run of 376 performances. Two more successes were to follow, *Difference of Opinion* (489) then *Who's Afraid of Virginia Woolf?* (which had started its run at the Piccadilly Theatre and had in all a total run of 426 performances. The theatre was closed from 20 June 1965 to 20 April 1966 for redecoration, and re-opened with a revival of *Thark*, but this had only 86 performances and was followed by the Peter Bridge revival of Shaw's *Too True to be Good*, which came over from the Strand to finish its run for 138 performances. More transfers and revivals followed: *Man and Superman* (232), *An Ideal Husband*, *Volpone* (a limited season). Then 'The Theatre of Comedy,' a season of Brian Rix farces in repertoire, *Stand by Your Bedouin*, *Uproar in the House*, *Let Sleeping Wives Lie* continued well into 1969. Roy Hudd and Rita Tushingham appeared in *The Giveaway*, to be followed by the 'Theatre 69' revival of *She Stoops to Conquer* with Tom Courtenay. In October Brian Rix

returned and presented *She's Done It Again*, which ran till
May 1970 when it was succeeded by a musical by Caryl
Brahms, Ned Sherrin and Alan Bennett with music by Ron
Grainer, *Sing A Rude Song*, starring Barbara Windsor as
Marie Lloyd, which had transferred from Greenwich. In
July came *The Two of Us* with Lynn Redgrave and
Richard Briers and on 10 February 1971 a comedy opened,
Don't Start Without Me, to be followed by another 'Don't'
—*Don't Just Lie There, Say Something*, opening in Sep-
tember 1971, and continuing until March 1973. After this a
transfer from St Martin's Theatre of *Sleuth* was to hold the
stage until the revival of Pinero's *Dandy Dick*, transferred
from Chichester, with Alastair Sim and Patricia Routledge,
was presented in October 1973 (when *Sleuth* moved over
to the Fortune to continue its run). Since then *The
Championship Season* and *Birds of Paradise* have been
staged.

16 · The Globe Theatre

(The Hicks Theatre)

Shaftesbury Avenue, W.1

Capacity: 907

Opened as the Hicks Theatre 27 December 1906 with a transfer from the Aldwych Theatre of *The Beauty of Bath*, a musical play by Seymour Hicks and Cosmo Hamilton, lyrics by Charles H. Taylor and music by Herbert E. Haines. Produced by Seymour Hicks under the management of Charles Frohman.

THE BUILDING

In April 1904 it was announced that Jack Jacobus, the owner of a shoemaker's establishment in Shaftesbury Avenue, had acquired, in association with Sydney Marler, an estate agent, from the almoners of Christ's Hospital an eighty-year building lease at a rent of £700 per annum, of a site including numbers 35–49 (odd) Shaftesbury Avenue. They also bought seventeen houses in Wardour Street, Rupert Street and Upper Rupert Street (now Winnet

Street). The intention was to enlarge Jacobus's
premises and to build two theatres on the site.

This is the land on which arose the Hicks, now the Globe,
Theatre and the Queen's Theatre. The Hicks, at the Rupert
Street corner, was the first to be completed; the Queen's
did not open until October 1907 (see No. 28). The architect
for the whole scheme was W. G. R. Sprague, who designed
the two theatres with similar elevations.

The Hicks Theatre was built by Charles Frohman and
Seymour Hicks, in association with the Jacobus–Marler
Estates, Ltd. The same group with J. E. Vedrenne in place
of Frohman were responsible for the Queen's. The builder
of both theatres was Walter Wallis of Balham.

The Hicks, a two-tier theatre, the gallery rising behind
the upper circle, its decorations of the Louis Seize period,
in Rose du Barri with ivory and gold enrichments, was rechristened the Globe in July 1909. There had been another
Globe Theatre in modern times in Newcastle Street; this
was shut in 1902 and swept away in the Strand (Aldwych–
Kingsway) improvements.

Today, apart from redecoration, the removal of the
boxes at the rear of the circle and the reshaping of
the stage boxes in 1950, and the recent conversion of the
gallery into a balcony by the addition of tip-up seats, the
theatre remains the same.

THE PLAYS

The opening took place on 27 December 1906 under the
name of the Hicks Theatre, and very appropriately the
first production was *The Beauty of Bath*, a musical play
by Seymour Hicks and Cosmo Hamilton, with music by
Herbert Haines, which had previously been presented at
the Aldwych earlier in the same year, and in which Hicks
and his wife, Ellaline Terriss, played the leading parts. Subsequent successes were scored by *Brewster's Millions*
(1907), in which Gerald du Maurier made a big success and
which ran for 321 performances; *A Waltz Dream* (1908),
an operetta by Felix Doerman and Leopold Jacobson, with
music by Oscar Strauss; and *The Dashing Little Duke*
(1909), a musical play by Seymour Hicks with music by
Frank E. Tours.

In July 1909 the name of the theatre was changed to the
Globe, and as such it reopened on July 6 with *His Borrowed
Plumes*, a play by Mrs George Cornwallis-West (Lady
Randolph Churchill). Subsequent successes were *A
Butterfly on the Wheel* (1911), presented by Lewis Waller,
and a musical comedy *The Pink Lady*, with music by Ivan
Caryll, which ran for 124 performances from April 1912,
after a number of short runs; in October 1913 Ethel Warwick
entered on a short season of management, presenting
People Like Ourselves with little success.

In March 1914 Oscar Ashe reappeared, after a tour in
Australia and South Africa, in a revival of *Kismet*, following
this in September of the same year with *Mameena*, which
was his own adaptation of Rider Haggard's *Child of the
Storm*. *Peg O' My Heart*, J. Hartley Manners's successful
play, originally produced at the Comedy in October 1914,
was transferred to the Globe in January 1916, when the
management of the theatre passed to Alfred Butt on the
death of Charles Frohman.

In 1917 *Suzette*, 'a musical affair' by Austen Hurgon
and George Arthurs, with music by Max Darewski,
ran for 255 performances with Gaby Deslys and Harry
Pilcer, and *The Willow Tree*, a Japanese fantasy by J. H.
Benrimo and Harrison Rhodes, started a run of 209
performances.

An important chapter in the Globe's history began in
January 1918 with the joint management of Marie Löhr
and her husband, Anthony Prinsep, lasting until 1927. It
opened with Somerset Maugham's *Love in a Cottage*, and
there followed a series of successful productions in which
Marie Löhr appeared. Among these were R. C. Carton and
Justin Huntly McCarthy's *Nurse Benson* (June 1918),
Victory (March 1919), a revival of *L'Aiglon* (June 1919),
Robert Hichens's *The Voice from the Minaret* (August
1919), a revival of Grundy's *A Marriage of Convenience*
(May 1920); and a revival of *Fedora* (October 1920). Also
during this period was produced *French Leave* (1920), by
Reginald Berkeley, the run of which began here but trans-
ferred to the Apollo, finally totalling 283 performances.

Other productions of note included a dramatisation of
Ethel M. Dell's popular best-seller, *The Knave of
Diamonds* (1921) and Michael Morton's *Woman to Woman*
in the same year. Also in 1921 came A. A. Milne's *The
Truth about Blayds*, and this was followed by a revival of
the same author's *Mr Pim Passes By* (1922), which had
previously been seen at the New Theatre in 1920.

After a sojourn in America Marie Löhr again appeared
in a series of successes at the Globe, commencing in September 1922 with a play very appropriately entitled *The
Return*, and following this with Sutro's *The Laughing
Lady* (November 1922) and Lonsdale's comedy *Aren't we
All?* (1923), after this Marie Löhr retired from the active
management of the theatre.

In September 1923 Somerset Maugham's *Our Betters*
was produced here and began a run of 548 performances.
This brilliant social satire and comedy of manners had
originally been seen in New York in 1917 and had waited
six years for a London production. In 1925 Noël Coward's
Fallen Angels ran for 158 performances.

Further productions by Anthony Prinsep included
Camilla States Her Case, *The Grand Duchess*,

Beginner's Luck, and *Lullaby* (1925), *By-Ways*, *Engaged*, *Our Dogs*, *There's no Fool . . .* , and a revival of *Trelawny of the 'Wells'* (1926), in all of which Margaret Bannerman appeared. Also during this period successes were attained with *All the King's Horses* and *Ask Beccles* (1926).

In June 1927 Strindberg's *The Spook Sonata* was presented, and in August *Potiphar's Wife*, by Edgar Middleton; in this play Jeanne de Casalis caused a great sensation by appearing in pyjamas. It ran for 143 performances.

In 1927 Prinsep terminated his management of the Globe. He had produced many outstanding successes and many notable plays and had also been responsible for an Italian season with Ruggero Ruggeri in 1926 and a French season with Louis Verneuil and Elvira Popesco. After this Alfred Butt was again in active control.

In October 1928 a comedy called *The Truth Game*, by H. E. S. Davidson (a pseudonym for Ivor Novello) began a run of 162 performances which terminated at Daly's Theatre. In 1929 *Canaries Sometimes Sing*, a Lonsdale comedy, began a run of 144 performances in October.

Maurice Browne became the manager in 1930 and brought an interesting season by foreign players, Moissi playing Hamlet and the Pitoëffs *Saint Joan*. A Japanese company also appeared. In the autumn of the same year came Elmer Rice's *Street Scene*.

The year 1931 opened with *The Improper Duchess*, a comedy by James Fagan, in which Yvonne Arnaud and Hartley Power made a great success. The play ran for 348 performances and was followed by a revival of *And so to Bed*, originally produced at the Queen's Theatre in September 1926. Barry Jackson presented Maugham's *For Services Rendered* in November 1932; and in January 1933 another Yvonne Arnaud success was *Doctor's Orders*.

Popular in 1933 was Ivor Novello's *Proscenium* and his *Murder in Mayfair* was also here in 1934. The same year Maurice Browne's lease ended and Harold Gosling became lessee. C. L. Anthony's *Call it a Day* ran for 509 performances from October 1935.

In February 1937 there was a revival of Shaw's *Candida* which ran for over a hundred performances. This was H. M. Tennent's first production at this theatre, which then became his headquarters, and in this year also Ruth Chatterton made her first appearance in England, in May, in a revival of Somerset Maugham's *The Constant Wife*. In November Owen Nares and Edith Evans appeared in St John Ervine's *Robert's Wife*, which ran for 606 performances.

The most interesting productions of 1939 were *Rhondda Roundabout*, a play by Jack Jones, and an 'all-star' revival of *The Importance of Being Earnest*, which has become a 'classic' production. After the outbreak of war productions included Clemence Dane's *Cousin Muriel* (1940),

with Edith Evans, Peggy Ashcroft and Alec Guinness;
Thunder Rock, with Michael Redgrave, originally produced
at the Neighbourhood Theatre (1940), and a revival of
Barrie's *Dear Brutus* (1940), with an 'all-star' cast.
London of the blitz days responded to the excellence of
this production as heartily as the war-weary London of
1917 had responded to the first production of the play at
Wyndham's Theatre. Emlyn Williams's *The Light of
Heart* also had a second run here during 1941, with the
author playing the part originally taken by Godfrey Tearle,
and at the end of the year came the same author's *The
Morning Star* on the theme of the war and London's air
raids. Its success was probably because, as one critic said,
'there is a certain amount of satisfaction to be had from
sitting in a theatre and watching the most grimly exciting
bit of your life enacted before your eyes'. In December
1942 came Robert Sherwood's *The Petrified Forest*, the
last play in which Owen Nares appeared in London before
his untimely death. Next came Priestley's *They Came to a
City* (1943) and then Terence Rattigan's comedy *While
the Sun Shines*, which opened in December 1943 and continued for 1154 nights. After this success only two revues
from the Lyric, Hammersmith, *Tuppence Coloured* (1947)
and *Oranges and Lemons* (1949) proved really popular,
until May 1949 brought Christopher Fry's *The Lady's Not
for Burning*, with John Gielgud and Pamela Brown; it
scored 294 performances and was followed by *Ring Round
the Moon* in January 1950.

The *Lyric Revue* from Hammersmith and *The Globe
Revue* occupied 1951 and 1952, but it was not until *The
Prisoner* with Alec Guinness in 1954 that the theatre had
another memorable production. *An Evening with Beatrice
Lillie* commenced in November of the same year and filled
the theatre for many months. In 1955 Emlyn Williams,
whose solo performance of Dickens had been seen at
several theatres, astonished London with *Dylan Thomas
Growing Up*. The next years brought *Mrs Willie* (1955),
A Likely Tale (1956), Coward's *Nude with Violin* (1956),
which had three leading men—John Gielgud, Michael
Wilding and Robert Helpmann—during its run which
lasted until February 1958. Then came Graham
Greene's *The Potting Shed*, Rattigan's *Variations on a
Theme*, and O'Neill's *Long Day's Journey into Night*, all
in 1958. Sybil Thorndike and Lewis Casson were seen in
Eighty in the Shade and later in 1959 *The Complaisant
Lover* was staged with Ralph Richardson, Paul Scofield
and Phyllis Calvert; it ran until June 1960. During the run
the lease of the theatre, together with that of the
Queen's, was acquired by the Prince Littler Group. The
next success was Robert Bolt's *A Man for All Seasons*
with Paul Scofield as Sir Thomas More, which began in

July and ran till March 1961. *The Rehearsal* by Anouilh followed from the Playhouse, Oxford, and proved a big success having to be transferred to the Queen's as the Globe was booked for *Dazzling Prospect;* this was a failure and *The Rehearsal* returned immediately, remaining until it transferred to the Apollo for a final season in December 1961. *Becket*, from the Aldwych, then held the stage till April 1962, to be followed by *The Private Ear and The Public Eye*, two plays by Peter Shaffer which ran for 547 performances. *Mary Mary* moved from the Queen's in September 1963 and ran in all for 396 performances until February 1964. The rest of the year consisted of a series of flops. In the following year, 1965, the longest run for a play was *Divorce Me Darling* (87), (Sandy Wilson's sequel to *The Boy Friend)* though *At the Drop of Another Hat*, with Flanders and Swann, chalked up 140 performances between September and February of the next year. Luck returned in June 1966 with *There's a Girl in My Soup* which later transferred to the Comedy Theatre. After this came *Play It Again Sam*, in September 1969, for a run of ten months, followed by a revival of Noël Coward's *Blithe Spirit* in June 1970. *Kean* opened in January 1971 and ran for nearly a year. *The Changing Room* started its run early in 1972, to be succeeded by *Notes on a Love Affair*, by Frank Marcus, *Parents' Day*, and a musical of *Rookery Nook* called *Popkiss*. Kenneth Williams appeared in a new comedy *My Fat Friend* early in 1973 and later in the year a revival of *Private Lives* transferred from the Queen's Theatre, running until succeeded in February 1974 by *Chez Nous* by Peter Nichols with Albert Finney and Geraldine McEwan.

17 · Haymarket,
The Theatre Royal

Haymarket, S.W.1

THE FIRST THEATRE
The Little Theatre in the Hay-Market

Opened 29 December 1720 with *La Fille à la Mode, ou le Badaud de Paris*, performed by the French Comedians of His Grace the Duke of Montague. Under the management of John Potter. Became the Theatre Royal in the Hay-Market, 1766.

THE SECOND THEATRE

Opened 4 July 1821 with *The Rivals*, preceded by an Occasional Address delivered by Daniel Terry and *Peter and Paul; or, Love in the Vineyards*, a vaudeville opening. Under the management of David Morris. Became known as the Theatre Royal, Haymarket, 1855.

Interior completely reconstructed
Capacity: 880

Opened 31 January 1880 with a revival of *Money* by Bulwer Lytton. Under the management of Mr and Mrs Bancroft.

Interior again completely reconstructed
Capacity: 906

Opened 2 January 1905 with a transfer of *Beauty and the Barge*, a farce by W. W. Jacobs and Louis N. Parker, preceded by *That Brute Simmons*, a play in one act by Arthur Morrison and Herbert C. Sargent. Produced by Cyril Maude. Under the management of Frederick Harrison and Cyril Maude.

*

The history of this theatre begins in 1720 when John Potter, a carpenter, built a small theatre on the site of an old inn called the 'King's Head' in the Hay-Market and a gunsmith's shop in Suffolk Street. He hoped to obtain a licence in spite of the Patent Theatres but was unable to do so. The theatre remained closed; it is said it was used by amateurs and some out-of-work actors from the Patent Theatres during the summer, but it was not until Potter gained the patronage of the Duke of Montague that he was able to open with a French Company sponsored by the Duke on 29 December 1720. The season was not a success, lasting only until May 1721. Potter then let the theatre for anything he could find that kept the doors open. We find Aaron Hill as manager, producing *Henry V* with an amateur company. In 1726 there was a mixed programme of opera, tumblers and Signora Violante on the tightrope. In 1729 *Hurlothrumbo; or, The Supernatural* was produced here: it ran for thirty nights and was the theatre's first success. In 1730 the burlesque *Tom Thumb*, first of the seven pieces by Henry Fielding, was produced. The theatre had been defying the Patent Theatres and a battle was long overdue.

In September 1733 Theophilus Cibber took charge with a company known as 'The Comedians of His Majesty's Revels,' actors who had revolted against the Drury Lane management. In 1735 Fielding became manager, with a company he called 'The Great Mogul's Company of Comedians.' He remained in charge until 1737, flouting the Patent Theatres and attracting the town with his crude satires which led to the introduction of censorship in 1737. In 1744 Macklin opened the theatre, which had been more or less closed since Fielding left. Among the company was an actor called Samuel Foote, who played Othello with no success. In 1747 Foote took the theatre, evading the licensing laws and making admission by invitation to partake of tea or chocolate, which allowed the recipients to witness his entertainment of impersonations of other actors or public characters. He began to write pungent satires on the topics of the day, and he himself was made the subject of a crude jest by the members of a party of guests of Lord Mexborough in 1766. They encouraged him to ride an unmanageable horse, the result of which was that he was thrown and injured his left leg, which had to be amputated. Among the guests was the Duke of York, who, to make some amends, obtained a Patent for Foote's Theatre, allowing it to open during the summer months when the other theatres were closed. Foote had become the owner of the theatre after John Whitehead, Potter's successor, sold out in 1760. He remained in sole control until he was forced to give up after a public scandal concerning his morals.

In 1776 Foote transferred his interest in the theatre to George Colman the elder, who remained in office until 1794. Foote died in 1777 and his Patent with him; the theatre was allowed to remain open as before, but on an annual licence. When Colman took over he slightly enlarged the house by the addition of a third tier of boxes, and he also re-roofed and generally renovated it. His son took over the reins from 1794 to 1803, and during this period many actors who were afterwards to become famous made their first appearance, including Charles Kemble, John Liston, John Bannister, R. W. Elliston and the elder Charles Mathews.

In 1805 occurred the 'Tailors' Riot' when hundreds of tailors, enraged at a revival of Foote's satire, The Tailors, assembled to barrack the performance and troops had to be called in to disperse them. Colman, who had taken his brother-in-law David Morris into partnership in 1805, found himself in deep waters through extravagance: and Morris, with some other associates, did his best to get rid of Colman. After many legal battles Morris gained control in 1817.

In 1820 London was being remodelled by John Nash, and it was decided to rebuild the theatre, this time a little to the south, so that a vista from St James's Square along Charles Street (now Charles II Street) could finish with the theatre. Morris obtained a 99-year lease of the land from the Crown at a rent of £356 9s. 6d.

The new building, designed by Nash, had the present exterior, with its well-known Corinthian portico. It cost £20,000 and opened on 4 July 1821 with a production of The Rivals. The interior of this new building was apparently uninviting and was variously described contemporarily as 'rude', 'naked', 'chilling', and even 'petrifying'. One contemporary account says that the theatre was 'in point of architectural beauty the most elegant in London but for the convenience of seeing and hearing the worst contrived'.

The old theatre remained standing by the new building for a little while. Eventually it was converted into shops and an eating house, the Café de l'Europe, which later became the Pall Mall Restaurant. This remained until extensive rebuilding between the wars swept it all away.

In 1822 Morris engaged Thomas Dibdin as his manager and though the theatre was successful the managerial ups and downs eventually led to Court proceedings. Morris remained at the theatre until 1837.

In September 1825 *Paul Pry*, a comedy by John Poole, with Liston in the name part and Madame Vestris singing 'Cherry Ripe', was an unprecedented success: it ran for 114 performances. During this run box prices were paid for seats in the gallery and Liston received between £50 and £60 per night.

On 12 November 1833 a theatrical sensation was caused when Julia Glover appeared as Falstaff in a production of *The Merry Wives of Windsor*. She had also played Hamlet in 1821 at the Lyceum.

From 1837 to 1853 Benjamin Webster was manager. He produced and acted in many of his own plays here. In 1837 Phelps made his first London appearance under this management, as Shylock, and in 1840 Macready appeared in *Money*. By the ending of the monopoly in 1843 the Hay-Market was acknowledged as the equal of Drury Lane and Covent Garden.

Webster was responsible for widening the proscenium, introducing gas lighting and placing 'orchestra stalls' between the orchestra and the pit. In connection with these improvements it is of interest to note that this was the last theatre in London to be illuminated by candles. A play-bill dated 28 April 1843 announced that 'a brilliant centre chandelier has been erected', and also that

by curtailment of the useless portion of the stage in front of the curtain and by advancing the orchestra and the lights nearer the actors and scenic effects, the Lessee, Mr Benjamin Webster, has been able to appropriate the portion so obtained to form a certain number of Orchestral Stalls, which can be retained by parties taking them for the whole evening. For the comfort of those visiting the Pit, backs have been placed to the seats.

This marks the loss of the fore-stage and the proscenium doors and is the next step towards the full picture-frame stage which was to come twenty years later. Altogether Webster spent £12,000 on the building. In June 1843 Webster appeared for the first time wth his constant associate, Madame Céleste. In the same year he offered a prize of £500 for the best English comedy. This was awarded by the judges to *Quid Pro Quo; or, The Day of Dupes*, by Mrs Gore, and was produced on 18 June 1844. It was received with 'uproar and ridicule'.

In 1848 there was further redecoration under the supervision of a Mr Sang and we read in an announcement that
'backs have been added to all the seats in the Circle'. In
his managerial address at the close of the season of 1848
Webster declared that in eighteen months he had lost £8000;
but he continued with the venture for another five years.
On 14 March 1853 his management closed and he moved
to the Adelphi Theatre. He had kept the house open for
sixteen years, paid £60,000 for rent, £30,000 for salaries
and had employed the best actors of his time. A presentation was made to him by the company.

He was immediately followed in management by J. B.
Buckstone. 'His control of the theatre was in every way
creditable. He surrounded himself with a body of actors
some of whom were famous, while none were undistin-
guished. Of his stage productions, amounting to between
one and two hundred, scarcely one was a failure, while
many were an unusual success.' During the summer closing
in 1853 he effected very considerable improvements in the
theatre, both in front of and behind the curtain. The work
was carried out under the direction of Mr G. Somers Clarke.
Among Buckstone's company were Henry Compton and
Barry Sullivan. In 1855 the hyphen was dropped and the
now-familiar form Haymarket was adopted. In 1861 history
was made when *Our American Cousin* was produced. It
introduced E. A. Sothern to London in the character of
Lord Dundreary and added a new word to the dictionary.
In 1863 Ellen Terry, aged fifteen, took the part of Britannia
in an extraordinary medley entitled *Buckstone at Home;
or, a Manager and his Friends*, 'Designed to introduce a
splendid panorama of the tour of the Prince of Wales in the
East.'

The year 1864 saw the first production of *David Garrick*,
by T. W. Robertson, also with Sothern. In October 1868
we read of redecorations including the introduction of an
allegorical group above the proscenium by E. C. Barnes,
and a new act-drop by Telbin. In 1873 'Morning Performances' or Matinées were introduced starting at 2 p.m. This
innovation, started the previous year at the Gaiety Theatre,
followed yet further interior decorations in 1871 again
under the direction of G. Somers Clarke, which were in
the Pompeian style. At this time, also, a picture in the
proscenium cove was painted by Thomas Ballard: this was
seen on the first night of Gilbert's *Pygmalion and Galatea*
with the Kendals on December 9.

Buckstone relinquished the management in 1878, a year
before his death, and he is still said to haunt the theatre. He
was succeeded by J. S. Clarke, who had really been more
or less in control for two or three years.

In 1879 the house was taken over by the Bancrofts as a
'new home' after their successful sojourn at the Prince of

Wales's (see No. 27). They began rebuilding, to designs by
C. J. Phipps directly the theatre closed on 30 September
1879, and opened on 31 January 1880 with a revival of
Money. At this opening there was a small riot because of
the abolition of the pit, which had always been considered
one of the best in London. Bancroft had completely rebuilt
the interior of the theatre, replacing the pit with stalls and
housing the pittites in a circle of their own. He completely
enclosed the stage with a proscenium on all four sides, the
first complete picture-frame stage.

Their period of management, in spite of this inauspicious
start, lasted successfully until 1885 and included revivals
of *School*, *Ours*, and *Caste*; two new adaptations from
Sardou, *Odette* and *Fedora*; new presentations of *The
Rivals* and of Tom Taylor's *Plot and Passion* (1881); *The
Overland Route* (1882) and a new comedy by Pinero, *Lords
and Commons* (1883).

The Bancrofts' farewell performance on 25 July 1885
was attended by the Prince and Princess of Wales, and they
retired with a profit, on the whole period of their management of the two theatres covering twenty years, of
£180,000.

From 1885 to 1887 Russell and Bashford took over without any success, and were succeeded on 15 September
1887 by Beerbohm Tree with a transfer of *The Red Lamp*
from the Comedy Theatre. He remained in charge (with
occasional absences in America) until he moved across
the road to the new Her Majesty's in 1896. He produced
plays by Shakespeare, Henry Arthur Jones, Sydney
Grundy, Oscar Wilde, and Haddon Chambers. One of
his most marked successes was *Trilby*, presented on
30 October 1895, which ran for 260 performances and from
the profits of which he built Her Majesty's Theatre.

This period also saw the first production of two of Wilde's
famous comedies, *A Woman of no Importance* (1893) and
An Ideal Husband (1895).

In October 1896 Cyril Maude and Frederick Harrison
became joint managers and opened with *Under the Red
Robe*, an adaptation of Stanley Weyman's novel. This
successful partnership lasted until July 1905. Other successful productions were those of *A Marriage of Convenience*
(1897), *The Little Minister* (1897), *The Manoeuvres of Jane*
(1898), *The Second in Command* (1900) and *Cousin Kate*
(1903). While Maude was on tour in 1900 Fred Terry produced *Sweet Nell of Old Drury* for the first time.

In 1904 the theatre closed, and alterations were made
under the direction of C. Stanley Peach. A manifesto tells
us:

> The work was completed in five months in which short
> time the whole of the interior in front of the curtain has
> been rebuilt from the foundations, steel brick and

concrete replacing the structure which existed till the end of last July. In arranging the new auditorium, the first consideration has been the safety and comfort of the public and the Pit—so long absent from this theatre—has been restored. The building has been erected by Messrs J. Jarvis and Sons of Tunbridge Wells, and the steel construction by Messrs Dawney and Sons. The decorations have been carried out, from the designs of the Architect, by Messrs Boekbinder and Co.

The famous Corinthian façade and a large proportion of the backstage premises were preserved.

Maude left the Haymarket in 1905 having acquired the Avenue Theatre (see Part IV, No. 7), leaving Harrison in control. From early in 1909 until 1912 the theatre was under the direction of Herbert Trench. One of his first important productions was that of Maurice Maeterlinck's *The Blue Bird*, translated by Teixeira de Mattos. Norman O'Neill, who composed the music for this, became musical director in 1909 and held this position until 1922.

Bunty Pulls the Strings, a Scottish comedy by Graham Moffatt, ran for 617 performances from 18 July 1911, after a trial matinée at the Playhouse. The backstage was renovated in 1909 and the roller act-drop installed by the Bancrofts replaced by a curtain.

On 14 July 1914 Ibsen's *Ghosts* had its first licensed performance here and in 1915 *Quinney's*, by H. A. Vachell, was a great success. From March 1917 *General Post*, a comedy by J. E. Harold Terry, ran for 532 performances.

In March 1920 Donald Calthrop entered into management and produced *The Young Person in Pink*, a comedy by Gertrude Jennings, which had a successful run. In the same year Barrie's *Mary Rose* began a run of 399 performances, followed by *The Circle* in 1921. Subsequent successes were *The Dover Road* (1922), *Havoc* (1923), one of the first serious plays on the Great War, *The Man with a Load of Mischief* (1925), *This Woman Business* (1926), *Yellow Sands* (1926, with a run of 610 performances), *The Fourth Wall* (1928), *The First Mrs Fraser* (632 performances from 1929), *Ten Minute Alibi* (878 performances from 1933), *Touch Wood* (1934), *The Moon in the Yellow River* (1934), *Full House* (1935), *The Amazing Dr Clitterhouse* (1936), *Comedienne* (1938), *Design for Living* (1939).

In 1926, when Harrison died, Horace Watson, his general manager for twenty-one years, succeeded to the management on behalf of Harrison's trustees. A great many of the successes mentioned above took place during his régime. He died in September 1934.

In July 1939 began the extensive alterations under the personal supervision of Stuart Watson, who had succeeded

106

Part 1. The West End

his father. The architect for these was John Murray, and
they included the enlargement of the stalls cloakroom and
the construction of a large lounge bar under the floor of
the stalls, decorated in keeping with the rest of the house
in Louis XIV style. The stalls foyer was also enlarged and
redecorated. Owing to the war this work was not completed
until March 1941.

After the outbreak of war in September 1939 was seen
No Time for Comedy, a revival of *The Doctor's
Dilemma*, and John Gielgud's production of *Love for Love*.

In the summer of 1944 John Gielgud, with H. M. Tennent,
announced a Repertory Season for the Haymarket. This
opened on October 11 with *The Circle*, *Love for Love*,
Hamlet, *A Midsummer Night's Dream* and *The Duchess
of Malfi* followed, and the season continued until August
1945. After this there was a revival of Wilde's *Lady Windermere's Fan* and Coward's *Present Laughter*, which had
first been here alternating with *This Happy Breed* in 1943.
Other successes were *The Heiress* (1949) and also *Waters of
the Moon* (1952) and *A Day by the Sea* (1953), both by N. C.
Hunter. *The Apple Cart* was revived with Noël Coward
and Margaret Leighton in 1954, and *The Matchmaker* by
Thornton Wilder ran from November 1954 well into the
next year. *The Chalk Garden* by Enid Bagnold opened in
April 1956, and on the death of Stuart Watson in September
his son, Anthony, became manager. The theatre still
remains in the hands of the Frederick Harrison Trust; one
of the directors of which, from 1946, was Charles La Trobe,
who had been associated with this theatre in various
capacities since 1908. He retired as Stage Director in 1960.
Flowering Cherry, *Two for the Seesaw* and *The
Pleasure of his Company* fill the three years until April 1960,
when John Gielgud again gave his Shakespearean recital,
Ages of Man. This was followed by Terence Rattigan's
Ross which ran until March 1962. After a week of Joyce
Grenfell, in April 1962 an all-star revival of *The School for
Scandal* ran until November, with changes of cast. This
was followed by *The Tulip Tree*, a new N. C. Hunter play
which ran for 139 performances after several flops and a
revival of *The Doctor's Dilemma* (84). The next success,
a transfer from the Lyric of *The Wings of the Dove*, totalled
324 performances. Then *Hostile Witness* ran for 444 performances from November 1964 to March 1965. A revival
of *The Glass Menagerie* which followed ran for only 43
performances, then Shaw's *You Never Can Tell* ran from
January to September 1966, 284 performances. A revival
of *The Rivals* with Margaret Rutherford and Ralph
Richardson which would total 360 performances, marked
the beginning of the 'Theatre Royal Haymarket Company'
under the leadership of Ralph Richardson. Richardson
then appeared in a revival of *The Merchant of Venice* for

100 performances. After this, in December 1967, came another revival, *Dear Octopus*, with Cicely Courtneidge and Jack Hulbert, a big success which transferred later to the Piccadilly and then the Strand. Oscar Wilde's *The Importance of Being Earnest* was revived in February 1968 and ran till October. After a revival of *Ring Round the Moon*, *Hadrian the Seventh* transferred in March 1969 from the Mermaid. The next new play was not needed until *A Bequest to the Nation*, by Terence Rattigan, opened in September 1970. In April 1971 there was a revival of *The Chalk Garden* that ran till the end of July, then *A Voyage Round My Father* opened on 4 August (first produced at the Greenwich Theatre) and ran into the latter part of 1972 when *Crown Matrimonial* was presented in October and ran until it was succeeded by a revival of *The Waltz of the Toreadors* with Trevor Howard and Coral Browne in February 1974. *Edith Evans and Friends* opened, for a limited season, on 15 April before a new thriller followed, *Who Saw Him Die?* in May 1974.

Full histories of the Haymarket are to be found in *The Haymarket Theatre* by Cyril Maude (1903), *Haymarket, Theatre of Perfection* by W. Macqueen-Pope (1948). Also of interest is *Through the Box-Office Window* by W. H. Leverton (1932), who was for fifty years the box-office manager, and *Excursions in Comedy and A Short History of the Theatre Royal Haymarket* by Harold Simpson (1930).

18 · Her Majesty's Theatre

(The Queen's Theatre, The King's Theatre, His Majesty's Theatre)

Haymarket, S.W.1

THE FIRST THEATRE

Opened as the Queen's Theatre 9 April 1705 with *The Loves of Ergasto*, an opera by Giacomo Greber. Preceded by an occasional prologue spoken by Mrs Bracegirdle. Under the management of William Congreve. Became the King's Theatre, 1714.

THE SECOND THEATRE
Capacity: 2500 (after reconstruction 1818)

Opened as the King's Theatre 26 March 1791 with an Entertainment of Singing and Dancing. Under the management of William Taylor; became Her Majesty's Theatre, 1837.

THE THIRD THEATRE
Capacity: 1890

Built as Her Majesty's Theatre 1868 and 1869; remained

empty and sold by auction 1874. Used for a series of
revivalist meetings given by Moody and Sankey from
15 April 1875. Again sold 1877.

Opened as an Opera House 28 April 1877 with *Norma*
by Bellini. Under the management of Colonel Mapleson.

THE FOURTH THEATRE
Capacity: 1261

Opened as Her Majesty's Theatre 28 April 1897 with
Seats of the Mighty, a play by Gilbert Parker, preceded
by an Inaugural Address delivered by Mrs Tree. Produced
by and under the management of Herbert Beerbohm Tree.

*

The troubles at Drury Lane between Rich and the actors,
combined with his mismanagement of the Theatre Royal,
gave Sir John Vanbrugh the idea of building a rival establishment, and he proceeded to make the designs. In 1703 he
wrote to his friend and correspondent Jacob Tonson that
he had negotiated the purchase of a site and that he intended
to call the theatre the Queen's, in honour of Queen Anne.
'The ground,' he wrote, 'is the second stable-yard going
up the Hay-Market. I give £2000 for it.' Other property
was also acquired.

With capital of £3000 advanced by 'persons of quality'
the scheme was proceeded with, and the foundation stone
of the new theatre was laid on 18 April 1704 by Lady Sunder-
land, the most celebrated Whig toast and beauty of her day;
a silver plaque inscribed 'The Little Whig' in compliment
to her Ladyship was placed under the stone.

Vanbrugh, with William Betterton from Lincoln's Inn,
where the rival company was operating, appointed
William Congreve as manager, and the theatre opened
on 9 April 1705. A special prologue was written by Garth
and spoken by Mrs Bracegirdle in which the building was
referred to as 'By Beauty founded and by Wit designed.'
The opening programme was a performance of Giacomo
Greber's *The Loves of Ergasto*, a pastoral opera with
Italian music of the kind then rapidly becoming fashionable; sung in Italian, it was the first to be given in its native
language.

The theatre was not successful and we read in a contemporary account that 'the convenience of a good theatre
has been sacrificed to exhibit a triumphal piece of architecture', and that 'not one word can be distinctly heard'.

The Confederacy, a comedy by Vanbrugh himself, was
produced in October 1705 in which Thomas Doggett, of
'Coat and Badge' fame, scored one of his greatest
successes. The vastness of the house unfitted it for drama
and also, as Colley Cibber tells us, 'The City, The Inns
of Court, and the middle part of the town, which were the

most constant support of a theatre, . . . were too far out of the reach of an easy walk, and coach hire is often too hard a tax upon the Pit and the Gallery.'

Writing to the Earl of Manchester, Vanbrugh says, 'I lost so much by the Opera last winter that I was glad to get quit of it,' he refers to the fact that in 1706 he let the theatre to Owen Swiney for a rent not exceeding £700 per annum. Swiney was equally unsuccessful and ran off in 1711, leaving a quantity of debts.

Meanwhile in 1709 the actors had been commanded to return to Drury Lane and the Queen's was left to become the cradle of Italian Opera in England and the first house in the country to be devoted entirely to that purpose. Just before Swiney's decampment in 1711 Handel's opera *Rinaldo* was given here—the first opera he produced in England. Handel had practically established himself in this country the previous year, and *Rinaldo* was such a success that he followed it up with a series of works of a similar nature. Royal patronage was given him, and permission to establish in 1720 a company of Italian opera singers at the King's Theatre, as it had now come to be called since the death of Queen Anne, under the title of 'The Royal Academy of Music.' This venture lost about £50,000 and eventually collapsed in 1728. After a short time Handel managed to start again and he produced *Esther*, the first oratorio heard in England, *Acis and Galatea* in 1732 and other operas. In 1734 the enterprise failed, largely owing to competition from an opera company established by Porpora, an Italian composer, at Lincoln's Inn. Handel's venture was terminated and, by an ironic stroke, Porpora succeeded him at the King's Theatre.

Opera continued to be performed with varying success under several managers. Two interior reconstructions took place, the first in 1778, and the second, by Michael Novosielski, in 1782. George Saunders, writing in *A Treatise on the Theatre* (1790), comments that 'Being confined to the original walls Mr Novosielski had not the opportunity of giving it greater width; the form therefore remained extremely bad, and the stage and appendages confined and inconvenient.' On 17 June 1789 the theatre was destroyed by fire, and the loss was estimated at £70,000. It was decided that another theatre should be erected immediately. The foundation stone was laid by the Earl of Buckingham on 3 April 1790 and the building went ahead to the designs of Michael Novosielski.

A private performance to inaugurate the new building was given to subscribers on 10 March 1791, when *Pirro*, an opera by Paisiello, was performed. The Opera House was opened to the public on March 26, it was at the time the largest theatre in England; it was generally regarded as one of the most resplendent theatres in the world.

While building was proceeding the opera company transferred to the Pantheon in Oxford Street, which was adapted and licensed for the purpose. When the new Opera House was ready, no full licence could be obtained and it was forced to open for music and dancing only. Opera had to be given in concert form, but when the Pantheon itself was burnt down in 1792 an arrangement was arrived at between the Opera and the Patent Theatres to the effect that neither party should invade one another's territory. Opera and ballet were then given continually at the King's except during the three seasons 1791–4 when Drury Lane was being rebuilt, and the company acted here, bringing with them their patent.

From 1816 the auditorium was remodelled and the exterior adorned with a colonnade of the Roman Doric order on three sides; the fourth side was occupied by an arcade, which remains to this day. This work, completed in 1818, was to designs by John Nash and G. S. Repton. The stage was at the Pall Mall end of the site but the house was entered from the colonnade in the Hay-Market. In 1821 the front of the theatre was adorned with a relief executed by Bubb, representing 'The Origin and Progress of Music.'

Although blamed for attempting to seduce the fashionable audiences and thus impoverishing the drama, the opera house was hardly a financial success for many years and according to a statement by Ebers it lost £3000 annually between 1820 and 1827 during his management.

The 'golden age' of the Italian Opera House, as it had become known, was from about 1830 to 1850, when it became the resort of the most brilliant and fashionable audiences. Throughout Europe it was venerated as the most brilliant of social spectacles, and was for this reason recommended in all guide books to London. Even the 'pittites' were required to wear full dress, and there was a note to this effect in Crutchley's *Picture of London*, 1834.

The theatre was not only associated with opera but with 'The Romantic Ballet' and its great stars. In 1837 the name was changed to Her Majesty's Theatre, Italian Opera House, which it retained throughout the reign of Victoria, except that 'Italian Opera House' was dropped when adopted by Covent Garden in 1847.

In 1842 Laporte, who had been in charge since 1828, was succeeded by Benjamin Lumley. Redecorations were carried out again in 1846, the work being done under the direction of a Mr Johnson. On 4 May 1847 was the début of Jenny Lind and the beginning of what came to be known as 'Lind Mania,' so great was her success. In 1850 further internal alterations were made so that promenade concerts could be given. Johnson was again the architect. A small

concert hall or 'Bijou Theatre' was included in the building
on the Haymarket Front.

The history of the theatre at this period, the story of
opera in England, is fully told by Dennis Arundell in *The
Critic at the Opera* (1957). A record of performances
between 1789–1820 is in *The Italian Opera and Contemporary Ballet* by William C. Smith (1955) and a history of
the theatre, *The King's Theatre 1704–1867,* by Daniel
Nalbach was published in 1972.

In 1851 *Fidelio* was performed for the first time in this
country, during the last season of operatic prosperity for
Her Majesty's. Covent Garden had abandoned the drama
in 1847 and its new interior was specially constructed
for opera. When Covent Garden was burnt down in 1856
Her Majesty's, which had been closed for four years,
was reopened for opera, continuing until its own destruction
by fire on 6 December 1867. The building was burnt down
in less than an hour. The fire broke out at eleven o'clock
at night, and it seems that the alarm was rather slow in
communicating with the headquarters of the brigade, then
located in Watling Street. It was said that the alarm was
not given until twenty minutes past eleven, by which time
the flames had attacked the roof. By midnight the scene
had become one of fearful grandeur, when the roof
collapsed amid a shower of sparks and fragments which
fell like so much hail in front of the clubs in Pall Mall.
Several houses round the theatre were gutted, principally
the shops in the adjoining Opera Arcade.

The theatre was reconstructed within the old remaining
shell by Charles Lee between 1868 and 1869 at a cost of
£50,000, the contractors being George Trollope and Son.
At the Charles Street end of the building was included
an hotel called The United and The Clergy Club, and
some shops and houses in Pall Mall. This structure
remained until it was demolished in 1892, and during this
time it had a chequered career. Lumley's lease did not
expire until 1891, but no tenant could be found for the new
building, which remained empty until it was sold for
£31,000 in May 1874 and opened with Moody and Sankey
'revival meetings' on 15 April 1875. The theatre was again
sold in the spring of 1877 and opera returned under Colonel
Henry Mapleson. He began his season on 28 April 1877
with *Norma* in which Titiens sang for almost the last time.
The first performance of *Carmen* was given on 22 June
1878. Other events of interest at this house were the Carl
Rosa seasons between 1879 and 1882, the first complete
performance in England of *The Ring* in 1882. Haverley's
American United Mastodon Minstrels had a season in
1880, *Uncle Tom's Cabin* was revived in 1882, Sarah
Bernhardt acted in 1886 and 1890. In 1889 the house was
even the scene of a boxing tournament. Pantomimes were

often given for Christmas seasons, and after one in 1890 the theatre closed. It was stripped by auction of its effects later in 1891 before it was demolished, the Royal Opera Arcade alone remaining.

The foundation stone of the fourth and present building was laid on 16 July 1896. The theatre 'covered the empty space which has for so long been an eyesore to this particular locality'. Only half the original site was used for the new theatre, which was built on the Charles Street corner. The rest of the ground was later occupied by the Carlton Hotel. On this ground is now New Zealand House, whose government owns the whole of the original site. The new Her Majesty's Theatre was built by Beerbohm Tree, who had been in management opposite at the Haymarket for many years. He had a great success with *Trilby*, an adaptation of Du Maurier's novel, and from the profits decided to build his own theatre. Designed by C. J. Phipps, the building was faced with Portland stone and crowned with a dome, the façade in French Renaissance style, and was built at a cost of £55,000. The contemporary manifesto tells us:

On the ground floor, level with the street, will be found Orchestral Stalls, Pit Stalls and the Pit.

The first floor will be devoted to the Dress Circle and Family Circle. The second tier consists of the Upper Circle, Amphitheatre and the Gallery behind.

The five doorways in the centre of the Haymarket façade underneath the loggia open into a vestibule exclusively for the use of the two classes of the Stalls and the Dress and Family Circles, and the Stalls have a third way out, level with the pavement in Charles Street . . .

The style adopted for the auditorium of the theatre is Louis XIV. There are private boxes on each of the tiers adjoining the proscenium and separated from it and other parts of the auditorium by marble columns. The hangings are of cerise-coloured embroidered silk and the walls generally are covered with a paper of the same tone.

The seating for Stalls, Dress and Family Circles is in arm chairs, covered with velvet the same colour as the curtains. The Tableau curtains are of velvet of a similar tone behind which is the Act Drop of tapestry copied from one of the Gobelin Tapestries now in Paris.

The whole of the theatre and annexes are lighted by the Electric Light taken from three centres, so that should any one centre fail, the other systems are always available. Hanging from the ceiling is a cut glass and brass electrolier and brackets of Louis XIV style are fixed round the box fronts and on the side walls.

The opening took place on 28 April 1897 with a production of *The Seats of the Mighty*, a dramatisation by

Gilbert Parker of his own novel. Tree's reign here was full of interest and he produced many plays, including spectacular revivals of Shakespeare. There is an elliptical bronze ornamental tablet on the north-east corner in Charles II Street, as it is now called, commemorating Tree's association with the theatre.

In 1902 the name of the theatre was changed to His Majesty's, by permission of Edward VII. In 1904 Tree instituted a Dramatic School in connection with the theatre which was eventually to become R.A.D.A.

Oscar Asche took over the management in September 1907 while Tree went abroad, and produced Laurence Binyon's *Attila* and revivals of *As You Like It* and *Othello*. The tradition of opera was kept alive by the production among others of *The Wreckers* by Dame Ethel Smyth (1909) and *Ariadne auf Naxos* by Richard Strauss, under Beecham (1913).

The Coronation 'Gala' Performance of 1911 was held here, and further 'Gala' Performances in aid of the King George V Pension Fund were held in 1914, 1915, 1917 and 1923. The original one in 1911 raised £4628 as a nucleus for the fund.

The full story of Tree and his productions can be read in his biography by Hesketh Pearson (1956), and a detailed history of the building is given in *The Survey of London*, vol. 29 (1960).

In 1916, while Tree was in America, Oscar Asche produced *Chu Chin Chow*, which had the phenomenal run of 2238 performances, the longest known until 1958, when it was exceeded by *The Mousetrap*. Described as a 'Musical Tale of the East, told by Oscar Asche, and set to music by Frederick Norton,' and opening on August 31, it cost £5300 to produce and netted £700,000 for its promoters. During the run Tree died and the theatre eventually came under the control of George Grossmith and J. A. E. Malone, with Joseph Benson as owner.

Cairo, which followed in October 1921, ran for 267 performances. Subsequent successes were Basil Dean's production of Somerset Maugham's *East of Suez* (1922) and James Elroy Flecker's *Hassan*, with incidental music by Frederic Delius (1923). A mixture of musical comedies followed; then came *The Co-Optimists* in 1925 and 1926 after which Gershwin's *Oh, Kay!* was produced in 1927. Diaghileff gave seasons of Russian Ballet in 1926 and 1928.

Noël Coward's *Bitter-Sweet* ran for 697 performances from July 1929 and Peggy Wood scored an instant success; 1931 saw the production of J. B. Priestley's *The Good Companions* and 1932 brought Anny Ahlers, of tragic memory, in *The Dubarry*. *Music in the Air* (1935), *Conversation Piece* (1934), *Henry IV, Part I* (1935) with

George Robey making theatrical history by his Falstaff, *The Happy Hypocrite* with Ivor Novello and Vivien Leigh (1936), and J. M. Barrie's much-discussed play *The Boy David* (1936) were also outstanding productions. In the late thirties the theatre housed many shows both musical and straight, often transfers, but none of them were outstanding successes.

During the war the theatre was mainly occupied with revivals of famous musical comedies, *The Merry Widow* (1943), *The Lilac Domino* (1944), and *Irene* (1945), though *Lady Behave* (1941) and *Du Barry was a Lady* (1942) had good runs. In 1945 the theatre was controlled by the Prince Littler Group, who used 'The Dome' as their office, though the block had become the property of the New Zealand Government. This was expected to threaten the existence of the theatre, but so far only the Carlton Hotel part of the site has been used.

In 1947 Robert Morley appeared in his own play, *Edward My Son*, with Peggy Ashcroft. Following years saw the successes of *Brigadoon* (1949), *Blue for a Boy* (1950), *The Tea House of the August Moon* (1954), *No Time for Sergeants* (1956) and *West Side Story* which ran from December 1958 until June 1961.

The theatre was then re-decorated and the next production was *Bye Bye Birdie*. When the run concluded in February 1962 it was followed by the two Guthrie Gilbert and Sullivan productions of *H.M.S. Pinafore* and *The Pirates of Penzance;* these continued in repertoire till June when *Lock Up Your Daughters* at last came to the West End from the Mermaid where it had just been revived. The next big hit was *The Right Honourable Gentleman* which ran for 572 performances from May 1964, then another success in October 1965, *Say Who You Are*, was followed by *Fiddler on the Roof* in February 1967 which ran till October 1971 for 2030 performances, succeeded by a short run, *The Ambassador. Company* came next, in January 1972, with the return of Elaine Strich, then late in 1972 *Applause* arrived, staying till October 1973, and was followed by *Pippin* for three months. A limited season of Pirandello's *Henry IV* opened, starring Rex Harrison, in February 1974. This was followed by Prospect's production of *Pericles* and, in July, a musical version of *The Good Companions*.

19 · The London Casino

(The Prince Edward Theatre, The Casino Cinerama Theatre)

Old Compton Street, Soho, W.1

Capacity: On opening as a theatre, 1800; as a cinema 1155

Opened as the Prince Edward Theatre 3 April 1930, with *Rio Rita*, a romantic musical comedy by Harry Tierney, book by Guy Bolton and Fred Thompson, lyrics by Joseph McCarthy. Produced by John Harwood, under the management of Lee Ephraim.

THE BUILDING

At the corner of Old Compton Street and Greek Street, Soho, just off Cambridge Circus, there had stood for close on a century a large draper's shop known as 'The Emporium', the property of William Reddun and Son. Run on old-fashioned lines, it counted Royalty among its clientèle, but changing times caused the business to close. The property together with other adjacent buildings was acquired by the Hay Hill Syndicate, Ltd, in 1929 and demolished.

The theatre erected by Griggs and Son on the site was designed by Edward A. Stone, the interior decorations were the work of Marc Henri and Laverdet. It was the first of the new theatres of 1930.

Its exterior of red and yellow brick was designed in the style of an Italian palace, its severity broken by rows of windows originally fitted with green shutters, and heavy over-shadowing eaves.

Much use was made of the then new decorative material Marb-L-Cote in the interior and the proscenium arch formed of a series of Lalique glass coves tinted in amber. The theatre remained in use only until 1935 when a new syndicate of owners converted it into a cabaret-restaurant at a cost of £25,000. A semi-circular dance floor was built up from the stage, stairways were constructed from the stalls to the dress circle, and the area under the stage was converted into kitchens. It reopened on 2 April 1936 as the London Casino.

It was restored to theatrical use in 1946 with again some structural alterations. It has undergone yet another change in recent years as in October 1954 it was converted for the screening of Cinerama, when a lease of the theatre was taken by Cinerama Exhibitors (London) Ltd.

THE PLAYS

The theatre opened under the name of the Prince Edward Theatre in compliment to the Prince of Wales on 3 April 1930 with a musical comedy *Rio Rita*, under the management of Lee Ephraim. This was not a great success nor were the others which followed, though *Nippy*, with Binnie Hale, scored 137 performances. Even the importation of Josephine Baker, the famous cabaret star, in October 1933 did not make the theatre popular. Non-stop revue from two till twelve was also tried, but was a failure here. The house had been wired for 'talkies' and for a period became the home of trade shows. It continued in this way for a year or so until eventually a syndicate decided to reconstruct it as a cabaret-restaurant. This syndicate was composed of M. Poulsen (of the Café de Paris), Major C. H. Bell, a consulting engineer well known in the cinematographic world who directed the installation of the original lighting, and E. A. Stone, the architect of the theatre. It took eighteen months to get the necessary licences from the authorities, but the building was eventually opened as the London Casino on 2 April 1936.

The stage show at the opening was *Folies Parisiennes*. The policy of the London Casino was an interchange of

shows, run by Clifford C. Fisher, between the French
Casino in New York, the Casino in Miami, U.S.A., and
the London Casino. Unfortunately ill-luck still dogged the
theatre; The French Casino in New York went bankrupt,
and the London Casino had to bear the full burden. In spite
of this there was a period during which it was declared
that more money was taken there than at any other place
of entertainment in London, a matter of £6000 to £7000 a
week not being unusual. In this manner the years passed
until 1940 when the blitz caused its closure.

In July 1942 the London Casino was converted into the
Queensbury All Services Club, which it remained for the
duration of the war.

Its first production after reconversion to a theatre in 1946
was *Pick-up-Girl* on 14 October, produced by Peter Cotes;
Tom Arnold and Emile Littler had assumed management
of the theatre. A revival of *The Dancing Years* was staged
in March 1947, followed by seasons of variety with
international stars heading the bills. Ballet seasons and
pantomimes kept the theatre occupied until 1949, when
Robert Nesbitt's *Latin Quarter* was staged; it ran successfully into several editions and other similar shows were
devised.

The year 1953 saw Cicely Courtneidge in a revue by
Vivian Ellis, *Over the Moon*, and a holiday-camp musical
Wish You were Here was the last show staged before
Cinerama arrived, on the largest of screens, in 1954.

On 1 May 1974 it was announced that, under the direction
of Bernard Delfont, the London Casino would be converted
into a dual purpose centre for both film and theatre at the
cost of £150,000 and would re-open with a pantomime,
Cinderella, at Christmas.

20 · The London Palladium

(The Palladium)

Argyll Street, Oxford Street, W.1

Capacity: 2325

Opened as the Palladium 26 December 1910 with a variety programme which included Nellie Wallace, Whit Cunliffe, Ella Retford, Ella Shields and Martin Harvey in a one-act play, *The Conspiracy*.

THE BUILDING

Before the erection of the Palladium in 1910, the site on which it arose had been associated with entertainment for many years.

Originally Argyll House, the London home of the Dukes of Argyll, was here. In the early 1800s it passed into the hands of the first Earl of Aberdeen, sometime Prime Minister, who lived here until his death in 1860. His long life had held up the march of building progress in the district, but after his death the house and gardens were

swallowed up by commercial interests. The house was
demolished and the land on which it stood was sold to a
firm of wine merchants, who excavated the site to a depth
of 25 ft and built bonded wine cellars. On the large surface
area the Corinthian Bazaar arose, but this was only a temporary structure.

In 1871 Frederick Charles Hengler acquired a ten-year
lease of the area, and opened his Hengler's Grand Cirque
in October 1871. Hengler, born and bred in the circus,
having been successful on tour, had acquired his own
show. Later he established himself in Liverpool. Excursions to other provincial centres and to London convinced
him that a permanent home in the capital would be a good
financial proposition. He was right to such an extent that,
in 1884, he was eventually able to enlarge his premises on a
grand scale, rebuilding them almost completely to the
designs of C. J. Phipps.

It was very much a one-man concern, and when Hengler
died in 1887, though his sons carried on for a while, the
popularity of the circus began to ebb. Another showman,
Edward Wulff, tried his hand with little luck; and in 1895
the ring was turned into the National Skating Palace, with
real ice.

Attempts were made five years later to resume circus,
but in 1900 the London Hippodrome opened in Charing
Cross Road, providing a mixture of circus, spectacle and
variety. This new building proved how out-moded was the
old Argyll Street Circus. The L.C.C. also demanded major
alterations, and improvements which were found financially
impossible to undertake, so in 1908 the lease of the site
passed into the hands of a syndicate, who announced plans
to build a music-hall to be known as the Palladium.

The prime mover behind the scheme was Walter
Gibbons, who wished to outdo his rivals in music-hall
management, Oswald Stoll, Edward Moss and Alfred
Butt, each of them with their own London headquarters
(the Coliseum, the Hippodrome and the Palace).

This was the height of the variety and music-hall boom,
and all the circuits were busily acquiring new premises.
The Victoria Palace was being built, the Middlesex (later
the Winter Garden, now the New London) was rebuilding,
central London also had the Tivoli, the Oxford, the Holborn
Empire, the Pavilion, the Alhambra and the Empire. Some
of these halls were soon to turn to the new form of spectacular revue for most of the time. The war saw the end of the
Tivoli and the conversion of the Pavilion and the Oxford
into theatres with the Middlesex soon to follow. Only the
Coliseum with its specialised form of entertainment
remained actively in this field until 1930. The Palladium,
the Victoria Palace and the Holborn Empire all strayed
from their original purpose as music-halls in the first ten

years of their life, but, in 1910, there were some sixty halls
in and around London. It seems now, looking back, that
the decline and death of music-hall and its traditional form
dated from the time it was given the accolade of a Royal
Command Performance in 1911.

The Palladium was designed by Frank Matcham, the
original estimate of £200,000 was exceeded by almost
£50,000. With a classic façade and an ample luxurious
vestibule, with its interior, as *The Era* of 24 December 1910
describes it:

> . . . brilliant in white and gold, with seating in warm red,
> the house sounds the last word in luxury and appointment,
> and the magnificent sweep of the dress circle presents
> a remarkable appearance from the stage.

In the great Palm Court at the back of the stalls, one
thousand persons can be comfortably served with tea.
This is a very striking feature of the Palladium and the
Palm Court is of all Norwegian Rose granite which,
especially, looks extremely attractive. In this Palm Court
a ladies' orchestra will play daily between performances.
The decorations are very beautiful, Rose du Barri
hangings adorn the boxes, and upholstery of the same
colour has been employed in the stalls, while the orchestra
is enclosed by a marble balustrade, Generally speaking,
the colour scheme of the walls is pink, white and gold,
with coloured marbles, and certainly there is not a dull
note anywhere. The walls of the main vestibule are
painted silver. Perhaps the most unique feature is the box
to box telephone that has been installed. It will therefore
be possible for the occupants of one box, recognising
friends in another box, to enter into conversation with
them.

All the seats in its two tiers were tip-up and prices were
very cheap. The area covered by the building stretched
behind Great Marlborough Street and Hills Place in Oxford
Street, having exits in each. The capacity was then second
only to the Coliseum. From 1934 the house has been
officially called the London Palladium.

THE PLAYS

The Palladium opened on 26 December 1910 and soon
became a popular home of variety. Its programmes often
included farce, melodrama and operatic representations as
well as the usual variety turns, and all the famous figures
of the halls appeared from time to time.

In 1912 Charles Gulliver took over control, giving two
performances nightly and three matinées a week. As the
days of music-hall gave way to spectacular revue, so the
Palladium changed with the fashion. In 1922 the outstanding production was Harry Day's great spectacle

Rockets, which ran for 490 performances, being followed
in 1923 with *Whirl of the World* with Nellie Wallace, Billy
Merson, Leslie Sarony, Nervo and Knox and Tommy
Handley, which ran for 53 weeks (627 performances),
written by Albert de Courville, Edgar Wallace and William
K. Wells, with music by Frederick Chappell.

In March 1925 came another de Courville success, *Sky
High* (309 performances), followed by *Folies Bergères*,
Palladium Pleasures and *Life* (1926) and *The Apache* (1927),
a musical play from the Hungarian which was presented
by Julian Wylie. Annual pantomimes were also a feature of
these years.

In 1928 the Palladium was bought by the General Theatre
Corporation, who turned it into a cinema, but this policy
only lasted three months. Towards the end of that year the
Palladium came under the direction of George Black, whose
policy was to speed up variety in competition with the ever
more popular cinema, which was just beginning to talk. The
Palladium under his management became famous for its
spectacular productions of revue and for his Variety. He
created the form of entertainment at the Palladium in 1932
known as 'crazy week', which proved so popular that it
developed into the Crazy Gang Shows, which were in fact
large-scale productions. Chief among these were *Life
Begins at Oxford Circus* and *Round About Regent Street*
(1935), *All Alight at Oxford Circus* and *O-Kay for Sound*
(1936), *London Rhapsody* (1937) and *These Foolish
Things* (1938).

Peter Pan made its annual Christmas home here from
1930 to 1938, the Peters being Jean Forbes-Robertson
from 1930 to 1934, and again in 1938, Nova Pilbeam in
1935, Elsa Lanchester in 1936 and Anna Neagle in 1937.

During the war George Black mounted several spectacular revues here, including *The Little Dog Laughed* (1940).

In 1946 George Black died and Val Parnell took over
control, the theatre becoming the property of Moss
Empires, Ltd. Shows, presented in the same tradition,
continued until 1948, when variety came back triumphantly,
and London had the opportunity of seeing the famous names
from across the Atlantic. This pattern, with a Christmas
pantomime and a spectacular revue, still continues to run its
successful course.

In 1960 the London Palladium came under the direction
of Leslie A. Macdonnell; and in November a take-over
bid for control by Charles Clore and his associates was
defeated by Prince Littler. The Palladium remains in the
Moss Empires Group with Sir Lew Grade as chairman
and under the direction of Louis Benjamin.

The name, London Palladium, has been used from
1934. The full story of the theatre has been told in *Top
of the Bill* by Ian Bevan (1952).

Timothy Birdsall
1980

21 · The Lyric Theatre

Shaftesbury Avenue, W.1

Capacity: 948

Opened 17 December 1888 with a transfer from the Prince of Wales' Theatre of *Dorothy*, being the eight hundred and seventeenth performance of the comedy–opera by B. C. Stephenson and Alfred Cellier. Under the management of Henry J. Leslie.

THE BUILDING

The Lyric was the second theatre in the new Shaftesbury Avenue, the first being the Shaftesbury Theatre, now demolished, whose opening preceded it by two months (see No. 5). It is situated in a block of buildings, which now includes the Apollo Theatre (not built until 1901) and the Windmill Theatre (1931), stretching from Great Windmill Street to Rupert Street, and facing Shaftesbury Avenue with Archer Street running behind.

The frontage of the Lyric Theatre stretches along the

whole of this block, except for the Apollo Theatre at the
Rupert Street end and bank premises on the Windmill Street
corner. Its stage-door and dressing-room block is in Great
Windmill Street and the gallery entrance until recently in
Archer Street.

The new theatre was built by Henry J. Leslie largely on
municipal ground, with the addition of some houses in
Archer Street and the old Hôtel de l'Etoile in Great Windmill Street, the site of the house in which Dr William Hunter
died. A plaque to this effect is now on the wall by the stage
door of the theatre. At the time of building the theatre was
almost on an isolated site.

Leslie financed the building of his own theatre out of the
profits he had made from *Dorothy*. This comic opera had
originally been produced by George Edwardes at the old
Gaiety Theatre on 25 September 1886. It was not a big
success but he nursed it for a while and transferred it to
the Prince of Wales' Theatre. Losing patience, he decided
to sell his interests to his accountant H. J. Leslie for £1000.
Leslie recast the title-role and introduced a song, 'Queen
of my Heart,' which Cellier had written for another purpose. The new version was seen in February 1887. It was
an instant success and ran on at the Prince of Wales' while
Leslie was building his own theatre, to which he eventually
transferred the production for its opening. He is said to
have made over £100,000 out of his deal.

The new theatre was designed by C. J. Phipps and built
in the short space of ten months by Messrs Stephens and
Bastow. A three-tier theatre, its gallery is now reseated
as a balcony.

A contemporary account of the building, taken from
The Theatre, February 1889, tells us that:

> The façade is of the Renaissance style in red brick and
> Portland stone, divided in the centre and two wings, each
> surmounted with a high pitched gable with recessed
> arcades.

Of the interior it says:

> The frame of the proscenium is of brown and white
> alabaster: the sides of the stalls and pit are lined with
> walnut and sycamore panelling, with handsome carved
> mouldings specially designed and manufactured in
> Germany. The Grand Hall of the second circle is early
> French Renaissance of the Henry II period, and the
> Stalls foyer and Smoking Room are in imitation of an
> early Dutch interior. The principal electrolier repre-
> sents an inverted bouquet of corn, barley and poppies
> in prodigal profusion.

In 1933 the theatre was completely redecorated by Michael
Rosenauer (except 'the Grand Hall of the second circle'

which remained as originally decorated). The vestibule crush room and bars were entirely reconstructed and other minor alterations made. Lock-up shops now occupy a large portion of the frontage at street level, with office premises above.

THE PLAYS

The revival of *Dorothy*, with which the theatre opened on 17 December 1888, was followed in April 1889 with the production of *Doris* by the same author and composer. This ran for two hundred performances and was succeeded by *The Red Hussar* by H. Pottinger Stephens, with music by Edward Solomon, which ran for 175 performances from November 1889. Marie Tempest and Hayden Coffin appeared in all these productions. The theatre was then taken by Horace Sedger and other successes which followed included *La Cigale*, a comic opera by F. C. Burnand, with music by E. Audran and Ivan Caryll, which ran for 423 performances from October 1890; *The Mountebanks* (1892), a comic opera by W. S. Gilbert, with music by Alfred Cellier, and *Little Christopher Columbus*, a burlesque by G. R. Sims and Cecil Raleigh, also with music by Caryll, which ran for 361 performances from October 1893. Also in 1893 the great Eleonora Duse made her first appearance in this country in *La Dame aux Camélias*, which was called on the programmes *Camille* from a mistaken notion that the play was familiar to English audiences under that name, as it was to the American public. She also appeared in *Fedora*, *Cavalleria Rusticana*, *La Locandicia*, *The Doll's House* and other plays.

In 1894 George Edwardes produced W. S. Gilbert's comic opera *His Excellency*, with music by F. Osmond Carr. William Greet then took the theatre, and Wilson Barrett's *The Sign of the Cross* ran for 435 performances from January 1896, followed by his *Daughters of Babylon*. *The Cat and the Cherub*, a Chinese play by C. B. Fernald, was produced in 1897.

In 1897 Réjane had a season and in 1898 Bernhardt was here; they both appeared as Frou-Frou. Other successes were *Dandy Dan the Lifeguardsman* (1897), *Little Miss Nobody* by Harry Graham with music by A. E. Godfrey and Landon Ronald, which ran for nearly two hundred performances, followed by *L'Amour Mouille* in April 1899, in which Tom B. Davis, who took over direction of the Lyric in 1898, introduced Evie Greene to London. It was Davis who gave Leslie Stuart his first commission and *Florodora*, a musical comedy by Owen Hall produced at the Lyric in November 1899, was Stuart's first musical comedy success, as well as the play in which Evie Greene made a triumph in the part of Dolores, and Ada Reeve scored as Lady Holyrood; the play was given 455 performances.

This success was followed by *The Silver Slipper*, an extravaganza by Owen Hall and Leslie Stuart, which had 197 performances from June 1901.

In 1902 Forbes-Robertson occupied the Lyric, appearing in *Mice and Men, Hamlet, Othello* in which Gertrude Elliott played Desdemona and Herbert Waring Iago; and in 1903 George Fleming's version of Rudyard Kipling's *The Light that Failed* ran for over one hundred performances.

Musical comedy returned to the Lyric at the end of Forbes-Robertson's season with *The Medal and the Maid*. This was a successful collaboration of Owen Hall and Sidney Jones, with Ada Reeve and Ruth Vincent, in April 1903, and was followed in October by *The Duchess of Dantzig*, a romantic opera based on *Madame Sans-Gêne*, by Henry Hamilton with music by Ivan Caryll. Evie Greene gave up the part which she had been playing for over two years at Daly's in *A Country Girl* in order to return to the Lyric and create the leading role in *The Duchess of Dantzig*, in which she was enormously popular. This play, a musical version of the story of Napoleon and Madame Sans-Gêne, was put on by George Edwardes, while Robert Courtneidge was responsible for the stage production; it ran for 236 performances.

Two musical comedies were successfully presented at the Lyric during 1905, *The Talk of the Town* by Seymour Hicks, and *The Blue Moon* with music by Howard Talbot and Paul Rubens. In the latter Florence Smithson made her first London appearance. In between these productions Martin Harvey had a season during which he produced *Hamlet, The Breed of the Treshams* and *The Only Way*.

In 1906 Lewis Waller became connected with the theatre and appeared in revivals of *Brigadier Gerard* and *Monsieur Beaucaire*, and a production of *Othello*, in which he played the name part with H. B. Irving as Iago and Evelyn Millard as Desdemona. Later in the same year he played in *Robin Hood*, a romantic play by Henry Hamilton and William Devereux; it was in this play that Waller was commanded to perform before King Edward VII and Queen Alexandra at Windsor Castle. In 1907 Waller revived Tom Taylor's *Clancarty*, and in 1908 was successful with Edward Milton Royle's drama *A White Man*, Maugham's *The Explorer*, a new version of *The Duke's Motto* (in which he was also commanded to appear at Windsor Castle), and *Henry V*. The two successes of 1909 were Conan Doyle's 'modern morality' play, *The Fires of Fate*, and William Devereux's *Sir Walter Raleigh*; and in 1910, his last year here, he staged *The Rivals*.

The year 1910 brought to London *The Chocolate Soldier*, an unofficial musical version of Shaw's *Arms and the Man*, with music by Oscar Strauss, which had over five hundred performances from September 10 and was revived at the

Lyric again in September 1914. Michael Faraday, who was a partner with F. C. Whitney in the production of this success, became sole director of the Lyric in 1911 and produced an interesting selection of musical plays, including *Nightbirds*, an English version of *Die Fledermaus* (1911), *The Five Frankfurters*, *The Girl in the Taxi* (1912) which was given 385 times, *Love and Laughter* (1913), *Mam'selle Tralala* (1914), the last three with Yvonne Arnaud, and *The New Shylock* (1914).

William Greet was succeeded by Edward Engelbach as lessee in 1914, and Grossmith and Laurillard presented *On Trial*, which was the success of 1915 with 174 performances, and then *Romance*, originally produced at the Duke of York's in October 1915, was transferred here to finish its remarkable run of 1049 performances. Owen Nares at the height of his matinée idol fame appeared opposite Doris Keane in this play. *Roxana* followed in 1918, and in April 1919 a memorable production of *Romeo and Juliet* was staged with a cast including Basil Sydney, Leon Quartermaine, Doris Keane, and Ellen Terry as the Nurse.

Matheson Lang entered on the Lyric management for a short time in 1918 with a successful production of *The Purple Mask*. *The Bird of Paradise*, a Hawaiian play, and *A Little Dutch Girl*, a musical comedy, were successes of 1919 and 1921. Later in 1921 *Welcome Stranger* by Aaron Hoffman began a run of 232 performances. Various managements used the theatre, but the lessee was now F. W. Tibbetts (1916–30).

Musical comedy again reigned at the Lyric with *Whirled into Happiness* (1922), a musical farce by Harry Graham, which had a run of 244 performances; *Lilac Time*, which started in December 1922 and had 626 performances, with Courtice Pounds in the leading role of Schubert; and *The Street Singer*, a musical play by Frederick Lonsdale, with music by H. Fraser Simson, with Phyllis Dare and Harry Welchman, which ran for 360 performances from June 1924.

In 1926 and 1927 two names became closely associated with the Lyric. Three plays by Avery Hopwood had outstanding runs: *The Best People*, written in collaboration with David Grey (1926), 309 performances; *The Gold Diggers* (1926), 180 performances; and *The Garden of Eden* (1927), 232 performances. In the last two appeared Tallulah Bankhead. She was at this time proving an enormous box-office attraction amongst the 'bright young people' of the Gay Twenties. She also appeared at the Lyric in *Her Cardboard Lover* (1928) and *Let Us Be Gay* (1929).

In 1929 Leslie Howard appeared in *Berkeley Square*, by John L. Balderston and J. C. Squire, which had previously been performed at the St Martin's Theatre in 1926 with Lawrence Anderson; and Frank Vosper's play *Murder on the Second Floor* began a run of 146 performances.

Eugene O'Neill's *Strange Interlude* (1931), Dodie Smith's first play *Autumn Crocus* (1931), J. B. Priestley's *Dangerous Corner* (1932), Rose Franken's *Another Language* (1932) with Edna Best and Herbert Marshall, and Rachel Crothers' *When Ladies Meet* (1933) all had good solid runs for their day.

In 1933 the theatre was redecorated when it came into the hands of Thomas Bostock, but a successful production was not found until January 1934 when Robert E. Sherwood's *Reunion in Vienna* was a big success for Alfred Lunt and Lynn Fontanne, who had appeared in the original American production of the play in 1931. Also in 1934 Sidney Kingsley's *Men in White* and Edna Ferber and George S. Kaufman's *Theatre Royal* had successful runs here. In 1935 Sherwood's *Tovarich* ran for 414 performances.

May 1936 saw J. B. Priestley's *Bees on the Boatdeck* with Ralph Richardson and Laurence Olivier, and Maurice Colbourne's *Charles the King*, in which Gwen Ffrangcon-Davies and Barry Jones appeared. Stephen Powys' *Wise To-morrow* (1937) was another success. In 1936 King Edward VIII removed the ban on stage personations of his great grandmother, Queen Victoria, and the play of 1937 was Laurence Housman's *Victoria Regina*, which was performed 337 times. Pamela Stanley repeated her remarkable success as Queen Victoria: the play had previously been given at the Gate Theatre in May 1935. The Gate, being a club, was therefore free from censorship.

May 1938 saw the Lunts again in *Amphitryon 38*, and September brought Charles Morgan's *The Flashing Stream* which attained 201 performances with Godfrey Tearle and Margaret Rawlings.

After the outbreak of war in 1939 it was some time before the Lyric achieved a solid run with *The Nutmeg Tree* in October 1941, which brought Yvonne Arnaud back to the theatre where she had made her early successes. In 1943 the theatre came under the control of Prince Littler. The Lunts returned to this theatre in Rattigan's *Love in Idleness* in 1944 and the same author's *The Winslow Boy* began its run of 476 performances in May 1946. The John Clements and Kay Hammond revival of *The Beaux' Stratagem*, though it commenced its run at the Phoenix, had the majority of its 532 performances at this theatre.

In August 1950 *The Little Hut* was first seen in London. It ran 1261 performances and it was not until September 1953 that its successor, *The Confidential Clerk* by T. S. Eliot, was staged. In April 1954 another long run began with *Hippo Dancing*, with Robert Morley scoring 443 performances. The luck continued with *My Three Angels* (1955) and *South Sea Bubble* by Noël Coward (1956).

Two musicals kept the theatre occupied from December

1956; first *Grab Me a Gondola*, which ran until *Irma La
Douce* opened in July 1958. When this finally closed in
March 1962 *Write me a Murder* followed. From September,
Breaking-Point ran until February 1963. For some time the
theatre was unlucky with generally short runs until *The
Wings of the Dove* opened in December running till April
when it transferred to the Haymarket. Then more produc-
tions flopped until *Robert and Elizabeth*, the musical
version of *The Barretts of Wimpole Street*, was presented
with June Bronhill, John Clements and Keith Michell in
October 1964. This success continued until February 1967,
totalling a run of 957 performances. Then came *Cactus
Flower*, with Margaret Leighton, running for 223 perform-
ances, and in November a revival for 166 performances of
Heartbreak House from Chichester. The next success was
Oh, Clarence! in February 1969 then the American one act
plays by Neil Simon, *Plaza Suite*, had a year's run. Next
were three short runs until a new play by Alan Ayckbourn,
How the Other Half Loves, settled in for a long run from
August 1970 until the autumn of 1972, succeeded in turn by
The Day After the Fair, based on a short story by Thomas
Hardy, adapted by Frank Harvey and bringing Deborah
Kerr back to the West End. It opened on 4 October 1972, and
filled the theatre for the next seven months till the return
of Alec Guinness in the summer of 1973 in *Habeas Corpus*.
This changed casts in 1974 and Alan Bennett, the play's
author, took over the part of Mrs Swabb that he had written
for Patricia Hayes, a unique West End transformation!

22 · The May Fair Theatre

Stratton Street, Berkeley Square, W.1

Capacity: 310

Opened 17 June 1963 with a revival of *Six Characters in Search of an Author* by Luigi Pirandello. Directed by William Ball under the management of Edward J. and Harry Lee Danziger.

THE BUILDING

The Danziger brother who owned the May Fair Hotel, which was originally built in 1927, transformed 'The Candlelight Room', which had been the Cabaret and Ballroom of the hotel, into a theatre.

'Modern hotels are no longer just blocks of rooms with

a restaurant and lounge. Real estate and taxes, especially
in central areas, are such that today every inch of space
in a building must be utilised. Today a hotel is a centre
of entertainment activity with bars, speciality restaurants,
shops and, in the case of the May Fair, even a cinema and,
now, a theatre,' said Harry Danziger in a radio interview.

'Being showmen we felt that a real licensed theatre
would be a unique crowning achievement for the entertainment centre we have created within the May Fair
Hotel. We hope the arrival of this theatre will add lustre to
the already rich cultural life of the elegant and historic
district of Mayfair,' added Edward Danziger in the same
broadcast.

The new theatre was designed by George Beech,
A.R.I.B.A.

The opening programme says:

The task was far from simple. The old Candlelight
Room, long remembered as the scene of Big Band
Broadcasting in the 30s, when Ambrose and Harry Roy
packed the place every night, had to be completely
demolished and a new enlarged structure, conforming
to strict L.C.C. and Lord Chamberlain's regulations
governing theatre construction, had to be designed and
built.

From the production standpoint the May Fair is
superbly equipped to stage almost any type of live
presentation. A glass enclosed control room at the rear
of the auditorium enables the perfect centring of lights
and balancing of sound by the stage manager and
operators who, in traditionally designed theatres, must
always work backstage, often at great inconvenience
and under considerable visual and acoustic handicaps.

A complete fly-gallery for flying scenery and props,
with the latest counter-weight equipment has been
built and, because the theatre is designed on the most
fluid lines, enabling it to be used in various forms, the
lighting equipment has been so designed that all parts
of the auditorium and stage can be covered by lighting
batons. A simple re-switching in the control room
allows control of any particular section of lighting
throughout the theatre. Hi-fi sound and provision for
television and film camera points enable filming of TV
transmission to take place at any time, including closed-
circuit transmission to other parts of the Hotel.

A special gallery has been constructed at the side
of the theatre for use by musicians. This is an innovation
in the sense that whatever presentation is made on
whatever stage area, it can always be accompanied by
an orchestra without interfering with sight lines of the
audience. Ancillary to the theatre is a self-contained

dressing-room block with bathrooms, wardrobe and make-up facilities.

The auditorium itself is basically a flat-floor area. All the seats are specially stepped so as to give the maximum sight conditions, all are on removable rostra and the stage area, too, is completely removable. This in itself means that by a simple arrangement of the rostra, the following four basic stages are available. Normal proscenium setting with audience; setting with apron and audience seated in front and on sides of aprons; platform stage with audience on two sides of platform area; theatre-in-the-round with audience completely surrounding stage.

It is not considered that these four positions are necessarily to be exploited all the time but when planning productions, the director is given a completely unrestricted choice of presentation.

Two of Mr Beech's greatest problems were sound insulation and ventilation. A self-contained refrigerated air conditioning system was specially designed for the May Fair Theatre and an acoustic isolation so conceived that no sound from the Theatre escapes to disturb the guests in the bedrooms or restaurants or no sound from the Hotel enters to disturb the performance. Original design has enabled the acoustics to be so well balanced that the sound level remains constant whether the auditorium is full or nearly empty.

Ralph Richardson 'unlocked the door' of the new theatre on 11 June 1963. The Danzigers sold the Hotel in 1964 and it is now run by The Grand Metropolitan Hotels Ltd.

THE PLAYS

On 17 June 1963 *Six Characters in Search of an Author* opened with Ralph Richardson and Barbara Jefford in the cast. It had a long and successful run of 295 performances until February 1964. *Beyond the Fringe* transferred from the Fortune Theatre in April and ran for well over two years till September 1966. Many short runs followed during the next four years. On 7 September 1970 *The Philanthropist*, first produced at the Royal Court, opened and continued until October 1973, becoming the theatre's longest running play. The leading role was created by Alec McCowen. After this came another transfer from the Royal Court. David Storey's *The Farm*, which enjoyed a short run and was succeeded by a transfer from the Hampstead Theatre Club of *The Ride Across Lake Constance*, by Peter Handke, which opened in December 1973. In January 1974 Roy Dotrice appeared in a revival of *Brief Lives*. Each Christmas a 'Sooty' entertainment has been presented for children.

23 · The New London Theatre

Parker Street, Drury Lane, W.C.2

Capacity: 907

Opened 10 January 1973 with *The Unknown Soldier and His Wife*, a play by Peter Ustinov. Directed by Peter Ustinov under the management of Bernard Delfont.

THE BUILDING

The present theatre is on the site of the Winter Garden Theatre which was closed in 1959, but which was not redeveloped until 1971–2.

There have been licensed premises at 167 Drury Lane since the days of the first Elizabeth and the name of Nell Gwynn, who had lived nearby, is associated with the

133

tavern on this site which by the latter end of the seventeenth century was known as the Mogul, after Aurengzebe, the great Mogul of Hindustan from 1658 to 1707.

Here from as early as 1828, under Henry Cook, glee clubs met and sing-songs were held in the usual adjoining hall. By 1838 it had gained a dubious reputation. The penny weekly, *Paul Pry*, says, 'We were agreeably surprised to notice the improvement which had taken place as regards order. We did not see a fight all the evening, neither did we see a police officer in the place.' The account goes on to say that 'The room is fitted up with good taste, and is as well adapted for its purpose as any place in London.'

On 27 December 1847 after some alterations, it was opened as the Mogul Saloon, under the management of a licensed victualler Edwin Winder, the Mogul Tavern remaining as part of the building. The hall seated some five hundred people. During the next years true music-hall gradually evolved, and became a popular form of entertainment and by 1851 Winder had renamed the premises the Middlesex Music-Hall. He remained here until he went to the Metropolitan in 1865. He was followed in management by Edward Wood and in 1866 by George Speedy and he in turn by H. G. Lake in 1868 who rebuilt the hall in 1872 making further alterations and improvements in 1875.

In 1878 J. L. Graydon, who had been behind the bar of the tavern early in his life, returned as manager. He made the place extremely successful, rebuilding it in 1891 at a cost of over £12,000.

Strangely enough throughout its career as a music-hall, the house was always known affectionately to Londoners as 'The Old Mo', for up to the end of its life as the Middlesex, the Mogul Tavern still existed.

In 1910 Graydon was joined by Osward Stoll and the music-hall was entirely rebuilt. It closed on 11 January 1910 and reopened on 30 October 1911 (a week before the Victoria Palace) as the New Middlesex Theatre of Varieties.

The Era for October 28 tells us:

> Built to the design of Frank Matcham the new house has been erected in red brick, Portland stone and polished granite, and occupies an advantageous position in Drury Lane, within earshot of the hurry and bustle of Holborn. The new theatre besides being a valuable acquisition to the thoroughfare, is a striking object lesson in the advance of refinement in the public amuse-ments of the people of this country . . . The New Middle-sex is the property of The Middlesex Theatre of Varieties Ltd of which Mr Oswald Stoll is chairman and managing director, and Mr J. L. Graydon so long and honourably

connected with the old Middlesex, a director taking
an active interest in the business . . . The new building
has the largest frontage of any variety theatre in London,
namely 155 ft to Shelton Street and 115 ft to Drury Lane,
and covers an area of 12,700 superficial feet. Thus the
original site of 10,000 ft, together with an important
property in the vicinity, has been absorbed. The main
entrance is at the angle of Drury Lane and Shelton Street
whence, through the main vestibule, staircases lead
direct to the stalls and circle. The stalls patrons pass
into a crush room, and thence by corridors direct to the
stalls, which are approached on either side. The auditorium is of ample dimensions—88 ft by 80 ft—is capable
of seating 3000 people, and contains two tiers constructed
on the steel cantilever principle without columns, so
that a clear and uninterrupted view of the stage is
obtained from every seat. The ground floor is divided
into orchestra stalls, stalls, and pit-stalls, all furnished
with comfortably upholstered seats, in common with the
family circle; while the balcony, as the gallery is named,
is provided with beautifully upholstered seats, equalled
in roomy comfort only in the dress circles of the best
theatres of the country. The theatre is heavily carpeted
in all parts. Every seat in the theatre including the
balcony is numbered, and consequently, is reservable
in advance. To facilitate further the work of this innovation, a large booking office has been established at
101 High Holborn.

The scheme of decoration in the auditorium is
Arabesque, in light tones of cream and gold, with tints
of pale green, and the hangings, seatings, and furnishing
generally, in warm crimson. The entrance to the building,
including the vestibules, the crush room for the stalls,
etc., are all in Renaissance, but the general tone of the
colour has been carried out throughout the house in
its entirety.

The Old Mogul public house has been entirely rebuilt,
and is in keeping with the modern theatre of which it
forms a part. An innovation, however, has been made
by the introduction of refreshment rooms on the first
floor, which is approached by a separate staircase direct
from the street, without passing into the Mogul itself.

This building remained in use as a music-hall, the home
of French revues, and later of touring revues, until it
closed on 1 February 1919.

The theatre was acquired by George Grossmith and
Edward Laurillard, who completely redecorated the
interior '. . . based entirely on the old French gardens
of the transitional period between Louis XIV and Louis
XV when the treillage style of architecture came into

vogue'. Some minor alterations were also made including
the abolition of the pit, and the changing of the main
entrance from the corner to the old pit entrance in Drury
Lane, but generally speaking no structural alterations
were made.

It was renamed the Winter Garden Theatre and reopened
as such in May 1919. The Old Mogul Tavern remained
incorporated in the fabric becoming the Nell Gwynn
Tavern and the stalls bar.

Grossmith and Laurillard reopened the theatre on 20
May 1919 with *Kissing Time*, a musical play by Guy Bolton
and P. G. Wodehouse, with music by Ivan Caryll, which
ran for 430 performances and seemed to establish the
success of the venture. This was followed in September
1920 by another musical play, *A Night Out*. This was an
adaptation by George Grossmith and Arthur Miller of the
French farce by Georges Feydeau (later to be seen at this
theatre as *Hotel Paradiso*) with music by Willie Redstone; it
secured a run of 311 performances. Leslie Henson played
in both these successes and most subsequent ones at this
theatre until 1926.

The partnership of Grossmith and Laurillard was
broken in 1921 by the retirement of Edward Laurillard,
who subsequently became lessee of the Apollo. A new
partnership was formed between Grossmith and J. A. E.
Malone. Malone was a man of considerable musical
experience, having been with George Edwardes from
1893 to 1915 and responsible for producing many of his
musical successes both in this country and America. As
might be expected the series of musical comedies at the
Winter Garden continued. In September 1921 came
Sally by Guy Bolton, with music by Jerome Kern (387
performances), followed by *The Cabaret Girl* by George
Grossmith and P. G. Wodehouse in September 1922 (361
performances), *The Beauty Prize* by the same author in
September 1923 (212 performances); Jerome Kern composed the music for both these. In April 1924 came a
revival of the Gaiety success of 1915, *Tonight's the Night*
(based on *The Pink Dominoes*) by Fred Thompson with
music by Paul Rubens (139 performances), followed in
September 1924 with *Primrose*, by George Grossmith
and Guy Bolton, with music by George Gershwin (255
performances), *Tell Me More* (May 1925) by Fred Thompson and William K. Wells, with music by George
Gershwin (263 performances) and *Kid Boots* (February
1926) by William Anthony McGuire and Otto Harbach,
with music by Harry Tierney (163 performances).

During this famous series of musical successes, besides
Leslie Henson, George Grossmith also appeared in
several, as did Dorothy Dickson and Heather Thatcher.
Grossmith and Malone gave up the theatre after *Kid*

Boots and it passed into the hands of William Gaunt, who kept up the tradition with *Tip-Toes* (April 1926) by Guy Bolton and Fred Thompson, with music by George Gershwin (182 performances), and *The Vagabond King* (April 1927), a musical adaptation by W. H. Post and Brian Hooker of *If I Were King*, with music by Rudolf Friml (480 performances).

In 1928 Laddie Cliff presented *So This is Love*, of which Stanley Lupino was part author, and they both appeared in the cast with Cyril Ritchard and Madge Elliott; it ran for 321 performances. With this production the theatre came into the hands of William Cooper and the next years saw the stage occupied by several transfers of established successes, including *Funny Face* and *The House that Jack Built*. In 1930 Sophie Tucker appeared in a musical comedy by Vivian Ellis, *Follow a Star*, and in 1932 Gracie Fields was here in a revue, *Walk this Way;* but from then on the theatre entered into a period during which it was more often closed than open and when it did reopen it was to little success. Between 1931 and 1939 there is nothing worth recording except that in November 1933 Bernard Shaw's *On the Rocks* was presented for the first time.

With the coming of the war an attempt was made to put the theatre on the map again; *Peter Pan* was given at Christmas 1942. In July 1943 Jack Buchanan returned with Elsie Randolph in *It's Time to Dance* by Douglas Furber and Arthur Rose, which ran for 259 performances. After this the theatre was kept open with various attractions, a Donald Wolfit season (1945), *The Ballet Jooss* also in the same year. This was followed in September by a play by Warren Chetham Strode, *Young Mrs Barrington*, which ran for 141 performances, and from May 1946 *No Room at the Inn*, by Joan Temple, ran for 425 performances. In 1947 the theatre passed into the hands of the Rank Organisation, but a success was hard to find. A gallant attempt to enlarge the scope of the Arts Theatre's policy was made by Alec Clunes in 1952, when he transferred the Club's work to this theatre, presenting *The Firstborn* by Christopher Fry and *The Constant Couple*, but the experiment proved only a moderate success. Following that there were several long runs at the Winter Garden: Agatha Christie's *Witness for the Prosecution* (458 performances from October 1953), *The Water Gipsies*, a play with music by A. P. Herbert and Vivian Ellis, which ran for 138 performances from August 1955, until *Hotel Paradiso* was produced, which scored 214 performances from May 1956. Two other noteworthy productions have been the revival of Shaw's *The Devil's Disciple* with Tyrone Power in 1956, and the transfer of Eugene O'Neill's *The Iceman Cometh* from the Arts Theatre in 1958. After a Christmas revival of *Alice in*

Wonderland in 1959 the theatre, as the Winter Garden, closed permanently.

Earlier in 1959 the Rank Organisation sold the theatre to a property development corporation and after it was closed in 1960 it was stripped of its fittings. In July it was announced:

London is to have a yet another new theatre.

It will stand on the site of the present Winter Garden, tucked into a big block of shops, flats and showrooms in the modern manner.

Behind this £450,000 scheme is the property firm, Pearson, Forsythe and Company. It bought the ailing Winter Garden from the Rank Organisation last year.

With the theatre came a covenant forbidding the new owners to put another theatre on the site. So plans for the new building were drawn up without a theatre and the L.C.C. turned them down. There had to be a theatre. Impasse.

So now the firm has bought some adjoining property, unhindered by covenants, and the new theatre is safely included. It will seat about 600 and will be very welcome.

Owing to certain outstanding leases, demolition was not begun and the theatre stood derelict. In September 1961 the site was sold to Charles Forte and a new development scheme was proposed.

The theatre was finally demolished in June – July 1965 and the site eventually cleared. Rebuilding was not carried out until 1971–2 when 'A complex incorporating a theatre, restaurant, shops, showrooms, flats and a large car park' was designed by Paul Turtkovic for the developers, Star Holdings Ltd.

'The New London Theatre itself rises up from the podium structure and is linked to this at the south end by an impressive, unbroken wall of glass. Many advanced innovations are incorporated in the theatre design and not only can the stage be revolved through 180° converting the setting from proscenium to theatre-in-the-round at the drop of a switch, but also the seats, lights, orchestra pit and walls can all be repositioned electrically.'

The architect for the theatre was Michael Percival, A.R.I.B.A. The press release said:

The New London is a theatre of the future. It is a theatre that moves; stage, seats, lights—even the walls can be made to change their positions.

Every type of production can be presented in a totally different way and yet can be performed within hours of each other. No longer will producers be constricted by the limitations of either 'proscenium' or 'in-the-round' for at the New London the use of modern technology has made both possible.

Almost one third of the theatre's floor is built on a revolve 60 ft wide which accommodates the stage, the orchestra pit and the first eight rows of the 911 seats. The walls along more than half the theatre length are faced with moveable panels extending from floor to ceiling. These are made to track and pivot in such a way that the shape of the auditorium can be completely changed. In a normal proscenium setting those at the edge of the stage turn to form the wings and proscenium opening whilst the remainder open out into a trumpet shape merging with the walls of the main auditorium.

The real magic becomes apparent when, at the throw of a switch, all of these elements—stage, seats, orchestra pit, walls—silently change their position to transform the theatre into an amphi-theatre. In just 4 minutes the revolve turns through 180 degrees bringing the stage to the centre of the auditorium and the 'front stalls' to where the backdrop had been. All of these 206 seats are then raised by electrically operated screw jacks to a steeper angle of raking. The wall panels slide and pivot into an unbroken half-circle at the back of the theatre.

The ceiling—composed of louvred panels like a horizontal venetian blind—is opened up to allow lights to project through, and scenery to be lowered, onto any part of the stage below.

Everything on the main revolve is movable; the orchestra pit across its centre is made up of three simple elevators any of which, when raised to floor level, reduces the size for when smaller groups of musicians are performing. Within the main revolve a smaller stage revolve is fitted as well as a set of traps reached from below.

The sound and lighting systems are the most advanced design with all controls centralised in a glass walled box high at the back of the auditorium. For many productions manual control will be unnecessary—a complete performance can be controlled automatically by a 'total memory' dimmer system. To ensure that sound definition achieves the highest possible standards the designers, at every stage, have consulted, with Dr Larsen Jorden, the Danish acoustics expert.

The New London is not a small theatre—it accommodates an audience of over 900—but, by massing the seating radially around the focal point of the stage, the designers have achieved an atmosphere of intimacy that belies the theatre's size.

No seat, including those in the circle, is remote from the stage, and carefully defined sightlines will ensure that the audience will have a clear, uninterrupted view of the performance.

Dressing accommodation for the performers is arranged on four floors at one side of the theatre with a lift giving access to the stage. The stars' dressing rooms are at stage level along with a large, comfortable Green Room. From a basement ramp lifts take the largest and heaviest pieces of scenery direct to stage and understage levels.

From the entrance foyer an escalator reaches up to the theatre's main reception—an area of 2400 sq ft immediately beneath and behind the rake of the theatre's auditorium. Here there are circular bars and a comfortable lounge area.

THE PLAYS

The theatre had its first audiences on 23 and 24 November when the B.B.C. invited guests for the television recording of Marlene Dietrich's solo performance.

The theatre opened officially on 10 January 1973 with Peter Ustinov starring and directing his own play *The Unknown Soldier and His Wife*, first produced in New York and later seen at Chichester in 1968. In June 1973 a new musical, *Grease*, was presented which ran until early in 1974. The theatre was 'dark' during the 'crisis' until *The Wolf* transferred yet again from the Queen's (it had come from the Playhouse, Oxford to the Apollo before moving to the Queen's) and ran until early summer.

24 · The Palace Theatre

(The Royal English Opera, The Palace Theatre of Varieties)

Cambridge Circus, Shaftesbury Avenue, W.1

Capacity: 1450

Opened as the Royal English Opera House 31 January 1891 with *Ivanhoe*, a romantic opera by Arthur Sullivan, words by Julian Sturgess. Under the management of Richard D'Oyly Carte.

THE BUILDING

The foundation stone of a new opera house was laid in 1888 on an island site at the Cambridge Circus junction of the new Shaftesbury Avenue (see No. 5). This site, bounded by Shaftesbury Avenue, Greek Street, Romilly Street and Cambridge Circus, was municipal land, on which D'Oyly Carte planned his home for English Opera.

Facing Cambridge Circus, it was designed by T. E.

141

Collcutt and G. H. Holloway, and took over two years to
build. It was a three-tier house. A contemporary account
tells us:

> For the façades of this beautiful theatre in Cambridge
> Circus, Mr Collcutt chose red Ellistown brick and
> Doulton terra-cotta, and with its grouping of arcaded
> windows, its deep balconies, its loggias, designed to be
> thrown open in summer, and its frieze and cornice,
> surmounting the second tier of windows, this front
> elevation will, doubtless, be regarded as a most attrac-
> tive example of balance and composition. The observant
> and critical visitor will not fail to notice the Grand Stair-
> case, to the left of the vestibule; this staircase descends to
> the stalls and ascends to the Royal Circle. The whole
> structure is supported on columned arches, the columns
> being of rich green marble, with gilded capitals and bases.
> The hand rail and plinth are in grand antique, the
> balusters in alabaster, and the steps in veined marble. It
> is lighted by upwards of 2000 electric lamps and the
> requisite power is generated on the premises. The pros-
> cenium arch is of costly Italian marbles, the smaller
> panels being of Mexican onyx.

After the collapse of D'Oyly Carte's hopes for English
Opera the name of the theatre was changed to the Palace,
when it became a variety theatre in 1892. In 1908 the
amphitheatre was reconstructed to designs by F. Emblin-
Walker, without a complete closure of the theatre. Today
the theatre retains the sumptuous atmosphere created by
D'Oyly Carte but for a few minor alterations (the removal
of the stage boxes), redecorations, recurtaining and reconditioning, particularly when it became a music-hall.

The roof and offices on the Shaftesbury Avenue side
were damaged in the blitz but have been rebuilt. A recent
redecoration has taken place, of which John Betjeman said
in November 1959, 'Alas, the veined marbles which were
so elegant and essential a part of its interior decoration
have lately been defaced by a coat of plum-coloured paint.'

THE PLAYS

The Royal English Opera House opened on 31 January
1891 with Sullivan's opera *Ivanhoe*, based on Scott's novel:
it ran for 155 performances. Unfortunately at the end of the
run D'Oyly Carte had not another English work ready for
immediate production and he was forced to fall back on a
French opera *The Basoche* by André Messager, giving it
its first English presentation. This was quickly followed
by a Sarah Bernhardt season during which she played
Sardou's *Cleopatra* and several other of her successes.
D'Oyly Carte, defeated in his original plans for an English
opera, sold the building to a company of which Augustus

Harris was managing director. He promptly renamed it the Palace Theatre of Varieties and opened it as a music-hall on 10 December 1892, after some redecorations and minor reconstructions. The next year the veteran Charles Morton was called in to put the music-hall on its feet, and on his death in 1904 it passed to Alfred Butt, who had been secretary since 1898 and assistant manager since 1899. Many stars of variety appeared here and among other artistes Marie Tempest made her first appearance on the variety stage, in a repertoire of songs in September 1906. In March 1908 Maud Allan, the dancer, created something of a sensation with her *Vision of Salome.*

On 10 April 1910 the great Pavlova made her first London appearance. She had been prima ballerina of the Maryinsky Theatre in St Petersburg, subsequently appearing at the Imperial Opera House of that city. Her London début was with Michael Mordkin. She scored an immediate success with *Le Cygne, L'Automne Bacchanale* and *Valse Caprice.*

In 1911 the house became known as the Palace Theatre and in 1912 Shaw's *How he Lied to her Husband* was introduced to music-hall audiences in a bill which also contained Beerbohm Tree in Kipling's *The Man who Was.* This year also saw the climax of the career of the Palace as a music-hall, when it was chosen as the venue of the Royal Command Variety Performance of which Oswald Stoll said, 'The Cinderella of the Arts at last went to the Ball.'

An interesting personality who played an important part in the history of this theatre was Herman Finck, who was associated with the Palace from its opening as a music-hall, when he was engaged as a pianist. He was subsequently employed as a violinist and became leader and subconductor under Alfred Plumpton in 1896. He was appointed sole musical director in 1900 and remained in that position for twenty years, composing the music for a great many of the Palace productions.

Just before the war in 1914 the revue craze hit the theatre and *The Passing Show* was produced. This revue by Arthur Wimperis and P. L. Flers introduced to London the American actress Elsie Janis, who met with immediate success. The production ran for 351 performances and was followed by *The Passing Show of 1915.* Other successful revues followed, including *Bric-a-Brac* (385 performances from 1915), *Vanity Fair* (265 performances from 1916), *Airs and Graces* (1917), *Pamela,* a musical comedy (1917), *Hullo, America!* (358 performances from 1918), and *The Whirligig* (414 performances from 1919).

The next chapter in the story of the Palace was a short period as a cinema, when it came under the control of C. B. Cochran. *The Co-optimists* were here for a long season and again films returned.

Irving Berlin's *The Music Box Revue* in 1923, and *The*

Co-optimists' third season in 1924 brought the Palace back into the list of living theatres and then there began a period of musical comedy.

No, No, Nanette ran for 655 performances from March 1925; 'Tea for Two' and 'I want to be Happy,' the popular numbers from this production, swept the country. The 'book' was by Frank Mandel, Otto Harbach and Irving Caesar, and the music by Vincent Youmans. This was followed by other successful musical productions including *Princess Charming* (362 performances from October 1926), *The Girl Friend* (421 performances from September 1927), *Virginia* (1928), *Hold Everything* and *Dear Love* (1929) and *Frederica* (1930). Later, in 1931 films were again shown and then, in the same year, C. B. Cochran made a brief attempt to restore variety, but the presentation of musical plays proved more successful.

According to *The Times* of 27 March 1930 an offer of £400,000 was made by a multiple store for the site, but the directors of the Palace refused it.

Subsequent successes were *The Cat and the Fiddle* (1932), *Dinner at Eight* and *Gay Divorce* (1933), *Why Not To-Night?* and C. B. Cochran's revue *Streamline* (1934), *Anything Goes* (1935), *This'll Make you Whistle* (1936), *On Your Toes* (1937), *Oh You Letty* (1937), *Dodsworth* (1938) and *Maritza* (1938).

From November 1938 the Palace became almost the permanent home of Jack Hulbert and Cicely Courtneidge in their musical comedy successes, *Under Your Hat*, *Full Swing* (1942), and *Something in the Air* (1943).

The next few years were occupied by *Gay Rosalinda* (1945), and *Song of Norway* (1946): this ran for 526 performances during which the theatre came under the control of Tom Arnold and Emile Littler. There was not another solid success until Ivor Novello's *King's Rhapsody* opened in September 1949; during the run of 839 performances its star and composer died.

Later came *Zip goes a Million* (1951), *The Glorious Days* (1953), and the many seasons of foreign companies who came under the banner of Peter Daubeny from all parts of the world, to make the Palace Theatre their home while in London.

Since 1951 Emile Littler has been in sole charge of the theatre. In 1957 *The Entertainer* with Laurence Olivier was transferred here from the Royal Court and musical comedy returned the next year with Norman Wisdom in *Where's Charley?* and revue, with *Fine Fettle* (1959). Rodgers and Hammerstein's *Flower Drum Song* began its run here in March 1960 and remained until the last Rodgers and Hammerstein collaboration, *The Sound of Music*, took its place in May 1961 where it stayed until January 1967 with 2385 performances. Then came *110 in the Shade* (101 performances), a revival of *The Desert Song* which transferred to the Cambridge Theatre to make room for Judi Dench in *Cabaret* (316 performances). This was followed by the flop of *Mr and Mrs*, then in February 1969 came *Two Cities*, a musical based on Dickens' *A Tale of Two Cities*, starring Edward Woodward. After a short run *Belle Starr* with Betty Grable was produced to be followed later the same year by *Phil the Fluter* with Evelyn Laye and Stanley Baxter. In April 1970 came a big success, a revue with Danny La Rue, *At the Palace*, which was to continue until April 1972. After a short revival of *The Maid of the Mountains*, success again came to the theatre with their next production, *Jesus Christ Superstar* by Tim Rice and Andrew Lloyd Webber, which opened on 9 August 1972, and continues to play to packed houses.

Charing Cross Road

Phoenix Street

25 · The Phoenix Theatre

Charing Cross Road and Phoenix Street, W.C.2

Capacity: 1028

Opened 24 September 1930 with *Private Lives*, an intimate comedy by Noël Coward. Produced by the author under the management of Charles B. Cochran.

THE BUILDING

The Phoenix was the second of the new theatres which opened in September 1930 (see No. 6). It was built on a plot of land stretching between Flitcroft Street and Phoenix Street, backed by Stacey Street. On this ground had stood some decaying property and a building which had once been a factory and had later become a far from high-class home of amusement called the Alcazar.

A contemporary account in 1925 describes it as

. . . a long narrow hall and the performances, which are of a music-hall order, are continuous from noon to midnight. But as London has shown that it finds mid-day a trifle early for variety entertainment, the doors are now opened at 2.30.

146

The most unusual features are three stage platforms and 'standing room only'. When a turn is completed on one stage the audience walks to another stage for the next turn. The originator of the experiment, M. Lucien Samett, hopes to extend the premises, so that there shall be room for tables, as well as the promenade. Then the Alcazar will approximate more nearly to the café chantants with which M. Samett has been identified in Paris.

Strictly speaking, he says, the Alcazar is a 'public audition centre'—London's first.

The public pays, but theatre managers in search of talent are admitted free. 'We have had more than 2000 visitors so far this week,' he added. 'I had not ventured to expect more than 1000 in the whole week. So I think I may claim that so far we are doing well.'

If 'Alcazars' are opened in all the big English towns there should be a decline in the number of unemployed artistes.

The 'one price only' for this was one shilling and sixpence, including tax. The experiment did not last long, and *The Stage* tells us it became 'finally a "fun city" with slot-machines and games of chance occupying the ground floor and such exhibitions as "Beautiful Artists' Models" posing as they do in Paris, on the second floor.'

The ground was owned by the Brinkman Estate and the new theatre which was to arise on this site was built by Sidney L. Bernstein. It was designed by Sir Giles Gilbert Scott, Bertie Crewe and Cecil Masey, with Theodore Komisarjevsky as art director. The construction was carried out by Bovis, Ltd.

The building includes shop and office premises on the Charing Cross Road frontage. The original main entrance and box office was in Charing Cross Road at the corner of Flitcroft Street, but it was later transferred to the Phoenix Street frontage. It is from this street that the theatre takes its name, *not* the Phoenix, an early seventeenth-century playhouse in Drury Lane, as is often supposed.

The Stage for 25 September 1930 describes the theatre thus:

The distinguished columns here are blues and pinks on a cream ground, and the whole is lavishly picked out with modelling in gold. Large windows in the adjacent promenade allow late-comers and others who might for some reason or other be prevented from getting to their seats to view the stalls level and the stage. The circle appears to come far forward and has a commodious upper circle above it. Care has been taken in the comfort of the seating. Each seat has sufficient body and leg room and is provided with its own hat rack. There are six roomy private boxes. The upholstery has a touch of the medieval, and is in a rare shade of dark pink with a touch of heliotrope or light purple in its pattern. In the front of the house rich reds, blues, and gold appear to be the prime colours. Bars and cloakrooms are well appointed, but no attempt has been made here in the shape of elaborate decoration. A striking feature in the interior decoration will be found in the fine reproductions of works by old masters. Here we have well executed copies of pictures by Titian, Giorgione, Tintoretto and Pinturicchio. The safety curtain carries Jacopo del Sellaio's 'The Triumph of Love' the original of which can be seen in the Oratorio di S. Ansano, Fiesole. These reproductions are the work of Vladimir Polunin.

An official unveiling ceremony by C. B. Cochran of the Charing Cross Road frontage took place on September 7, 'to a fanfare of trumpets, the clicking of cameras, and a talky-machine, that recorded his inaugural speech'.

THE PLAYS

The theatre opened to the public on 24 September 1930 under Cochran's management with *Private Lives*. This play was one of Noël Coward's outstanding successes and was written in Shanghai in roughly four days during convalescence from an attack of influenza. The original cast included the author, Gertrude Lawrence, Adrianne Allen and Laurence Olivier. 'We were an immediate hit,' said Coward, 'and our three months limited engagement was sold out during the first week.' 'We closed,' he adds, 'at the end of our scheduled three months knowing that we could easily have run for another six.' The play had a run of 101 performances. It then had a successful presentation in America.

The next success at the Phoenix was Louis Weitzenkorn's *Late Night Final* (132 performances from June 1931). After this the theatre ran into an unsuccessful patch. In 1932 it changed hands and came under the control of Victor Luxemburg. The theatre went non-stop, with variety but this was a failure and it returned to another run of unsuccessful plays until a policy was adopted of transferring established successes from other theatres.

In January 1936 Noël Coward once again brought prosperity to the Phoenix with his programmes of one-act plays under the title of *Tonight at 8.30*; these plays ran for 157 performances, but the prosperity was short-lived and short runs and transfers were again the order of the day.

In the autumn of 1938 there appeared a series of plays sponsored by Michel St Denis and Bronson Albery in connection with the London Theatre Studio and these included

The White Guard, adapted by Rodney Ackland from the Russian of Bulgakov, and *Twelfth Night*. For a period between 1938 and 1939 the theatre showed films, then it passed into the hands of Jack Bartholomew and *Judgment Day* by Elmer Rice was revived in November 1939.

Outstanding productions later in the war were *Sky High* (June 1942), John Gielgud's revival of Congreve's *Love for Love* (April 1943), an interesting production of Tolstoy's *War and Peace* (August 1943) introducing a cinematic technique, Ivor Novello's musical play *Arc de Triomphe* (November 1943), and a dramatisation of Kate O'Brien's novel *The Last of Summer* (June 1944).

In 1942 the theatre was taken over by Tom Arnold, and in May 1944 by Prince Littler. It was then merged into the Associated Theatre Properties (London) Ltd.

Strangely enough the Phoenix could never manage to maintain its place in the theatre list consistently, and except for *The Skin of our Teeth*, which had its first production in May 1945, it did not achieve a major run until Cicely Courtneidge appeared in *Under the Counter*, which scored 665 performances from November 1945.

In 1948 Sir John Vanbrugh's *The Relapse* had the exceptional run of 252 performances, after a transfer from the Lyric, Hammersmith. Next came Rattigan's double bill entitled *Playbill* consisting of *The Browning Version* and *Harlequinade*.

Subsequent productions included *Death of a Salesman* (1949), *Dear Miss Phoebe* (1950), John Gielgud's production of *The Winter's Tale* (1951), and *Much Ado About Nothing* (1952), Noël Coward's *Quadrille* with the Lunts (1952), *The Sleeping Prince*. Terence Rattigan's Coronation play written for the Oliviers (1953), and John Van Druten's *Bell, Book and Candle* (1954).

From December 1955 to July 1956 the stage of the Phoenix was occupied with the Paul Scofield–Peter Brook season, during which were seen *Hamlet*, *The Power and the Glory* by Grahame Greene, and a revival of T. S. Eliot's *The Family Reunion*. The next success was *The Diary of Anne Frank* at the end of 1956. From September 1957 until September 1960 only two plays were needed to fill the theatre, firstly *Roar Like a Dove* by Lesley Storm, and from March 1960 *A Majority of One* with Molly Picon and Robert Morley. This was followed by the short runs of *The Last Joke* and *Out of this World*, quickly succeeded by *The Geese are Getting Fat* in December which lasted for only 45 performances.

Then there were ten different occupants of the stage. Six of them new plays and four transfers; John Osborne's *Luther* from the Royal Court accounted for seven months between August 1961 and March 1962. The new play, *All Things Bright and Beautiful*, which opened just before

Christmas, failed to see in the New Year. *All in Good Time*, from the Mermaid, was a success with 211 performances in 1963. After this, very short runs were the order of the day. From September 1965 *Ivanov* ran for 134 performances and *Incident at Vichy* ran from January to April. Then the theatre was closed until a revival of *Lady Windermere's Fan* in October achieved 181 performances.

In March 1966 the lease of the theatre returned to the family of the original owners and Gerald Flint-Shipman and his wife, Veronica, assumed management, opening with *In at the Death* on 21 April 1967. Redecoration took place and new bars were constructed. (A Noël Coward Bar in the Phoenix Street foyer was opened by the Master himself in 1969). *Let's all go Down the Strand* occupied the stage from October until January 1968 with 117 performances.

It was not until March 1968 that the theatre's luck returned with *Canterbury Tales* which ran for over 2000 performances. The next musical, this time from Broadway, a send-up of Shakespeare's *Two Gentlemen of Verona*, opened in April 1973, and in November a revival followed of *Design for Living* with Vanessa Redgrave. This Coward play had not been seen in the West End since its first production in 1939. It continued with success well into 1974.

26 · The Piccadilly Theatre

Denman Street and Sherwood Street,
Piccadilly Circus, W.1

Capacity: 1150

Opened 27 April 1928 with *Blue Eyes*, a romantic musical play by Jerome Kern, book and lyrics by Guy Bolton and Graham John. Produced by John Harwood under the management of Lee Ephraim.

THE BUILDING

On ground which was covered by derelict stables, the Piccadilly Theatre Company, with the impresario Edward Laurillard, built a theatre. It was designed by Bertie Crewe in conjunction with Edward A. Stone. The interior decoration was by Marc-Henri, the contractors were Griggs and Sons. The corner site embraces a public house, the Queen's Head, and some shops between the frontage and the sideway to the stage door. A simple white Portland stone frontage curves round the corner and the original interior decorations were carried out in green and gold,

with natural English walnut woodwork. This has given way
to a completely new scheme of interior decoration carried
out in 1955.

THE PLAYS

The theatre opened on 27 April 1928 with a musical
comedy *Blue Eyes* with Evelyn Laye. This transferred to
Daly's Theatre in August to finish its run of 276 performances.

The theatre then fell to the prevailing craze of the 'talkies'
and was taken by Warner Brothers for the showing of Vita-
phone films, and among these Al Jolson was seen and heard
in *The Singing Fool*.

The stage was not used again until November 1929 when
The Student Prince was revived. The theatre had its first
triumph with *Folly to be Wise*, a revue by Dion Titheradge,
with music by Vivian Ellis in January 1931, which ran for
257 performances. James Bridie's *A Sleeping Clergyman*,
considered by some people to be his best play, and in which
Ernest Thesiger and Robert Donat both scored singular
successes, had 230 performances from September 1933, and
was followed by *Counsellor at Law* by Elmer Rice in April
1934 and *Queer Cargo* (August 1934) by Noel Langley.
After this came a bad patch in this theatre's history, during
which the Windmill extended its activities to the Piccadilly.

In December 1937 an entirely new form of entertainment
was presented here by Firth Shephard. This was called
Choose your Time and consisted of a mixture of news-reel,
a 'swingphonic orchestra', individual turns, a Donald Duck
film, and a short comedy called *Talk of the Devil* by
Anthony Pelissier, in which Yvonne Arnaud and John
Mills appeared. After this the theatre was used for transfers
of long runs at reduced prices. From the outbreak of war
the Piccadilly was closed until Noël Coward's *Blithe Spirit*
in July 1941 started its run, but soon transferred. After
this, among other plays, were Gielgud's *Macbeth* (1942),
and two musical comedies, *Sunny River* and *Panama Hattie*
(1943). During the attacks from flying bombs the theatre
was damaged by blast and remained closed for some months,
but reopened with Agatha Christie's thriller *Appointment
with Death* in 1945. At this date the theatre came under
the control of the present owners, The Piccadilly Theatre,
Ltd.

Later productions included Noël Coward's revue *Sigh
No More* (1945), *A Man about the House* (1946), *Antony
and Cleopatra* with Edith Evans and Godfrey Tearle (1946),
The Voice of the Turtle (1947). A period of short runs and
transfers ensued until *A Question of Fact* by Wynyard
Browne in December 1953. Then again good fortune was
elusive until *A Girl Called Jo*, a musical version of *Little
Women*, in December 1955, and Peter Ustinov's *Romanoff*

and Juliet in May 1956, *A Dead Secret* and *The Rape of the Belt* (1957), *Hook, Line and Sinker* (1958), *The Marriage-go-Round* with John Clements and Kay Hammond in 1959. At the end of this success in 1960 came two flops in quick succession, *The Golden Touch* and *Bachelor Flat*, the latter scoring only four performances in May. Then foreign dance companies, for a season, the Dublin Festival Company's revival of *The Playboy of the Western World* and *Toys in the Attic* kept the theatre open.

In December it was announced that an offer for the theatre had been made by Bernard Delfont, and had been quickly challenged by another from Donald Albery, who emerged the victor.

The new régime soon instituted a scheme of redecoration and back-stage improvements. Ian Albery was appointed general manager bringing a third generation of the family into active participation of the London theatre scene. *The Amorous Prawn* transferred from the Saville in February 1960 and ran for the next twelve months but the theatre was not able to secure an established success, although it staged a Festival of French Theatre, two visits of Marcel Marceau and several interesting plays. Late in 1962 *Fiorello!* the American political musical proved a great disappointment and this was followed in December by *The Rag Trade*, based on a popular TV series which also failed to appeal and came off after a short run of only 85 performances. Then in 1963, until September, came seasons of ballet, an Italian musical and some French plays, followed by a transfer from the Savoy of *The Masters* which continued until early in the new year. The next big success to come in was *Who's Afraid of Virginia Woolf?* until it was transferred in July to make room for a musical, *Instant Marriage*, in August 1964, which ran for 366 performances. After this came more flops, interspersed with seasons of folk dancers and more ballet. *Barefoot in the Park* ran for 243 performances between November 1965 and June 1966 and a revival of *Oliver* in April 1967 had 331 performances. The next musical, *Man of La Mancha* with Keith Michell, opened in April 1968 and a musical, based on Daisy Ashford's novel, *The Young Visiters*, in December 1968 ran over the holidays. The following year saw a revival of *Man of La Mancha*, this time with Richard Kiley (who had created the part in New York) in the lead. Prospect Productions presented a transfer from the Mermaid of *Richard II* and *Edward the Second* early in 1970. In April came *Who Killed Santa Claus?* and in October *Vivat Vivat Regina!* by Robert Bolt, from Chichester, enjoyed a big success and ran for just over a year. In November 1971, again from Chichester, came *Dear Antoine* and in February 1972 yet another revival from Chichester, *Reunion in Vienna*. After this came a transfer from the Prince of Wales of *The*

Threepenny Opera, then in July 'a spanking new British musical for kids of all ages', *Pull Both Ends*. In November another musical was presented, but *I and Albert* was an expensive failure. Then in May 1973 success arrived at last with *Gypsy* starring Angela Lansbury, who was later succeeded by Dolores Gray. In March 1974 *A Street Car Named Desire* was revived with Claire Bloom in the lead.

27 · The Prince of Wales' Theatre

(The Prince's Theatre)

Coventry Street, W.1

THE FIRST THEATRE

Capacity: 1062

Opened as the Prince's Theatre 18 January 1884 with a revival of *The Palace of Truth*, a Fairy Comedy by W. S. Gilbert. Produced by the author and preceded by a revival of *In Honour Bound*, a comedy in one act by Sydney Grundy. Under the management of Edgar Bruce.

THE SECOND THEATRE

Capacity: 1139

Opened 27 October 1937 with *Les Folies de Paris et Londres*. Produced by and under the management of Alfred Esdaile.

THE BUILDING

The actor-manager Edgar Bruce took the Prince of

155

Wales's Theatre in Tottenham Street (the site later occupied
by the Scala), after the Bancrofts had left to go to the
Haymarket in 1880. He remained there until the theatre
was condemned by the Metropolitan Board of Works two
years later. With the profits he had made out of *The
Colonel*, a burlesque of the aesthetic movement, by F. C.
Burnand, he decided to build his own theatre on land he
acquired on the corner of Coventry Street and Oxenden
Street, stretching across to Whitcomb Street, between
Piccadilly Circus and Leicester Square.

The Era, 12 January 1884, tells us:

> The important block of buildings which has gradually
> been rising in Coventry Street, comprises the Prince's
> Hotel and Restaurant in Whitcomb and Coventry Streets,
> and the Prince's Theatre at the corner of Coventry and
> Oxenden Streets. The last is now completed, and will be
> opened to the public on the 18th inst. Although externally
> the two buildings form ostensibly one grand pile, yet
> they are entirely distinct, and separated by an open space
> at the rear. The theatre has been built for Mr Bruce by
> Messrs W. and D. McGregor from the designs and under
> the superintendence of Mr J. C. Phipps . . . The scheme
> of the theatre includes stalls and pit on the street level,
> balcony of six rows on the first floor, first circle of six
> rows on second floor, and gallery on the third floor, with
> eight private boxes on either side of the proscenium.
> Round each there is a corridor with brick walls separating
> them from the auditorium and every entrance staircase
> is external to the walls of the theatre proper.

Of the auditorium and its decorations the report
continues:

> A picture painted by Mr Padgett forms the central
> feature in the tympanum of the pediment. From this part
> the ceiling slopes up to the very back of the gallery, the
> circular line of the front of the gallery being carried on
> to the ceiling by mouldings, from which springs, what
> may be called a series of fan shaped panels to pilasters
> and flat arches at the back. The general tone of the
> decoration is ivory white, cream colour and gold, the
> gilding being in large masses. Rich colour is derived from
> the hangings, which are of red orange plush, terracotta
> being used for the background on the walls. Mr Padgett's
> picture represents 'Pan and the Nymph,' the deep blue
> of the background showing up the figures in strong relief
> . . . The audience to the stalls after leaving the vestibule
> descend by a spacious staircase through a foyer, which
> is decorated and fitted up in the Moorish style, and under
> the vestibule is a circular room, also in the Moorish style,
> for smoking, having a grotto constructed under the street.

The theatre was renamed the Prince of Wales' in 1886, the old house of that name had ceased to be a theatre, the Salvation Army having taken it over as a hostel.

In 1936 it was announced that the theatre was to be completely rebuilt and the last performance took place on 16 January 1937.

The new theatre was designed by Robert Cromie, who by giving careful attention to planning, enlarged the capacity of the house and also provided a bigger stage. Access to seats was made easier, as the stalls level was raised to street level. The circle front was brought forward to within 21 ft of the orchestra and is only 11 ft above the stalls. The auditorium of the new building is 80 ft by 60 ft compared with 43 ft by 57 ft in the old theatre.

In addition to the theatre proper the building [a contemporary tells us] also contains a Cocktail Bar and an American Bar at circle level, as well as a Stalls Bar. In the latter there is a dance floor and a feature of the bar itself is a 46 ft counter built of glass blocks lit from behind. The stage has a revolving centre, and there are no footlights, but the acting area is floodlit from the front of the circle. Instead of floats there is an illuminated glass panel which extends round the orchestral pit, to form a promenade for the chorus. The idea aimed at in the auditorium is twofold; first, to create an atmosphere in harmony with the show, and second to avoid period decoration. The motif is one of stylised drapery, and the gold stage tableau curtains are repeated in gilded plaster on the side walls and are draped round false windows. The stalls are panelled in figured walnut with pilasters and architraves of engraved peach. The exterior of the building, with a corner tower designed partly to conceal taller buildings behind it, is in white artificial stone. The tower contains the boiler house and the air conditioning plant.

The builders were Marfix, Ltd. The foundation stone was laid by Gracie Fields on 17 June 1937 and the theatre was opened on 27 October of that year. The theatre was completely redecorated in 1961 and in 1963 the proscenium, the orchestra, and the stage were remodelled.

THE PLAYS

The first theatre opened on 18 January 1884 as the Prince's. The play was a revival of W. S. Gilbert's *The Palace of Truth* with Tree in the cast. Edgar Bruce acted in the curtain raiser *In Honour Bound*. On 29 March 1884 Charles Hawtrey's famous farce *The Private Secretary* was first produced. Some one had given him a copy of a German play *Der Bibliotheker* and he had it in his pocket during a holiday in Biarritz and quickly made his own

adaptation. Although this play has since met with terrific
success and has been revived fourteen times in the West
End, the original production was a failure with Tree in the
title role. It was condemned out of hand by the critics and
existed for barely two months, but Hawtrey had faith in it
and transferred it to the old Globe with W. S. Penley in
the part of the curate. Hawtrey purchased all the rights
and made a profit of about £100,000 on his lucky deal, for
it developed into one of the most complete and genuine
successes of the year, running for 785 performances.

Called Back, by Hugh Conway and J. Comyns Carr,
followed in May 1884. In January 1885 Lillie Langtry began
a season and appeared in *Princess George,* followed by a
revival of *The School for Scandal,* with William Farren as
Sir Peter and Tree as Joseph. This was succeeded by a
revival of *Peril* in April, and in October was produced *The
Great Pink Pearl,* then Mrs Langtry returned for another
season of revivals until May 1886.

In 1886 the name of the theatre was changed to the Prince
of Wales', when the comic opera *La Béarnaise* by André
Messager was produced on October 4. During the run in
December at matinées was first given a dramatised version
of *Alice in Wonderland* by H. Saville Clarke and music
by Walter Slaughter. The next production was *Dorothy* in
February 1887 which was brought from the Gaiety where
it had not been over-successful. The full story of this will
be found under the history of the Lyric Theatre (see No. 21).
The next big success to arrive was not until 1889 when
Marjorie, a comic opera by Walter Slaughter, had a
successful run of 193 performances, a foretaste of the many
popular musical productions with which the theatre was
destined to be associated in the future. Since 1887 the
theatre had been under the control of Horace Sedger, who
remained until 1891. His last presentation was a run of 250
performances accorded to the 'wordless play', *L'Enfant
Prodigue,* by Michael Carré with music by André Wormser,
which re-introduced Pierrot to London.

In 1892 an epoch-making production presented by George
Edwardes was *In Town* described as 'a musical farce' by
Adrian Ross and J. T. Tanner with music by Osmond Carr.
This was really the prototype of musical comedy. It was
afterwards played at the Gaiety, but started its career of
292 performances at the Prince of Wales'. The success of
In Town was a step towards the gradual increase in the
popularity of this particular form of entertainment. In 1893
it was followed by *A Gaiety Girl,* which had a run of 413
performances and was one of the first important successes
of Sidney Jones; it was later transferred to Daly's to
conclude its run.

In 1895 *Gentleman Joe,* 'a musical farce' by Basil Hood
and Walter Slaughter, ran for 392 performances with

Arthur Roberts in the title role. The following year, when Henry Lowenfeld took the theatre, saw the first production in London of Audran's *La Poupée* in which Willie Edouin played the doll-maker.

Between 1898 and 1899 Mrs Patrick Campbell and Forbes-Robertson appeared here. One of their outstanding successes was Maeterlinck's *Pelleas and Melisande*; this was presented in the summer of 1898 and in September 1899 they produced *The Moonlight Blossom*, a Japanese play by C. B. Fernald and Louis N. Parker. Between their seasons, among other plays was seen *The Only Way*, transferred on 1 April 1899 from the Lyceum, where it had been first staged the previous month. It achieved in all 167 performances on its first presentation. Martin Harvey returned in February 1900 with a romantic play *Don Juan's Last Wager*, followed by a triple bill including *Ib and Little Christina*.

In August 1900 Marie Tempest, after severing her connection with George Edwardes and musical comedy, appeared here under the management of Frank Curzon in a play called *English Nell* by Edward Rose and Anthony Hope, from the latter's novel *Simon Dale*. She followed this with a version of Charles Reade's *Peg Woffington*, and in 1901 with *Becky Sharp* by Robert Hichens and Cosmo Gordon Lennox, her second husband, taken from Thackeray's *Vanity Fair*. As a result of these performances Marie Tempest became acknowledged as a comedy actress of the first rank.

Tonie Edgar Bruce succeeded her father as proprietor of the theatre on his death in 1901, and she retained that position until the house changed hands in February 1935. Frank Curzon, who became manager in 1900 and lessee in 1902, remained until 1915.

In 1903 the theatre renewed its connection with musical comedy and a successful chapter opened under the management of George Edwardes. The series of musical comedy 'hits' include *The School Girl* (1903), *Lady Madcap* (1904), *The Little Cherub* and *See See* (1906). The next productions were under Frank Curzon's own management and mostly starred his wife Isabel Jay; they were *Miss Hook of Holland* (1907), *My Mimosa Maid* (1908), *The King of Cadonia* (1908), *Dear Little Denmark* (1909), *The Balkan Princess* (1910).

This series did much to increase the reputation of Paul Rubens, who was an important figure in musical comedy development. As well as composing the music of five of the above plays he was also responsible for the part authorship of three and the sole authorship of one. After this era Charles Hawtrey appeared in a series of comedies and then between 1912 and 1918 there was an assortment of successes including *At the Barn* (1912) and *Art and Opportunity*

(1912), both with Marie Tempest, *Broadway Jones* (1914), *Mr Manhattan* (1916), *Anthony in Wonderland* (1917), *Carminetta* (1917), *Yes, Uncle* (1917), and *Fair and Warmer* (1918).

From 1918 to 1926 André Charlot, who became lessee in 1917, presented his revues here. These included *Bran Pie* (1919), *A to Z* (1921), *Charlot's Revue* (1924), and *Charlot's Show* (1926). Other outstanding productions during this period included a dramatisation of H. de Vere Stacpoole's *The Blue Lagoon* (1920), *The Gipsy Princess* (1921), the second season of *The Co-Optimists* (1923), *So This is London* (1923), *The Rat* (1924), and later *The Blue Train* (1927), *Alibi* (1928), and *By Candlelight* (1928).

In 1930 the theatre came for a short while under the management of Edith Evans for the production of *Delilah*, which failed to attract. In November 1931 M. E. Benjamin became licensee and general manager, and in March 1932 Novello's *I Lived with You* was produced. The early thirties were bad days for the theatre, and in 1932 Non-stop Revue took possession and the theatre passed into the control of Charles Clore. These revues developed into a form of English Folies Bergères. In 1935 the theatre passed entirely into the hands of Alfred Esdaile, who continued with the same policy. The last revue before the theatre was rebuilt was *Encore Les Dames*, and after a nine-months' closure the new theatre opened on 27 October 1937 with *Les Folies de Paris et Londres*. Others followed in similar vein until this era was broken by a musical comedy *Present Arms* in May 1940, and later Charles Chaplin's film *The Great Dictator* was shown here.

After a short return to the old non-stop entertainment, the theatre passed to the control of George Black and so eventually into the hands of Moss Empires, Ltd. Black first presented *Happidrome*, and this was followed by a stage version of James Hadley Chase's *No Orchids for Miss Blandish* in August 1942. *Strike a New Note* in 1943 brought Sid Field to the West End, and in 1944 he starred in *Strike It Again* and then *Piccadilly Hayride* (1946). The next few years saw mixed styles of entertainment here. Mae West in *Diamond Lil* (1948), Katherine Dunham and her dancers paid their first visit to London in 1948 to great success; and *Harvey*, with Sid Field, began its run of 610 performances in January 1949. This was his last part, and his early death was a great loss to the theatre. After an American revue, *Touch and Go*, in 1950, the theatre became entirely devoted to Variety or 'spectacular and fabulous' Folies Bergère style revues, which have starred such artists as Frankie Howerd, Norman Wisdom, Benny Hill, Winifred Atwell and others. After a return to musical comedy no great success was scored until the play *The World of Susie Wong* was presented in November 1959.

A new production was not needed until August 1961 when Sammy Davis Jnr appeared in a variety season.

In October an American musical, *Do-Re-Mi* opened and ran till February 1962 and was followed by *Come Blow Your Horn* which ran for 582 performances. Stage alterations were made in 1963 and the theatre reopened with *Round about Piccadilly* on 28 March 1964, running for 408 performances. Some short runs of plays and musicals followed in the next two years, the most interesting of these was *Funny Girl*, with Barbra Streisand, 109 performances from April till July 1966. *Way Out in Piccadilly*, a revue, ran for 427 performances from November 1966. The next big success was *Sweet Charity* in October 1967 which had 484 performances to its credit. April 1969 saw *Cat Among the Pigeons* by Georges Feydeau, followed in October by *Promises Promises*. No new production was required until February 1971 when *Catch my Soul* started a run till July. In August The *Avengers* opened and quickly closed, then *Big Bad Mouse* was revived in September (it had been presented at the Shaftesbury Theatre in 1966). February 1972 saw a revival of *The Threepenny Opera*, which later transferred to the Piccadilly Theatre. Sacha Distel starred in his West End revue in April and *Smilin' Through* came in July and smiled through only 29 performances. A musical version of Pinero's *Trelawny of the 'Wells'*, under the title of *Trelawny*, by Julian Slade and Audrey Woods, first seen at Sadler's Wells, transferred for a short season in August. Then came Anthony Newley and Leslie Bricasse's new show *The Good Old Bad Old Days* from December till a revue, *The Danny La Rue Show* opened in December 1973.

28 · The Queen's Theatre

Shaftesbury Avenue, W.1

Capacity: 989

Opened 8 October 1907 with *The Sugar Bowl*, a comedy by Madeleine Lucette Ryley. Produced by and under the management of Herbert Sleath.

THE BUILDING

The Queen's Theatre, at the Wardour Street corner of the Shaftesbury Avenue block of buildings, was built as a pair to the Hicks Theatre (now the Globe Theatre), and was the second to open in this building scheme of Jack Jacobus and Sydney Marler (see No. 16). The Queen's was originally a slightly larger house than its companion; both were designed by W. G. R. Sprague with similar elevations. Seymour Hicks was again connected with the enterprise and J. E. Vedrenne was the original lessee.

There seem to have been many discussions on the names for these new theatres. The Piccadilly and the Wardour

162

were among those discarded. Bernard Shaw wrote to Granville Barker about their associate Vedrenne. 'The papers say he is going to call his theatre the Central, as if it were a criminal court or a railway terminus.' Later, when its present name was decided upon, he commented, 'He is after a knighthood . . . it is not for nothing he called his theatre the Queen's . . . though why not the Alexandra?'

There had been a previous theatre of the same name, the Queen's, in Long Acre. This was closed in 1887 and eventually pulled down. The site was covered by Odhams Press, now demolished.

The Stage of 10 October 1907 describes the new theatre, the construction of which was carried out by Walter Wallis of Balham, thus:

> A two-tier house, the Queen's holds about 1200 persons, representing some £300 in money. The colour scheme of the walls and roof is white and gold, while green is the hue of the carpets, hangings and upholstery, and of the very charming velvet tableau curtain. From a spacious and lofty entrance-hall, with passages leading down into the stalls, one ascends by a handsome marble staircase to the dress circle, which runs out over the pit; and there is a fine and roomy saloon at the top. Mr Vedrenne makes a point that 7/6 will be charged for seats in the first three rows only of the dress circle, while but 5/- will be the price of the remaining eight rows, also unreserved, in which evening dress will be optional. On the second tier of the Queen's, which is in the Old Italian Renaissance style and in the building of which the cantilever principle has been adopted, are the upper circle and the shilling gallery. The auditorium is lighted up agreeably with electric lamps and an electrolier, and ample refreshment room and other accommodation will be found to have been provided.

The theatre was badly damaged by a bomb on 24 September 1940; a large portion of the front of the premises and the back of the circles was destroyed. It was not until February 1958 that plans were published for the reconstruction of the theatre. The architects were Westwood, Sons and Partner, who, while creating a modern exterior and front of house, contrived to retain, in co-operation with Hugh Casson, the old Edwardian atmosphere of the auditorium, decorating it in red, gold and white. It reopened on 8 July 1959.

THE PLAYS

The opening comedy, *The Sugar Bowl*, presented by Herbert Sleath with his wife, Ellis Jeffreys and Edmund Gwenn in the cast, 'failed to attract', which gave Shaw no cause for complaint, as the successful production of

The Devil's Disciple was transferred from the Savoy with Barker himself replacing Matheson Lang as Dick Dudgeon.

In the days when a settled policy for a theatre was still the rule the new Queen's did not seem to be able to find its feet—plays and musicals followed with varying success. *The Dairymaids*, a revival with Phyllis Dare; *The Belle of Brittany* and *The Persian Princess*, both with Ruth Vincent, among others, account for the first two years of its history. By now Vedrenne had surrendered his lease to H. B. Irving, who produced a succession of new plays and revivals of his father's successes, *The House Opposite*, *Dr Jekyll and Mr Hyde*, *Princess Clementina*, *The Bells*, *Louis XI*, *Hamlet*, and other productions which occupied the years until 1911.

In 1913 'Tango Teas' were instituted at which patrons could indulge in the latest craze of tango dancing, watch a dress parade, and have tea, at tables placed in the stalls, for an inclusive charge of half a crown.

It was not until 14 April 1914 that the theatre found its first long run with *Potash and Perlmutter*, with two lovable American comedians Augustus Yorke and Robert Leonard (Ernest Milton was the juvenile): this was to run for 665 performances, and to be followed by a sequel. From then no settled success was found until Alfred Butt, who had been the lessee from 1913, was joined by Owen Nares, who presented *The House of Peril*, *The Cinderella Man* and *Mr Todd's Experiment*.

The gay twenties were occupied with *Bluebeard's Eighth Wife*, a transfer of *Stop Flirting* with the Astaires, a revival of Barrie's *The Little Minister* with Owen Nares and Fay Compton, the experimental American play *Beggar on Horseback* with A. E. Matthews, *And so to Bed* with Yvonne Arnaud, *Crime*, and *Queen High*, to name only a·few productions. Every actor of note seems to have played at this theatre during these years when plays regularly transferred from theatre to theatre. Here too London audiences participated for the first time in *The Trial of Mary Dugan*.

September 1929 heralded the régime of Sir Barry Jackson with the Malvern Festival production of Shaw's *The Apple Cart*, with Cedric Hardwicke and Edith Evans, but before he could settle in Maurice Browne brought the Old Vic production of *Hamlet* to the theatre and the West End saw John Gielgud's memorable performance for the first time.

The names of the plays both old and new which figured on the posters in the next four years are theatrical history: *The Barretts of Wimpole Street*, *The Immortal Hour*, *The Farmer's Wife*, *Heartbreak House*, *Evensong*, to list but a few. *The Old Folks at Home*, with Marie Tempest, brought Harold Gosling's name to the programme as lessee, for the first time in December 1933. In 1935 *Short Story*, Robert Morley's first play, was produced with a glittering cast including Marie Tempest, Sybil Thorndike, Margaret Rutherford, Ursula Jeans, A. E. Matthews, and Rex Harrison. Transfers of *Love from a Stranger*, *Jane Eyre* and *The Wind and the Rain* all form a pattern in the success of the theatre.

The name of H. M. Tennent appears for the first time on the programme of *Retreat from Folly*, H. M. Harwood's play again starring Marie Tempest on 24 February 1937. This was followed by Emlyn Williams's play *He Was Born Gay*, 'a brilliant failure', with the author, Gwen Ffrangcon-Davies and John Gielgud in the cast. On September 6 of the same year Gielgud opened his own season with *Richard II*, followed by *The School for Scandal*, *The Three Sisters*, and *The Merchant of Venice*, with Peggy Ashcroft as leading lady and a supporting cast which now reads like an 'all-star matinée': Michael Redgrave, Alec Guinness, Anthony Quayle, Léon Quartermaine, Harcourt Williams, George Devine, Glen Byam Shaw, Harry Andrews, Dennis Price, George Howe, Ernest Hare, Richard Ainley, Gwen Ffrangcon-Davies, Angela Baddeley, Athene Seyler, Carol Goodner, Dorothy Green, Rachel Kempson. The last production before the outbreak of war was Dodie Smith's *Dear Octopus*, and when the theatres were allowed to reopen H. M. Tennent's revue *All Clear* in December 1939 helped to brighten the blackout. *Rebecca*, by Daphne du Maurier, with Owen Nares, Celia Johnson and Margaret Rutherford, was at the height of its successful run when the theatre was hit by a bomb, and its doors were closed until July 1959, when the theatre reopened with John Gielgud's Shakespearean recital *Ages of Man*. After a short season of *Hamlet*, given by the Youth Theatre, the successful run of *The Aspern Papers* began in August. After the run finished, *Joie de Vivre*, a musical version of Rattigan's *French Without Tears*, achieved four nights in July 1960. Robert Bolt had the unique honour of having two plays in adjacent theatres when his *The Tiger and the Horse* opened at the Queen's in August. Shortly after its reopening the lease of the theatre together with that of the Globe was offered for sale by the descendants of the original owners. It was acquired by the Prince Littler Group (Associated Theatre Properties).

After *The Tiger and the Horse* finished its run in March 1961 it was followed by a revival of Ibsen's *The Lady from the Sea* which ran until June when *The Rehearsal* arrived for its month's stay. This was followed by the musical *Stop the World—I Want to Get Off*, and a new production was not needed till November 1962 when *Vanity Fair*, in a musical version was staged but it lasted for only 70 performances. The next five plays all had short runs except

Mary Mary which opened in February 1963 and transferred to the Globe in September. From then till April 1965 many productions were seen for short runs, including a season of the National Youth Theatre with *Coriolanus* and *A Midsummer Night's Dream* in 1964, until a revival of *Present Laughter* in April 1965 ran for 289 performances. The new Noël Coward plays, under the title of *Suite in Three Keys*, were presented for a limited season, from April till July 1966, followed by the National Theatre Company Season. In October 1966 Neil Simon's *The Odd Couple* began its run of 405 performances, then in November 1967 Peter Ustinov's comedy *Halfway Up A Tree* arrived for 440 performances. In March 1969 Joe Orton's *What the Butler Saw*, with Ralph Richardson and Coral Browne, had a short run, then *Conduct Unbecoming* was presented in July 1969 for a good run. Several short runs followed until late 1971 when Kenneth More appeared in *Getting On* which continued until May 1972, when Marlene Dietrich was at the theatre for a short season. John Gielgud's revival of Noël Coward's *Private Lives*, with Maggie Smith and Robert Stephens, started a well-acclaimed run in September 1972, and transferred to the Globe Theatre in July 1973 to make room for a new musical *The Card*, adapted from Arnold Bennett's novel, with Jim Dale and Millicent Martin. This was followed in November by a new thriller starring Roy Dotrice, called *Gomes*, which achieved only six performances and in December *The Wolf* transferred from the Apollo Theatre though it moved on to the New London in April 1974 when *Bordello*, the Toulouse-Lautrec musical opened. From June, a revival of *Hair* for the summer season opened with its delayed 2000th performance.

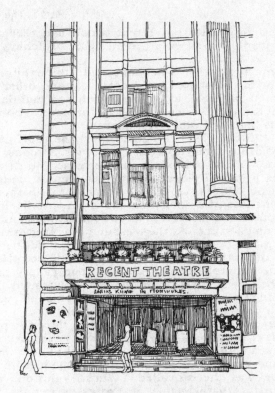

29 · The Regent Theatre

(The Marlborough Hall, The Polytechnic Great Hall,
The Polytechnic Theatre, The Cameo-Poly Cinema)

307 Regent Street, W.1

Capacity: 518

Built 1911–2. Used for a Founders' Day meeting 16 January 1911 during the rebuilding of the entire premises, which were opened 11 March 1912 by King George V and Queen Mary. The Hall was used for lectures and opened to the public as a cinema. Reconstructed and opened as the Polytechnic Theatre 11 April 1923 with *The Wonderland of Big Game*, a travel film. Opened as the Regent Theatre, 27 March 1974, with *Flowers*, A Pantomime for Jean Genet, devised and directed by Lindsay Kemp. Under the management of Michael Codron, in association with Larry Parnes.

THE BUILDING

The Royal Polytechnic was founded in 1838 for 'the Exhibition of Novelties in the Arts and Practical Science' in

premises at 309 Regent Street which had recently been
constructed. It was enlarged in 1848 stretching back to
Cavendish Square.

'Originally,' an 1875 account said, 'the exhibition consists, for the most part, of mechanical and other models,
distributed through various apartments; a hall devoted to
manufacturing processes; a theatre, or lecture room; a very
spacious hall; and other apartments.

'The "Great Hall" is lighted from the roof, and about
midway around the apartment extends a roomy gallery.
The latter contains models and designs. The floor of the
hall was principally occupied by two canals, containing a
surface of 700 feet of water, attached to which were the
appurtenances of a dockyard: locks, water-wheels, steam-
boat models, &c. But these have been removed as occupying too much space. At the west end is a reservoir, or tank,
fourteen feet deep; this, with the canals, holds nearly 5000
gallons of water, and can, if requisite, be emptied in less
than one minute. Beneath the west end gallery hangs the
diving-bell, which has, from the commencement, been the
chief and standing attraction of the Polytechnic, especially
with the young folk and country cousins.

'Courses of lectures are delivered on the principal topics
of the day, and indeed upon almost every subject connected
with human interest, accompanied with dioramic illustra-
tions, and various optical illusions; not the least interesting
of these was the so-called "Ghost" illusion, which is
associated with the name of Professor Pepper, and has
obtained great popularity in all the various shapes, dramatic
and other, which it has assumed from season to season.
The manufacture of spun-glass also has been carried on in
the large room almost from the commencement with great
success.'

Beside the dramatic sketches, especially 'Pepper's
Ghost,' a speciality of the Polytechnic from its outset, lan-
tern lectures on popular scientific subjects and Dissolving Views of travel were always part of the daily
programme.

In 1878 they were advertising *Pilgrim's Progress*, adapted
by W. G. Wills, with 'libretto' read 'with the assistance of
several actors and actresses and illustrated by Dissolving
Views and stage Tableaux'. Reserved seats 'In the Large
Theatre' were divided between upper and lower balcony,
stalls and private boxes as well as seats 'in the Small
Theatre'.

By 1860 classes, apprenticeship schools and technical
lectures were being held by the Polytechnic Institution and
College. In 1880 Quintin Hogg bought the building, retained
the old name, and it became the first of the 'People's
Universities.'

It was badly damaged by fire in 1881 but rebuilt with

further premises at 307 (which became the Marlborough Hall) and 311. Its rapid expansion early in the century led to a complete rebuilding in 1909–1911, designed by Frank T. Verity (exterior) and George A. Mitchell (interior) with still further additions up the street. The Great Hall (the Polytechnic Large Hall) at 307 was built and used for lectures, concerts and films, particularly travel films, carrying on the old tradition.

In 1923 the hall was remodelled as the Polytechnic Theatre. It was described as 'The Father of All Cinemas and the Home of Projection.' The new Theatre held 630 people in balcony and stalls. The opening film, on 11 April, was *The Wonderland of Big Game*. The cinema was run by a management 'By special arrangement with the Governors of the Polytechnic' and for many years they continued the policy of travel films, often with lectures, as well as occasional feature films of an instructive and suitable nature. It was yet again reconstructed by the architect, F. J. Wills and reopened with *Chang* on 3 March 1927. As the vogue for this style of film declined the cinema became a News Theatre and a centre for foreign and 'art' films, eventually known as the Cameo-Poly.

A lease of the cinema was acquired in 1974 by Laurie March and Larry Parnes and, after redecoration, it was renamed The Regent Theatre and opened on 27 March, with *Flowers*, which had previously been seen at the Bush Theatre, a theatre upstairs in a public house at Shepherds Bush. From 1 April 1974 Lunch Time Theatre was presented, commencing with two J. M. Barrie one act plays, *The Will* and *The Twelve Pound Look*.

There had been an earlier Regent Theatre in Euston Road, Kings Cross. It opened as the Euston Palace of Varieties in 1900 and became the Regent under Nigel Playfair in 1922. It was subsequently run for some years by Barry Jackson. It eventually became a cinema in 1930 and was demolished in 1971.

30 · The Royal Court Theatre

Sloane Square, S.W.1

Capacity: 401

Opened 24 September 1888 with *Mamma!* a farcical comedy (from the French *Les Surprises du Divorce*) by Sydney Grundy, preceded by *Hermine*, a play in one act by Charles Thomas. Under the management of Mrs John Wood.

THE BUILDING

The present theatre is the second to bear the name of the Royal Court, but the earlier building did not stand on the same site as that now occupied by this theatre. The existence of two separate buildings has been the cause of considerable confusion to historians. The first theatre had three names during its existence, the New Chelsea Theatre, then the Belgravia, and finally the Royal Court Theatre.

In 1818 when Sloane Square was still an open space, simply enclosed with wooden posts connected with iron chains, a dissenting chapel was built on ground on the south side. This ground eventually, when rebuilding and improvements were made in the square in 1887, was covered by a row of houses and gardens, lying between

Lower Sloane Street and Sloane Avenue (then calling itself Lower George Street).

The chapel fell into disuse and in 1870 was converted into a theatre called the New Chelsea, which opened on April 16, the same night as the Vaudeville Theatre.

The Era for April 17 tells us:

Among the many Easter novelties we have to record the opening of fresh theatres, one of which, the New Chelsea in Sloane Square, under the management of Arthur Morgan and B. Oliver, for the first time became a candidate for popular favour yesterday evening. The crowded south western district of London not possessing anything like a Theatre nearer than the Haymarket and St James's, it occurred to the gentlemen above named that a dissenting chapel (close by the aristocratic neighbourhood of Eaton Equare) which had, perhaps, been the means of converting thousands, might itself be advantageously converted—into a Theatre. With this end in view, in an incredibly short time, they have turned pews into pit and galleries into boxes, raising a theatrical gallery far above, and devoting pulpit space and its surroundings to the erection of a stage where a different style of elocution is to be practised to that which was heard in the Ebenezer or Bethel out of which this place of amusement is formed. The alterations have been well carried out, and though the house is by no means large, it is commodious, and the decorations with which it abounds are tasty. It is still in a very incomplete state, which was admitted by Mr Walter Holland in apologetic speech, in which he said that the management having pledged themselves that the Theatre should be opened on the 16th April, they resolved to keep their word, although at two o'clock that day the paint on the scenery was wet. He further added that having firmly believed that Chelsea can support a Theatre, they tried the experiment, and from week to week would supply the Drama, with a diversified programme, like that of a Music-Hall. Chelsea, moreover, he stated, owed something to the Theatres for it was through Nell Gwynn that Charles the Second built Chelsea Hospital. What encouragement will be given to the new Theatre as it proceeds the future must tell, if Mr Holland's programme is adopted, no doubt it will have plenty of support, and the reception all the performances met with at the opening justify the belief that proclivities of this generation will lead them to extend sufficient support to it. Drama, comedy, farce, ballet and burlesque, with a strong company, comprised the amusement on the first night. The Mathews family

gave their drawing room entertainment and Mr J. H.
Millburn sang some of his capital songs. The sisters
Laura and Ada Fenoulhet gave the scene from the
burlesque of *Kenilworth* wherein Leicester narrates
to Amy Robsart his experiences of London life, concluding with the Pyne and Harrison duet; and a clever
ventriloquist Professor Hilton created a great deal of
amusement by giving specimens of his difficult art.
Miss Patty Goddard and Miss Julian were also on the
list; and the original drama of *Mabel*, the plot of which
is simplicity itself, two honest people being suspected
of dishonesty, and the honour being established before
the curtain falls, was furnished for giving the perfect
theatrical air to the bill. In this piece Messrs Young
Walter Holland, Charles Chamberlain, Harry Rivers,
Ashley Charles, Nicolson, Wareham, Howard, and
Fenwick, and Miss Ada Attawell acquitted themselves
well; and *The Spectre Bridegroom*, which was the
concluding piece, showed most of those gentlemen,
with the addition of Mr B. Oliver, Miss Fanny
Morelli and Miss Bessie Walters took equal advantage
in a screaming farce. Considering that it was the first
night, the proceedings went off with a minimum of
hitches.

The venture was not a particularly successful one, and
before long the name was changed to the Belgravia, but
by the end of the year the theatre was again in the hands of
the builders and a much more drastic reconstruction
took place. The architect was Walter Emden, who
converted the interior into

. . . a bright brilliant little theatre capable of seating
comfortably 1100 persons. It is gorgeous in gilding,
profuse in ornamentation and its hangings and box
curtains are of a pinkish mauve satin, which has a
novel and very satisfactory effect. Two huge griffons,
or dragons, flank the proscenium boxes on each side
of the house. The frescoes over the proscenium, by
Mr Gurden Dalziel, representing incidents in the
life of St George of England, are very skilfully
painted. [*Illustrated London News*, 4 February 1871.]

The new manageress was Marie Litton and she opened
on 25 January 1871 with *Randall's Thumb* by W. S. Gilbert,
with *Turn Him Out* as the preceding farce. An opening
address by John Oxenford was spoken by Mrs Herman
Vezin.
     The biggest success of this period was Gilbert's bur-
lesque *The Happy Land*, which aroused much controversy
owing to its political satire, causing the intervention of
the Lord Chamberlain. In 1875 Mr and Mrs Kendal

and John Hare took over the management and the prestige
of this theatre was established. When they left in 1879
the Polish actress Helena Modjeska appeared here
under the management of Wilson Barrett, who was
also her leading man. It was her London début.

The next landmark is in 1881 when John Clayton took
the reins. The theatre was again completely altered and a
new porch added under the supervision of Alexander
Peebles.

In 1885 the now famous series of Pinero farces began,
which brought fame and fortune to all concerned. First
The Magistrate, then *The Schoolmistress* (1886), and
Dandy Dick (1887), all scored exceptionally long runs
for their day.

Unfortunately it had been decided to make improvements in Sloane Square which involved demolition of
the theatre, but John Clayton arranged to build a new
theatre on a nearby site. The old theatre closed on 22 July
1887. The present Royal Court Theatre was erected on
part of the Cadogan Estate on the east side of the square,
beside the entrance to the Metropolitan railway. It was
designed by Walter Emden and W. R. Crewe, and opened
on 24 September 1888.

The front of the new theatre was of stone and red
brick, freely treated in the Italian Renaissance style. The
entrance was panelled in oak and had a painted ceiling.
The interior was decorated in Empire style. A contemporary account (*The Builder*, 29 November 1888)
says:

> The decoration is not much better than theatre decora-
> tion usually is, and the large vases and *fronton* (we
> borrow a French word for what we have no precise
> English for) with nothing behind it, which forms the
> centre feature of the skyline of the façade, belong to
> the most commonplace order of architectural acces-
> sories. The worst point, architecturally, is the manner
> in which the drum of the octagonal dome over the
> centre part of the auditorium hangs in the air in front
> of the gallery. Nothing could look more unarchitec-
> tural and inconstructive.

A three-tier theatre, it had a gallery rising behind
the upper circle. The building has undergone several
changes since that date. It originally held 642 people.
When J. H. Leigh took the theatre in 1903 structural
alterations and redecorations were carried out by C. E.
Lancaster Parkinson. Once again, in 1921, Lord Lathom
spent a large sum on further improvements.

The theatre was sold in 1934 for £7500 to become a
cinema, after further reconstruction under Cecil Masey.
It was put out of use in November 1940 when bombs

fell on Sloane Square Station and remained derelict until
it was completely renovated by Robert Cromie for the
London Theatre Guild in 1952. The new interior shut
off the old gallery, transforming it into offices, and
reducing the capacity.

Since the coming of the English Stage Company in
1956 several completely new colour schemes of interior
decoration have been introduced and an apron stage
constructed, turning the lower boxes into stage doors,
with balconies above. The theatre was closed from
March to September 1964 during reconstruction.

The old rehearsal room of the theatre was used as a
restaurant for the club premises incorporated in the
theatre, and many cabaret artists appeared there from
1952.

In 1971 the room was opened on 23 November as the
Theatre Upstairs for open stage experimental productions (Capacity, 80).

THE PLAYS

The new theatre opened on 24 September 1888 with
Mamma! under the joint proprietorship of Mrs John
Wood and Arthur Chudleigh. This partnership lasted
until 1891 and amongst the successes produced were
The Weaker Sex by Pinero with the Kendals, *Aunt Jack*
(1889), Pinero's *The Cabinet Minister* (1890), and *The
Late Lamented* (1891). Mrs John Wood left the partnership and Arthur Chudleigh continued on his own, presenting *The Guardsman* (1892) and *The Amazons* by Pinero
(1893).

In November 1893 was produced a triple bill, in which
the third item, *Under the Clock* by C. H. Brookfield and
Seymour Hicks, though calling itself an extravaganza,
was in fact a topical burlesque of current theatrical
activities and has been said to be the forerunner of the
modern intimate revue. This was followed by a number
of short-lived productions both straight and musical,
among which should be mentioned Robert Buchanan's
Sweet Nancy, in which Martin Harvey made an early
appearance away from the Lyceum company (1897).

In 1897 the theatre was taken for a season by John
Hare and his opening performance, a revival of Pinero's
The Hobby-Horse, was attended by the Prince and
Princess of Wales and the Duke of York. On 20 January
1898 was the production of *Trelawny of the 'Wells'*,
which proved a great success and ran for 135 performances. After this success, in 1899, Dion Boucicault
joined Chudleigh in management. Plays presented under
their joint banner included *A Court Scandal* in which
Seymour Hicks played the part which his wife, Ellaline
Terriss, was later to play in the musical version, *The*

Dashing Little Duke. At the turn of the century the Court Theatre came under the control of a company with H. T. Brickwell and Frederick Kerr as managers. In 1901 Martin Harvey produced *A Cigarette Maker's Romance*, which proved a huge success. For some time after this the theatre fell on evil days, and in 1904 it was taken by J. H. Leigh. He presented a series of Shakespearean revivals in which he and his wife, Thyrza Norman, appeared. They began with *The Tempest* in October 1903 followed in 1904 by *Romeo and Juliet* and *The Two Gentlemen of Verona*, in which Granville Barker acted and produced, and for this production J. E. Vedrenne joined Leigh as business manager. Barker in conjunction with Vedrenne persuaded Leigh to allow them to present special matinées of Shaw's *Candida*, from this began the famous management which was to remain at this theatre until June 1907. They established what Bernard Shaw called 'that congregation'. It was not so much a repertory season as a season of short runs. Nearly a thousand performances were given altogether, and among the plays presented were Gilbert Murray's translations of the *Hippolytus, Troades* and *Electra*, Maeterlinck's *Aglavaine and Selysette*, Galsworthy's *The Silver Box*, St John Hankin's *The Charity That Began at Home* and *The Return of the Prodigal*, Elizabeth Robins's *Votes for Women* and Shaw's *John Bull's Other Island, You Never Can Tell, Man and Superman, Candida, Major Barbara, The Doctor's Dilemma* and others. It was one of the most notable theatrical ventures in the history of the stage. Thirty-two plays were presented in all, by seventeen authors. The policy and partnership were so successful that in 1907 removal to the Savoy Theatre was justified. The full story of this era is told in Desmond MacCarthy's *The Court Theatre* (1907) and the many other books on Shaw and Barker.

In 1907 Otho Stuart became manager and produced, among other plays, *Lady Frederick* by Somerset Maugham, which scored his first great success. He relinquished the management in February 1908. Many others came and went in the following ten years.

Between 1910 and the end of the 1914–18 War the Court Theatre often became the home of many distinguished visitors. In May 1910 the Abbey Theatre Company from Dublin gave a London season here and in 1911 there was a season by Lydia Yavorska (The Princess Bariatinsky), and the Irish National Theatre appeared again here in that year and in 1913 and 1914. The year 1915 brought Frank Benson's production of *A Midsummer Night's Dream* at Christmas and in 1917 H. V. Neilson presented *Hush!* which was extensively advertised as 'a play that must be seen by every maiden,

wife and mother'. The Court was often used by amateurs
and play-producing societies and apart from the special
seasons, was more often than not closed during the
decade which followed the Vedrenne-Barker management.

After the war J. H. Leigh sold the theatre to Lord
Lathom and J. B. Fagan became manager in 1918,
producing *Damaged Goods, Twelfth Night, The School
for Scandal, The Lost Leader* by Lennox Robinson, and
The Merchant of Venice, in which Maurice Moscovitch
made an instant success. In 1920 a dramatic version of
Daisy Ashford's *The Young Visiters* was produced here.
In October 1921 Shaw's *Heartbreak House* had its first
production here, then Fagan staged a number of Shakespearean revivals. In 1922 J. T. Grein and Leon M. Lion
presented a season of Galsworthy's plays, but once again
the theatre seemed destined to have bad luck. In 1924
it was taken over by Barry Jackson, with the Birmingham
Repertory Company, who began his tenancy with Shaw's
'play cycle in five parts'—*Back to Methuselah*, produced
between February 18 and 22, one part each night. This
was followed by *The Farmer's Wife* by Eden Phillpotts,
which had a phenomenally long run of 1329 performances
from 11 March 1924, finishing in January 1927.

After this he presented Macbeth and *The Taming of the
Shrew*, both in modern dress. In 1928, Elmer Rice's
The Adding Machine, an interesting 'impressionist
play', was produced. During Barry Jackson's régime
other noteworthy plays were presented here, and after
he left the Macdona Players performed Shaw plays for
seasons in 1929, 1930 and 1931. In 1932 the last play to
be seen here for many years was staged: it was *The School
for Husbands*, and after this the theatre remained closed.

In 1934 the theatre came onto the market and in March
1935 two plays were put on for a week each, then it was
used as a repertory cinema but closed again with the
coming of the blitz in 1940.

After several abortive attempts to reopen the theatre,
it was eventually purchased by Alfred Esdaile and the
London Theatre Guild, Ltd. It was reconditioned and
reopened on 2 July 1952 with *The Bride of Denmark
Hill*. During the next two years were produced *Miss
Hargreaves* with Margaret Rutherford and several
other less notable productions. In 1954 Laurier Lister took
the theatre and presented intimate revue, *Airs on a
Shoestring*, which ran for 772 performances. Then came
another dull patch until London first saw the Brecht-Weill
version of *The Beggar's Opera* entitled *The Threepenny
Opera* in February 1956. This transferred to the Aldwych
and Comedy Theatres and totalled in all 140 performances. In April of the same year the English Stage
Company took over the theatre. Its Artistic Director,

George Devine, announced a policy of repertory, but
this system was eventually abolished and plays presented
for limited seasons. In their first two years, they were
able to claim that they had produced thirty plays, the
majority of which were new works. Their most talked-of
discovery during this period was John Osborne with his
plays *Look Back in Anger* and *The Entertainer*. The next
most discussed playwright was Arnold Wesker, whose
Roots (part of the eventual trilogy), and *The Kitchen* and
Chips with Everything, made him a national figure.
The Royal Court once again became the centre of new
movements in the modern theatre.

Through the next few years many new plays were seen
and *Period of Adjustment* (1962), *The Ginger Man*
(1963), *Inadmissible Evidence* (1964), *Little Malcolm
and his Struggle Against the Eunuchs* (1966), *Restoration of Arnold Middleton* (1967), *Time Present* (1968),
Hotel in Amsterdam (1968) and a revival of *Look Back in
Anger* (1968) were all later seen in the West End with
mixed success. George Devine died in 1966 and William
Gaskill became artistic director of the Company until
succeeded by Oscar Lewenstein in 1972. Three new
plays, presented during 1969, were Edward Bond's
Saved, *Narrow Road to the Deep North* and *Early
Morning*. April the same year saw David Storey's play
In Celebration and in July a production by the Bread
and Puppet Theatre of America entitled *Cry of the
People for Meat*, was followed quickly by *Captain Oates'
Left Sock* and a revival of *The Double Dealer* by Congreve. In September came a French season with the
Compagnie Renaud-Barnault which was followed in
October by David Storey's *The Contractor* which transferred to the West End. At Christmas *The Three
Musketeers Ride Again*, an entertainment based on the
novel by Alexandre Dumas, was presented. In January 1970
Three Months Gone was produced, and this too later
transferred to the West End. In February *Uncle Vanya* was
revived and followed in April by *Widowers' Houses*.
June's presentation was *Home*, by David Storey (later
to transfer), followed in August by *The Philanthropist*,
by Christopher Hampton, another play transferred to
the West End, which had a very long run at the May
Fair. The rest of 1970 saw several new plays produced with
a transfer of *Lulu* to the Apollo (January 1971).

During 1971 a revival of *The Duchess of Malfi* was
seen and among other productions were *Man is Man*,
One at Night, *Slag*, *The Lovers of Viorne*, *West of
Suez* (which transferred to the Cambridge) and *The
Changing Room* (transferred to the Globe). Early in the
new year of 1972 came *Alpha Beta* (transferred to the
Apollo); *Veterans*, with John Gielgud and John Mills in

March; April saw *Big Wolf* followed by *Crete and Sergeant Pepper*, then *The Old Ones*, which was succeeded by *Richard's Cork Leg*, *A Pagan Place*, and in December a new play by John Osborne, *A Sense of Detachment*. The new year, 1973, saw *Krapp's Last Tape* and *Not I*, a Beckett double bill, *The Freedom of the City* and *Savages* by Christopher Hampton (transferred to the Comedy). Then followed *The Sea*, by Edward Bond; *Magnificence*, *The Removalists* and *Cromwell* and *The Farm* by David Storey (the latter transferred to the May Fair). *The Merry Go Round*, by D. H. Lawrence, was the last in a series of first productions or revivals of his plays which had started in 1967.

1974 has, so far, not been especially eventful. In fact, in March a 'pay what you like' policy was adopted to 'sell' *Runaway*, a new play, to a reluctant public. For the 'Almost Free Theatre' offers of admission ranged from 2p to 25p, both of which were accepted! At least this was an advance on the occasion in 1969 when, under similar circumstances, *Life Price*, another new play, was thrown open free to the public. In all fairness this was done with the consent of the Arts Council from whom a £135,000 subsidy was available in the last financial year. In April 1974 David Storey came up with yet another new play, *Life Class*, starring Alan Bates, which was seen later at the Duke of York's.

31 · The Royalty Theatre

Portugal Street, Kingsway, W.C.2

Capacity: 922

Opened 23 June 1960 with *The Visit*, a play by Friedrich Dürrenmatt, adapted by Maurice Valency. Directed by Peter Brook under the management of H. M. Tennent, Ltd, and Two Arts, Ltd.

THE BUILDING

The present theatre is on part of the site of the London Opera House opened on 13 November 1911. This building later became the Stoll Picture Theatre and then the Stoll Theatre. The idea of a vast opera-house in the newly-constructed Kingsway was conceived by Oscar Hammerstein, the American impresario, as a rival to the Royal Opera House, Covent Garden.

Excavations on a site stretching from Portugal Street to Sardinia Street began in October 1910; the area covered

24,500 sq.ft, on which a holy well of supposed healing qualities was situated. Hammerstein spent over £200,000 on the building, which was designed by Bertie Crewe.

The exterior [says a contemporary account] is treated in French Renaissance design with a façade of Portland Stone with Norwegian grey granite bases. At each side, after the first 50 feet, are red brick facings. The main façade is divided into two storeys, each nearly 40 feet high, the lower half is heavily rusticated. The lines of the upper storey are broken by coupled Corinthian pilasters, the carved capitals having square volutes. A notable feature is a central window 39 feet high. On the main cornice are twelve statues sculptured by Thomas Rudge of Clapham. At the ends are groups of three figures representing Melody and Harmony, and over the central window are seated figures representing Inspiration and Composition; between these and the end groups are four single statues of Comedy, Tragedy, Dance and Song.

The entrance hall is flanked by white and gold fluted columns surmounted by bas-reliefs of famous composers. The seating accommodation is 2250.

(At the time of demolition the capacity was given as 2420.)

The interior matched the exterior in elegance and extravagance. It was everything a Grand Opera House of its period should be.

Hammerstein announced a grand opening season of twenty weeks, to begin on 13 November 1911 with a production of an opera new to London, *Quo Vadis?* by Jean Nouguès.

Though full of good intentions, the impresario found he was up against The Syndicate who ran Covent Garden. They had all the popular operas firmly fixed in their repertoire and the greatest singers of the day under contract. Hammerstein was left with works that were new or less familiar to the public.

The first season lasting until March 1912 was announced to continue for another summer season of twelve weeks to open on April 22, divided between Italian and French works. Among his singers remembered today were Orville Harrold, Maurice Renaud, Lina Cavalieri, Félice Lyne and Marguerite d'Alvarez.

When the Covent Garden season opened in April 1912, Hammerstein soon discovered it was useless to carry on against the odds he had to fight and was forced to close on July 13. He returned to America having lost, it was said, £47,000.

The theatre remained closed until Christmas 1912 when Fernand Akoun, a French impresario, gave a season of variety and films. Hammerstein disposed of his interest in the building to the London Opera House, Ltd, who experimented again with variety followed by a revue, in the same programme, *Come Over Here*, which ran from April 1913 for 217 performances.

A patriotic play *For England Expects* was staged at the outbreak of war followed by a pantomime *Aladdin* which failed, a strange occurrence for a pantomime. After this period the theatre was more often closed than open, though *Charley's Aunt* was here for Christmas 1915.

In 1916 control passed to Oswald Stoll, who after staging, among other attractions, a revue *Look Who's Here*, and a pantomime *Cinderella*, followed this by the curious experiment of a Jewish 'Bing Boys' called *The Other Bing Boys*, with Augustus Yorke and Robert Leonard of *Potash and Perlmutter* fame, and Ella Retford as the other 'Emma.' All these efforts failed to establish the reputation of the theatre. In the summer of 1917 Stoll, who had been taking an interest in film-making at the Cricklewood Studios, turned the Opera House into a cinema, renaming it the Stoll Picture Theatre.

As a cinema the building at last achieved success. Part of the programme always consisted of a stage presentation of an orchestra with a singer or instrumentalist. The resident Grand Orchestra and organist in silent days were justly famous, even in the days of the 'talkies' stage shows were from time to time presented.

The building returned to completely 'live' entertainment in 1941 when twice-nightly variety was staged, followed by a Christmas pantomime with Nervo and Knox, Jay Laurier and Tessa Deane. Sir Oswald Stoll died in January 1942 and the theatre eventually passed into the control of Prince Littler whereupon the name of the Stoll Theatre was adopted.

Under the new régime were presented revivals of famous musical comedies, *Rose Marie*, *Lilac Time*, *Show Boat*, and *The Student Prince*. These and transfers from other theatres, Christmas entertainments and varied attractions kept the theatre busy until 1947, when Tom Arnold commenced his series of Ice Spectacles. The vast stage was converted into an ice rink, and nearly everything that had been performed in music hall or circus seemed to be transferred on to skates.

It was not until two years later that musical comedy reigned again with a revival of *Wild Violets* and a transfer of the record-breaking *Oklahoma!* moved here from Drury Lane to finish its fourth year.

In 1951 *Festival Ballet* was founded by Anton Dolin, who with Markova drew large audiences for its opening season. From then until the end of its life the theatre mainly housed ballet, dance and opera seasons, with a few excursions back into musical comedy with varying success.

The most remarkable sensations of the last years were *Porgy and Bess*, Gershwin's Jazz Opera, staged in October 1952, Ingrid Bergmàn in *Joan at the Stake* (October 1954), and *Kismet*, the eastern musical to the melodies of Borodin, which from its opening in April 1955 with Alfred Drake, Doretta Morrow and Joan Diener, ran for 648 performances, the longest success of this theatre.

There is little more to add: some Italian opera and finally a triumphant five-week season of the Stratford Memorial Theatre production of *Titus Andronicus* with Laurence Olivier and Vivien Leigh, which had just returned from a European tour. The theatre closed with a packed house on 4 August 1957.

By then it was known that a building development corporation under the direction of Charles Clore had purchased the site and was to build a block of offices. Demolition and rebuilding permission was not given by the L.C.C. unless another theatre could be provided in the plans for the new building. After consideration this was agreed upon and the Stoll Theatre completely vanished under the pick-axe.

In September 1959 the first details of the new theatre were given. Among other things, it was learnt that it was to be called the Kingsway. The previous theatre of this name in Great Queen Street, opened in 1881 (as the Novelty), was later a blitz casualty and eventually, after several promises of rebuilding, was completely demolished, a block of offices rising on the site in 1959. It was not until April 1960 that more information was released, then it was announced by the owners that the final choice of name was the Royalty Theatre, once again that of a previous building with a long history.

Fanny Kelly (Lamb's 'Barbara S—') built a small theatre on the yard and stables of her house at 73 Dean Street, opening it as a school of acting in 1840. After struggling for nearly ten years she had to close and the theatre became the New English Opera House, the Royal Soho Theatre and eventually the Royalty in 1861. During its life it had many reconstructions but eventually became outmoded and was finally closed in 1939. Many schemes were suggested for its rehabilitation, but after it had been severely damaged in the blitz it was pulled down and a block of offices called Royalty House arose on the site.

The Royalty has a place in stage history, for among the first London productions within its walls were *Trial by Jury* (1875), *Ghosts* (1891), *Charley's Aunt* (1892), *Widowers' Houses* (1892), *Milestones* (1912), *The Vortex* (1924), *Juno and the Paycock* (1925), *While Parents Sleep* (1929).

There had been an even earlier Royalty Theatre in Wellclose Square in the East End of London, built by John

Palmer, the actor, in 1787. He hoped to obtain a licence but was opposed by the patent theatre and had to give up after only two performances. The following year Macready the elder opened it with a burletta licence and it had a precarious existence under several subsequent managements.

In 1818 it was known as the East London Theatre and was burnt down in 1826. When it was rebuilt and reopened as the Brunswick in 1828 it had been so badly constructed that it collapsed during a rehearsal killing fifteen people and injuring many others three days after it had opened. Certainly the new theatre in Kingsway bears a name well recorded in theatrical annals.

A dedication stone in the vestibule of the new Royalty Theatre was unveiled by Dame Edith Evans at a private view on 15 June 1960.

Constructed below ground level in the centre of a vast office block, it has its entrance in Portugal Street, the façade reaching almost from Kingsway to Sheffield Street. It was the first new West End theatre since the Saville was opened in 1931.

The architects, Lewis Solomon, Kaye and Partners, have designed a theatre on a mixture of traditional and modern lines. The Press manifestos stated:

The auditorium, 73 ft deep, 71 ft wide and 32 ft high, has been designed to afford excellent sight lines from all parts of the House. Special care has been taken in the shape of the auditorium and its decor to ensure that acoustics are first class.

Seating is on two levels. The Stalls can seat 689 people and the Circle 288, which with 20 seats in the boxes totals 997.

The large box on the left side of the auditorium is the Royal Box and is provided with a retiring room to which access can be gained direct from Kingsway. The decor has been designed to combine the dignity of the Georgian theatre and the lushness of the Victorian theatre in present-day terms. The walls, for acoustics, are panelled in timber which is covered with a sheet plastic resembling leather. The material, which has never been seen in this country before, has been specially imported from America. The colour scheme is in shades of grey-green, gold and white, with carpets, seating and curtains in red.

The light fittings have been specially designed in satin brass and cut glass to give the sparkle of the old-fashioned chandelier in a more contemporary form.

This theatre introduces a new principle in stage design. The proscenium opening is adjustable and can be varied from full width of 43 ft, suitable for a large-scale musical play, to a minimum width of 36 ft, suitable for a straight play with a small cast. The height of the opening is fixed at 20 ft. The stage is 33 ft deep, but, by raising the large door of the Scene Dock at rear of the stage an extra 12 ft depth can be obtained. The grid, from which the scenery is suspended, is 52 ft above the Stage. An electric hoist provides for raising and lowering scenery from the Scenery entrance, which is 16 ft above the stage.

The Orchestra Pit can accommodate 40 musicians. It is equipped with a lift which can rise to stage level. In this position it can serve as an Apron stage, extending 7 ft into the Auditorium. The footlights, working interdependently with the lift, can be electrically rotated to provide a flush stage level affording no interruption to the use of the Apron stage.

In the centre of the Stage is a compound revolve, consisting of an inner circle 15 ft diameter, and an outer ring 25 ft diameter. These can be made to rotate independently of each other, at varying speeds and directions and at the same time the complete inner circle can act as a lift, serving from the floor of the Stage basement to a level 4 ft above Stage level.

On either side of the Proscenium opening, concealed in the panelling, are Doors with openings above, features of the Theatre during the Restoration and Georgian periods.

Entrance to the theatre is beneath a projecting canopy in Portugal Street, round the corner from Kingsway. The edge of the canopy is faced with Emerald Pearl Granite, the walls below with White Pentelicon Marble and Black Mosaic and the Entrance Doors and display windows are of Silver Bronze. A warm air curtain has been provided inside the main entrance for warmth when the doors are open. On the stone panel above the entrance are five figures and a crest. These have all been executed in three-dimensional mosaic. The figures represent Tragedy, Comedy, Harlequinade, Dancing and Music. The crest is the insignia of the Royalty Theatre, and it will be found repeated at intervals in the interior decor of the building.

The Foyer is panelled in Burmese Rosewood, and has a ceiling of Rosewood and Maple panelling. Also a photo-mural of Kingsway and the London Opera House as it looked when it was built in 1911.

From the Foyer the Staircase sweeps down to the Circle, Stalls and Lounges. The wallpaper has a red flock pattern of the Royalty crest, on a gold and ivory background, which is repeated throughout.

On the Circle level the Foyer is again panelled in Burmese Rosewood with relieving areas of wallpaper and gold and white Vinyl. The walls around the bar are panelled with American Black Walnut. The feature of this Bar is the large rear illuminated concrete and glass screen which depicts a royal procession.

On the Stalls level the panelling is in Lido Marble, Burmese Rosewood and American Black Walnut. The long zig-zag Bar is reflected in the mirror facetted Back Bar Fitting, which is illuminated to sparkle like a giant cut diamond.

A long lease of the theatre was taken by Bernard Delfont.

THE PLAYS

The opening production, *The Visit*, presented by H. M. Tennent, Ltd, and Two Arts, Ltd, was first seen in London at a Gala Preview in aid of King George's Pension Fund for Actors on 23 June 1960. The theatre was officially opened to the public on the following night.

This play was first toured in the provinces with Alfred Lunt and Lynn Fontanne in late 1957 as *Time and Again*, but it did not reach London. They returned to America and opened the rebuilt and renamed Lunt-Fontanne Theatre in New York with this play, retitled *The Visit*, on 5 May 1958, after a long tour in America. They appeared at last in the play in London, strangely enough again to open a new theatre. After this finished its run in October, Zizi Jeanmaire appeared in 'An Evening of Song and Dance' followed by Antonio and his Company at the end of the year.

The new theatre seemed unable to put itself on the map and several plays came and went. In May 1961 the run of *The Miracle Worker* which had opened in March was broken and it transferred to Wyndham's when it was announced that Metro-Goldwyn-Mayer had taken a long lease of the theatre and would transfer *Ben Hur* there from the Empire (then closing for re-building). Films came back to Kingsway on 29 May. The theatre was closed for most of 1962 and did not re-open till November when *Mutiny on the Bounty* was first shown.

It remained a cinema on and off under various managements until it was taken over by Paul Raymond and once again became a theatre on 2 April 1970 with an all male revue, *Birds of a Feather*, which ran for only a month. This was followed by the success of *Oh! Calcutta!* Kenneth Tynan's 'evening of elegant erotica' which ran here until transferring to the Duchess in January 1974. The theatre was then closed until March 1974 when Paul Raymond's spectacular extravaganza, *Royalty Folies*, opened.

32 · The St Martin's Theatre

West Street, Shaftesbury Avenue, W.C.2

Capacity: 550

Opened 23 November 1916 with *Houp La!* a comedy with music by Fred Thompson and Hugh E. Wright, music by Nat D. Ayer and Howard Talbot. Produced by Frank Collins. Under the management of C. B. Cochran.

THE BUILDING

The theatre, almost at the corner of Upper St Martin's Lane, was planned as a companion to the Ambassadors (opened 1913; see No. 4), but the outbreak of the First World War held up building, and the theatre was not completed until 1916; even at the last moment its first night had to be postponed.

Designed by W. G. R. Sprague (the architect of the Ambassadors) for Lord Willoughby de Broke (the father of the present owner), with B. A. Meyer as licensee. The builders were Lenn Thornton and Company.

An account of the theatre in *The Architectural Review* says:

. . . this building shows a change that has slowly been taking place during recent years. Its interior, instead of revelling in a lavish display of modelled plaster work, tricked out with gold leaf and paint, has an intimate, almost domestic character. In general style it tends to be what is known as English Georgian and gives one the impression of being a private theatre provided by some patron of the dramatic arts for the entertainment of his guests. The façade comprises a range of columns standing on a plain base and entablature and parapet. On this cornice, at the centre, is a large bronzed cartouche with flags grouped around, and on either side are vases. The proscenium and flanking walls of the auditorium are panelled their full height in Italian walnut with a range of columns and pilasters on either side, with gilded capitals and bases, carrying a bold entablature which is continued across the proscenium.

The Coat of Arms above the cartouche on the facade was blown down in the blitz and has not been replaced. The vases also have disappeared. The theatre is in two tiers with dress circle and upper circle rising above the stalls. The theatre remains today almost as originally built, and in 1960 when it returned to the hands of the son of its original owner, a complete redecoration and renovation was put in hand, which was not finished until the following year.

THE PLAYS

The theatre opened on 23 November 1916 with Gertie Millar and George Graves in *Houp La!* a comedy with music, by Fred Thompson and Hugh E. Wright, music by Nat D. Ayer and Howard Talbot, under the direction of Charles B. Cochran, who was the original lessee of the theatre. This ran for 108 performances and was succeeded by a very different fare, a revival of Brieux's *Damaged Goods*, adapted by John Pollock. The play had been given a private performance at the Little Theatre in February 1914, but this was the first public performance in this country. It ran for 281 performances and was followed by yet another very different type of play, *Sleeping Partners*, 'a garden of Eden episode' by Seymour Hicks (from the French), which was produced in December 1917 (129 performances); it was revived here in March 1919. A musical play called *The Officers' Mess* ran for 200 performances from November 1918 and in 1920 Frank Benson appeared in John Masefield's *Pompey the Great* and *Hamlet*. From March 1920 to 1925 the theatre was under the management of Alec Rea and Basil Dean, who formed the company known as 'Reandean'. Alec Rea was

lessee of the theatre from 1920 to 1937 and was afterwards
chairman of the company known as 'Reandco', which
succeeded 'Reandean'. Both these ventures gave notable
plays notably acted, and amongst them were John Galsworthy's *The Skin Game* (349 performances from April
1920) and Clemence Dane's *A Bill of Divorcement* (401
performances from March 1921). The latter play was the
one in which Clemence Dane found fame as a playwright
and in which the promising young actress Meggie Albanesi
established herself, before her death in December 1923 at
the early age of twenty-four. A plaque with a bas-relief
portrait is in the foyer of the theatre, a memorial to a great
actress who unfortunately did not live long enough to
achieve the fame which would have undoubtedly been hers.
Other successes which followed these two early productions were John Galsworthy's *Loyalties* (407 performances) from March 1922, and *R.U.R.* (*Rossum's Universal
Robots*), which ran for 126 performances from April 1923:
this was a translation by Paul Selver from the Czecho-
slovakian of Karel Čapek, adapted by Nigel Playfair.
Capek was obsessed with the mechanisation of modern
life and this play was first produced in Prague in January
1921. In the latter half of 1923 came Charles McEvoy's *The
Likes of Her* (228 performances from August 1923), a play
of East End slum life in which Hermione Baddeley at the
age of seventeen gave a remarkable performance.

Subsequent successes were John Galsworthy's *The
Forest, In the Next Room*, by Eleanor Robson and Harriet
Ford (203 performances) both in 1924, and Lonsdale's
Spring Cleaning (262 performances from January 1925),
which raised storms of protest because into it the author
introduced a 'street walker'.

During 1923 and 1924 'The Playbox Theatre'—giving
matinée performances—proved a highly successful
experiment.

In November 1925 Arnold Ridley's comedy thriller *The
Ghost Train* was first produced here, and thus the St
Martin's was responsible for its send-off on a run of ulti-
mately 655 performances, after transferring to other
theatres.

The year 1926 brought a mixed selection of plays all of
which ran for over a hundred performances: Patrick
Hastings' *Scotch Mist*, Sidney Howard's *They Knew what
they Wanted*, later to become the musical *The Most Happy
Fella*, Noël Coward's *The Queen was in the Parlour*, and
J. L. Balderston and J. C. Squire's *Berkeley Square*. The
successes of 1927 were Reginald Berkeley's *The White
Chateau*, which he had written during convalescence from
wounds in 1917 and had first been played by the officers
at the Reserve Battalion Theatre and which some critics
consider to be the best play of its kind; Lynn Starling's

comedy *Meet the Wife*, and Sidney Howard's *The Silver Cord*.

In 1928 Walter Hackett scored two successes here with *Other Men's Wives* (143 performances from April) and 77 *Park Lane* (which ran for 308 performances from October). Another Hackett success was *Sorry You've Been Troubled* (157 performances from September 1929). In all three Marion Lorne appeared. The years 1930 and 1931 saw the production of no less than eight plays at the St Martin's, the chief successes of which were Roland Pertwee's *Honour's Easy* (128 performances) and Neil Grant's *Petticoat Influence* (283 performances) both in 1930, and Ronald Jeans' *Lean Harvest* with 123 performances, and *The Nelson Touch* in 1931.

A dramatisation of Mary Webb's *Precious Bane* appeared in 1932, but the play was not so successful as the book. The greatest success of 1932 was Rodney Ackland's *Strange Orchestra*, which transferred here from the Embassy Theatre in September and ran for 135 performances—not a long run—but much was thought of the work which was the first modern play to be produced by John Gielgud. 1933 opened with Mordaunt Shairp's *The Green Bay Tree*, which ran for 163 performances, and in October that year began the run of Merton Hodge's *The Wind and the Rain*. This, Hodge's first play, was originally produced at the Arts Theatre Club as *As it was in the Beginning*; rewritten, it was produced in Manchester under the title of *The Wind and the Rain*, and then it came to the St Martin's; transferring first to the Queen's and then to the Savoy, it ran continuously for over two years with 1001 performances.

In 1935 Dion Titheradge's *Man of Yesterday*, Martin Vale's *The Two Mrs. Carrolls*, and James Parish's *Distinguished Gathering* were produced here, the latter coming from the Embassy Theatre. 1936 saw several productions of which the most outstanding were *Heroes Don't Care* by Margot Neville (149 performances from June) and Geoffrey Kerr's *Till the Cows Come Home* (117 performances from October).

In 1937 J. W. Pemberton acquired an interest in the St Martin's and during that year a run of 161 performances was begun with *Autumn*, a play by Margaret Kennedy and Gregory Ratoff, from the Russian, produced by Basil Dean, with Flora Robson. In 1938 a run of 161 performances was scored by Thomas Browne's *Plan for a Hostess*, and J. B. Priestley's *When We are Married* began a run of 175 performances. It was also a Basil Dean production.

After the outbreak of war in 1939 various productions appeared at the St Martin's with little success, and there were some transfers. *Love in a Mist* by Kenneth Horne ran from November 1941, and *Claudia*, by Rose Franken,

558 performances from September 1942. In 1943 the lease
of the theatre was disposed of by J. W. Pemberton to
Bernard Delfont.

The Druid's Rest by Emlyn Williams (January 1944)
was followed in August of the same year by the Arts Theatre
Club production of Bird in Hand, the Arts Company thus
extending its sphere of influence by playing in a West End
theatre. They followed this by The Magistrate in
November. In 1945 Laura, starring Sonia Dresdel, was
followed by The Shop at Sly Corner by Edward Percy
which ran 863 performances, with Kenneth Kent, Ada
Reeve and Cathleen Nesbitt. During the run the theatre
again changed hands, coming under the control of J. M.
Cook. The next years were filled with productions many
of which had incredibly short runs, though the following
successes should be mentioned: a revival of The Wild Duck
(1948) with a star cast, a revue Penny Plain with Joyce
Grenfell (1951), Small Hotel (1955), The Rainmaker (1956),
Plaintiff in a Pretty Hat (1957) and The Grass is Greener
(1958).

During 1959 the theatre returned into the hands of the de
Broke family and Bertie Meyer once again came into
control. 1960 saw the production of Double Yolk, Inherit
the Wind, a transfer from the Cambridge Theatre of John
Mortimer's The Wrong Side of the Park, and in July a
farce, The Brides of March. In November this was succeeded by a transfer from the Piccadilly of The Playboy of
the Western World, and it was announced that Associated-
Rediffusion had taken a long lease of the theatre.

The next long run was Guilty Party, which held the stage
from July 1961 until June 1962, then Kill Two Birds opened
in October, and lasted 100 performances, followed by
Stephen D for 120 performances. A transfer from the Arts,
Where Angels Fear To Tread, brought success to the
theatre for 261 performances, but several very short runs
followed until Past Imperfect opened in June 1964 and
transferred to the Savoy the following February. Eric
Portman had a good run in The Creeper from July 1965
till January 1966. Bertie Meyer then returned to the theatre
as Licensee for Lord Willoughby de Broke, and for almost
the next three years it was run by Peter Bridge, but unfortunately either short runs or transfers were the order
of the day. The lease was then taken up by Peter
Saunders. Out of the Question, with Gladys Cooper,
opened in October 1968 to a good run of 9 months. The next
success was Sleuth, which opened in February 1970, later
to transfer to the Garrick in March 1973, and then to the
Fortune, in the following October. After this came a flop,
Lover, quickly followed by Say Goodnight to Grandma,
both in March 1973. Later in the year saw a transfer of
Lloyd George Knew my Father from the Savoy then, in

January 1974, *Dead Easy* appeared, though for only a few performances. *The Collector*, previously seen at the Bush Theatre in Shepherd's Bush in 1972, followed until *The Mousetrap* crossed the passageway on 25 March 1974 to continue its twenty-second year's run.

33 · The Savoy Theatre

Strand, W.C.2

THE FIRST THEATRE
Capacity: 986

Opened 10 October 1881 with a transfer of *Patience; or, Bunthorne's Bride*, an 'aesthetic opera' by W. S. Gilbert and Arthur Sullivan. Under the management of Richard D'Oyly Carte.

THE SECOND THEATRE
Capacity: 1122

Opened 21 October 1929 with a revival of *The Gondoliers* by W. S. Gilbert and Arthur Sullivan. Under the management of Rupert D'Oyly Carte.

THE BUILDING
The story of the Savoy Theatre is bound up with the fortunes of Gilbert, Sullivan and D'Oyly Carte. The partnership had had its foundation at the Royalty Theatre in Dean Street, Soho, where D'Oyly Carte was the business manager and Gilbert and Sullivan collaborated in the one-act dramatic cantata *Trial by Jury*. (They had written *Thespis; or, the Gods Grown Old* together for the Gaiety Theatre in 1871 with little success.) It was D'Oyly Carte who suggested further partnership, and the result was the formation of the Comedy Opera Company to present the work of Gilbert and Sullivan.

The first opera was *The Sorcerer*, produced at the Opera Comique in 1877, followed by *H.M.S. Pinafore* (1878), *The Pirates of Penzance* (1880) and *Patience* (1881).

During the run of *H.M.S. Pinafore* Carte had become sole lessee and manager of the theatre, and when his lease was nearing its end, he decided, instead of seeking renewal, to build his own theatre, especially suited to the requirements of the new school of comic opera.

After some difficulty he found a suitable site, a rough sloping patch of ground situated close by the Thames Embankment, within the precincts of the ancient Savoy Palace and adjacent to the Chapel Royal. The approach from the Strand was down the precipitous Beaufort Street, where Rimmel, the famous perfumers, had their works. He purchased the freehold, plans for the theatre were drawn up by C. J. Phipps, and it was built by Messrs Patman and Fotherinham in a few months. The main frontage was placed at the embankment end of the plot and the side stretched up Beaufort Street. Later, after the Savoy Hotel was built, the entrance to the theatre was made in its courtyard off the Strand. This was done, when extensive redecoration and repairs were carried out under the direction of A. Bloomfield Jackson in 1903. Later the entrance was given a 'face lift' to bring it into line with a reconstruction of the Savoy Hotel.

D'Oyly Carte in his inaugural statement dated 6 October 1881, said:

I think I may claim to have carried out some important improvements deserving special notice. The most important of these are in the lighting and decoration. From the time, now some years since, that the first electric lights in lamps were exhibited outside the Paris Opera House, I have been convinced that electric light in some form is the light of the future for use in theatres, not to go further. The peculiar steely blue colour and the flicker which are inevitable in all systems of 'arc' lights, however, make them unsuitable for use in any but very large

buildings. The invention of the 'incandescent lamp' has
now paved the way for application of electricity to lighting houses, and consequently theatres . . . This is in fact
the first time that it has been attempted to light any public
building entirely by electricity. What is being done is an
experiment, and may succeed or fail. It is not possible,
until the application of the accumulator or secondary
battery—the reserve store of electric power—becomes
practicable, to guarantee absolutely against any break-
down of the electric light. To provide against such a
contingency, gas is laid on through the building, and the
'pilot' light of the central sunburner will always be kept
alight, so that in case of accident the theatre can be
flooded with gas light in a few seconds. The greatest
drawback to the enjoyment of the theatrical performances are, undoubtedly, the foul air and heat which
pervade all theatres. As everyone knows, each gas burner
consumes as much oxygen as many people, and causes
heat besides. The incandescent lamps consume no
oxygen, and cause no perceptible heat. If the experiment
of electric lighting succeeds, there can be no question of
the enormous advantages to be gained in purity of air
and coolness—advantages the value of which it is hardly
possible to over estimate. . . . I venture to think that,
with some few exceptions, the interiors of most theatres
hitherto built have been conceived with little, if any,
artistic purpose, and generally executed with little com-
pleteness, and in a more or less garish manner. Without
adopting either the styles known as 'Queen Anne' and
'Early English', or entering upon the so-called aesthetic
manner, a result has now been produced which I feel sure
will be appreciated by all persons of taste. Paintings of
cherubim, muses, angels, and mythological deities have
been discarded, and the ornament consists entirely of
delicate plaster modelling designed in the manner of the
Italian Renaissance. The main colour tones are white,
pale yellow and gold—gold used only for backgrounds
or large masses and not following what may be called,
for want of a better or worse name, the Gingerbread
School of Decorative Art—for gilding relief work or
mouldings. . . . The stalls are covered with blue plush of
an inky hue and the balcony seats are of stamped velvet
of the same tint, while the curtains of the boxes are of
yellowish silk, brocaded with a pattern of decorative
flowers in broken colours.

Only the auditorium was lit by electricity on the opening
night; it reached the stage on 28 December.
  Another innovation was the inauguration of the queueing
system for pit and gallery. Until then, it had been everyone
for himself in a general rush and crush, but from this time,

the method of first come, first served began, gradually
spreading to other theatres.

The theatre, a three-tier auditorium, was completely
rebuilt in 1929, the old interior being swept away, leaving
only its main walls, and a new two-tier theatre was designed
by Frank A. Tugwell, with interior decorations by Basil
Ionides. The work was carried out by the Pitcher Construction Company.

Once again the main entrance was transferred to the
embankment, but soon they re-used that in Savoy Court,
which was refaced with stainless steel, to conform with
another renovation of the Savoy Hotel.

The reconstruction started directly after the performance
of *Journey's End* on 3 June 1929 (the play transferred to
the Prince of Wales'), and the theatre was ready for reopening on October 21.

Christopher Hussey writing in *Country Life*, 16 November 1929, says:

> The new Savoy Theatre is the first really outstanding
> example of modern decoration applied to a public place
> on a commercial basis. . . . Every part bears evidence of
> imagination. . . . It is the colouring and lighting that next
> strikes the eye. The general effect is one of glowing sun-
> shine. Only gold and silver leaf are employed on the
> walls, and all the lighting is indirect; through the coffers
> of the proscenium lintel, in great flutes or gadroons on
> the ceiling beneath the gallery, and in the base of the
> gallery parapets. In this way the auditorium is suffused
> with a golden light, which the autumnal colours of the
> seats and curtain warm into a glow. The lighting is so
> arranged that it picks out in vivid gilding the clean lines
> of the decoration, thus livening up the otherwise prevail-
> ing flat treatment. The walls are lined with broad vertical
> flutes which, in fact, are ventilating shafts.

The metal grilles have a Japanese motif, followed out in
the decoration of the proscenium walls.

THE PLAYS

The first theatre opened on 10 October 1881 with
Patience, transferred from the Opera Comique where it
had been first produced on 23 April 1881. A more brilliant
audience than that which attended has seldom been seen
in any theatre other than Covent Garden, royalty heading
the list of those present. The Savoy was maintained as a
permanent home for the Gilbert and Sullivan Operas, which
were produced as follows: *Iolanthe* (25 November 1882),
Princess Ida (5 January 1884), *The Sorcerer* in a slightly
revised version, and *Trial by Jury* (1 October 1884), *The
Mikado* (14 March 1885), *Ruddigore* (22 January 1887), *The*

Yeoman of the Guard (3 October 1888), *The Gondoliers* (7 December 1889), *Utopia Ltd* (7 October 1893).

During the interval between *The Gondoliers* and *Utopia Ltd*, the period covering the estrangement between Gilbert and Sullivan, various pieces were produced, and after *Utopia Ltd* there were a number of productions which were comparatively unsuccessful. These include *Haddon Hall* by Sydney Grundy and Arthur Sullivan (1892), *Jane Annie* by J. M. Barrie and Conan Doyle, with music by Ernest Ford (1893), *The Chieftain* by F. C. Burnand and Sullivan (1894).

On 7 March 1896 *The Grand Duke* by Gilbert and Sullivan was produced but was a failure. It was the last work of the famous collaborators. Gilbert's last opera *Fallen Fairies* with music by Edward German was produced here in 1909.

From 1897 beside revivals of previous 'G. and S.' successes, the Savoy tradition was maintained with, among others, *The Beauty Stone* by Pinero, Comyns Carr and Sullivan (1898), *The Rose of Persia* by Basil Hood and Sullivan (1899), *The Emerald Isle* by Basil Hood with music by Sullivan and completed after his death by Edward German (1901), *Merrie England* by Basil Hood and Edward German (1901), and *The Princess of Kensington* by the same collaborators (1903). This brought the comic opera régime to a close.

William Greet, who had been lessee since 1902, handed over to J. H. Leigh, with Vedrenne as his manager. Among other noteworthy occasions was the Mrs Browne-Potter season in 1904–5. Lena Ashwell was here in *The Shulamite* in 1906 after a season in 1907 by the D'Oyly Carte Company of Gilbert and Sullivan revivals, J. E. Vedrenne and Granville Barker transferred their very successful partnership here from the Court Theatre. Shaw's *The Devil's Disciple* and *Caesar and Cleopatra* were among the plays staged, and there were some notable Shakespearean productions by Granville Barker between 1912 and 1914. These included *The Winter's Tale* (1912) with Henry Ainley as Leontes, Dennis Neilson-Terry as Florizel, Lillah McCarthy as Hermione, Cathleen Nesbitt as Perdita and Esmé Beringer as Paulina; *Twelfth Night* (1912) with Henry Ainley and Lillah McCarthy, and *A Midsummer Night's Dream* (1914) with Nigel Playfair as Bottom, Dennis Neilson-Terry as Oberon, Donald Calthrop as Puck, Laura Cowie as Hermia, and Lillah McCarthy as Helena. In 1911 the original production of *Where the Rainbow Ends* took place at this theatre.

In 1910 H. B. Irving became lessee, a position he kept until he died in 1919, and then his executors held the theatre until 1929. During these years he often appeared here as an actor-manager and was seen in *The Sin of David*

(1914), *Searchlights* and *The Case of Lady Camber* (1915),
The Barton Mystery (1916), and *Hamlet* (1917).

Successes were also scored by *Nothing But the Truth*
(which ran for 578 performances from 1918), *Paddy the
Next Best Thing* (867 performances from 1920), *The Young
Idea* by Coward (1923), *The Sport of Kings* (1924), *The
Unfair Sex* (1925), *Young Woodley* by Van Druten (1928),
and *Journey's End* by R. C. Sherriff (594 performances in
1929). Robert Courtneidge was in management between
1920 and 1929.

In 1929 the theatre was entirely reconstructed and given
the form which we know today. The new theatre opened on
21 October 1929 with a revival of *The Gondoliers*. There had
not been a D'Oyly Carte season since 1909 at this theatre.
The first lessees of the new theatre were Killick and
Payne-Jennings.

The Gilbert and Sullivan revivals of 1929–30 and 1932–3
were very popular. Other successful productions were
Wonder Bar (1930), *Jolly Roger* and *Please!* a Charlot
revue (1933), *The Aunt of England* (1935). There were
also seasons of *The Camargo Ballet* in 1932 and *The Ballet
Jooss* in 1933, but during the last part of the thirties
the theatre mainly housed transfers of successes from
other theatres. After the outbreak of war in 1939 the
outstanding productions were a Cochran revue *Lights
Up!* in 1941 and *The Man Who Came to Dinner*, which
ran for 709 performances from December 1941; this
was presented by Firth Shephard, who remained at the
theatre until his death in 1949. This was followed by *My
Sister Eileen* (1943), and a revival of *The Last of
Mrs Cheyney*, with Jack Buchanan and Coral Browne
(1944).

Later successes were *Life with Father* (1947) and *A La
Carte*, an Alan Melville revue (1948). Stanley French continued the Firth Shephard Company until 1951 presenting
The Human Touch and *Young Wives' Tale* (1949), among
other plays. D'Oyly Carte returned for a season in 1951
and again in 1954, followed by *The Spider's Web* by Agatha
Christie (1954), *Subway in the Sky* (1957), *Free as Air*
(1957), *A Day in the Life of . . .* (1958), *The Ring of Truth*
(1959), *The Gazebo* (1960–1) and *Sweet Bird of Time* (June–
November).

A season by the D'Oyly Carte Company, during which
the copyright on the Operas expired, was held from
November 1961 until April 1962. Noël Coward's *Sail Away*
commenced its run in June and continued for a successful
run of 252 performances until January 1963. After a short
run of *Trap for a Lonely Man*, *The Masters* was produced
in September 1963. It eventually transferred to the Piccadilly and the D'Oyly Carte Opera Company returned for
a Christmas season. 1964 was an unsuccessful year for the

theatre. A revival of Pinero's *The School-mistress* ran
for only 85 performances, then in November Noël Coward's
Blithe Spirit was presented as a musical, *High Spirits*, but
ran only until the end of January 1965. Later the same year
saw a revival of Maugham's *The Circle* for a limited season.
The Savoy's next big success was *Alibi for a Judge*, opening
in August 1965 and running on for 704 performances.
According to the Evidence was presented in September
1967 and continued for 259 performances. The next hit,
under Peter Gale's management, *The Secretary Bird*,
started its long run in October 1968 and continued well into
its fourth year, closing in June 1972. The following month
came another success, *Lloyd George Knew my Father*,
later to transfer to the St Martin's. In October 1973 *At the
End of the Day* was presented and ran till March 1974,
when it was followed by *A Ghost On Tiptoe* with Robert
Morley.

The theatre is at present owned by a company of which
Bridget D'Oyly Carte is the family representative.

The story of the Savoy Theatre in its early years is told
in *Gilbert, Sullivan and D'Oyly Carte* by François Cellier
and Cunningham Bridgeman (1927), and the many other
books on the partnership.

34 · The Shaftesbury Theatre

(The Princes Theatre)

Shaftesbury Avenue, W.C.2
Capacity: 1250

Opened as the Princes Theatre 26 December 1911 with a transfer from the Lyceum Theatre of *The Three Musketeers*, a version of the Dumas novel by Arthur Shirley and Ben Landeck. Produced by and under the management of Walter and Frederick Melville.

THE BUILDING

The last new theatre to open in Shaftesbury Avenue was built on land which had been covered by a maze of derelict property, at the New Oxford Street end of the Avenue where it crosses the junction of St Giles's High Street and Broad Street (now High Holborn). The theatre was situated on the corner of Shaftesbury Avenue and High Holborn and backed by Grape Street. It was designed by Bertie Crewe for Walter and Frederick Melville, who called their

company Popular Playhouses, Ltd. It was to be the home
for melodrama with prices from sixpence to five shillings
and run on lines similar to those which the Melvilles were
then successfully pursuing at the Lyceum.

The Era of 23 December 1911 says:

> The new house has three frontages, which enable the
> house to be cleared in a few minutes. Externally an
> example of Modern Renaissance, internally the house is
> eclectical French in its decorations. Above the main
> entrance, at the corner, rises an elegant tower. The
> interior decoration is in cream and gold, with side panels
> in autumnal tints, and groups of statuary over the boxes.
> The saucer-domed ceiling is ornamented with symbolic
> groups representing 'The Light of the World,' 'En-
> deavour,' 'Love,' 'The Crowning Success,' and 'The
> Torch of Destiny,' and four life-size groups which sur-
> mount the boxes are emblematic of Comedy, Tragedy,
> Poetry, and Music. The ten boxes are parted by Ionic
> columns, with figured drums fluted and enriched; and
> bas-relief groups adorn the proscenium arch. The
> crimson velvet of the upholstery goes well with the rose
> and white marbles, the alabaster, and the gold mosaic
> of the walls.
>
> The New Princes is a two-tier theatre, and each tier has
> its own saloon adorned with oak panelling, wrought iron
> fittings and tapestries. The Stalls saloon is Elizabethan,
> the circle saloon Jacobean. A central ring of electric
> lights is suspended from the ceiling of the auditorium,
> supplemented by four large wrought brass chandeliers.
> The arrangements for heating and ventilating by the
> 'Plenum' system of forced air will ensure a gradual
> change of atmosphere six times an hour.
>
> 'Heat Waves' are met by the provision of a sliding roof.

For the first three years of its life the theatre was
officially known as the New Princes Theatre. In recent
years the gallery was divided into two parts, the front rows
having been reseated as an upper circle.

THE PLAYS

The theatre opened on 26 December 1911 with *The Three
Musketeers*, transferred from the Lyceum. Under the
management of the Brothers Melville many popular melodramas were presented, including *The Apple of Eden*
(1912), a revival of *Women and Wine* (1912), *The Story of
the Rosary*, Walter Howard's romantic drama (December
1913), *On His Majesty's Service* (December 1914), and
When London Sleeps (1915). *For England, Home, and
Beauty*, another melodrama (1915) ran for one hundred
performances.

In December 1916 Seymour Hicks assumed management,

opening with a revival of *Bluebell in Fairyland* and then reviving *The Catch of the Season* (February 1917). This he followed with other old favourites.

In April 1919 came *Monsieur Beaucaire*, presented by Gilbert Miller, described as 'a romantic opera' with André Messager's music. In this production the part of Lady Mary Carlisle was played by Maggie Teyte, the well-known opera singer. It ran for 221 performances. The Princes was gradually increasing its scope and changing from the original policy of 'Lyceum melodrama.' Cochran became lessee in 1919.

From September 1919 to the end of January 1920 there was a season of Gilbert and Sullivan revivals during which all but three of the operas were performed.

From February 1920 *Pretty Peggy*, a musical play by Arthur Rose and Charles Austin, with music by A. Emmett Adams, ran for 168 performances. In April 1921 Sarah Bernhardt appeared as Daniel, the title-role of Louis Verneuil's play, and Diaghileff's Russian Ballet had a season. October 1921 brought another season of D'Oyly Carte's Gilbert and Sullivan operas which lasted until April 1922 and subsequent successes were the Guitrys in a season of plays, a musical play called *The Cousin from Nowhere* by Fred Thompson, with music by Edward Kunneke (1923), *The Return of Sherlock Holmes*, founded on the stories of Arthur Conan Doyle by J. E. Harold Terry and Arthur Rose, in which Eille Norwood played the great detective (1923), *Alf's Button* by W. A. Darlington (1924), and *Frasquita*, a musical play by Lehár, produced by Oscar Asche, with José Collins (1925). There were very successful seasons of Gilbert and Sullivan Opera revivals in 1924 and 1926. Sybil Thorndike appeared in *Macbeth* with Henry Ainley (1926) and in *The Greater Love* (1927), and Diaghileff also brought his ballet here again in 1927.

In December 1927 George Robey entered into management for a time, presenting his revue *Bits and Pieces*. In December 1928 an explosion of gas-main pipes caused an upheaval in several main thoroughfares in the West End of London and the Princes Theatre was compelled to close its doors for several weeks owing to 'the impassability of the roadway to vehicular traffic.' This interrupted the run of *Funny Face* which had been produced in the November. Sydney Howard made a great success in this Gershwin musical comedy which ran for 263 performances, with the Astaires and Leslie Henson.

The year 1929 brought W. H. Berry in *A Warm Corner*, with a run of 238 performances, while his success of 1930 was *Oh, Daddy!* a farce adapted from the German by Austin Melford, which ran for 195 performances. These introduced Firth Shephard to this theatre, he was to remain here in management on and off until 1946. The next few years were mainly occupied with short runs and revivals. In 1933 Charles Macdona revived *Diplomacy* with an all-star cast, and in 1934 *Merrie England* and *The Rose of Persia* were again seen.

The years 1936–37 saw the production of two of Ian Hay's adaptations of Edgar Wallace stories, *The Frog* (1936) and *The Gusher* (1937): these ran for 483 and 137 performances respectively. In 1938 Bert Hammond became lessee on the death of the Melvilles. Subsequent successes were *Wild Oats* (260 performances from April 1938), and *Sitting Pretty* (1939). Wartime productions included *Shepherd's Pie* (December 1939), *Fun and Games* (August 1941), in which Carol Raye made a considerable impression at the age of eighteen; *Wild Rose* (August 1942), which was a revised version of *Sally*; *Old Chelsea* (February 1943), *Halfway to Heaven* (December 1943), and seasons of ballet and opera by the Sadler's Wells Companies in 1944.

In 1945 Evelyn Laye appeared in Oscar Strauss' operetta *Three Waltzes* and in 1946 *Merrie England* was again staged in a revised version. Later the same year came a revue *The Shephard Show*, with Arthur Riscoe, Richard Hearne, Douglas Byng and Marie Burke. In 1947 the Princes came under the direction of Bertram Montague though the new productions were not so successful as the ballet seasons from many parts of the world and the annual pantomimes.

The next play to achieve a long run was *His Excellency*, with Eric Portman, which began in May 1950. Other short runs in between ballet seasons kept the theatre fairly busy until the end of Montague's management in 1952. After this the theatre was more often closed than open, though occasional seasons had their success. These included Maurice Chevalier (1952), *Antony and Cleopatra* from Stratford-upon-Avon, with Michael Redgrave and Peggy Ashcroft in 1953. Two American musicals, *Pal Joey* (1954) and *Wonderful Town* (1955) had good runs, as also did *Summer Song*, from an English stable, in 1955. The D'Oyly Carte Company returned to their old home in 1942, 1956, 1958 and 1960, but apart from this, little success attended the Princes. It remained in the Melville family until 1961; after Bert Hammond retired in 1957 the theatre was directed by Andrew Melville.

The first change of ownership was announced in June 1961 when Jack Hylton, who had been a lessee from November 1951, bought the theatre and adjoining property. The following August the freehold was acquired by Television Wales and the West. In October the freehold was again sold, this time to Charles Clore, but not until September 1962 was it confirmed that a new partnership between Clore and E.M.I. (Electrical and Musical Industries) was to control the theatre. It was also announced that the theatre would be completely and drastically redecorated and reconditioned as well, a new stage and lighting equipment being installed.

For two years the old theatre was only spasmodically active with *King Kong*, the South African musical (February–October 1961) and several uneventful productions until *Gentlemen Prefer Blondes* opened in August 1962. This moved to the Strand when the theatre closed for reconstruction on 3 November 1962.

The theatre was renamed the Shaftesbury (see No. 5) and reopened in March 1963 with the American musical success *How to Succeed in Business Without Really Trying*, which ran for 520 performances. A musical version of J. M. Barrie's *The Admirable Crichton*, called *Our Man Crichton*, played from December 1964 till June 1965. After this the theatre was dark until for only 43 performances the ill-fated *Twang!* was seen between December and January 1966. Again the theatre was closed until October when success returned with *Big Bad Mouse* with 635 performances to April 1968. *Hair* followed in September, the day after censorship ended, and ran till its ill-timed end when part of the theatre ceiling collapsed, on 19 July 1973, just as it was about to celebrate its 2000th performance. Meantime the freehold had changed hands several times and in March 1973 the threat of redevelopment as an office block loomed, and after the forced closure a campaign, similar to that which raged around the St James's, was mounted. Eventually, in March 1974, the theatre was placed on the Statutory list of buildings of Special Architectural or Historic Interest, by the Department of the Environment.

35 · The Strand Theatre

(The Waldorf Theatre, The Whitney Theatre)

Aldwych, W.C.2

Capacity: 1082

Opened 22 May 1905 with *Il Maestro di Capella*, an opera by Ferdinand Paer, followed by *I Pagliacci* by Leoncavallo, in a season of opera alternating with dramatic performances given by Eleanora Duse and her company. Under the management of Henry Russell.

THE BUILDING

The Waldorf, at the corner of Catherine Street and the newly created Aldwych, was the first theatre to be opened in the block of buildings planned to include the Waldorf Hotel in the centre and the Aldwych Theatre at the Drury Lane corner (see No. 3).

The Waldorf, at the corner of Catherine Street and the wych by nine months, was designed by W. G. R. Sprague, architect of both theatres. They were given identical exteriors.

The theatre was erected by a group of businessmen calling themselves The Waldorf Theatre Syndicate, Ltd, and leased for twenty-one years to the American impresarios, the Shubert brothers. In effect this was only Lee Shubert owing to the untimely death of his brother Sam in a railway accident early in May 1905.

The building operations were carried out by S. and J. Waring. It was the last three-tier theatre to be built in London, the L.C.C. having then decided against this form of building in the future.

The Era of 20 May 1905 says:

The decorative scheme of the interior is in the Louis XIV style. The walls of the crush room and main staircase are adorned with alternate stripes of dove coloured and violet marble, and the balustrade of the staircase is a wrought iron copy of one of Baron's famous designs. On the first tier level is the refreshment saloon, decorated in cream and gold. In the auditorium the colour scheme is Rose du Barri, relieved by richly gilt circle fronts, and by a touch of green in the French tapestries upholstering the stalls and dress circle; a qualifying note being struck in the brown French walnut of the seat frames. One of the notable features is a magnificent circular ceiling in modelled plaster with finely gilt centre piece and outer border, and a boldly treated picture sweeping round the two, painted after the style of Le Brun. The bas relievo modelling of the tympanum which surmounts the proscenium represents Apollo in his chariot drawn by four spirited horses, and attended by goddesses and cupids. The action is full of vigour, combined with delicacy of touch. A deep cornice in Louis XIV style runs round the theatre, and over the proscenium opening and boxes. The proscenium opening and the dress and upper circle are supported by pilasters of Fleur de pêche marble with gilt capitals; and between the smaller pilasters on the dress circle and stalls level lofty mirrors reach to the cornice. The prevailing tone of Rose du Barri is continued in a deep velvet pile carpet of the same colour.

The name of the theatre remained the Waldorf until 1909 when it became the Strand. Its name was again changed in 1911 to the Whitney, but returned permanently to the Strand in 1913. A previous theatre, the Royal Strand, had existed until 1906 in the Strand itself where Aldwych tube station is now situated, and the Sans Pareil from 1814 to 1819 (when it became the Adelphi) intermittently called itself the Strand Theatre.

In 1930 the theatre was redecorated and partially reconstructed at which time the boxes round the back of the dress circle were entirely removed. But for this, and a further redecoration in more recent years, the theatre remains much as it was when built.

This was the only theatre in London where a solicitous management placed a warning painted on a wall in letters nearly a foot high facing the occupants of the gallery admonishing them to 'Beware of Pickpockets,' possibly because it still remained unreserved until 1962. It was closed for a time until it became a re-seated balcony in December 1963.

Ivor Novello occupied the flat over the theatre for many years.

THE PLAYS

The theatre opened as the Waldorf on 22 May 1905 with a season of opera alternating with plays given by Eleanora Duse and her company. It had originally been intended to present *Cavalleria Rusticana* and *I Pagliacci* on the opening night, but at the last moment Calvé, who was to sing Santuzza, was unable to appear and *Il Maestro di Capella* was substituted. The first dramatic performance in the theatre took place the next night, when Duse appeared in an Italian version of Pinero's *The Second Mrs Tanqueray*. During the first year the theatre housed Beerbohm Tree and his company from His Majesty's in *Oliver Twist*, while repairs were carried out to a sudden defect in the proscenium arch of Tree's theatre, and in October H. B. Irving appeared in a play, from the German, *Lights Out*.

After the destruction of the Avenue Theatre in 1905 (see Part IV, No. 7) and until it was reopened in 1907 as the Playhouse, Cyril Maude made his headquarters at the Waldorf, from January 1906 presenting *The Superior Miss Pellender*, revivals of *She Stoops to Conquer*, *The Heir at Law*, and *The Second in Command*, and *Shore Acres*, a new play by James Herne.

After Cyril Maude left the next event of importance was the visit of E. H. Sothern and Julia Marlowe, who brought their company from the States and presented during their season *The Sunken Bell*, *Jeanne d'Arc*, *Twelfth Night*, *As You Like It*, *Hamlet*, *Romeo and Juliet*, and *When Knighthood was in Flower*. This season was succeeded by several uneventful productions and in October 1909 the theatre was taken over by J. A. Harrison, who changed the name to the Strand Theatre, reopening on October 23 with *The Merry Peasant*, an operetta by Leo Fall. This was not a success. Several lessees came and went in the next two years until May 1911, when the theatre again changed its name to the Whitney Theatre, having been purchased by the American manager F. C. Whitney, whose

first production was a comic opera, *Baron Trenck*. He
followed this with *The Spring Maid*, neither of which were
great successes, and after several other failures the theatre
returned to its former title of the Strand under the direction
of Louis Meyer with *The Son and Heir*, a play by Gladys
Unger on 1 February 1913. The theatre had its first solid
success with Matheson Lang, who appeared first in *The
Barrier* and then in *Mr Wu*, which ran for 403 performances
from November 1913. The war years saw a number of
transfers and revivals, and in 1915 Fred Terry and Julia
Neilson had the theatre for a twelve months' season,
presenting *Mistress Wilful*, *The Argyle Case*, and revivals
of *Sweet Nell of Old Drury*, *Henry of Navarre* and *The
Scarlet Pimpernel*. During the run of the latter the theatre
was damaged by German bombs in an air raid, but the play
continued to be performed until the end of the season.

After the death of Louis Meyer, the theatre was acquired
in 1916 by José Levy. During 1917 *Under Cover*, a play by
Roi Cooper-Megrue, ran for 195 performances and a
dramatisation of Elinor Glyn's popular novel, *Three Weeks*,
by Roy Horniman, ran for 122. *The Hidden Hand* by
Laurence Cowen had a successful run in 1918 and in this
year also Grossmith and Laurillard presented *Scandal* by
Cosmo Hamilton, beginning in December.

From November 1919 to 1923 Arthur Bourchier was in
control, and during this period many outstanding productions appeared. His tenure began with George Broadhurst's
melodrama *The Crimson Alibi* (125 performances) and
continued with A. E. Thomas's *Come out of the Kitchen*
(111 performances from March 1920), A. E. W. Mason's *At
the Villa Rose* (227 performances from July 1920), Ian Hay's
A Safety Match (229 performances from January 1921),
The Love Match (1922) and *Treasure Island*, a dramatisation of R. L. Stevenson's story, at Christmas 1922. He
revived this here each Christmas until 1926. Other managers then presented plays, though Bourchier remained
proprietor until his death in 1927. Eugene O'Neill's
Anna Christie was produced at the Strand in 1923 and
ran for 103 performances with Pauline Lord in the title
role.

Monsieur Beaucaire had a revival in February 1924 and
was followed by *Stop Flirting*, the musical comedy originally produced at the Shaftesbury which was transferred
here in March 1924. A play called *Broadway* by Philip
Dunning and George Abbot produced in December 1926
ran for 252 performances.

From 1927 to 1929 George Grossmith was in charge of
the theatre, the control of which had passed to Kyrle Bellew,
Bourchier's second wife. During the next few years the
record is not particularly distinguished as far as production is concerned. Fred Terry and Julia Neilson were here

for a season from December 1928 and several successes from other theatres transferred. A well-remembered chapter of the theatre's history lasted from 1930 to 1934 when Leslie Henson and Firth Shephard were co-lessees. This partnership is interesting since it was at this theatre that Henson made his first appearance on the West End stage in *Nicely Thanks* (1912). The Henson-Shephard partnership began with *It's a Boy*, a farce by Austin Melford, in October 1930. This ran for 366 performances and was followed by *Counsel's Opinion* (1931), *It's a Girl, Party*, and *Night of the Garter* (1932). Later came the farces with music, *Nice Goings On* (1933) and *Lucky Break* (1934).

In 1935 José Levy again became the proprietor of the theatre (he died the following year) and *1066 and All That*, 'a comic history with music', by Reginald Arkell, from the book by Sellar and Yeatman with music by Alfred Reynolds was produced in April 1935 running for 387 performances. May 1936 brought Vernon Sylvaine's *Aren't Men Beasts!* 283 performances with Alfred Drayton and Robertson Hare.

In 1937 there was a revival of Edgar Wallace's *The Squeaker*, followed by Elmer Rice's *Judgment Day*, which ran for 116 performances, and another of Vernon Sylvaine's successes, *A Spot of Bother*, scored 178 performances, from July 1937, then came Ben Travers' *Banana Ridge*, April 1938, with Hare and Drayton. This team also appeared in another farce by Ben Travers, *Spotted Dick*, just before the outbreak of war, and they resumed their association with this theatre in Vernon Sylvaine's farce, *Aren't Women Angels!* in 1940. During the blitz Donald Wolfit kept the theatre open with 'lunch-time' Shakespeare and in March 1942 there was a production of Offenbach's *Tales of Hoffman*. On December 23 of the same year began the run of *Arsenic and Old Lace*, which lasted for 1337 performances. During this the theatre passed from the hands of the executors of José Levy into those of the Send Manor Trust, with Lionel Falk as director, who had been connected with this theatre since 1936. After the run of *Arsenic and Old Lace* it was some time before the theatre once again had an established success, though *Cage Me a Peacock* (1948) had a pleasant run and in 1949 came *Queen Elizabeth Slept Here*, which ran well into 1950. Then came *Will any Gentleman?* (1950) and several transfers including *And So to Bed* (1951), and *The River Line* (1952). In November 1954 *Simon and Laura* by Alan Melville was seen and in the following February 1955 *Sailor, Beware!* began its long run of 1082 performances which lasted into 1958. After several disappointing runs came the revue *For Adults Only*, which was a huge success. The theatre after this was unlucky, though *Rollo* (October 1959) and

The More the Merrier (February 1960) had good runs. This was followed by a transfer of Ionesco's *Rhinoceros* with Laurence Olivier from the Royal Court. In August a strange mixture of 'Ballet and Song,' *The Princess*, was produced, receiving a disastrous press, upon which the management threw open the theatre without payment for a week in a vain attempt to save the day—then a unique event in theatrical history. From October, *Settled Out of Court* occupied the stage until *Belle* opened in May 1961. The Oxford Playhouse production of *Hamlet*, with Jeremy Brett, then came to London for a few weeks. *Goodnight Mrs Puffin* opened in July but quickly moved over the road to the Duchess to make way for *The Affair* which ran for a year. *The New Men* in September 1962 was a disappointment and gave way to a transfer of *Gentlemen Prefer Blondes* in November which ran till March 1963.

A Funny Thing Happened on the Way to the Forum, from October 1964 until July 1965, was the next long run, a total of 761 performances. Then came a revival of Shaw's *Too True to be Good*, which transferred to the Garrick in October, and late in that same year a revival of Oscar Wilde's *An Ideal Husband*, with Margaret Lockwood, ran until it too transferred, to the Piccadilly. The Wilde revival was succeeded in July 1966 by a thriller, *Wait Until Dark*, which later moved to the Duchess to make room at the Strand for a revival of Bernard Shaw's *Getting Married*, from April to August 1967. Two short runs followed and then in November came *Number 10* with Michael Denison and Dulcie Gray, which ran for 110 performances. The next big success was to be a farce, *Not Now Darling*, which opened in June 1968 and was followed by several short runs and a transfer until a revival of J. B. Priestley's *When We Are Married* arrived in November 1970, running until *No Sex Please—We're British* opened in June 1971. This is now in its fourth successful year, a record for this theatre.

36 · The Vaudeville Theatre

Strand, W.C.2

THE FIRST THEATRE
Capacity: 1000

Opened 16 April 1870 with *For Love or Money*, a comedy by Andrew Halliday, followed by a burlesque, *Don Carlos; or, the Infante in Arms!* by Conway Edwardes, and preceded by an Address by Shirley Brooks spoken by H. J. Montague. Produced by Thomas Thorne under the management of H. J. Montague, David James and Thomas Thorne.

THE SECOND RECONSTRUCTED THEATRE
Capacity: 740

Opened 13 January 1891 with *Woodbarrow Farm*, a comedy by Jerome K. Jerome. Preceded by *The Note of Hand*, a one-act play by Herbert Keith under the management of Thomas Thorne.

THE THIRD RECONSTRUCTED THEATRE
Capacity: 659

Opened 23 February 1926 with *R.S.V.P.*, a revue by Archie de Bear. Under the management of J. M. and R. Gatti.

THE BUILDING
Wybrow Robertson (the husband of Marie Litton) acquired premises in the Strand on which he built a theatre designed by C. J. Phipps.

The Era of 17 April 1870 tells us:

> This elegant little theatre has been erected upon the site occupied by Nos. 403 and 404 Strand, and the premises of the defunct Bentinck Club in the rear. It extends nearly as far as Maiden Lane in the north and to Lumley Court towards the east. . . . The principal entrance is in the Strand, by a spacious hall leading to the stairs, on the level with the Strand; and by a staircase, 6 feet wide, to the balcony and boxes. The pit is approached by a separate corridor 5 feet wide level with the Strand. The gallery entrance is in Lumley Court approached both from the Strand and Maiden Lane. The plan of the auditory is strikingly original as well as elegant, it consists of a balcony, the front forming a semicircle, opening out by curves of a contrary flexure to the proscenium columns. Behind this at a higher level is the dress circle tier, the front of the upper circle being on the same vertical line as the division between the balcony and the dress circle. Behind the upper circle is a spacious gallery. The front of the upper circle is carried round over the proscenium opening, from which springs a groined ceiling joining the main ceiling over the auditory at its diameter line. There are, on either side between the balcony and the stage openings on the grand tier, three private boxes, divided by pillars having enriched capitals, and surmounted by semicircular arches, each containing a figure-subject. Below these again, on the pit level, are two more private boxes on either side. . . . There are six rows of armchairs in the stalls, a commodious pit, three rows of armchairs in the balcony, four rows of seats in dress circle, two more private boxes behind same, two rows of upper circle and spacious gallery. . . . The colour decoration has been executed by Mr George Gordon. They are principally on the flat, there being no raised ornament on the ceiling or box fronts, except the upper and lower mouldings. The general character is Romanesque. The ceiling is divided into compartments with white ornaments on a blue ground. The panels in the cove over the proscenium are of varied design and colours on a grey ground. The front of the balcony tier is the most elaborate, being ornamented in rich colour on a gold ground; this

front is slightly out of the perpendicular, so that the whole
light from the sun-burner pouring on the gold ground pro-
duces a most rich effect. The lunettes in arches over the
private boxes have been painted by Mr W. Phillips and
represent on either side subjects from the Fairy portion of
A Misdummer Night's Dream, and *The Tempest*. The
hangings for the boxes are the richest hue of golden-
coloured figured satin, the effect of which is enhanced by
the warm crimson and gold colour with which the walls
are lined.

The new system of lighting caused comment, as a later
historian says:

Strode's sun-burners radiated their brilliance from the
centre of the ceiling; the footlights, contrary to the
practice then obtaining, were entirely out of sight of the
audience, and turning downward, the product of the com-
bustion was taken away in a large iron cylinder running
parallel with the front of the stage and carried off through
the main wall. One advantage gained by this invention
was the removal of the unpleasant vapour screen, which,
in the old manner, was constantly rising between the
audience and the scene. The performers were thus enabled to approach the footlights without risks, and a piece
of gauze could be placed over without ignition.

The frontage of the existing buildings in the Strand seems
to have been retained and an entrance to the theatre made
through the ground floor of one of them, alterations being
made only at street level.

The first managers, on a twenty-one-year lease, were
David James, H. J. Montague, and Thomas Thorne, and
the theatre was opened on the same night as the New
Chelsea Theatre (later to become the first Royal Court:
see No. 30).

In 1891 when Thorne, the last of the original management
to remain, renewed his lease, the theatre was reconstructed
under the supervision of the original architect. *The Era* of
10 January 1891 reports:

The frontage, which was not rebuilt when the theatre
was constructed in 1870, comprised Nos. 403 and 404,
Strand. These two houses have now been pulled down,
and a handsome façade in Portland stone erected; this
is of four storeys in height.

The ground storey has a centre archway leading into the
vestibule, with two side doorways respectively leading to
the pit, and also the vestibule. The doorways to the
vestibule are recessed, so as to leave a porch, 6 foot
wide, closed to the thoroughfare by the patent Bostock
iron gates, which neither swing, nor fold, but slide away
to nothing behind the piers, causing no obstruction. The

vestibule is in the same position as formerly, but now forms a handsome entrance hall, some 20 feet square. The pit entrance is at the eastern side, in the position formerly occupied by a flower shop.

On the first storey a loggia, 6 foot wide, is formed under an arcade of five arches. Opening on to this, through five French casement windows, is the grand foyer or saloon, 26 feet by 20 feet, with elaborate ceiling, fireplace and fittings. Here will be found a buffet for refreshments, while the loggia will form a pleasant lounge for smoking in the summer. The walls of the staircase are decorated with an elaborately designed Japanese leather paper in gold and red. The vestibule and foyer have similar hangings on the walls, while the floors are of marble, and the ceiling of ornamental plaster of geometric design.

The auditorium, as regards its seating capacity, is unaltered, but the private boxes and side corridors on the stalls level have been removed. New stall seats covered in peacock-blue plush have been erected and placed sufficiently far apart to admit of easy passing between the rows. A more striking change in the auditorium, which has entirely changed the character of the theatre, has been the removal of small rooms on either side of the amphitheatre, and the cove over the proscenium. A new ceiling with groins springing from the outer walls, gives a wonderful idea of enlarged space, and the space above the proscenium opening has been crowned by a pediment. The scheme of colour adopted in the auditorium has been French white and grey with gold, the seating peacock blue, the carpets and hangings to the private boxes of rose colour, and the walls of a greenish grey. The favourite little theatre thus becomes to all intents a new one, replete with every convenience.

The 'new frontage' is the one that remains to this day. In 1892 Thorne sold his lease to the Brothers Gatti, Agostino and Stephano, who beside their restaurant and theatre interests were also proprietors and developers of an electric generating station off Maiden Lane. The throb of the new electrical monster had caused trouble between Thorne and the Gattis and was heading towards litigation, which was averted by their purchase of the theatre.

This building remained except for redecoration (notably in 1902) until 1925, when its interior was gutted. It closed on November 7 and reopened the following February 23. The architect Robert Atkinson and the builders Bovis, Ltd, worked in a remarkably short space of time. The roof was raised, part of the basement lowered, the proscenium enlarged, new stairways were built, and the stage and

auditorium completely reconstructed. The new auditorium
was made oblong instead of horseshoe-shaped as before.
A new back elevation and stage door was made in Maiden
Lane, but the 1899 façade in the Strand remained unaltered.
This is the theatre as we know it today; except it has had
several redecorations, most recently after the long run of
Salad Days ended in March 1960, before the opening of
Follow that Girl, and when the theatre was taken over by
Peter Saunders in 1969, Peter Rice gave the theatre a
completely 'new look' during and between runs.

THE PLAYS

The opening took place on 16 April 1870 under a trium-
virate management, consisting of H. J. Montague, David
James and Thomas Thorne. On this occasion Montague
spoke an address, written by Shirley Brooks, followed by
a double bill consisting of *For Love or Money* and *Don
Carlos; or, the Infante in Arms!*, a burlesque. An early
success was scored by *The Two Roses* in June 1870. This
was a comedy by James Albery, and was the play in which
Henry Irving first rose to fame as Digby Grant. It had
a long run for those days, 294 performances, and was
revived at the same theatre in 1874 and 1879.

Montague seceded from the management in 1871 and
James and Thorne continued in partnership until 1882 when
James dropped out and Thorne became the sole lessee.

In January 1872 a revival of *London Assurance* ran for
165 performances with John Clayton and Amy Fawcett,
and in July of the same year a revival of *The School for
Scandal* (Henry Neville as Charles, John Clayton as Joseph,
William Fawcett as Sir Peter, and Amy Fawcett as Lady
Teazle) scored 404 performances, the record run for this
play, and in December of the same year Robert Reece's
'Classical Burlesque,' *Romulus and Remus*, ran for 169
performances. Another outstanding run was that achieved
in November 1873 by a revival of *The Road to Ruin* by
Thomas Holcroft. Incidentally this play was again revived
at the Vaudeville in December 1879, July 1882 and July
1886.

All previous successes in the annals of stage history were
left far behind by the record run of *Our Boys*, a comedy by
H. J. Byron, which ran for 1362 performances from 16
January 1875 until 18 April 1879. It was immediately
succeeded 'without the intermission of a single night' by a
new comedy from the same author called *Our Girls*, but
this was not so successful, only running 131 performances.

In June 1880 Robert Reece, under the pseudonym of
S. G. Lankester, obtained a run of 164 performances with
his farcical comedy *The Guv'nor* (also revived here in
January 1893); George R. Sims' *The Half-Way House* ran
for 106 performances from October 1881, and two successes

of 1882 were the revivals of *Money* (152 performances from June) and *The Rivals* (227 performances from December). From May 1883 Joseph Derrick's comedy *Confusion* ran for 457 performances.

In 1884 came *Saints and Sinners* by Henry Arthur Jones; this was an early attempt at a 'problem play' and was responsible for some animated controversy, because a section of the audience, on the first night, resented its use of biblical quotations. However, it ran for 182 performances. There followed a series of 'pleasingly romantic and mildly humorous plays' between 1884 and 1889. These included *Loose Tiles* (1885), a farcical comedy by J. P. Hurst, which ran for 126 performances, and *Sophia* (1886), a comedy by Robert Buchanan from Fielding's *Tom Jones*, which ran for 100 performances.

Cyril Maude was engaged to play here in 1888 in *Joseph's Sweetheart*, a comedy by Robert Buchanan based on the novel *Joseph Andrews*. He followed this appearance (the play ran for 261 performances) with further parts in *That Doctor Cupid* by the same author (147 performances from January 1889), *Angelina* (1889), *The Old Home* (1889), a revival of *The School for Scandal* in which he played Joseph Surface to Winifred Emery's Lady Teazle (1890), *Clarissa* (1890) adapted by Robert Buchanan from the novel *Clarissa Harlowe*, and *Miss Tomboy*, also by Robert Buchanan and founded on *The Relapse* (1890). The theatre then closed for reconstruction. The reopening on 13 January 1891 was with *Woodbarrow Farm*, a comedy by Jerome K. Jerome, still under the management of Thorne. In 1891 Ibsen's *Rosmersholm* and *Hedda Gabler* were given their first performances in England, the former in February and the latter in April, with Elizabeth Robins playing Hedda; they were performed at matinées.

In 1892 the management of the theatre was taken over by the brothers Gatti who revived *Our Boys*, which was again a success and ran for 137 performances. In 1895 *The Strange Adventures of Miss Brown* ran for 255 performances with Weedon Grossmith, who also became manager. Great success was achieved by *A Night Out*, a farce by Charles Klein from the French of Feydeau, which ran for 531 performances in 1896. In October 1897 *Never Again* (118 performances) and in October 1898 *On and Off* (226 performances) were successful productions.

From September 1900 Seymour Hicks and Ellaline Terriss appeared in a series of long runs, under Charles Frohman and the Gattis. The first play was *Self and Lady* by Seymour Hicks and this was followed by a revival of the musical version of *Alice in Wonderland* (by H. Saville Clarke with music by Walter Slaughter), in which Hicks played the part of the Mad Hatter. In 1901 came Basil Hood's *Sweet and Twenty* (235 performances from April),

J. C. Buckstone's *Scrooge*, in which Hicks made a great success of the name part, and *Bluebell in Fairyland*, a musical dream play by Seymour Hicks with music by Walter Slaughter, which ran from December for 294 performances. In September 1902 J. M. Barrie's *Quality Street* was first produced, with Hicks as Valentine Brown and Ellaline Terriss as Phoebe Throssel; this play ran for 459 performances and had the honour of a command performance at Windsor Castle. In 1903 came *The Cherry Girl*, a musical play which Hicks wrote and for which Ivan Caryll supplied the music; it ran for 215 performances from December and was succeeded in September 1904 by *The Catch of the Season*, which proved an immense hit; it was written by Hicks and Cosmo Hamilton with music by H. E. Baines and Evelyn Baker, and ran for 621 performances. *The Belle of Mayfair*, April 1906, came next by C. H. Brookfield and Cosmo Hamilton with music by Leslie Stuart; it ran for 416 performances. Hicks then left for the new Aldwych Theatre.

The next chapter of the theatre's history is connected with Charles Hawtrey, who appeared here in a series of comedies which included Louis N. Parker's *Mr George* (April 1907), Charles Brookfield's *Dear old Charley* (January 1908), and Somerset Maugham's *Jack Straw* (March 1908), which ran for 321 performances. Between 1909 and 1915 outstanding productions included James Forbes' play *The Chorus Lady* (102 performances from April 1909), F. Anstey's farce *The Brass Bottle* (244 performances from September 1909), *The Girl in the Train*, a musical play by Leo Fall (340 performances from June 1910), *Little Miss Llewellyn*, a comedy by Sydney Blow and Douglas Hoare (192 performances from August 1912), and H. V. Esmond's *The Dangerous Age* (May 1914).

In August 1915 Willard Mack's drama *Kick In* ran for 128 performances and then another definite chapter opened in the history of the Vaudeville. It became the home of a long series of revues presented by André Charlot. Charlot, who had a great deal of experience in connection with various Paris theatres and music-halls, had been managing director of the Alhambra and made a speciality of revue production. He began his association with the Vaudeville by transferring from the Playhouse the revue *Samples* in September 1915. This finished a run of 242 performances and was followed by *Some* (273 performances in 1916), *Cheep* (483 performances in 1917–18), *Tabs* (268 performances) and *Buzz-Buzz* (1918), the latter scoring a then record revue run of 612 performances. *Just Fancy* (333 performances in 1920–21), *Puss! Puss!* and *Now and Then* (1921), *Pot Luck* (1921) with 284 performances, *Snap* (230 performances in 1922), *Hats* (258 performances in 1923) and *Yes* (1923). Authors and composers connected with these productions included Harry Grattan, Ronald Jeans, Arthur Wimperis, John Hastings Turner, Dion Titheradge, Douglas Furber, J. W. Tate, Ivor Novello, Herman Darewski, Philip Braham and Kenneth Duffield. In January 1924 a revue called *Puppets* by Dion Titheradge with music by Ivor Novello began a run of 255 performances and in July of the same year this was followed by another revue *The Odd Spot* by Dion Titheradge and Peter Santon with 106 performances. After this some plays followed and *The Punch Bowl*, an Archie de Bear revue, transferred from the Duke of York's.

The last performance took place on 7 November 1925 and then the theatre was again reconstructed. The reopening took place on 23 February 1926 with Archie de Bear's revue *R.S.V.P.*, which contained a ballet and incidental music by Norman O'Neill. This ran for 297 performances and subsequent successes included *Vaudeville Vanities* (November 1926), *Blue Skies* (June 1927), *Lord Babs* (1928), *Charlot's 1928 Revue*, Somerset Maugham's *The Breadwinner* (158 performances from September 1930), *After Dark*, a revue by Ronald Jeans (1933), *Charlot's Char-a-bang! Stop-Go*, and *The Sleeping Beauty or What a Witch!* (1935), *Stars and Stripes*, *Red, Bright and Blue*, and *Charlot's Non-Stop Revue* (1937).

In 1937 the theatre was redecorated, but a success could not be found. In March 1938 Walter Hackett entered on a short lease, producing *Toss of a Coin*. From October 1938 Robert Morley's *Goodness, How Sad!* had a run of 229 performances. After the outbreak of the war the first success was in March 1940 when a revue called *Moonshine* was presented by Archie de Bear. In October Robert Atkins had a season of Shakespeare, and in December 1940 Jean Forbes-Robertson assumed the management for a revival of *Berkeley Square*. Subsequent successes during the war years were Mary Hayley Bell's *Men in Shadow* (1942), Enid Bagnold's *Lottie Dundass*, Mabel and Denis Constanduros' *Acacia Avenue* (1943), and Esther McCracken's *No Medals*, which ran for 742 performances from October 1944.

After the war important productions were *Now Barabbas . . .* (1947), *The Chiltern Hundreds*, which ran for 651 performances from April 1947, *Bonaventure* (1949), *Ardèle* and *Women of Twilight* (1951), and *Murder Mistaken* (1952). On 5 August 1954 *Salad Days* began the run which was eventually to break the record for a musical production previously held by *Chu Chin Chow*. At the end of its run in March 1960 it had achieved 2329 performances. After a very short closure for redecoration, another Julian Slade and Dorothy Reynolds musical, *Follow that Girl*, was presented on 17 March, but failed to rival its predecessor. The next two plays came and went all too quickly, but in

November success returned with Ronald Millar's comedy *The Bride Comes Back*, which ran until July 1961.

The new Slade-Reynolds musical, *Wildest Dreams*, which followed had only a short run and then *Teresa of Avila* was produced for a season. In December *Critic's Choice* was produced and it ran till May 1962. *Chips with Everything* transferred from the Royal Court in June and ran until February 1963.

The next few years did not provide any successful new plays. There were seasons by dance companies and several revivals for limited seasons. It was not until May 1965 that any entertainment ran over 84 performances, then *Portrait of a Queen* with Dorothy Tutin as Victoria ran from May 1965 until January 1966 with 274 performances. A revival of *Arsenic and Old Lace*, with Sybil Thorndike and Athene Seyler, ran for 300 performances during the year. Several more short runs, revivals and transfers followed in 1967 until the next success arrived in July 1968, *The Man Most Likely To*—it was to continue its run till the summer of 1970.

The theatre was bought by Peter Saunders from the Gatti family in April 1969 and a scheme, by Peter Rice, for its redecoration, both before and behind the curtain, commenced and was carried out over the next two years.

In June 1970 *Lady Frederick*, a revival of W. Somerset Maugham's play, held the stage with Margaret Lockwood in the lead and was later to transfer to the Duke of York's to make room, in September, for Alastair Sim in *The Jockey Club Stakes*. This later also moved over to the Duke of York's, in March 1971, to make room for *Move Over Mrs Markham*, an apt title, and after a long run, to February 1973, came *A Private Matter*, with Alastair Sim and a male frontal nude. This continued for several months until *Signs of the Times* was produced in June. The next show, in December, was a revue, *Cockie*, based on the life and work of Charles B. Cochran, which ran until February 1974 and early in the next month *Snap*, a V.D. comedy, with Maggie Smith, was produced.

37 · The Victoria Palace

(Moy's Music-Hall, The Royal Standard Music-Hall,
Victoria Palace Theatre)

Victoria Street, S.W.1

Capacity: 1565

Opened 6 November 1911 as a music-hall with a variety entertainment which included Lizzie Glenroy, Betty Barclay, Herbert Sleath and company in a one-act play *The Deputy Sheriff.*

THE BUILDING

In 1911 at the height of the rush to build new music-halls, Alfred Butt acquired the Royal Standard Music-Hall, Pimlico, which he demolished, and on its site erected the Victoria Palace.

219

In the days before the coming of Victoria Station, there was at Pimlico in Stockdale Terrace a tavern called the Royal Standard built in 1832. Here were held 'Select Harmonic Meetings' two or three times a week. By 1840 the proprietor John Moy, who had been there for some years, had obtained a licence for both singing and dancing and following the pattern which was evolving in other similar places he enlarged his premises and gradually regular music-hall bills took the place of the sing-songs. The 'Room' became known as Moy's Music-Hall and from 1854, the Royal Standard Concert Rooms.

In 1863 his successor, Robert Alfred Brown, reconditioned the hall, which was partly over the public house and partly over stables and a mews, and he reopened it on December 26, as the Royal Standard Music-Hall. It became a 'popular resort where the stage jutted into a room on the first floor and the performers were able to exchange pleasantries with the audience who sat around at little tables'.

The arrival of Victoria Station and later the construction of Victoria Street considerably altered this locality and eventually the Standard was rebuilt in 1886 by its then owner Richard Wake.

An advertisement in *The Era Almanack* of 1891 announced that it was:

> . . . Entirely Re-built Enlarged, and Re-decorated, being at the present time the most comfortable Hall of entertainment in London. No expense has been spared both on the Stage and in the Auditorium, to study the comfort of the Public. The lighting of the Hall by electricity has now been completed, and by the brilliance of light and coolness throughout, testifying to its complete success. The Refreshment department has always been the careful study of the Proprietor. There is a large and Handsome Grill Room, open from 12 a.m. to 12 p.m.; Billiard Room, with two tables by Burroughes Watts; large Public Bars on the ground floor; and the continued and increased popularity of this Establishment sufficiently attests the estimation in which it is held.

Its last owner, Thomas S. Dickie, still a licensed victualler, who took over in 1896, sold his interest to Alfred Butt in 1910, and what had become the oldest premises to hold a music-hall licence in London was demolished.

The new building, to be called the Victoria Palace, almost on the corner of Allington Street, in which it has its stage door, was designed by Frank Matcham and built by Henry Lovatt, Ltd. Its white exterior of classical design embellished with statues, originally had a figure of Pavlova poised on the tower. This figure of gilded metal copied from a statuette by Mrs Langworth was Butt's act of homage to the dancer he had introduced to London with such success at the Palace in 1910. This tribute was not appreciated by the superstitious ballerina, who would never look at her image as she passed by on her many travels from Victoria Station. It is said that the car blinds were always drawn at this part of the journey. The statue was taken down for safety during the blitz and has since completely disappeared.

The Era of 4 November 1901 describes the interior of the new house:

> In the scheme of internal treatment the main object has been to combine a maximum of comfort and convenience with a prevailing note of simplicity. The handsome entrance hall through which the visitor passes to the stalls, dress circle, and boxes has walls of grey marble with embellishments of old gold mosaic and pillars of white Sicilian marble. Left and right from this vestibule there are cloakrooms and an elegant boudoir devoted to the comfort of the ladies.
>
> From the vestibule to the stalls, dress circle, and boxes it is but a very few steps and this ease of accessibility will be appreciated by all who, having entered the house, desire to reach their places in as little time as possible. For the further convenience of visitors to the tea room, dress circle and box levels there has been installed a lift, a feature which, doubtless, will be greatly appreciated. An elaborate heating system has been installed, which enables an even temperature to be kept throughout the winter, and in the summer the magnificent sliding roofs of the auditorium and main vestibule permit the house to be kept delightfully cool.

The theatre cost £12,000 to build.

THE PLAYS

The Victoria Palace opened on 6 November 1911 with a variety bill, and under Alfred Butt all the famous music-hall names of the period took the stage. In 1920 Butt was joined by R. H. Gillespie in management. A fairy play called The Windmill Man, by Frederick Bowyer, with Bert Coote as the mad gardener made its annual home here at Christmas each year from December 1921 to December 1929 and again in December 1931.

The Victoria Palace managed to avoid the craze for revue until Gracie Fields appeared in Archie Pitt's The Show's the Thing in 1929. After this Butt left the theatre in the hands of Gillespie and a series of revues followed including The Chelsea Follies (1930), and The Hour Glass (1931). Gillespie was joined by Charles

Gulliver in 1932. He was replaced by George Black later
the same year, but he only remained here for a short
period and variety returned. In 1933 *Daddy Long-Legs*,
with Renée Kelly, had a Christmas season, but difficult
times had hit the variety theatres, and in time the Victoria
Palace joined the ranks of the regular theatres, calling
itself the Victoria Palace Theatre in September 1934
with the production of *Young England*. This play was
written by Walter Reynolds, proprietor of the Theatre
Royal, Leeds, in all seriousness, as a full-blooded patriotic
melodrama, but it was unrestrainedly guyed by audiences
and rapidly became a cult. A squad of 'chuckers-out' was
instituted by the management to deal with over-
obstreperous members of the audience. A quarter of a
million people saw the play which was transferred to
the Kingsway Theatre and then to Daly's, the total
run lasting six months. One playgoer boasted of 150
visits and three others claimed to have spent £150 on seats.

In May 1935 another chapter in the history of this
theatre was opened under the management of Seymour
Hicks, who presented *The Miracle Man*. This was followed
by revivals of *Vintage Wine* (1935) and *The Man in Dress
Clothes* (1936). After this repertory was tried for a season.

During 1936 and 1937 a series of revues was presented
here by Kurt Robitschek. The first of these, *Let's Raise
the Curtain*, was described as an 'all-in-one show' and
featured Florence Desmond, Elizabeth Welch and
George Gee. This was succeeded by *Laughter over
London*, with George Robey and Billy Bennett, and
Wonderful World, 'a coronation revue' with Florence
Desmond (May 1937).

On 16 December 1937 was the first night of the remarkable run of *Me and My Girl*, a musical comedy by L.
Arthur Rose and Douglas Furber, with music by Noel
Gay. At the outbreak of war in 1939 this play had scored
1046 performances. It was revived here in 1944 and had
another long run. Wartime productions included George
Black's *Black Vanities*, *La-Di-Da-Di-Da*, with music
by Noel Gay, *The Love Racket* by Stanley Lupino
(1943), afterwards transferred to the Princes, and *Meet
Me Victoria* (1944).

In February 1945 the Victoria Palace renewed its connection with Variety for a season. From 1937 the
theatre had reverted to its original name of the Victoria
Palace, and on 17 April 1947 the Crazy Gang took
possession of the theatre with enormous success and
Together Again was presented by Jack Hylton for 1566
performances. Then, for some years, apart from some
rather unsuccessful excursions into other fields, the
Gang was the mainstay of the theatre with *Knights of
Madness* (1950), *Ring out the Bells* (1952), *Jokers Wild*

(1954), *These Foolish Kings* (1956) and *Crown Jewels* (1959). After a revival of *Rose Marie* (August 1960), the Crazy Gang returned for what was announced to be their farewell show, *Young in Heart*, in December. The last night of the Crazy Gang was on 19 May 1962; *The Black and White Minstrels* immediately followed and did not finish their run until 1970, after giving 4344 performances— a unique achievement. It was followed by *The Magic of the Minstrels* in November 1970 which did not have such a magnificent run and was succeeded by *The Max Bygraves Show* in November 1972. In October 1973 the 'Carry on' film series came to the stage with Barbara Windsor in *Carry On London*.

Since 1948, the theatre has been under the direction of Moss Empires, Ltd.

38 · The Westminster Theatre

Palace Street, Buckingham Palace Road, S.W.1

Capacity: 603

Opened 7 October 1931 with *The Anatomist*, a play by James Bridie. Produced by Tyrone Guthrie, under the management of Anmer Hall.

THE BUILDING

On the corner of what is now Palace Street and Palace Place, stood a church, a chapel of ease to St Peter's, Eaton Square. It had been built in the 1830s, but eventually outlived its original purpose, fell into disrepair and was sold. A new frontage was added to the old chapel walls, the interior was partially reconstructed and redecorated. It opened in 1924 as a cinema, called the St James' Picture Theatre. In 1931 the cinema was taken over by Anmer Hall and once again alterations were made, the old chapel crypt was transformed into dressing-rooms, a green-room, and a stalls bar. Some changes were also made in the exterior. A contemporary notice says:

> The interior scheme of decoration gives an effect of daintiness and brightness pleasing to the eye and restful to the senses—this effect is mostly achieved by the pink, blue, cream shaded to pink, colourings. Miss Molly MacArthur, who is responsible for this, has shown much brilliance and artistry in her choice of furnishings scheme of decoration. In her employment of pink panellings and elephant grey carpets, she has succeeded in no uncertain manner in making this theatre into a lovely and intimate place.
>
> The whole of the reconstruction was from the designs of Arnold Dunbar Smith . . . The exterior is carried out in a pale grey brickwork. Its simplicity is very pleasing. The vestibule of the house follows the line of the exterior tower and is decorated the same restful grey.

There is only one circle and there are boxes placed behind this, as well as two stage boxes. The colour scheme and the name chosen for the theatre were from Anmer Hall's old school, Westminster. His real name was A. B. Horne. Anmer Hall was his ancestral home in Norfolk.

The date of the opening of the theatre, October 7, was the evening before the curtain was to rise at another theatre, the Saville (see Part IV No. 9).

THE PLAYS

The theatre opened on 7 October 1931 with a production of James Bridie's *The Anatomist*, a play dealing with the famous 'resurrectionists' of the nineteenth century which was remarkable for Henry Ainley's playing of the title role. Anmer Hall's policy was to present distinguished plays at popular prices and he controlled the destiny of the theatre for about seven years, presenting plays by Ibsen, Shaw, Granville Barker, Eugene O'Neill, T. S. Eliot and other outstanding dramatists. Amongst his successful presentations were *The Unquiet Spirit* by Jean Jacques Bernard, and *A Pair of Spectacles* (1931), *Six Characters in Search of an Author* by Pirandello, *Tobias and the Angel* by Bridie, *Love's Labours Lost* and *The Kingdom of God* by Sierra (1932), *Waste* by Granville Barker (1936), *Anna Christie* and *Mourning Becomes Electra* by O'Neill and *Heartbreak House* by Shaw (1937), and *The Zeal of Thy House* by Dorothy Sayers (1938).

In 1934 a repertory company under J. Baxter Somerville took a lease of the theatre. The Dublin Gate Theatre

appeared here in 1935, 1936 and 1937 and the Group Theatre
in 1935. Anmer Hall ceased production at the Westminster
in 1938 and later in the same year the London Mask
Theatre appeared here under the direction of J. B. Priestley,
Ronald Jeans and Thane Parker, with Michael Macowan
as producer. Outstanding productions of this régime were
Marco Millions, Eliot's *The Family Reunion*, and
Priestley's own play *Music at Night*, the first play to be
produced in London after the outbreak of war in 1939.
They ceased operations at the Westminster in 1940.

Later wartime productions included Afinogenov's
Distant Point, *Little Women* (1941), Lajos Biro's *School
for Slavery* (1942), a Shakespearean season with Robert
Atkins, a season by Donald Wolfit including *The Imaginary
Invalid*, and *The Master Builder* (1943). James Bridie's
Mr Bolfry, later transferred to the Playhouse, started here
in 1943.

In the same year the theatre came under the direction of
Robert Donat and he began his own management with a
successful revival of Wilde's *An Ideal Husband*. In a note
printed in the programme the policy of the new theatre was
thus set forth: 'We do not aspire to reform the theatre,
nor do we seek to save it. We merely hope to fill it,
with good plays and good audiences. We believe in the
commercial theatre, we have to. A theatre that cannot pay
its way cannot survive.'

An Ideal Husband, having broken all records for the
Westminster Theatre with 266 performances, was followed
by a new play by James Bridie, *It Depends What You Mean*,
which in turn was followed by *The Cure for Love* by Walter
Greenwood (1945). Then came the return of Cedric Hardwicke to the London stage after seven years in Hollywood
in a revival of *Yellow Sands*, in the same year. Donat then
left the theatre actively and various managements were
in charge for the next few years; among the plays seen was
Message for Margaret (1946). Later the same year the
theatre was bought by the Oxford Group (a Moral Re-
armament Movement) and for some time was off the professional map. It returned to the fold under Kenneth Lindsay in 1948 with a revival of *The Anatomist*. In 1949 a new
era opened for the theatre with Alec Rea and E. P. Clift
in management. Their first success was *Black Chiffon* by
Lesley Storm. This ran for 409 performances from May
1949, but their other productions were not so successful.

In 1952 the Mask Theatre returned and their biggest
success was *Nightmare Abbey*. Later the same year James
Sherwood presented *Dial M for Murder*, which ran for 425
performances. The Mask Theatre's production of *Carring-
ton V.C.* from July 1953 scored 205 performances. In 1954
Ralph Birch became lessee and a revival of *The Duenna*
with music by Julian Slade ran 134 performances. *Dead*

on Nine (1955), *Night of the Fourth* (1956), and *Dear Delinquent* (1957) all had good runs. In 1958 Ralph Birch retired from the management, and the most noteworthy production of the year was *Any Other Business*, which ran for 178 performances. After this there are no big commercial successes to record.

The Moral Re-armament movement took active control in 1960 and began its own policy of films and plays with 'a message'. This pattern continued over the next few years and a Christmas play for children, *Give A Dog A Bone*, which first appeared in 1964, was to become a regular Christmas attraction. After its 1965/6 season, the theatre was closed for renovations and rebuilding to include 'The Peter Howard Memorial Building'.

The alterations comprised an extension over the old courtyard behind the theatre, creating a new entrance and foyer, dressing rooms, restaurant, etc., designed by John and Sylvia Reid. A full description of this work is told in *The History of the Westminster Theatre* by K. D. Beldon, published in 1965.

The theatre reopened on 8 December 1966 with its usual Christmas attraction. In February 1968 they had a success with a new musical, *Annie*, which ran for 243 performances. In November 1969 the theatre returned to commercial management for a revival of *The Old Ladies*, by Rodney Ackland, adapted from the novel by Hugh Walpole, with Joyce Carey, Flora Robson and Joan Miller. This production transferred to the Duchess Theatre in December to make room once more for Moral Re-armament and *Give A Dog A Bone*. Another return to commercialism was made with Noël Coward's *Relative Values*, which was revived with Margaret Lockwood in September 1973 but closed in December when came 'The 10th Gala Season' of *Give A Dog A Bone*, to be followed by Gershwin's *Oh, Kay!*, with Amanda Barrie, in March 1974, under the management of Henry Sherwood.

39 · The Whitehall Theatre

Whitehall, S.W.1

Capacity: 628

Opened 29 September 1930 with a transfer from the Duke of York's Theatre of *The Way to Treat a Woman*, a play by Walter Hackett. Produced by the author and Thomas Reynolds, under the management of Walter Hackett.

THE BUILDING

In Whitehall just below the point where it enters Trafalgar Square stood Ye Old Ship Tavern, established in 1650. This was demolished and the business removed to the opposite side of Whitehall. On the vacant site stretching back to Spring Gardens was built the Whitehall Theatre.

The promoters were Whitehall Theatre, Ltd, and Walter Hackett was the original licensee. The building was designed by Edward A. Stone and the interior decorations were by Marc-Henri and Laverdet. *The Times* of 29 September 1930 said:

At any rate there can be no doubt from the first glance at its tower-like façade with tall windows, the Whitehall Theatre prepares you for something brisk and up to date. What it suggests is the atmosphere of combined comfort and altertness, not without a certain heartlessness, which becomes the modern comedy.

And Professor C. H. Riley in the *Architect's Journal*, 14 January 1931, says:

The Whitehall Theatre . . . so clean and simple in its line that it makes the new Government offices, Banks, and Public Houses of that great thoroughfare look as if they need a shave.

Another contemporary calls it:

A dream in black and silver . . . the ceiling to the auditorium of which is designed to represent a silver cloud, and has the effect of being suspended in mid-air. The front of the circle is silver with floral designs in pastel shades. All the seats have a perfect line of sight. Great columns of modern design sweep on to the recessed stage and are flooded with silver light from a concealed source. The vestibule is executed in satinwood, with the main staircase in ebony. The circle bar is cast in the form of a saloon on a liner—a delicate compliment to the Old Ship Inn. . . . Hitherto black has been entirely avoided as it was always thought to be too sombre, but here it has been so skilfully used that, when blended with silver and green it presents one of the gayest schemes of decoration to be seen anywhere. Very skilfully, too, this scheme manages to use the dresses of the ladies in the audience to enhance, not only its own beauty, but to throw up the splashes of colour provided by them. The lighting used throughout has been specially designed to please lady patrons. There are no hard tones anywhere, the very mirrors being rose-tinted.

This was the third new theatre to be opened in the month of September 1930 (see No. 6).

THE PLAYS

The theatre opened on 29 September 1930 with a transfer of *The Way to Treat a Woman*, by Walter Hackett, originally produced at the Duke of York's on 11 June 1930. It completed its run here of 263 performances. This was succeeded by another of Hackett's comedies *Good Losers*, in the writing of which he had the collaboration of Michael Arlen and which ran for 134 performances from February 1931. Subsequent successes were scored with *Take a Chance* and *The Gay Adventurer*, both by Hackett and both in 1931, the latter running for 290 performances; *Road House* (340 performances in 1932), and *Afterwards* (208 performances in 1933). All these four plays were written by Hackett, but in 1934 he left the theatre.

Viceroy Sarah, a play by Norman Ginsbury, was produced here in February 1935 and ran for 158 performances. This play was originally produced at the Arts Theatre in May 1934, and later in the same year came St John Ervine's great success, *Anthony and Anna*, which ran for 789 performances through 1936 to 1937; it had originally been produced in 1926 at the Liverpool Playhouse. In December 1937 *I Killed the Count*, a play by Alec Coppel, began a run of 184 performances. July 1938 brought *Lot's Wife* by Peter Blackmore, which ran for 236 performances and in March 1939 there was a revival of Shaw's *The Doctor's Dilemma*.

After the outbreak of war the policy of 'modern comedy' fell by the wayside and varied fare was provided. In 1942 the theatre came under the direction of Alfred Esdaile and light entertainment was the order of the day, with a revue *Whitehall Follies* and Phyllis Dixey 'Non-Stop'. In October 1943 the theatre came under the direction of Bernard Delfont and Rodney Ackland's *The Dark River* was staged and later in the same year there was a dramatisation of John Steinbeck's *The Moon is Down*. There were then more non-stop revues featuring Phyllis Dixey, who took over the theatre herself in May 1944. She remained in control of the theatre until 1947, when it passed to H. J. Barlow during the run of *Worm's Eye View*. This play by R. F. Delderfield was first produced at this theatre on 18 December 1945 and ran for 500 performances. Its career was interrupted, and after a short tour, it returned on 5 May 1947 for another 1745 performances. After some uneventful productions *Reluctant Heroes* was produced in September 1950. It was presented by Brian Rix. His successful management of the theatre included the presentation of *Dry Rot* (1954), *Simple Spymen* (1958), *One for the Pot* (1961) and *Chase Me Comrade* (1964). In May 1966 Danny La Rue appeared in *Come Spy With Me*, a highly successful run of 468 performances. Brian Rix had another big success, *Uproar in the House*, in October 1967 which ran until March 1969. In January 1971, as sitting tenant, Paul Raymond bought the remaining 60 year lease from Mrs Felice Cooper (whose husband became licensee in 1944). His production, *Pyjama Tops*, opened in September 1969, and continued into 1974.

40 · The Windmill Theatre

Great Windmill Street, W.1

Capacity as theatre: 322

Opened 22 June 1931 with *Inquest!* a play by Michael Barrington. Produced by Campbell Gullan. Under the management of the Windmill Theatre Company, Ltd.

THE BUILDING

This part of London has a rural history. A windmill stood here from the reign of Charles II until late in the eighteenth century. This gave its name to the footpath leading to the mill from Piccadilly at the top of the Hay-Market over Windmill Fields. From here could be seen the towers of Westminster and its palace. Great Windmill

Street now runs from Coventry Street (Piccadilly Circus) up to Brewer Street, crossing Shaftesbury Avenue. In 1910 a cinema, the Palais de Luxe, was opened at the corner of a block of buildings which included the Apollo and Lyric Theatres (see Nos. 5 and 21) at the point where Archer Street joins Great Windmill Street just off Shaftesbury Avenue. This cinema was one of the first of the little West End homes of the early films. With the rise of the large super-cinema, it descended the scale and its programmes consisted of foreign films and classics. The property came into the possession of Mrs Laura Henderson who, in association with Bernard Isaac and J. F. Watts Phillips (The Windmill Theatre Co, Ltd), converted it into a theatre. The general manager was Vivian Van Damm. The architect, Howard Jones, remodelled the exterior in the style of a traditional windmill and the interior was entirely reconstructed to become a one-tier theatre of miniature size.

THE PLAYS

The theatre opened on 22 June 1931 with a new play by Michael Barrington called *Inquest!*, with Mary Glynne, Hilda Trevelyan and Herbert Lomas in the cast. This was only a mild success and once again films were shown which included *The Blue Angel* and *Sous les Toits de Paris*. In December 1931 it was announced that a policy of non-stop variety would be tried. Mrs Henderson gave her manager Vivian Van Damm *carte blanche* to try and help the variety profession which had been hit by the coming of the 'talkies'.

On 3 February 1932 this innovation began and *Revudeville* was introduced, a programme of continuous non-stop variety of a nature then new to London. The idea originated in Paris and proved most popular, drawing crowded audiences. The performances ran from 2.30 p.m. until 11 p.m.

During the first years the project lost £20,000, but the tide turned and the theatre became an established part of the London scene.

The Windmill was the only theatre in London which never closed, except for the twelve compulsory days between 4 and 16 September 1939, throughout the blitz, the performers often sleeping night after night in the theatre during the worst of the attacks from the air.

The death of Mrs Henderson in 1944 was a great loss to the Windmill, but it was announced that the policy of the theatre was to remain unchanged under the direction of Van Damm. After his death in December 1960 the theatre was carried on by his daughter Sheila, who had become his partner. Many famous comedians of today made their first impact here and a roll of honour was fixed to the exterior of the theatre. The full history of the venture has been told in *To-Night and Every Night* by Vivian Van Damm (1954). The last edition of *Revudeville* was seen in 1964.

In October the theatre was sold to the Compton Cinema Group and it closed on 31 October 1964 and was reconstructed as a cinema and casino. In 1973 a campaign was started to revive 'The Old Windmill Days' and re-claim the theatre. Eventually, in February 1974, the theatre was bought by Paul Raymond, from Laurie Marsh, who transferred a 114 year lease to him. Raymond announced his intention of making it a home for nude shows 'a la *Revudeville* but without the comic element'.

41 · Wyndham's Theatre

Charing Cross Road, W.C.2

Capacity: 760

Opened 16 November 1899 with a revival of *David Garrick*,
a play by T. W. Robertson. Produced by and under the
management of Charles Wyndham.

THE BUILDING

Towards the end of the century Charles Wyndham, who
had been at the Criterion since 1875, decided to build his
own theatre. Mary Moore, in her privately printed
reminiscences, tells us that in 1897 Joseph Pyke began
to negotiate for a site between Charing Cross Road and
St Martin's Lane which was part of the Salisbury Estate.
He was told that the then Marquess would not permit a
theatre to be built on his land, or if he did it would only be
for Wyndham, for whose acting he had great admiration.
Pyke therefore approached Wyndham with a view to an
association. If Wyndham were to secure the site and clear
it at a cost of £10,000 he, Pyke, would advance the money
for the building charging six per cent on his outlay and
hold a mortgage on the cleared site as security. Unfortunately Wyndham, at that period, could not put up the

234

money. Mary Moore, his leading lady and later his wife, found ten friends who acted as guarantors to her bank for £1000 each for one year, on which she was to pay the interest. When the building was completed, an increased mortgage on the theatre was to repay the bank. The site acquired stretched from Charing Cross Road to St Martin's Lane with St Martin's Court on both sides at the Charing Cross Road end, and crossing it midway.

The theatre was built on the Charing Cross Road end of the plot, so that it was isolated on all sides. The remainder of the ground was later in 1903, to be occupied by the New Theatre (see No. 2).

The theatre was designed by W. G. R. Sprague, its exterior in a classical style.

The Era of 18 November 1899 says:

The house is not very large, being built on a site of only 7000 square feet. The reserved portion includes twelve private boxes, 157 stalls, 160 dress circle and 180 family circle seats. The pit is small, but particularly good, and the gallery is large and admirably planned. The theatre being isolated, the exits from the various parts of the house are many and direct. In addition to the staircases, which to the dress circle and balcony are of white marble, there is a lift which runs to each floor and to the roof, where, if the L.C.C. will permit, Mr Wyndham proposes to have a Winter Garden. The stage, in common with that of the Criterion Theatre, is flat, but it is some 6 ft wider and 10 ft deeper. The scheme of decoration is that of the Louis XVI period, and the colours used are turquoise blue and cream, relieved by judicious gilding. The proscenium is set in cream and gold bordering, which is continued along the front of the stage, thus hiding the footlights, and forming a complete frame. At the top are allegorical figures, and portraits of Sheridan and Goldsmith. The ceiling of the auditorium contains paintings after Boucher, which are illuminated by a ring of concealed electric lights and a central sunlight covered by a crystal pendant and surrounded by eight smaller lights. Round the dress and family circle there are clusters of electric lights, tempered by cream silk shades. The vestibule is decorated in 'old rose'.

Among the 'allegorical' decorations above the proscenium, in the centre, is a bust which bears a strong resemblance to Mary Moore.

It is a two-tier theatre, and the unreserved gallery, which became a bookable balcony in 1961, rises behind the upper circle. The decorations and seating remained in perfect order, very much as they were at its opening, until a reconditioning after the Second World War.

For many years the complete picture frame, on all four

sides, of the proscenium, was the only one left in London
of the style originally devised by Squire Bancroft for the
Haymarket in 1880, but now only the original curtain
remains unaltered.

THE PLAYS

The theatre opened on 16 November 1899 with a revival
of *David Garrick*, and on this occasion Wyndham handed
over the total receipts, £4000, to the Aldershot Branch
of the Soldiers' Wives and Families Association. This
magnanimous gesture was widely supported and a contemporary account of the opening night speaks of it
'as a great patriotic manifestation'. The Band of the
Coldstream Guards filled the stage and played 'God Save
the King,' 'God Bless the Prince of Wales,' and 'Rule
Britannia.'

The first new production was *Cyrano de Bergerac*,
translated from Rostand by G. Stuart Ogilvie and Louis N.
Parker. This was in April 1900 and subsequent productions
included Henry Arthur Jones's *Mrs Dane's Defence*
(October 1900), which ran for over two hundred performances, *The Mummy and the Humming Bird*, and revivals
of several of Wyndham's old successes.

In 1902 Frank Curzon entered on the management and
successes were scored by *Mrs Gorringe's Necklace* by
Hubert Henry Davies, which ran for 160 performances from
May 1903, and J. M. Barrie's *Little Mary*, 'an uncom-
fortable play' which ran for 208 performances from September of the same year, R. C. Carton's *Public Opinion*
(1905), *The Girl Behind the Counter*, a musical comedy
with music by Howard Talbot and Mrs de la Pasture's
Peter's Mother (1906). The original production of *When
Knights were Bold* by Charles Marlowe (a pen-name for
Harriet Jay) then had a run of 579 performances from
January 1907. In January 1909 was produced *An English-
man's Home*, which was announced as 'a play by a
patriot'. After a sensational first night it became common
knowledge that the author was Gerald du Maurier's soldier
brother, Guy. At the time Lord Roberts's stirring appeals
to Britons to realise their national danger were echoed
from public platforms all over the country. Here was a
stage picture of what would happen to those who refused to
listen. For six months Wyndham's Theatre was crowded.
Shortly after this Frank Curzon was joined in the management by Charles Hawtrey and during their partnership *The
Little Damozel* and *The Naked Truth* ran for over 150
performances in 1909 and 1910. In September 1910 Curzon
was joined by Gerald du Maurier, who remained connected
with the theatre for fifteen years. The successful productions of this era included *Nobody's Daughter* (1910), *Mr
Jarvis*, *Passers-by*, and *The Perplexed Husband* (1911), *The*

Dust of Egypt, Jelf's, and *Doormats* (1912). In March 1913 came a revival of *Diplomacy,* which ran for 455 performances. In 1914 came *The Clever Ones, Outcast,* and a revival of *Raffles* and in 1915 *Gamblers All* and *The Ware Case.* In March 1916 J. M. Barrie's 'fancy', *A Kiss for Cinderella,* was first produced and later in the same year *The Old Country* and *London Pride,* 'a London play for London people', which ran for 280 performances.

After a revival of *A Pair of Spectacles* in 1917 came the first production of *Dear Brutus,* which ran for 365 performances, and in which du Maurier scored a great success in the part of Dearth, with Faith Celli as Margaret the dream child. Du Maurier then joined the Army. From August 1918 *The Law Divine* by H. V. Esmond ran for 368 performances. In September 1919 du Maurier returned in Sutro's *The Choice* (316 performances) and his record of successes was continued with *The Prude's Fall* (1920) with 227 performances, *Bulldog Drummond* (430 performances from March 1921), *The Dancers* (1923), which ran for 344 performances and introduced Tallulah Bankhead to the London stage, and *To Have the Honour* (1924), which ran 193 performances.

The next chapter is associated with the plays of Edgar Wallace, under the management of Frank Curzon. As far as this theatre is concerned the series began with *The Ringer,* which ran for 410 performances from May 1926, and apart from an interim under Leon M. Lion, who presented *The Lady in Law* and *The Way of the World,* and plays by Shaw and Galsworthy, the series continued until 1932. The subsequent productions were *The Calendar* (September 1929), *On the Spot* (April 1930), *Smoky Cell* (December 1930), in which the audience were asked to believe that they were witnessing an actual electrocution in an American prison and the theatre ticket was a reproduction of the card of admission granted to American newspaper men; *The Old Man* (May 1931), *The Case of the Frightened Lady* (191 performances from August 1931), and *The Green Pack,* produced on the day before Wallace's death in Hollywood in 1932.

After this chapter of 'thrillers' there appeared plays of various kinds under the management of Howard Wyndham and Bronson Albery, many of which were outstanding and amongst which should be mentioned *Service* by C. L. Anthony (Dodie Smith) in 1932, *Clive of India,* which ran for 409 performances from January 1934; *The Maitlands,* the second, and unfortunately the last, play from that highly promising young dramatist Ronald Mackenzie (1934); *Sweet Aloes* by Jay Mallory (Joyce Carey), which began a run of 476 performances in October of the same year; then followed *Three Men on a Horse* and *Mademoiselle* (1936), *George and Margaret* (1937) which had a run of 799 performances, *She too was Young* and *Quiet Wedding*, both in 1938, the latter running for 227 performances.

Wyndham's was one of the earliest theatres to reopen after the compulsory closure in 1939 and *Diversion*, an intimate revue which ran into a second edition, was one of the shows which helped to keep London amused during the early days of the war. Subsequent successes were *Cottage to Let* and *Quiet Week-End*, a sequel to *Quiet Wedding*, which broke the long run record for Wyndham's with 1059 performances; Peter Ustinov's *The Banbury Nose* (September 1944) and in January 1945, Daphne du Maurier's *The Years Between*.

The first new post-war production was *Clutterbuck* by Benn Levy in August 1946 and subsequent successes were *Deep are the Roots* (1947), and a revival of *You Never Can Tell*, which scored 312 performances from October 1947. In March James Bridie's *Daphne Laureola* began its run of 367 performances with Edith Evans. From 1951 *The Love of Four Colonels* by Peter Ustinov ran for 812 performances, and in April 1953 it was followed by *The Living Room*, and then came *The Boy Friend* on 14 January 1954, which scored 2078 performances. Then two Theatre Workshop productions, *A Taste of Honey* (February 1959) and *The Hostage* (June 1959) kept the theatre full. The latter ended its run of 427 performances in June 1960 and was succeeded by *Call it Love*, with songs by Sandy Wilson, which lasted only a few nights. The remainder of the year was filled by Shaw's *Candida*, a revival from the Oxford Playhouse, which transferred from the Piccadilly and scored the play's longest run to date, and *Chin-Chin* with Celia Johnson and Anthony Quayle in November. When this play finished in March 1961 another Joan Littlewood production, *Sparrers Can't Sing*, from Stratford, East, came to town. *The Miracle Worker* transferred from the Royalty in May and ran until October when another Shaw success from Oxford, *Heartbreak House* ran until displaced by a transfer of *Bonne Soupe* from the Comedy in February 1962. In July another transfer, *Period of Adjustment* from the Royal Court occupied the stage until Michael Redgrave appeared in *Out of Bounds* in November 1962, until June 1963 for 241 performances, quickly followed by *Oh, What a Lovely War*, from the Theatre Royal, Stratford, for 501 performances. The next play, in June 1964, from the Arts Theatre, was *Entertaining Mr Sloane* which after a few months transferred to the Queen's Theatre. *Inadmissible Evidence* arrived in November 1965 for 251 performances. The next real success was *The Prime of Miss Jean Brodie* in May 1966. Scoring 588 performances by September 1967. The next three plays were *Wise Child* (125), *The Italian Girl* (315) and a revival of *The Cocktail Party* in November 1968. The American play, *The Boys in the Band*, opened in February 1969 and ran until May 1970 when *Abelard and Heloise* started its long run which was to continue to January 1972, when the American rock musical, *Godspell*, by John Michael Tebelak and Stephen Schwartz, opened, having been 'tried out' at the Round House. This is now well into the third successful year.

The theatre is run in connection with the Criterion and the Albery by Wyndham Theatres, Ltd.

PART 2

The Outer Ring

The Outer Ring

INTRODUCTION

In this section we are dealing fully only with those out-lying theatres which pursue a definite policy and are almost part and parcel of the West End theatre list.

Of the vast number of suburban music halls which arose in most districts of London between the nineties and the First World War, some became cinemas in the 'talkie' boom, others kept the flag of variety, or touring revue, flying up to the bitter end. Some of these are now derelict and, like the Putney Hippodrome, await demolition; a few have been converted to other uses: the Shepherd's Bush Empire has become a B.B.C. television studio and the Hackney Empire is a Mecca Bingo Casino and a listed building.

The Metropolitan, Edgware Road, the last of the old music halls of London kept open spasmodically, was finally demolished in 1963, leaving Wilton's in Wellclose Square, Whitechapel, and Macdonald's in Hoxton (both Listed buildings) alone in their glory.

For almost every suburban music hall there was an equivalent local theatre which housed touring companies of various sorts. These were the first to suffer eclipse after the war; some became cinemas, some tried repertory with varying success. Remaining today are the Camden Theatre, empty but still in existence, and the Coronet, Notting Hill Gate, now a cinema; one is Listed and the other Protected. The Embassy, Swiss Cottage, of a later vintage, has become the home of the Central School of Speech, Training and Dramatic Art, but most buildings have passed completely into oblivion.

In the 1930s Streatham Hill Theatre (now used for Bingo), The Lewisham Hippodrome (now demolished) and Golders Green, still in existence, Listed but unused, formed a link in the circuit which presented London productions direct from or before their West End run.

With the loss of so many places of entertainment around London in the past fifty years, the strange phenomenon has arisen of variety, ballet, 'pop' and Christmas productions being staged at the large cinemas,

like the New Victoria and the Rainbow (The Finsbury
Park Astoria). This is an indication that live entertainment
can make a popular comeback to new audiences, when
housed in the comfort of the local super-cinema which,
after all, was forecast in the early thirties at the time of
their building, when it was announced that they were fully
equipped for stage productions. Did they foresee, though,
the decline of the suburban cinema?

In the outer ring there were also working amateur
theatres, the Questors, who have built a modern theatre for
themselves at Ealing; the Tavistock Repertory Company
(from the Tavistock Little Theatre at the Mary Ward
Settlement, Russell Square) at the Tower Theatre, Canon-
bury; and Unity Theatre, which opens periodically in
King's Cross, as well as those new theatres built in office
blocks like the City banks, Shell Centre, etc., London
University (The Collegiate), The Central School of Arts and
Crafts (The Jeanetta Cochran), L.A.M.D.A., R.A.D.A.
(The Vanbrugh)—all have specially built and equipped
theatres, as has the Inner London Education Authority
with the Cockpit, Toynbee Hall, and The Curtain, among
others. Some of these have been used at times for professional productions.

A small theatre which has had a long existence in both
amateur and professional fields is the Twentieth Century,
Archer Street, Bayswater, W.11. Built in 1863 and opened
at the latter end of that year as the Victoria Hall, its
early life was entirely devoted to amateur activities. In 1866
it became known as the Bijou Theatre, but it retained the
original name on its licence and continued to use this from
time to time as occasion demanded.

It was partially destroyed by fire in 1891 but rebuilt and
reopened in 1893; from that time it was used extensively for
copyright performances, then needed by law, and several of
Shaw's early plays first saw the light on its stage in this
form. It was also used professionally in the early years of
the new century until it became a cinema from 1911 to
1918. In July 1924 it was taken by Lena Ashwell and used as
the headquarters of her 'Once a Week' players (The Lena
Ashwell Players) who toured the town halls in and around
London. In 1936 the premises were sold to the Rudolf
Steiner Association, who again changed the name to the
Twentieth Century Theatre and it was occasionally used for
try-outs, etc. It held some 300 people. Though it is Listed it
is now an antiques warehouse.

The summer of 1972 saw, after the many abortive
schemes to resurrect 'The Globe' or a 'Back to
Shakespeare' Theatre, Sam Wanamaker's Bankside
Festival in a temporary theatre, erected on Bankside. This
was a courageous but ill-fated project, and though many
interesting productions were seen during the two seasons of

its existence, the good work was defeated and the theatre destroyed by the elements in 1973.

In the last year there has been a spate of cinema conversions both in and out of the West End—the Regent, formerly the Cameo-Poly Cinema, Regent Street, opened in March 1974; the King's Road (Essoldo) Cinema, temporarily housing *The Rocky Horror Show*, is to be rebuilt; the State, Kilburn (the old Kilburn Empire) is also on the list. News of a new Lyric, Hammersmith, came in April 1974.

We have added to this section the Greenwich Theatre, the Round House, the Shaw Theatre and the Young Vic.

1 · The Greenwich Theatre

(Crowder's Music Hall, The Parthenon, Barnard's,
The Greenwich Hippodrome, etc.)

Crooms Hill, Greenwich, S.E.10

Capacity: 426

Opened 21 October 1969 with *Martin Luther King*, a play with music, by Ewan Hooper. Directed by Alan Vaughan Williams under the management of the Greenwich Theatre Trust.

*

The Greenwich Theatre, at the foot of Crooms Hill, stands on ground long associated with entertainment. The Rose and Crown Public House, still part of the building, though unconnected, started the usual music hall entertainment in the Large Room in the 1850s, in the fashion of

the time, under the direction of the Licensee, Charles
Crowder. He enlarged his premises and opened as
Crowder's Music Hall on 28 October 1871. During the
following years many names were used, the Rose and
Crown Palace of Varieties, the Parthenon Palace of
Varieties, Barnard's Palace of Varieties among them. It was
completely rebuilt in the contemporary mode in 1895 as the
Greenwich Hippodrome. Music hall and pantomimes were
presented till 1924 when it became a cinema which it
remained until 1949, when it closed. After becoming a warehouse it was due for redevelopment. A campaign to
rebuild the theatre as a new arts centre was launched by
Ewan Hooper in 1962 when the old Hippodrome was
bought by the Council for demolition. After years of cam-
paigning and fund-raising, the new theatre, a one tier
auditorium with an open stage in the shell of the old
building, including a restaurant, coffee bars and exhibition
area designed by Brian Meeking, was finally opened in
1969 and run by a Trust with civic support under the
direction of Ewan Hooper. *The Greenwich Theatre Book*
was published in the same year. The first production at the
new theatre was Ewan Hooper's *Martin Luther King*, and in
November *Spithead*, another documentary, was produced.
At Christmas, for the children, *The New Adventures of
Noah's Ark* was presented. In February 1970 came their
first production to transfer to the West End, *Sing a Rude
Song*, with Barbara Windsor and Denis Quilley, a musical
based on the life of Marie Lloyd. March saw a strange
version of the old drama, *The Corsican Brothers;* the
following month a revival of *Medea* and in May a new play,
Lorna and Ted. A play by Iris Murdoch, *The Servants and
the Snow*, came in September 1970 and in October *Dan the
Archer* was followed by the success of *A Voyage Round my
Father*, by John Mortimer, again to be seen later in the
West End. In April came another success, *Forget-Me-Not-
Lane* by Peter Nichols, also to transfer to the West End. A
revival of *The Glass Menagerie* in May preceded *A Fish
Out Of Water*, with Fenella Fielding, which was followed
by *The Sandboy* and a revival of *Antigone* and the
Electra of Sophocles, then a new play in November, *A
Liberated Woman*. The Christmas 1971 attraction was *Jack
and the Beanstalk*.
   A policy of summer music hall with well known stars
harked back to the fund raising days, when 'old time'
music hall was seen at the Green Man on Blackheath, and is
now continued in the Tram Shed at Woolwich, an addition
to the Theatre's *extra mural* activities in 1973. Children's
Theatre (the Bowsprit Company), pop concerts, Art
Exhibitions and late night shows have kept the theatre
premises, with its restaurant, open at all times of the day.
   In 1972 *The Little Giant* and a revival of *Electra* and

Brussels, presented in conjunction with the Royal Court Theatre Upstairs, a play about a Boy Scout Troop at a summer camp, was followed by a revival of *A Doll's House* with Susan Hampshire, then *The Rose and the Ring* was presented for the festive season. In January 1973 a new company formed by Robin Phillips gave its first performance with a revival of *The Three Sisters*. Their first season, which lasted till June, included *The House of Bernarda Alba; Rosmesholm* and *The Provoked Wife*. After various visiting attractions Robin Phillips returned with *Cat's Play*, which brought Elizabeth Bergner back to the stage. Late November saw a new American musical, *Zorba*, which was directed by Robin Phillips and was the final production of his second season.

Early in 1974 another exciting season commenced under the direction of Jonathan Miller and was called Family Romances. The plays were *Ghosts, The Seagull* and *Hamlet*. Between *The Seagull* and *Hamlet*, Glenda Jackson, Susannah York and Vivien Merchant appeared in *The Maids*, by Jean Genet, directed by Minos Volonakis. Then the Family Romances were performed in repertoire. *The Norman Conquest*, three plays by Alan Acykbourn, opened in May on their triumphant way to the West End.

2 · The Lyric Theatre

(The Lyric Opera House, The New Lyric)

Bradmore Grove, Hammersmith, W.6

THE FIRST THEATRE
Capacity: 550

Opened as the Lyric Hall, 17 November 1888 with M. d'Arc's *French Marionettes,* presenting a programme which included a drama, a Christy Minstrel troupe and a panto-mime *Blue Beard* (a week after its opening it was being called the Lyric Hall and Opera House in advertisements, though the original ones only give the Lyric Hall as its name). Under the management of Charles Cordingley.

Reconstructed and opened as a regular theatre, the Lyric Opera House, 17 November 1890 with a triple bill con-sisting of *The Waterman,* a ballad opera by Charles

Dibdin, *His Last Legs*, a farce by W. B. Bernard, and the first performance of *Puck*, an after-dinner version of *A Midsummer Night's Dream*. Under the management of Charles Cordingley.

RECONSTRUCTED THEATRE
Capacity: 755

Opened 20 July 1895 with *A House of Lies*, a drama by Charles Hannan, followed by a revival of *Dora*, a pastoral play by Charles Reade, founded on Tennyson's poem, and preceded by an Occasional Prologue spoken by Lillie Langtry. Under the management of Acton Phillips and Son. Demolished 1972.

*

In 1886 a project to build a theatre was put forward by Charles Cordingley, the proprietor and editor of *The West London Advertiser;* he acquired some vacant land and old properties in Bradmore Grove for the purpose. Unfortunately his original plans did not find favour with the authorities, though eventually it seems Cordingley went ahead without the approval of the Metropolitan Board of Works. The Lyric Hall, designed by Isaac Mason, was completed and opened on 17 November 1888 with Marionette performances which finished on the 29th. (An advertisement announced the opening night for November 12, and a gospel meeting is reported as taking place on Sunday the 11th, but it was not in regular use till a week later.) A carved brick name 'The Lyric Hall 1888' remained to the end on the building. It consisted of a large hall on one floor without galleries, seating 550, which could be used for theatrical performances, and a small upstairs room available for auctions and sales. The premises were advertised as being suitable for concerts, entertainments, public meetings, balls and similar social functions. Though not a regular theatre, for a dramatic licence could not be obtained, companies played one-night engagements here on their rounds of Town Hall, Corn Exchange and similar buildings. G. P. Hawtrey's *Pickpocket* company performed on 8 December 1888 and *East Lynne* was presented on 21 January 1889 (a programme in the G.L.C. archives gives the name of the Hall definitely as the Lyric Hall and Opera House).

Cordingley soon began to have trouble with both the L.C.C. which succeeded the Board of Works in 1889 and the Licensing Authorities. Plans to bring the property into line with the necessary requirements by the original architect were refused and finally in 1890 the Hall was redesigned and converted into a regular theatre by F. and H. Francis and Sons.

The Era for 23 November 1890 tells us:

A spacious balcony, a commodious gallery, and four new boxes have been put up; and the whole appearance of the place has completely changed. The decorations in pleasing Pompeian style, are chaste, and effective; and the lounges, smoking saloons, and buffets, add to the comfort and convenience of the patrons of the establishment. The stalls and fauteuils, covered in silk plush, increase the luxury of the seating accommodation, which is in every respect liberal; and the stage curtains of blue plush, and the drop with its picturesque landscape scene, also contribute to the general effect of brightness and tasteful harmony in the interior. Nor has the safety of the audience been less carefully considered than their pleasure and convenience. The theatre is constructed entirely of fire-resisting materials, iron, concrete, and stone; and there are eight large exits from the auditorium. The intention of the new management is to offer to the inhabitants of the Western suburbs a light, popular musical and dramatic entertainment, introducing from time to time, original operettas, comic operas, extravaganzas and dramatic pieces.

This idea of reviving light opera with a mixed bill was not a success, and before a year had passed the theatre was closed and Cordingley sold the property to Acton Phillips and his son, who were then running the Temple Theatre of Varieties in King Street (this later became the Hammersmith Palace).

They reopened the Lyric on 19 October 1891 with the policy of presenting melodramas old and new with a stock company. They began with Watts Phillips's *Lost in London*.

In 1895 it was decided to rebuild the theatre almost completely to the designs of Frank Matcham. How he altered the house is told in *The Era* of 20 July.

Whereas in the old building the pit floor was considerably above the ground level, it is now below it. The present dress circle occupies the position of the old pit and the new gallery occupies that of the old balcony. There are no less than ten exits—two from each part of the house and all the doors are provided with safety bolts. The stalls, dress circle, and upper circle have velvet tip-up seats, and retiring rooms and saloons are provided. The raised plaster decorations are rich in detail, and the colouring in shades of cream and blue is very tasteful. Artistic paintings fill in the four panels of the ceiling, and there are two figure paintings on each side of the proscenium. The stage opening has the shape of an arch, and with the private boxes, is luxuriously draped in terra cotta plush. The two projecting sides of the proscenium are cleverly treated. The private boxes are well placed for a good view of the stage. The pit is a fine one, and has a good rake. It is comfortably fitted with upholstered seating. The pit walls are covered with coloured tiles, which are very effective. The new stage is much deeper than the old one, and has scene docks on each side, with property rooms and everything necessary for the staging of large productions. The height to the roof, gained by lowering the theatre, enables the scenery to be taken up without folding; and the floor of the stage is fitted with traps and bridges so that any mechanical effects can be produced.

The theatre opened on 20 July. A Prologue spoken by Mrs Langtry started the evening; this was followed by the first production of a drama by Charles Hannan called *A House of Lies*, in which Charles Warner and his daughter Grace appeared. It was followed by a revival of *Dora*, a pastoral play founded by Charles Reade on Tennyson's poem.

For the next few years the theatre was occupied either by touring companies or seasons by a resident stock company. An annual pantomime was produced under the direction of John M. East, who was the general manager for the Phillips' during most of their régime.

In 1899 further alterations and improvements were again made to enlarge the theatre, which was so successfully giving local audiences the kind of entertainment that appealed to them.

The Era of 21 October 1899 says:

At the rear of the dress circle is a large and handsome saloon, and this occupies the vacant space over the entrance vestibule and offices, etc. The saloon is fitted up and furnished in a most artistic manner, the ceiling being raised in decoration and the walls covered in leather paper, and the whole richly furnished and lighted by electricity. The approach to this room is by a wide staircase, the walls and ceiling being similarly decorated. A large retiring room has been added, and fitted up with all the latest improvements. . . . The old buildings which used to fall back some distance from the main wall on the first tier, has now been brought forward, and it greatly enhances the appearance of the exterior. The front consists of yellow bricks pointed with red stone ornamentations. The handsome windows are provided with ornamental leaded lights. There is a quantity of elaborate iron work, and a graceful balcony at each end of the building. All the woodwork and doors are of 'post office' red, which gives a warm appearance and harmonises with the stonework. The entrance hall is new, the walls being of Hendon stone and faience work, with

ceilings of raised Cordova work delicately decorated.
The whole of the entrance hall and the dress circle tier,
from which the approach to the new saloon bar runs, have
been handsomely adorned, and velvet curtains of a rich
terra cotta colour have been added.

Frank Matcham was again responsible for the alterations.
The policy of Acton Phillips, who had died earlier in the
year, was continued by his son until 1904, when the theatre
passed to Samuel James. The opening of the King's Theatre
a few minutes away, in December 1902, had caused the
theatre to lose many of its patrons, and during the next
few years it was to pass through many transitory
managements.

The G.L.C. demanded alterations in 1907 which were
completed to allow Wentworth Crocke to reopen in
1909 calling it the People's Popular Playhouse. When the
cinema swept popular melodrama from the stage, there
was no place for this style of theatre, and it became known
locally as the 'Blood and Flea Pit,' being used for any event
which would keep its doors open, though they were more
often closed.

It was in this state that it was discovered in 1918 by Nigel
Playfair who redecorated it, turning the bar over the
entrance hall into an office, and launched the seasons which
have become part of theatre history. He changed the name
to the Lyric Theatre after his first production. Since his
day only renovation and redecoration took place and the
theatre remained an unspoilt example of a late Victorian
Playhouse. The original name of the Lyric Opera House
was revived in 1958.

The full story of the Playfair régime has been told by its
founder in The Story of the Lyric Theatre, Hammersmith
(1925) and Hammersmith Hoy (1930). The theatre reopened
with a Christmas production, Make Believe by A. A. Milne,
on 24 December 1918. The first success of the early years
was John Drinkwater's chronicle play Abraham Lincoln,
produced in February 1919, which ran for a year. Next he
produced St John Ervine's John Ferguson and in April a
revival of As You Like It, the cast including Playfair himself, Ivan Sampson, Herbert Marshall and Athene Seyler.

On 5 June 1920 Nigel Playfair presented his celebrated
revival of The Beggar's Opera by John Gay, with the music
rearranged by Frederick Austin. It ran for 1463 performances, three and a half years. The décor which put the
Lyric 'on the map' theatrically was the work of Claud Lovat
Fraser. Revivals of this production were given in June
1925, May 1926, February 1928, March 1929, and May
1930. In 1924 there was a revival of The Way of the World,
which ran for 158 performances with Edith Evans unfor-
gettable as Millamant. Also in 1924 came Midsummer

Madness by Clifford Bax, with music by Armstrong Gibbs, which was notable for the reappearance of Marie Tempest in a singing part; and later in the year there was a production of Sheridan's *The Duenna;* 1925 brought revivals of *The Rivals, The Cherry Orchard*, and *Lionel and Clarissa*, a comic opera by Isaac Bickerstaff, seldom heard since its original Covent Garden production in 1768. It was also in November 1925 that Ellen Terry made her last appearance on the stage in Walter de la Mare's *Crossings*.

On 10 April 1926 there was produced *Riverside Nights*, an entertainment by A. P. Herbert, arranged by Nigel Playfair. In 1927 outstanding productions were *The Beaux' Stratagem, When Crummles Played*, and the Old Vic Company in a season while their own theatre was being renovated.

There was another Isaac Bickerstaff revival in 1928 when *Love in a Village* had a run of 124 performances. Another success of this year was *A Hundred Years Old*, a comedy adapted from the Spanish by Helen and Harley Granville-Barker. In 1929 A. P. Herbert wrote a new version of Offenbach's *La Vie Parisienne*, and subsequent successes included a black and white production of *The Importance of Being Earnest* (1930), and *Tantivy Towers* (1931) and *Derby Day* (1932), both by A. P. Herbert.

After Playfair left in 1933 there was a sharp decline in the fortunes of the theatre. Arthur Phillips ran a series of Shakespeare revivals in 1935 and 1936. Then, after a closure, a 'season of thrillers' was announced but only *Dracula* appeared. The theatre was mostly dark until J. Baxter Somerville took it in 1944. First a number of C.E.M.A. productions were staged, including Flora Robson as Thérèse Raquin in *Guilty*. Then in October 1945 the Company of Four began their long association with the theatre.

During the next eleven years, almost every star of the London stage came to Hammersmith and many plays which moved 'up west' were first seen here. In 1952 John Gielgud gave a season in which he revived *Venice Preserved, Richard II*, and *The Way of the World*. Not only were classics produced but revues were staged which made both stars and writers.

When the theatre came under the direct control of Baxter Somerville in 1956 there was a mixed assortment of presentations, for both the popular and discerning audience. The plays put on by Michael Codron brought several new writers to the theatre, including Harold Pinter and John Mortimer. The 59 Theatre Company presented a remarkable production of Ibsen's *Brand*. Programmes included such diverse entertainment as *Valmouth, The Demon Barber*, a 'Third Programme Revue'—*One to Another, New Cranks, Tomorrow—with Pictures!* and *Hooray for*

Daisy! at Christmas 1960, all of which made interesting theatre-going.

Activity in the next two years was spasmodic, with the theatre unfortunately more often closed than open, but success returned unexpectedly with the Canadian revue *Clap Hands* which opened in November 1962 but quickly transferred to the new Prince Charles Theatre for its opening on Boxing Day; Maeterlinck's *The Blue Bird* was revived for Christmas.

After the death of J. Baxter Somerville in January 1963 a gallant attempt to run the theatre by his trustees failed and the theatre closed in the summer. It did not reopen until June 1964 (as the New Lyric, Hammersmith) with *Man on the Stairs*. This marked the beginning of a new management who had acquired the lease of the theatre (John Grogan, Paula Stone and Desmond Ainsworth). The theatre had been completely redecorated and refurbished. The illustrious names, from Playfair to Gielgud, which had been on the plaster-work cartouches round the proscenium and on the boxes had been painted out, not an auspicious beginning!

Four weeks of Old Time Music Hall in July and August were followed by short seasons. The Lyric was closed for most of 1965 but a pantomime, *Puss in Boots*, was seen at Christmas, with *The Sooty Show* in the mornings. Two odd Sunday performances in March and June finished the life of the theatre and it was finally used as a location for several film and television productions.

The Acton family, who were the original Freeholders, sold the theatre for redevelopment in 1968, and after much discussion the auditorium plasterwork was preserved and stored by order of the G.L.C., and the theatre was eventually razed to the ground in June 1972.

In April 1974 it was announced in *The Stage:*

At its meeting on April 17, Hammersmith Council approved plans for a new theatre to replace the Lyric. It is due for completion in 1978 at a total cost of £2 to £3 million.

The theatre will be leased and operated by the Contemporary Dance Trust, which will contribute up to a million pounds, to include the cost of a building to house its school of dance. The theatre will be part of the St Martin's Property Company's development in King Street, adjacent to Hammersmith Broadway, and the developers are contributing £160,000 for the foundations, substructure and podium. Theatre Projects Ltd and David Hicks Associates have been appointed to advise on the preparation of a brief and on the designs used in a feasibility study which has been carried out.

Another chapter has begun on this famous Theatre.

3 · The Mermaid Theatre

Puddle Dock, Upper Thames Street, Blackfriars, E.C.4

Capacity: 498

Opened 28 May 1959 with *Lock Up your Daughters*, a musical play by Laurie Johnson, lyrics by Lionel Bart. Adapted by Bernard Miles from Henry Fielding's *Rape upon Rape*. Produced by Peter Coe under the management of the Mermaid Theatre Trust.

*

The whole idea of an Elizabethan-style theatre in London originated when Bernard Miles and his wife Josephine Wilson converted the hall of the old St John's Wood School in Acacia Road into a theatre.

The stage was constructed to the designs of Michael Stringer and C. Walter Hodges, and the hall turned into an auditorium with Ernst Freud as architect. The theatre, holding 200, was opened on 9 September 1951 with Purcell's opera *Dido and Aeneas* in which Kirsten Flagstad and Maggie Teyte sang. Twenty performances were given alternatively with Julius Gellner's production of *The Tempest* and various song recitals. The following year the opera was revived, and *Macbeth* produced in Elizabethan speech. Thomas Middleton's *A Trick to Catch the Old One* was also staged.

In 1953, as part of the Coronation festivities, the
Mermaid Stage was set up in the quadrangle of the Royal
Exchange in the City of London, being adapted to suit its
surroundings. Performances of *As You Like It, Dido and
Aeneas, Eastward Ho!* by Ben Jonson, Chapman and
Marston, and *Macbeth*, were given between May and July
to some 10,000 people.

This was said at the time to be the first theatre within
the City boundaries for over 200 years, but the existence
of the City of London Theatre in Bishopsgate Street,
Norton Folgate, flourishing from 1835 to 1868, and the
New City Subscription Theatre in Milton Street, Fore
Street, which had a short life from 1831 to 1836, must not
be overloooked.

The success of the Coronation season gave rise to the idea
of building a permanent Mermaid Theatre in the City. The
site eventually chosen was Puddle Dock, a blitzed and
disused wharf near Blackfriars Station. A new theatre of
modern design, carried out by Elidir L. W. Davies, arose,
re-using the old dock walls. The open stage was again from
the design of Michael Stringer and C. Walter Hodges.
Building began in 1957 and the theatre with its adjoining
restaurant opened the following year. The raked auditorium
stretching down to the open stage, the spacious vestibule,
and stairways strike a new note of severe simplicity in
theatre architecture.

The whole scheme and the gathering in of financial
support for the enterprise was due to the enthusiasm of
Bernard Miles and his wife, and the immediate success of
their opening production enabled the theatre to be without
debt before the end of the first year, and to begin its
second production *Treasure Island* (which became almost
an annual event) on a financially secure basis.

Henry V in battledress, the next production, was a
curious experiment by Julius Gellner, attempting to make
Shakespeare's play applicable to modern warfare; it opened
in February 1960. It was followed by *Great Expectations*
(April), Brecht's *Galileo* (June), *Mr Burke, M.P.* (October)
and *Emil and the Detectives* at Christmas.

The following year saw several revivals by famous
authors, including *John Gabriel Borkman; 'Tis Pity She's a
Whore; The Shewing-Up of Blanco Posnet; Androcles and
the Lion.* In 1962 there were several productions of plays
by Sean O'Casey: *Purple Dust, Red Roses for Me* and
The Plough and the Stars, as well as a revival of *Lock Up
Your Daughters*, which transferred to Her Majesty's
Theatre. In November there was a revival of *The Witch of
Edmonton* by Thomas Dekker. 1963 saw four transfers to
the West End, first, in January, *The Bed Sitting-Room*,
which went to the Duke of York's Theatre; secondly,
All in Good Time went to the Phoenix Theatre;

thirdly, *Virtue in Danger* continued its run at the Strand Theatre, and fourthly, *Alfie* moved to the Duchess Theatre. During 1964 there were revivals of *Macbeth*, *The Maid's Tragedy* and *The Shoemaker's Holiday* and in September the Living Theatre of New York presented a prison play, *The Brig*. In 1965 there were revivals of *Dandy Dick* and *Fanny's First Play*. In November came *Spring and Port Wine* by Bill Naughton, later to transfer to the West End. The next year came revivals of *The Philanderer* and *The Imaginary Invalid* and several new plays, as well as a production of Sardou's *Let's Get a Divorce* which transferred to the Comedy Theatre. During the following year, 1967, there were productions of *The Shadow of a Gunman; The Trojan Wars* and *The High Bid* by Henry James. In February 1968 Edith Evans appeared in Shaw's *The Black Girl in Search of God*, and in April *Hadrian the Seventh* started its successful run before transferring to the Haymarket Theatre. The Christmas season saw *Gulliver's Travels*, in place of the usual *Treasure Island*. In March 1969 came yet another revival of *Lock Up Your Daughters*, followed by Henry James' *The Other House*, and in September Prospect Productions brought, from Edinburgh, *Edward the Second*, by Christopher Marlowe, and the following evening Shakespeare's *Richard II* with Ian McKellan in the title roles. Both plays later transferred to the Piccadilly Theatre. The first new production in 1970 was Bernard Kops' *Enter Solly Gold*. In March came a revival of Shaw's *The Apple Cart* and April saw a revival of *Henry IV Part I* and the following month came *Henry IV Part II*. Then in June *The Tempest* was presented; later in the year a production of *Saint Joan* was staged. In November came *Exiles*, by James Joyce, and for the holiday season *Dick Turpin* was presented, quickly to be followed on 30 December by Saki's *The Watched Pot*. In 1971 there were revivals of *John Bull's Other Island* in May; in September, *Othello*, and in November, Shaw's *Geneva*. *Dick Turpin* was again seen in December. In January 1972 *The Price of Justice*, by Camus, appeared, and in March a revival of *The Caretaker* was followed by a successful revival of *Journey's End*, later to transfer to the Cambridge Theatre. This was succeeded by the highly entertaining *Cowardy Custard*, a delightful pastiche of the words and music of Noël Coward, directed by Wendy Toye. No new production was needed until July 1973 when a revival of *Juno and the Paycock* came on and in August another revival was seen, *An Inspector Calls* by J. B. Priestley. At Christmas, for a change, a musical version of *Treasure Island*, with music by Cyril Ormadel, was performed. 1974 did not start successfully and a stopgap season of vintage films was shown until Constance Cummings appeared in

Children in April. This was followed later in the summer
by *Cole*, a Cole Porter pastiche.

Threats of clearance in the large redevelopment taking
place around the theatre have been met and the Mermaid
remains the centre of much interesting theatrical activity at
all times of the day.

4 · The Old Vic

(The Royal Coburg Theatre, The Royal Victoria Theatre, The New
Victoria Palace, The Royal Victoria Hall, and Coffee Tavern)

The New Cut and Waterloo Road, S.E.1

Capacity: 948

Opened on 11 May 1818 with a melodramatic spectacle,
Trial by Battle; or, Heaven Defend the Right, by William
Barrymore, preceded by a Harlequinade *Midnight Revelry;
or, Harlequin and Comus,* and followed by a grand Asiatic
ballet *Alzora and Nerine,* by Leclerq. Produced by William
Barrymore under the management of Joseph Glossop.

*

An interesting publication called *The Nic-Nac or Literary
Cabinet,* in its issue dated 25 September 1824, gives the
following account of the birth of this theatre:

Mr Jones, who formerly rented the Surrey Theatre in
St George's Circus, Lambeth, becoming insolvent, his
assignees let that house to Mr Elliston for a term of

years. Elliston's management terminated in 1814 and
Jones' lease of the premises expiring soon after, the
ground landlord, Temple West Esq., demanded a great
increase upon the old rent. The offer of Jones'
assignees was refused, but as they still had the lease
under which performances had been carried on at the
Surrey Theatre and which had been granted to Jones, they
imagined that they would be able to make their own
terms. West, however, obtained another licence for performances at the Surrey, and Jones' assignees, thus
disappointed, issued proposals for building another
house, as follows:

Proposals for the Royal Coburg Theatre. Mr. Jones
(late proprietor of the Royal Circus, or Surrey Theatre)
having agreed for a piece of land near the foot of
Waterloo Bridge, on the Surrey side of the river, for the
purpose of building a new theatre, and having obtained the
patronage of H.R.H. The Princess Charlotte of Wales
and His Serene Highness the Prince of Saxe-Coburg,
proposed to dispose of a part, by way of subscription,
as follows: the whole is estimated at £42,000. A sub-
scriber of one-eighth of that sum to be considered a joint-
proprietor. Subscribers for one share of £100 to receive
interest at 5 per cent, and each share to entitle the
holder to a personal free-admission, transferable each
season. The holder of five shares to be eligible to be
elected as a trustee; and the holder of two shares to be
entitled to vote on all occasions.

For the present, subscriptions are received at Sir John
Pinhorn and Co's, Bankers, Southwark. . . . Each sub-
scriber to pay down 25 per cent monthly until the whole
is paid and 35 per cent at the time of subscribing. As soon
as £4,000 shall have been subscribed, a general meeting
of the subscribers to be called for the purpose of framing
regulations for the government of the concern, and elect-
ing trustees, treasurers and other officers. Materials, to
the amount of several thousand pounds are already purchased. The whole property in scenery, dresses, etc. at
the Surrey Theatre have been removed to this concern,
and the Theatre is intended to be opened at Christmas
next. Subscriptions are also received and further information will be communicated by Mr Jones, near the
Obelisk, St. George's Fields; and Mr Chippendale,
solicitor to the Theatre, Great Queen Street, Lincolns
Inn Fields.

Few subscribers came forward to back this scheme,
which originated with Jones, Dunn the last tenant of the
Surrey, and Serres a marine painter; the first on the
strength of his former connections, and having procured
the ground; the second having a stock of scenery,

dresses, etc. and the third having interested the Prince and
Princess of Coburg to procure a licence, which was issued
at the Surrey Quarter Sessions on 16 October 1816.

The building, however, for want of money proceeded
slowly, until the spring of 1817, when Joseph Glossop, the
son of a wealthy Soho merchant, advanced a few hundred
pounds, lent him by his father. The workmen then proceeded until the day before Good Friday 1817, when they
struck—and carried off the scaffolding. In this state the
building remained until the autumn, and it was expected
ever to remain so, but Glossop made arrangements for
taking the management into his own hands, proceeded
speedily with the building, and it was opened on 11 May
1818, in a still unfinished state.

The site was formerly known as Lambeth Marsh. The
theatre today is bounded by Waterloo Road and Webber
Street; it faces onto the Cut. The projectors of the scheme
purchased the materials from the old Savoy Palace in the
Strand, which had been pulled down to form an opening to
Waterloo Bridge. The building of the theatre cost £12,000,
and the first stone was laid by Alderman Goodbehere, and
bore the following inscription: 'This first stone of the Royal
Coburg Theatre was laid on the 14th day of September in
the year 1816, by His Serene Highness the Prince of Saxe
Coburg and Her Royal Highness the Princess Charlotte of
Wales, by their Serene and Royal Highness's proxy
Alderman Goodbehere.'

The architect of the theatre was Rudolph Cabanel, of
Aachen. The opening took place on Whit Monday, and it
may be of interest to quote from a playbill announcing this:

Royal Coburg Theatre, opposite Waterloo Bridge
Road, Lambeth. The Nobility, Gentry and the Public are
respectfully informed that the above new and splendid
theatre, which has been erected according to the plans
and designs and under the superintendence of the
celebrated architect Mr. Cabanel, will open on Whit
Monday, the 11th May 1818, under the immediate
patronage of His Royal Highness of Saxe Coburg, with
entirely new entertainments now preparing on a scale of
magnitude and great expense. The audience part of the
theatre will be lighted by a superb Central Lustre, while
others of a most costly description will shed a beautiful
and brilliant light over the whole house. The Decorations
of the interior and Grand Panoramic Marine Saloon
designed and executed by Mr. Serres (Marine Painter to
His Majesty). The ceiling and proscenium designed by
Mr. Cabanel and executed by Mr. Latilla and Assistants.

The burnished gold and silver ornaments by Mr Collet
and Assistants.

The company already engaged include many per-

formers of High Celebrity from the London and principal
Provincial Theatres. The scenery is entirely new and
painted by the following celebrated artists: Messrs
Serres, Latilla, Morris, Scruton, Stanfield, S. Morris and
Assistants.

The scheme of decoration was fawn and gold, and the
drop curtain was adorned with a view of Claremont
House.

The original company included Thomas Blanchard,
George Davidge, Benjamin Webster, with William Barrymore as producer. At the opening performance *Trial by
Battle* was preceded by a harlequinade, *Midnight Revelry;
or, Harlequin and Comus*, and followed by a Leclerq ballet,
Alzora and Nerine, but this order of precedence was only
settled after another trial by battle at the beginning of the
evening. Norman, the stage manager and clown, wanted the
harlequinade to be the first item, as he also had to perform
at Covent Garden. Glossop disagreed, wanting it to be the
last item, and even locked up the clown's costume and
arranged with Richard Usher to perform as clown.
Norman had distributed bills among the audience, detailing
his grievance; and when Munro (the theatre's first villain)
advanced to deliver an opening address, Norman appeared
too, and the house was in uproar. Barrymore intervening,
he and Munro were pelted with orange peel and apple
cores, and eventually Glossop had to give way to
Norman's request; and so the pantomime was given as the
first instead of the last item of the evening, when
Blanchard, who was to be the hero of *Trial by Battle*,
proved to be more popular as Pantaloon than Norman as
the clown.

The theatre became established as a home of successful
melodrama, and visits by well-known West End actors
soon followed. In 1824 it was announced that 'this
splendid theatre has been entirely re-embellished on a most
costly and magnificent scale and rendered without
exception the most commodious and elegant in Europe'.

A looking-glass curtain was installed, which was one of
the sights of London, but it had eventually to be dis-
mantled and abandoned, owing to the strain which it
imposed upon the roof. The curtain was used later, in
pieces, to decorate the walls and to make dressing-room
mirrors.

Edmund Kean opened for six performances at £50 a
night in 1831, under the management of George Davidge
(who held the theatre from 1824 to 1833).

On 1 July 1833 the theatre, once again redecorated, was
opened by Abbot and Egerton as the Royal Victoria
Theatre, with a production of *Black-Ey'd Susan* (first seen
at the Surrey in 1829). On 17 June 1834 Paganini made his

farewell appearance here. In 1840 the management passed
into the hands of David Osbaldiston and in 1841 we read that
a fire damaged some calico scenery stored in the theatre,
but the building itself escaped injury.

It must be remembered that since its opening the house
had been a 'Minor' theatre—only allowed a burletta licence
and forbidden to present the legitimate drama, the
property of the two patent theatres, Drury Lane and
Covent Garden (and the Haymarket in the summer
months). Though ways and means were found to evade the
law, it was not until the passing of the Theatres Act of
1843 that the Victoria came under the authority of the Lord
Chamberlain and was allowed to present Shakespeare; from
that time the term ''Minor'' theatre lost its meaning and
gradually went out of use. Unfortunately the Victoria
made little use of the new-found freedom and in 1845 a
'fourpenny gallery' was introduced. Eliza Vincent, who
had been a leading lady here, became the manager in the
mid-1850s.

In 1858 serious loss of life was caused by a false alarm of
fire which started a stampede in the gallery. Sixteen people
lost their lives and a great number were injured.

The bad days followed when the theatre sank to the level
of a Blood-Tub. From 1867 things were a little better under
the management of J. A. Cave, but in 1871 the theatre was
sold by auction. The new owners partially reconstructed the
interior and reopened as the New Victoria Palace, but this
did not help, and another sale soon followed. The theatre
finally closed at the Whitsun of 1880. It was taken over by
Emma Cons, a social reformer. The whole of the interior
was rearranged by J. T. Robinson, the architect, about
£3000 spent and it reopened on 27 December 1880 for
concerts, under the name of The Royal Victoria Hall and
Coffee Tavern. During the previous years it had attained
a rather lurid reputation; Miss Cons undertook its purifica-
tion, and set about transforming it into a 'cheap and
decent place of amusement on strict temperance lines'.
William Poel was her manager from 1881 to 1883. The
project was considerably helped by Samuel Morley, a
textile manufacturer and M.P. for Bristol; and from that
time the theatre went forward until in 1888 it was possible
to buy the freehold, and the title deeds were presented by
Emma Cons to the Charity Commission.

The year 1900 saw the first opera produced there, *The
Bohemian Girl*, under the conductorship of Charles Corri,
who was for many years in charge of the musical
direction of the theatre.

In 1912 the management passed from Emma Cons to her
niece Lilian Baylis (who had been acting manager since
1898), of whom Tyrone Guthrie has said: 'Lilian Baylis . . .
saw a job to be done at the Vic and thenceforward that job

was her whole life. First she introduced the new "moving pictures" then she obtained a dramatic licence so that operatic concerts could be turned into full Opera Performances; then, on the proceeds of the penny cinema shows she organised Symphony Concerts, and lost all she had made.' From 1914 to 1919 the theatre was largely kept alive by an annual grant from the City Parochial Foundation, from the Carnegie United Kingdom Trust, and by large helpings from Lilian Baylis's private purse; it was also helped by sympathisers' public subscriptions, and other charitable bequests. In October 1914 Miss Baylis made one of the boldest experiments in theatrical history, against the advice of every theatrical manager in London, by presenting Shakespeare at popular prices. If for no other reason—and there are several—the Old Vic would be famous for the fact that it was the first theatre in the world to have produced the whole of the plays of Shakespeare contained in the First Folio. The plays were produced between October 1914 and November 1923. This is a record which was not equalled until the 'Five-Year Plan' of 1953–8.

On 25 October 1918 the theatre celebrated its hundredth birthday and received a visit from Queen Mary and the Princess Royal.

A financial crisis was brought about in 1921 when the L.C.C. ordered the theatre to be largely reconditioned. This meant rehousing Morley College which had occupied part of the backstage premises since 1894. The total amount required to make all the necessary alterations was £30,000. Every effort was made to get the required sum. A fund was started which never looked like attaining the total until Sir George Dance came forward with the whole of the amount, and work began, the theatre remaining open during the repairs until 1927.

In November 1923 Princess Mary was present to commemorate the Tercentenary of the publication of the First Folio. In 1927 the main reconstruction started and the autumn season was held at the Lyric, Hammersmith. The theatre reopened in its changed form with *Romeo and Juliet* on 14 February 1928.

On 5 May 1931 was the first performance of ballet, at which Anton Dolin was the guest artist. This marked the original formation of the Vic-Wells Ballet Company under the direction of Ninette de Valois. (Lilian Baylis had rebuilt and reopened Sadler's Wells Theatre in January 1931; see No. 7.)

The mixed seasons of opera and Shakespeare and other revivals, which had been the policy, now alternated between the Old Vic and the new Sadler's Wells Theatre. After a time this became too awkward and expensive, and eventually in 1935 the Wells became the home of the opera and ballet companies and drama remained at the Old Vic.

To list all the famous actors who have appeared here would be a 'Who's Who in the Theatre' of the last fifty years. From the time the Old Vic became 'West End' in the mid-thirties up to the outbreak of the war in 1939, its reputation went from strength to strength. Lilian Baylis died in 1937 leaving a living memorial.

The Old Vic did not reopen for the 1939–40 season, but performances of *The Tempest* and *King Lear* were given with John Gielgud in 1940. The theatre received severe bomb damage in May 1941 and was closed until 1950, when it reopened, on November 14, completely renovated, partially reconstructed, taking its place as the national Theatre 'pro tem'. The architect for the reconstruction was Douglas W. Rowntree, with Pierre Sonrel as consultant for the fore-stage area (this has been modified and partially redesigned since the reopening). On 18 March 1958 the Queen opened the Old Vic Annexe, a building to house the wardrobe and workrooms, situated on the opposite corner of Webber Street.

The Old Vic Company ceased its existence in 1963 with a performance of *Measure for Measure* on 15 June in the presence of Princess Marina, Duchess of Kent.

The theatre was then taken over by the National Theatre Company, under the direction of Laurence Olivier (succeeded by Peter Hall in 1974), to be used until their new theatre was built on the South Bank. The opening production was *Hamlet*, with Peter O'Toole, on 22 October.

The story of the theatre has been told in several books and the accounts of its companies both here and at the New Theatre in the war are well covered. Those interested can read *The Old Vic* by John Booth (1917), *The Old Vic and Its Associations* by H. Chance Newton (1922), *The Old Vic* by Cicely Hamilton and Lilian Baylis (1926), *The Old "Old Vic"* by Edwin Fagg (1936), *The Vic-Wells, The Work of Lilian Baylis*, edited by Harcourt Williams (1935), *A Theatre for Everybody* by Edward J. Dent (1945), and *Old Vic Saga* by Harcourt Williams (1949).

For the productions, references should be made to *These Players* by Doris Westwood (1926), *Four Years of the Old Vic* by Harcourt Williams (1935), *Four Seasons of the Old Vic Company, 1944–9*, *Old Vic Drama* (1948), and *Old Vic Drama 2* (1957) by Audrey Williamson, *The Old Vic 1949–50* by Lionel Hale (1950), *The Old Vic in Photographs* by John Vickers (1949), *Scrapbook of the Old Vic* by Mary Clarke, 5 volumes (1953–58).

The full history of the National Theatre Company's twelve years' sojourn has yet to be told before the company move to their new theatre in April 1975.

5 · The Open Air Theatre

Queen Mary's Gardens, Inner Circle, Regents Park, N.W.1

Capacity: 1200

Opened 5 June 1933 with *Twelfth Night.* Produced by Robert Atkins, Under the management of Sydney W. Carroll and Lewis Schaverien.

*

Open-air productions of Shakespeare in the Royal Botanical Gardens, as they were then called, had been given by Ben Greet and his Woodland Players from 1900 for some years.

The idea was revived by Sydney Carroll, in association with Lewis Schaverien, in July 1932. By arrangement with the Office of Works who controlled the Gardens, four matinée performances were given of Robert Atkins's production of *Twelfth Night,* in black and white, which was then running at the New Theatre.

The success of the venture led to the creation of a permanent open-air theatre, beginning the following year. From then on each summer with only a few exceptions during some of the war years and after, it has presented pastoral Shakespeare and other suitable plays. The casts have included distinguished actors and actresses from the West End stage and often casting innovations from other fields.

Nigel Playfair's production of *The Fantasticks* by Rostand was transferred from the Lyric, Hammersmith, in July 1933 for some special performances, the young Robert Helpmann, in his first year in London, dancing in the *pas de six.*

It was here, strangely enough, in 1934 that the first performance of a play, *The Six of Calais* by Bernard Shaw, took place. Even opera and ballet at times have formed the programme.

Sir Ben Greet, as he had become, returned to the Park in his last years as Master of the Greensward from 1933 to 1935. Robert Atkins, who had produced at the theatre since the beginning, assumed its direction in 1939.

268   Part 2. The Outer Ring

Though the vagaries of the English climate made each new season a gamble during the days of rising costs, he managed to keep alive this unique part of London's theatrical entertainment until he retired. Performances were given in a marquee when wet.

The theatre did not open during 1961, but under the new management of David Conville and with a reconstructed stage, it has had successful seasons each summer since 1962 of *al fresco* Shakespearian productions.

At the end of the 1974 season the theatre will be reconstructed at the cost of £90,000, to be reopened in June 1975.

6 · The Round House

Chalk Farm Road, N.W.1

Capacity: 400–600

Opened as a theatre June 1968 with *Themes on the Tempest* devised and directed by Peter Brook. Presented by Experimental Theatre.

*

The Round House is part of the railway buildings which began to grow at Chalk Farm early in the last century. *Old and New London* (1875) says:

When in 1831–2 the London and Birmingham Railway [as this line was originally called, before it became the London North Western] was first projected, the metropolitan terminus was at Chalk Farm, near the north-east

corner of Regent's Park. It was not until 1835 that a bill
was brought into Parliament, and carried after great
opposition, for bringing this terminus as near to London
as what was then termed 'Euston Grove'. Up to the
year 1845, for fear of frightening the horses in the streets,
the locomotive engines came no nearer to London than
Chalk Farm, where the engine was detached from the
train, and from thence to Euston Station the carriages
were attached to an endless rope moved by a stationary
engine at the Chalk Farm end of the line.

In 1846, when an amalagamation of several lines took
place, George Stephenson, who had built the railway
originally, constructed new assembly and engine sheds,
including the now famous Round House, which was built in
1847.

Old and New London says:

The circular building which projects into the Chalk
Farm Road near the Adelaide Hotel was built to
accommodate the locomotive engines in the early days of
the London and Birmingham Railway. It is about 120
feet in diameter, and has in its centre a turn-table, by
means of which the engines can be shifted to the up and
down lines, and to the various sidings. Externally, the
building is not very attractive, but its interior is light, the
arched roof being supported on graceful iron pillars.

It remained in use until the days of further railway
expansion, and when no longer needed in 1869 it became
a warehouse for W. S. Silbey until 1964, eventually
being Listed as a building of architectural and historic
importance for which a use had to be found.

In 1960 Arnold Wesker, the playwright, founded Centre
42 as 'An Association not for profit and registered as a
National Charity', stating:

The 42 movement is a bid by a new generation of
writers, actors, musicians, painters, sculptors and architects to assume responsibilities in the shaping of our
culture by returning art to the community, where, through
familiarity and participation, they can revitalise their
work by confronting a new audience and transforming
their art into a creative force.

In 1962, Centre 42 mounted six People's Festivals, in
co-operation with the local Trades Councils in Welling-
borough, Nottingham, Leicester, Birmingham, Bristol
and Hayes. The purpose of these Festivals is to
establish the habit of participation in the arts. Further
Festivals are planned for the near future and a centre
in London.

In 1966 they announced they had acquired the Round

House and began raising funds 'for its conversion to a multi-purpose Arts Centre for national and local use to be open to the public in the spring of 1967'. They did not do well financially and after many difficulties the scheme was salvaged by George Hoskins, who established a Round House Trust, and the interior was fitted out as a theatre in 1967 by the architects, Bickerdale, Allen, Rich and Partners to accommodate an audience of 400 to 600 people according to the seating and staging.

The building was used under a temporary licence for 'Pop' concerts and other club activities until it was fully equipped and licensed by the end of 1967. The first public performance, according to the published report, was Peter Brook's production in June 1968 of *Themes on The Tempest* which made theatrical history in its free use of a large open space. In the autumn John Arden produced, in conjunction with the I.C.A., his own play *The Hero Rises Up*—a take-down of Nelson; in January 1969 Daniel Barenboim and the New Philharmonia Orchestra recorded Beethoven's major works for his centenary; through the winter London Weekend Television did five broadcasts of a 'Round House Forum' when many speakers debated their causes.

It was finally accepted, if not by the Press, on 17 February 1969 with a production of *Hamlet*, presented by the Free Theatre, a new Company, who issued the following statement:

> For many people the theatre is anachronistic. The idea of planning an evening in advance, buying tickets, plush seats, is an anathema. Free Theatre is determined to make the theatre available and alive for just this audience.
>
> This can only be done by emphasising what is most unique in theatre—its presence. It is just this presence that the proscenium theatre has weakened and debilitated, despite the revolution already achieved by writers whose work, subject and attack could never have found a stage before.
>
> Now a new revolution is needed to destroy, finally and completely, the form of the proscenium theatre and the social habits that go with it. To restore impact to the theatre, it must be liberated from the tyranny of any form. Each production can have its own shape of stage and audience. Each will then be unique.

As their aims were said to coincide with so many of the aims of Centre 42 the Company was welcomed by the Round House Trust. The cast included Nicol Williamson as Hamlet, and Marianne Faithfull as Ophelia. It had a mixed reception and an interrupted run, until the production, with the addition of Constance Cummings as Gertrude, moved to America in May. In September

the National Youth Theatre's production of *Macbeth*
was seen. From November companies from all over the
country gave London seasons. The Phoenix, Leicester,
brought a new play by Dennis Potter, *Son of Man*.
A week later the Freehold Company presented *Antigone*,
then The Meadow Players, in February 1970, brought
The Blacks by Genet. March saw *The Foreign Field*,
this time presented by the Contemporary Theatre. In
May Arnold Wesker directed his own play, *The Friends*,
then in July came the first success, which put the Round
House 'on the theatre map', a revue presented by Michael
White, *Oh! Calcutta!* written by various authors, and later
to move into the West End, first to the Royalty Theatre
and later to the Duchess. In November the Royal
Shakespeare Company held a Theatre-go-Round Festival,
and the year concluded with a rock version of Shakespeare's
Othello under the title of *Catch My Soul*, which continued
its run eventually at the Prince of Wales. In March Jean-
Louis Barrault's adaptation of *Rabelais*, the first in English,
and directed by Barrault, arrived for a seven week season.
After this, among other plays, were: *Confrontation, Maybe
That's Your Problem, Titus Andronicus, Pork, Skyers*
and *1789*. Then came a big success with the American
musical based on the Gospel according to St Matthew,
Godspell, which promptly transferred to Wyndham's in
January 1972. During the first half of 1972 were seen *Mother
Earth, The Black Macbeth, Quetzecoate* and *The Wheel*.
Later in the year plays included *Rock Carmen, Stand and
Deliver!* and *Bible One*, Frank Dunlop's successful re-
working of the Bible, earlier seen at Edinburgh and the
Young Vic, Part I, *The Creation to Jacob* and Part II *Joseph
and the Amazing Technicolor Dreamcoat*, by Tim Rice and
Andrew Lloyd Webber. This arrived at the Albery early in
February 1973. During the next year the much discussed
Peter Coe production of *Decameron 73* was seen after a
postponement of the first night and Prospect Theatre
Company, in the summer of 1973, presented a season of
three plays, *The Royal Hunt of the Sun, Twelfth Night*
and their up-dated *Pericles. A Feast of Fools* was presented
for a Christmas season and 1974 started with *Le Grand
Magic Circus*, described as an account of 5000 years of
love and adventure. This ran till March since when there
has been little of note to record.

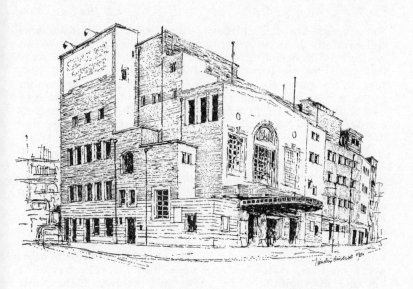

7 · Sadler's Wells Theatre

Rosebery Avenue, Finsbury, E.C.1

Capacity: 1499

THE PRESENT THEATRE

Opened 6 January 1931 with Shakespeare's *Twelfth Night*. Produced by Harcourt Williams, under the management of Lilian Baylis.

*

The history of this theatre really begins in 1683, when some workmen digging in the grounds of Thomas Sadler, an inspector of Highways in Clerkenwell, discovered a well which was identified as once having belonged to the Priory of Clerkenwell, and which in the Middle Ages had been associated with miraculous powers. In a very short time people were flocking to drink these 'excellent steel waters' and Sadler enclosed the gardens and converted them into a pleasure resort. In partnership with Francis Forcer, a dancing master, he also erected a wooden Musick House, with a platform serving as a stage, which was opened as Sadler's Musick House on 3 June 1683. Sadler was succeeded by Forcer, who took a Mr Miles into partnership and in 1699 the place became known as Miles' Musick House for a short time, but soon returned to its original name, but by 1718 it was simply called Sadler's Wells. Miles died in 1724 and Forcer in 1730, after which Forcer's

son carried on for thirteen years until he in turn was
followed by John Warren, under whose régime the Wells
became 'villainously disreputable'. At this time there were
four or five performances a day, the number of performances and their length being determined by the number
of people waiting to gain admission. In 1744 a Grand Jury
had cause to put on record a verdict in which the place was
condemned as 'of great extravagance, luxury, idleness and
ill-fame'.

Thomas Rosoman, a builder, became manager in 1746. In
1753 he engaged a regular company and the Musick House,
which had housed mainly singers, dancers and acrobatic
displays, became a regular theatre. He demolished the
original wooden building in 1765 and built a stone theatre at
a cost of £4225. The entire demolition and reconstruction
occupied, it is said, only seven weeks. The theatre opened
with a mixed programme on 8 April 1765. Rosoman did
much to improve the status of the theatre and the tone of its
performances. After his retirement in 1772, Thomas King
became manager for ten years and brought fashionable
audiences there to patronise him, as he had been for many
years associated with Drury Lane, and after a while the
interior was entirely remodelled. The theatre from 1772 had
been held by a group of shareholders, which included
Richard Wroughton, Henry Siddons (husband of the famous
actress), Charles Dibdin, the elder, and his two sons: they
delegated the active management of the theatre to various
of their number. In 1783 the great attraction was a company
of performing dogs. In 1786 Maria Romanzini, afterwards
better known as Mrs Bland, made her first appearance here,
and other famous appearances included those of Braham,
Boyce the Harlequin, and the famous clown Joseph
Grimaldi, who played here from 1781 to 1805. In 1801 a
boy actor, Master Carey, afterwards the great Edmund
Kean, made an early appearance.

In 1804 under the management of Charles Dibdin, a
series of nautical dramas were presented, featuring real
water in a tank fed by the New River. The theatre was
sometimes known as the Aquatic Theatre at this period.

In 1817 Grimaldi became a shareholder, a speculation
which resulted in a heavy loss, and a succession of
managers followed. During 1821 the first plays of Douglas
Jerrold were produced here, *More Frightened than Hurt*
and *The Chieftain's Oath;* these were melodramas in the
'aquatic tradition', and in the latter we read that there was
'a spacious lake of real water' and that 'the destruction of
Maclean's camp by fire was grand in the extreme'.
Grimaldi made his farewell appearance in 1828.

In 1832 the theatre was under the management of Fanny
Fitzwilliam and W. H. Williams, and in 1834 there was a
fire, caused by gas lighting, which did some damage to

scenery, and the theatre underwent a thorough renovation in 1838.

The year 1841 saw the production of *Giselle; or, The Phantom Night Dancers* on August 23. In the final scene Dibdin's water tank was used for real fountains, with suitable lighting effects. The ballet and incidental dances were arranged by Frampton, and Fenton designed the scenery. (This was a dramatic version by William Moncrieff of the famous ballet which was not produced, at Her Majesty's theatre, until 1842.)

The year 1844 is in many respects one of the most important dates in the history of old Sadler's Wells. In this year it was let to Samuel Phelps and Mary Warner. Phelps's own announcement of his aim is particularly interesting:

> Mrs Warner and Mr Phelps embark on the management of Sadler's Wells in the hope of eventually rendering it what a theatre ought to be—a place for justly representing the works of our great dramatic poets. This undertaking commences at a time when stages which have been called 'National' are closed, or devoted to very different objects from that of presenting the real drama of England, and when the law has placed all theatres upon equal footing of security and respectability . . . These circumstances justify the notion that each separate division of our immense metropolis, with its two million of inhabitants, may have its own well conducted theatre, within a reasonable distance of its patrons.

The breaking of the monopoly of the Patent Theatres in 1843 made it possible for the Minor Theatres to present the plays of Shakespeare. Phelps's work at the Wells was one of the most important outcomes of this change in the law. He identified the theatre with the presentation of Shakespeare, producing thirty-four of the plays. It was a bold experiment to transform a theatre with a reputation extending over nearly two centuries for having the roughest audiences in London and for being the home of the lower forms of dramatic entertainment, into a home for legitimate drama. Phelps's management began on 27 May 1844, with a production of *Macbeth*. Mrs Warner retired from the partnership in 1846, and after considerable alterations to the theatre it was announced it was to be under the management of Phelps and Greenwood. Greenwood retired in 1860, and Phelps terminated his management two years later, having added an important chapter to the history of the theatre. His revival of *Antony and Cleopatra* in 1849 was the first for a century, and that of *Pericles* in 1854 the first since the Restoration. Phelps's importance is considerable, for his success coincided with the low-water mark of the poetic drama at the metropolitan theatres. At the time of his retirement he had given between three and four thousand performances in all. During this period the name Theatre Royal, Sadler's Wells, was adopted.

Captain Morton Price and Miss Lucette succeeded Phelps, with light entertainment for a season, and then it came into the hands of Robert Edgar from 1863 to 1871. Edgar's wife and leading lady was Alice Marriott, one of the most famous female Hamlets of her day. After Edgar's régime ended, the theatre sank to the lowest depths. It was a skating rink, a pickle-factory, the scene of a prize-fight, and was eventually closed as a dangerous structure and left derelict.

It was sold for £1020 and eventually the interior was reconstructed at a cost of £12,000 to designs by C. J. Phipps. The life of the theatre was revived by Mrs Bateman from the Lyceum, with her daughter Kate as leading lady. Reopening on 9 October 1879, she claimed that it was 'one of the largest and most commodious theatres in London, providing accommodation for 2500 persons, not one of whom, it is believed, will fail to command a good view of the stage'.

On the death of Mrs Bateman in 1881 her younger daughter Isabel carried on the management for a while, but the theatre then, like so many of its suburban counterparts, became the home of crude melodrama. 'The Saturday night gallery contained the most villainous, desperate, hatchet-faced assembly of ruffians to be found in all London.'

In November 1893 it became a music-hall under the management of George Belmont. In June 1901 renovations were undertaken by Bertie Crewe, for a new manager F. Macnaughton. The work was carried out without interfering with any of the performances and the scaffolding was taken down each day. The contractors for this work were John Weibkind and Sons, who achieved a remarkable piece of reconstruction.

Eventually the theatre became a cinema and in 1906 closed altogether and once again became derelict. In 1921 it was reported that it had been acquired by Ernest Rolls, who intended to convert it into a 'Cabaret' Theatre, but this project came to nothing.

In 1927 began the next important chapter in the history of Sadler's Wells, when Lilian Baylis and Sir Reginald Rowe launched an appeal for its rehabilitation, with a view to making it a north London counterpart of the Old Vic. As funds came in so work began on the complete demolition of the old theatre. A new building gradually arose, designed by F. G. M. Chancellor, the money having been raised by a committee under the chairmanship of the Duke of Devonshire. The Carnegie Trust contributed £14,200 and the Finsbury Borough Council £2000. The theatre was constituted under a Charity Commission scheme similar to that of the Old Vic.

An account in *The Times* of 29 November 1930 says:

Externally the New Sadler's Wells may be described as an impressive composition of masses in brick, with a Georgian flavour. There is a canopy over the principal entrance and a group of three stone dressed windows and a decorative panel, by Mr Herman Cawlthra above, but the building relies for architectural effect chiefly on the proportion of the masses and the texture of the wall surfaces.

Cawlthra was also responsible for the panel in relief over the proscenium of a scene from *A Midsummer Night's Dream*.

The theatre reopened on 6 January 1931 under the management of Lilian Baylis and in conjunction with the Old Vic, with *Twelfth Night*, the cast being headed by John Gielgud and Dorothy Green.

Between 1931 and 1937 about fifty operas were performed, and the Ballet Company formed at the Old Vic in 1931 developed into Sadler's Wells Ballet Company (now the Royal Ballet at Covent Garden).

At first the company from the Vic and Wells alternated between theatres but this scheme was eventually dropped in 1934 and the Wells became completely devoted to Opera and Ballet.

In 1938 improvements were carried out as part of the memorial to Lilian Baylis. These included the building of a new rehearsal room, a greatly enlarged stage, a new scene dock, new dressing-rooms and shower-baths. The newly acquired site comprised a wide new frontage in Arlington Way, connected by a strip of land at the back of the stage wall, with an extension of the frontage next to the stage door in Rosebery Avenue. The architects were Stanley Hall and Easton and Robertson.

In September 1940 the theatre was closed and became a rest home for 180 people bombed out in the locality. It remained as such for nearly a year until it suffered minor damage from enemy action.

On Thursday, 7 June, 1945, the theatre reopened with Benjamin Britten's opera *Peter Grimes*. Once the Vic-Wells Ballet Company went to Covent Garden, and with the later-formed Sadler's Wells Theatre Ballet became the Royal Ballet, the Opera Company became resident at the Wells, except for visiting companies. In 1958 the company from the Moscow Art Theatre was there for a season.

In 1959 alterations were made to improve the acoustics. A canopy was built, suspended high over the orchestra and a redesigned proscenium arch by Hope Bagenal has completely obscured the Shakespearean decoration. The theatre was also redecorated at the same time in an

entirely new scheme. In 1960 a new storey was added to
part of the building to give increased wardrobe accommodation. The original well is to be found under a trap
door at the back of the stalls. In 1968 the Opera Company
moved to the London Coliseum, taking with it its sub-
stantial grant from the Arts Council. The theatre
reverted to the Governors of the Sadler's Wells Trust, for
whom Douglas Craig is now the Administrator of the
theatre. Since then visiting companies of Ballet, Opera
and plays have, with a Christmas D'Oyly Carte Season,
kept the theatre open. In 1971 financial difficulties led to a
public appeal. As Douglas Craig said in his report in
June 1973:

In 1968, for very good reasons, Sadler's Wells Opera
moved down to the London Coliseum. It was agreed
that Sadler's Wells Theatre should be kept open as 'a
theatre for the public'—a view strongly endorsed by the
Arts Council. Unfortunately the theatre was not given too
good a start in playing its role because the publicity
given to the move to the Coliseum contrived to suggest
that not only was Sadler's Wells Theatre no longer good
for the Opera Company (which had outgrown it) but that it
was no good for anything, and this impression was con-
veyed very strongly to the Greater London Council
representatives who inspected the premises.

It was agreed to let the theatre to visiting companies
at an economic rental. Hindsight reveals that unfortunately the figure chosen was pitched too low, so that the
first year's work showed a deficit of £31,000. The Arts
Council complained about this, having, they said, been
given assurances that the theatre would run without
need of further subsidy, but neither they nor the G.L.C.
were disposed to offer financial help, for various
reasons—they had already committed large sums to
'Sadler's Wells', there was no more money available for
London, etc.

Moreover, it later proved an embarrassment to the new
administration that during this period some 'old
friends' such as the Handel Opera Society and the
London Opera Centre were offered the use of the theatre
at a specially reduced figure.

It was finally decided that Sadler's Wells Trust could
no longer bear the theatre's deficit, the two organisations
decided to separate and legal advice was sought in
negotiations which at times became acrimonious and
which are in fact still not wholly concluded and could at
any moment be reopened by anyone who had a mind to
do so.

Since, therefore, the theatre was operating at a loss
which could not be covered by any of the obvious sources

—the Trust, the Arts Council of Great Britain or the Greater London Council—the Governors decided in the autumn of 1971 to launch a public appeal, at the same time codifying their policy; a suitable shop window for important foreign companies; a platform for worthy home-based companies in need of a properly equipped and sited metropolitan show-case; an important London link in a DALTA-type circuit of high quality touring presentations; the encouragement of student performances. This, incidentally, is fully in line with the scheme of the Charity Commissioners under which Sadler's Wells Theatre was reopened in 1931 and with the Arts Council's report on opera and ballet published in December 1969.

Meantime the theatre continues with difficulty to keep to its aims and purpose.

The story of the Wells can be read in *Some London Theatres, Past and Present* by Michael Williams (1883), *Old Sadler's Wells* by Edwin Fagg (1935), *A Theatre for Everybody* by Edward J. Dent (1945), *The Memoirs of Charles Dibdin, the Younger*, edited by George Speaight (1956), *The Story of Sadler's Wells* by Dennis Arundell (1965) and many books on the Ballet and Opera Companies which give a full account of the work of the past years.

8 · The Shaw Theatre

100 Euston Road, N.W.1

Capacity: 458

Opened 5 July 1971 with a revival of *The Devil's Disciple* by George Bernard Shaw. Directed by Michael Croft and presented by the National Youth Theatre, Dolphin Theatre Company.

*

The opening programme contained the following note:

The Shaw Theatre is part of the St. Pancras Library complex. It takes its name from George Bernard Shaw who was a member of the old St. Pancras Borough Council between 1897 and 1903. When Camden Council was looking for a name for its new theatre it had the happy thought of honouring Shaw's long association with the borough in this most befitting manner.

Plans for a library building on the Euston Road were first conceived as long ago as 1907. The present architects—Elidir Davies and Partners—took over the scheme from the then St. Pancras Borough Council in 1960. Since that time, the original concept of the building has gone through a number of changes, and the theatre is probably the one part of the complex which has changed most of all.

In 1960 the architects were asked to design a comparatively simple Assembly Hall which would be suitable for conferences, lectures and concerts, and which would be capable of being rapidly converted from one use to another. When the original library concept was enlarged, the Council was persuaded to enlarge the hall as well, and in 1965 the architects were asked to install an orchestra pit for chamber opera. The concept was again enlarged in 1968 when Camden decided to put the emphasis on drama, and the hall was adapted for this purpose. The auditorium seating was increased to its present capacity, a flying tower was added, dressing room space was enlarged and a small administration block was attached so that the theatre would be able to house a permanent company.

The theatre consists of one tier of seats rising from stage level. The whole complex was opened by Princess Anne on 2 April 1971 and the theatre had its first performance in the presence of Princess Margaret and Lord Snowdon on the following 5 July.

The National Youth Theatre was founded by Michael Croft in 1956. The story of its London seasons and tours is told in *The National Youth Theatre* by Simon Masters, 1969. The first theatre programme tells:

For five years the National Youth Theatre had been seeking a permanent home. In 1965 Camden Council had already offered it a site at Swiss Cottage for this purpose. However, as a result of many planning delays and financial problems, this NYT project never got off the ground. Thus in 1968, when the plans for the Shaw Theatre were finally settled, the Council offered to lease it to the NYT.

The terms of this lease represent an extraordinary act of theatre patronage by a local council, and one for which it is difficult to find a parallel.

The lease has been offered to the NYT, in the first instance, for seven years. The theatre has been leased at a peppercorn rent and with the free provision of certain essential services such as lighting, heating and maintenance. In addition, the Council has made an annual

grant of £9000 to the NYT to meet the salaries of front
of the house and security staff. At the same time,
while providing such generous financial help, the Council
has agreed not to interfere in any way with the NYT's
artistic policy.

A professional company, the Dolphin Theatre Company,
was formed to alternate with the Youth Theatre productions
and other presentations. Their first production was Shaw's
The Devil's Disciple, with a cast headed by Tom Bell and
directed by Michael Croft. The next few months saw some
new plays and revivals including *The Shoemaker's Holiday*,
(the debut of NYT in their own theatre), *The Samaritan*,
The Long and the Short and the Tall, *Romeo and Juliet*
and *Twelfth Night*, with Vanessa Redgrave. In May 1972
Mia Farrow made her first London stage appearance in a
revival of J. M. Barrie's *Mary Rose*, a Manchester
Theatre 69 production. In September 1972 the National
Youth Theatre was seen in a revival of *Zigger Zagger*, by
Peter Terson, first seen in 1967 and later this had a short
run in the West End at the Strand Theatre. Early in 1973,
from Edinburgh, Bill Bryden's play, *Willie Rough*, arrived;
later in the year came a revival of *Macbeth*. Sheila Allen
played Lady Macbeth and First Witch in this production.
Early in 1974 *Mind Your Head*, by Adrian Mitchell, first
presented at Liverpool Everyman Theatre, had a London
season, followed by a Dolphin Company production of *The
Importance of Being Earnest* and other revivals.

9 · The Theatre Royal

Angel Lane, Stratford, E.15

Capacity: 500

Opened 17 December 1884 with *Richelieu* by Bulwer Lytton, followed by a comedietta (with songs by Lucy Hawthorne). Produced by and under the management of William Charles Dillon.

*

In July 1884 a licence was granted to William Charles Dillon to build a theatre on the Salway Estate at the corner of Salway Road and Angel Lane, Stratford-by-Bow (a wooden booth theatre had been near the site in earlier days), as *The Stage* reports on 11 July 1884:

> Despite the opposition of the Rev. R. P. Pelly, vicar of St. John's Church, Stratford, who appeared to object. He produced a petition against it, signed by the clergy of the district, and urged 'that a theatre would not tend to the moral elevation of the people of the neighbourhood'; that it would injuriously affect a home close by; and that 'probably a low class of drama would be provided, so that it would become the resort of the lowest classes'. The intolerance of such one-sided arguments was at once apparent to the justices, and Colonel Howard, the chairman, met the clerical opposition boldly by saying 'the bench had a duty to perform to the public'. The licence for the new theatre was therefore granted, on the usual terms of being renewed annually. In arriving at this decision the justices expressed an opinion that a 'well conducted theatre would be a benefit to the neighbourhood'.

William Charles Dillon must not be confused with the famous tragedian Charles Dillon (1819–81) who, strangely enough, does not appear to have borne any relationship to the East End actor-manager, who billed himself W. Charles Dillon, and who had a liking for playing the parts associated with his namesake. His real name was

Silver, and his sister was married to Fred Fredericks,
senior. He and his family partly financed the building of
the theatre.

In November 1884 *The Stage* reports that the theatre
would be ready for opening in the December with a
Stock Company. *The Era* for December 20 duly reported
the event.

> The outside of the building we must describe as ugly
> in the extreme, but the interior presents a very pretty
> and attractive appearance. The Theatre, which it is
> estimated will accommodate about one thousand, has
> been built by Messrs David G. Laing and Sons, from
> designs and under the direction of the well known Mr
> James George Buckle, A.R.I.B.A., of Adam Street,
> Adelphi. The lines of the house are so arranged that
> a good view of the stage is obtained from every seat,
> and the auditorium is ventilated by means of a sunlight and
> large extraction cowl over the gallery. A similar cowl
> ventilates the stage and there is ample provision for
> fresh air. . . . The theatre has been built in accordance
> with all the recent regulations imposed on metropolitan
> theatres, and the woodwork throughout, not excepting
> the seats, has been coated with Astrophy's patent
> Cyanite, a fireproof solution recommended by Captain
> Shaw. The interior fittings of elegant and very elaborate
> description, but in truth it must be said that the approaches
> are in an exceedingly rough state, and there is a per-
> vading smell of paint which is anything but refresh-
> ing. . . . The estimated cost of the building is between
> £3000 and £4000.

After describing the production of *Richelieu* the reporter
goes on to say:

> Mr Dillon won much applause. He worked under
> difficulties and in one important scene had to interrupt
> the action of the play in order to reprove some inatten-
> tive gods who were appeasing their appetites. At the
> end of the act Mr Dillon very properly delivered the
> dwellers on high a lecture on the sin of cracking nuts,
> and it is to be hoped they will profit by his very earnest
> reproof. 'You treat me fairly,' said Mr Dillon, 'and I
> will treat you fairly, and give you good entertainment;
> but I will certainly not have the beautiful lines of this
> play spoiled and my artists insulted by your rude
> behaviour.'

Of the leading lady the reviewer continues:

> Her presence was very attractive, and a sergeant of
> police who took a seat next to us remarked in confidence,
> 'If that 'ed of 'air's hall 'er hown, sir, it's a very fine
> one and she ought to be proud on it'.

We are told that *Hamlet* and *Richard III* are in rehearsal
and *Proof* would be performed on Boxing Day.

The local press, *The Stratford Express*, was not very
encouraging:

> The so-called Theatre Royal, Stratford has been
> opened this week, we are not aware of any solid ground
> for the adoption of the 'Royal' title and if this is a
> prophecy it is rather a hardy one. If it is used to give
> an impression that the management desires to give
> only good plays and make the theatre really desirable
> to Stratford, we hail the promise with pleasure.

After noting the plays produced the critic has to admit
that their choice shows a determination to avoid 'the dreary
pieces in which the uninstructed delight—to witness a
murder every twenty minutes'.

At this time the productions seemed to have been
changed almost nightly. Dillon took his benefit in April
in *Ingomar* and the theatre was announced as available for
touring companies before the resumption of the Stock
Season. He continued this policy with revivals of famous
plays until the spring of 1886 when the theatre was taken
over by Fred Thomas, who continued in the same manner
with a Stock Company, but the plays from this time on
were more of the nature anticipated by the first local critic.

In June 1887 little Ada Reeve, who had been a child
actress at the Pavilion Whitechapel since her first appearance there in 1878, came to the Royal with her father
Charles Reeve to play Ned in Henry Pettitt's *The Black
Flag*. She also appeared with him in a comedietta in the
same programme.

Thomas was succeeded by Albert Fredericks in April
1888 with Hugh Moss as his general manager. The
Fredericks family, the brothers Fred and Albert, and
their children and in-laws, were one of the largest
managerial families in the East End. They were also
responsible for building the Borough Theatre and Opera
House not far away in Stratford High Street, which
opened on 31 August 1896 with a more 'West End' star
touring policy, but is now no longer in existence. Under
their management the Royal continued with annual
pantomimes and touring melodrama until this class of
entertainment was gradually rivalled by the cinema.

The stage was enlarged in 1891. A fire at the theatre
in 1921 caused some damage back-stage. In 1927 a policy
of twice-nightly variety and revue was established, the
prices being 1/6 to 4d. By this time Fred Fredericks
junior was the manager; he retired in 1932; the theatre
passed out of the family's hands in 1957.

A return to twice-nightly 'blood and thunder' melodrama in a repertory season was tried in 1935 for eighteen

months at a big loss, and from 1946 to 1949 David
Horne presented seasons of plays of the first quality.
He was followed by other managers who tried to keep
the theatre alive in Stratford against the prevailing odds
but without avail and in 1952 it became the Palace of
Varieties for a brief spell with twice-nightly revue and
music-hall. (It had twice-nightly variety between 1943 and
1946.)

In 1953 the Royal was taken by Theatre Workshop; they
acquired the lease in 1957 and in 1959 completely
redecorated and reconditioned it to the designs of
John Bury, reopening in the October.

Theatre Workshop, 'A British People's Theatre', was
founded by Joan Littlewood in 1945 with headquarters at
the Theatre Royal, Kendal. They toured Cumberland
and Westmorland and in 1946 moved south to Ormesby,
which became their home from which tours of this country
and the continent were organised. In 1952 they were first
seen in London at the Embassy Theatre, Swiss Cottage,
and the Comedy Theatre when they produced *Uranium
235*. It was in February 1953 that the company took
over the Theatre Royal, Stratford, and two years later
they had their first big success with *The Good Soldier
Schweik*, which was later transferred to the Duke of
York's. They were also invited to take part in the Paris
International Festival. With support from the Arts
Council and local Councils, they rose to become a strong
influence on the contemporary theatre. The conquest of
the West End was completed with *A Taste of Honey* (1958),
The Hostage (1958), *Make me an Offer* (1959), *Fings
Ain't Wot They Used t'Be* (1959), *Sparrers Can't Sing*
(1960), and *Progress to the Park* (1960), which all began
their careers at Stratford.

Theatre Workshop suffered a temporary eclipse in the
summer of 1961 when Joan Littlewood retired from active
participation in the company; although the theatre remained
open, on and off, with visiting productions, it had little
success. Joan Littlewood and Theatre Workshop returned
in October 1962 with the production of *What a Crazy
World!* a Cockney musical.

The theatre then went through an uneventful period
until March 1963 when Joan Littlewood directed *Oh!
What a Lovely War*, which transferred, with great success,
to Wyndham's in June. The theatre continued to be busy
for the next year, but by June 1964 came a change of
tenancy. The first production under the new management,
Stage Sixty, was *Edge of Reason* in September. At
Christmas came *The Rose and the Ring*. The following
year there were revivals of *Widowers' Houses*, *Ghosts*
and *Saint's Day*, which went to the St Martin's. A musical
based on *Cold Comfort Farm* was seen in October under

the title of *Something Nasty in the Wood Shed* and was the last play produced by Stage Sixty.

Little happened in 1966 and Joan Littlewood returned to direct *Macbird* in April 1967 and the following month she was responsible for *Intrigues and Amours*, a play based on Sir John Vanbrugh's *The Provoked Wife*. In June a two handed play, *Green Julia*, was presented and in September an 'affectionate lampoon', *Mrs Wilson's Diary*, was staged and transferred to the Criterion. In November *The Marie Lloyd Story* had its first night, but was not a success. After this the theatre closed until October 1970 when Joan Littlewood was back again, directing a play by Kenneth Hill, *Forward, Up Your End*, and in December *The Projector* followed. The theatre again closed and did not re-open until March 1972 with *The Londoners*. Joan Littlewood returned to Theatre Workshop with a revised version of her earlier success *Sparrers Can't Sing*, with new music by Lionel Bart, quickly followed by 'a present day rethink' of *The Hostage*. Then came a new farce by Henry Livings, *The Finest Family*, a new musical, *Costa Packet*, and on Boxing Day, 1972, a full scale pantomime for the whole family, *The Big Rock Candy Mountain*.

In May 1973 there was a successful revival of *Sweeny Todd*, which was succeeded by various evenings of light entertainment until the end of 1973. Early in 1974 *Gentlemen Prefer Anything* was staged but in March the theatre was again threatened with financial difficulties and closure. During the last few years the entire surroundings of the theatre have been razed to the ground and the theatre, which is Listed, has been isolated in a vast area of 'no man's land' awaiting development. The theatre is to reopen as Theatre Workshop during the summer.

10 · Wimbledon Theatre

Broadway, Wimbledon, S.W.19

Capacity: 2000

Opened 26 December 1910 with a pantomime, *Jack and Jill; or, the Hill, the Well and the Crown.* Under the management of J. B. Mulholland.

*

Wimbledon was the last of the Mulholland Theatres in the suburbs. These included the Metropole Theatre, Camberwell, (built 1894, demolished 1937 and replaced by an Odeon Cinema) and the King's Theatre, Hammersmith (built 1902, demolished 1963).

Wimbledon theatre was designed by Cecil Masey and Roy Young.

The Era 24 December 1910 said:

The exterior is very simply constructed in a Georgian renaissance style, particularly suitable for a building of its size. The main feature is the tower at the corner, which is surmounted by a dome, above which is a balcony with columns and entablature, which in turn support a crystal ball with a winged figure above. The height of this figure is exactly 100 feet above the pavement. At night the crystal ball will be powerfully illuminated by the mercury vapour process, which throws out violet rays, and will be a beacon light for many miles round. It practically commands ten miles of railways. The figure is also illuminated in a unique and effective manner.

The main entrance is beneath the tower at the corner of Merton Road [now Broadway] and Russell Road and leads through a spacious entrance hall and lounge to the circle and stalls. One is immediately struck by a notable departure from the orthodox line of theatre construction in the fan-shape of the building. The proscenium opening forms, so to speak, the handle end of the fan, and the building widens out from the proscenium wall, the width at the back of the pit being nearly double that at the front of the stalls. The result is an immense gain in holding capacity.

The decorations of the auditorium are in the Georgian and Italian renaissance styles. The decorations are in cream and white, brown, rose-pink, and blue and gold. The main ceiling is semi-circular, slightly coved, and divided up by heavy beams intersecting painted panels, these beams converging to a semicircular opening, over which is the sliding roof. The paintings between are very beautiful, and are the work of Signor Buccini.

There are no boxes on the ground floor. There are ten boxes in all—miniature drawing-rooms. The ground floor is composed of orchestra stalls pit, all handsomely upholstered, and the slope is so effective that everyone has an uninterrupted view of the stage. Over this again is the amphitheatre and gallery tier. The fronts of the boxes and of the tiers are of pierced and hammered brass with bronze enrichments, which not only hold, but reflect the lights. The draperies and carpets all match in shades of old rose and gold, the seats being in crocodile skin of a darker colour, the whole blending with a most pleasing effect.

It was a touring house, run in conjunction with the King's, Hammersmith, with an annual pantomime. All the stars of the period appeared within their walls. In the 1930s repertory was tried at both theatres with the Wilson Barrett and Jevan Brandon-Thomas Company. After the War (during which the Globe and Statue were a casualty) the theatre continued to keep going in difficult times with a company under the direction of Peter Haddon (1955–1962). Management by Audrey Lupton and Arthur Lane followed, but by the 1960s the theatre, like so many others up and down the country, was threatened with closure. After a local campaign the theatre was bought from the Mulholland family by the local council (Wimbledon and Merton) and is now run as a commercial touring theatre by the Merton Civic Theatre Trust. After redecoration it re-opened on 8 November 1968 and has gradually become re-established locally as the centre for the Merton Festival and other artistic activities.

The first London season of the Actors Company, in March–May 1974, successfully brought the theatre once again to the attention of the West End playgoer and the critics.

11 · The Young Vic

The Cut, S.E.1

Capacity: 456
(with an adjoining Studio Theatre seating 150)

Opened 11 September 1970 with *The Cheats of Scapino*, adapted from Molière and directed by Frank Dunlop. Under the management of the National Theatre.

*

The conversion of old shops with the added new building was a brain child of Frank Dunlop, who wished to introduce a young audience to good theatre in intimate surroundings. The opening was described in *The Stage*, 17 September:

Accompanied by the deafening boom of amplified music from a pop group and fireworks from the roof, London's newest theatre, the Young Vic, opened. A couple of hundred yards across the road from the parent Old Vic Theatre, the new one is designed, by William Howell, specifically for the under twenty-fives and its unconventional atmosphere is intended to take the boredom out of theatre-going for this age-group.

Whether or not young people do find traditional theatre a boring experience is an arguable point, and this is perhaps not the place to discuss it. There can be little argument, however, about the success of the new building, with its studio theatre for dancing during the interval and after the show and small productions, and its licensed coffee bar complete with juke-box. In fact, it is something of a fun-place, and the simplicity of the seat-buying arrangements—all unreserved—makes attendance at a play as easy as buying a coke at a coffee bar.

The theatre itself is a large square room with concrete breeze-block walls and chamfered corners, wooden bench seats on three sides in stepped tiers and a gallery round the greater part of the area. The woodwork is

painted red, like the railings round the edge of a Japanese
Noh Theatre platform, and the platform stage along one
side thrusts forward into the centre of the room, so that
every member of the audience is almost nose-to-nose with
the actors.

On the opening night, sitting among the young people
and virtually incognito—for there is no red carpet or
fanfare treatment at this theatre—Sybil Thorndike looked
ecstatic, commenting in a stage whisper, 'A theatre after
my own heart.' It was not difficult to imagine her longing
to be down on the stage adding her own lively contri-
bution to the commedia dell arte high jinks.

The Cheats of Scapino was a very free adaptation of
Molière's play, *Les Fourberies de Scapin*, by Frank
Dunlop, who also directed, and the settings were by Carl
Toms, whose work here has remained an inspiration
through the years.

By Christmas 1970 they had produced their seventh play,
a revival of *The King Stag*. During 1971 there were revivals
of *Waiting for Godot, End-Game, Taming of the Shrew,
Oedipus, Happy Days* and *Romeo and Juliet*, played in
repertoire.

In 1972 were seen *Sweet Mr. Shakespeare, She Stoops
to Conquer, The Chains, The Maids, Deathwatch, The
Alchemist* and a double bill by Harold Pinter and Ted
Hughes, *The Dwarfs* and *The Wound*, among other note-
worthy plays. The following year, 1973, saw two John
Osborne revivals, *Epitaph for George Dillon* and *Look
Back in Anger*. Then *Rosencrantz and Guildenstern are
Dead* and a most entertaining revival of *French Without
Tears*, followed by *Much Ado About Nothing*. Early
in 1974 the Young Vic Company paid a visit to America
with a repertoire of their plays and the theatre was let to
visiting companies during their absence.

PART 3

Club Theatres

Club Theatres

INTRODUCTION

Between the wars a large number of halls, attics and basements in and around the West End became Club Theatres, for experimental productions, but by 1963 the only little theatre left which pursued its original policy was the Arts Theatre Club.

The story of these little theatres which sprang up between the two world wars has been fully told by Norman Marshall in *The Other Theatre*, published in 1947. This book puts on record the efforts of this class of theatre which was swept away by rising costs, a more liberal censorship and some few enlightened managements who risked public production of the more non-commercial play.

To say that all passed away is not strictly true. The Hovenden Theatre Club survived many ups and downs through the enthusiasm of its founder, Valerie Hovenden, and became an anachronism in a modern age. Started in 1950 as a band of actors presenting period plays in historic London houses, it found a more permanent home in the A.I.A. Gallery at 15 Lisle Street. Moving from there to the basement of the Church house of the bombed St Anne's Soho, it came to rest in an upper room in a building in Garrick yard, off St Martin's Lane, where, after various managements, it is still in existence as the Little Theatre Club. Its production policy is erratic, though its doors as a club are always open. It has staged some interesting revivals, but it has not, as yet, found a new masterpiece.

A very strange manifestation of the late 1950s was the springing up at almost every street corner and alleyway in Soho of Revue Bars and Strip-Tease Clubs. Though these have no part in our history, mention must be made of the Irving Theatre in Irving Street, between Charing Cross Road and Leicester Square. It opened with *10–15*, an intimate revue, on 6 September 1951. Consisting of club premises and a restaurant upstairs, the theatre, on street level, had previously been an art gallery. Plays were staged with late-night revues following, in which many of today's

younger artists found their feet. Gradually revue became its
mainstay and with the 'Strip' craze it housed non-stop nude
revue—strange fare for only the second theatre in this
country named after our first actor knight. (The first was in
Seacombe in Cheshire in 1899!) The Irving closed and
became a restaurant in 1964.

Another addition to theatre club activities in outer
London is the Hampstead Theatre Club founded by James
Roose Evans. Its first season took place at the Moreland
Hall, 3 Holly Bush Vale, N.W.3, opening on 24
September 1959 with *King's Daughter*, translated by Emyr
Humphreys from the Welsh of Saunders Lewis. The pro-
ductions there were staged for irregular performances at
periods when the hall was not in use for other purposes.
It was next door to the Everyman, one of the first of the
little theatres of the twenties, which had a distinguished
career in its day but is now a cinema. Their production in
January 1960 of two one-act plays by Harold Pinter, *The
Dumb Waiter* and *The Room*, was later seen at the Royal
Court Theatre. After their last production in July, a double
bill, Ionesco's *Jacques*, and *George* by John Anthony West,
their activities were in abeyance for over two years. On
16 December 1962 they opened a newly built theatre in
Avenue Road, Swiss Cottage, N.W.3 with a production of
The Seagull. This new theatre seated 160 people, was
designed by D. A. Gough, and will eventually become part
of the Hampstead Civic Centre. It was later moved bodily
to another part of the site and enlarged. The scheme is
described as 'London's First Civic Theatre', but it still
remains a club open only to members.

Since the last edition of this book a surprising
resurgence of the club theatre has taken place, similar to the
phenomenal 'Off Broadway' theatre which sprang up a
little earlier in New York. Both are symptoms of theatrical
economics and the need for a 'platform' (one must not say
stage) for the newer than new dramatist and the out of
work actor. The all consuming television has brought back
the short play and concise writing, so often a failure when
expanded to West End length, but unfortunately this has
also bred playwrights unable to sustain a whole evening's
thought. The new, ever-increasing attic, basement, public
house or open space theatre, either at lunch time or pub
time in and around London, has attempted to involve the
spectator more than ever.

We do not intend to list or describe these new theatres.
They must be chronicled with hindsight and their value
assessed by another Norman Marshall in the distant future.

1 · The Arts Theatre

6 and 7 Great Newport Street, W.C.2

Capacity: 339

Opened 20 April 1927 with *Picnic*, an intimate revue. Produced by Harold Scott and presented by the club.

*

The building of premises on a site between St Martin's Lane and Charing Cross Road to provide 'the amenities of a London Club and a congenial place for those interested in the theatre on both sides of the curtain', was begun in 1927 under the direction of Walter Payne, Bronson Albery, and W. E. Gillespie, with Bernard Isaac and Lionel Barton as managing directors. The designs by P. Morley Horder included a small private theatre. The club had to stage productions of unusual plays and also to let the theatre to outside companies. Being a club it was outside the censorship regulations.

In February 1928 John Van Druten's *Young Woodley* was staged during its ban by the Lord Chamberlain. Other successes later transferred to the West End included another Van Druten, *Diversion*, *The Lady with a Lamp*, *The Infinite Shoeblack*, *People Like Us*; Frank Vosper's play on the Thompson-Bywaters case, appeared in 1929 but was not publicly produced until 1948. Other first performances included *Nine to Six*, *After All*, *Musical Chairs*, *Party*, *The Lake* and *Viceroy Sarah*. Visits by foreign artists and companies were also arranged. *La Compagnie des Quinze* appeared in 1931, Yvette Guilbert had a season, and Karsavina danced. During the Second World War the theatre became the home of Lunch-Time Ballet, and in 1942 Alec Clunes's regime began. The club and theatre were taken over by the Arts Theatre Group of Actors and from then until 1953 achieved the status of 'a pocket National Theatre'. It presented new plays and revivals, staging seasons of English Comedy; many of its productions were transferred to the West End.

A full list of these productions, and an account of Alec Clunes's work there can be found in the *Theatre World* Monograph on this actor by J. C. Trewin, published in 1958.

The theatre then came under the direction of Campbell Williams and his wife, who pursued a policy of staging new and unusual plays, some of which made noteworthy entrances into the West End theatrical world. These included *Waiting for Godot* in 1955, and *The Waltz of the Toreadors* in 1956. The relaxed censorship limited the appeal of the private theatre, but the management continued to provide stimulating fare.

The premises are under a threat of demolition. The ground is now owned by a development corporation, and in January 1962 the lease was sold to Nat Cohen, the film producer, who took possession in March; this did not affect the recently negotiated tenancy taken by the Royal Shakespeare Company to use the Arts as an experimental theatre for six months with an option to extend.

The Stratford Company opened on 13 March 1962 with *Everything in the Garden* and then presented seven new plays and revivals, but the venture was not a financial success and the lease was not renewed.

After this both club and theatre were completely redecorated and several new plays, late night entertainments and films were produced.

In 1966 Alfred Esdaile took over the lease and the following year Peter Birtwistle became director of the Club and Caryl Jenner and her Unicorn Theatre for Children became responsible for the theatre. It has remained its headquarters since her death, with intermittent productions by other managements.

2 · The Players' Theatre

(The Arches, The Hungerford, Gatti's, Charing Cross
Music-Hall)

173 and 174 Hungerford Arches, Villiers Street, Strand, W.C.2

Capacity: 300

The Arches licensed for music and dancing to Carlo Gatti
1867. Opened as the Players' Theatre 14 January 1946
with a programme of 'Late Joys'.

*

On the site of Charing Cross Railway Station, the
London terminus of the South-Eastern Railway, built in
1863, had stood Hungerford Market through which access
was gained to Hungerford Bridge. In this Market Carlo
Gatti and his brother Giovanni and their partner
Guiseppe Monico had for seven years run 'coffee and ice

rooms' in Hungerford Hall, which was part of the market.
It was Licensed for Music in 1858 and used as a Music Hall.
When the market was demolished in 1862 they received a
compensation of £7750. Monico went into the West End to
open on his own, while Gatti and his brother crossed the
river to Lambeth. Gatti's in the Westminster Bridge Road,
at first a restaurant, was to become a music-hall, in the
prevailing fashion, in 1865 when they eventually managed
to obtain the necessary licence. This building was throughout its life to be known by the name of Gatti's Music-
Hall.

Under the new station was created a series of arches for
which various uses were soon found. It seems that two of
them at least had been used as licensed premises from the
outset and called the Arches, as in 1866, one George Burry
Goodman had tried unsuccessfully to obtain a music
licence.

In 1867 Carlo Gatti, giving his address as Wharf Road,
Caledonian Road, St Mary, Islington, and describing himself as a licensed victualler, sent a petition to the Middlesex
Justices. He said that in the previous October he had
taken possession of premises in Villiers Street, being two of
the Arches under the South-Eastern Railway, numbered 174
and 175, and known by the name of the Arches. He had
taken a lease of the premises which consisted of two large
rooms, one being used as a billiard room, 250 ft long,
containing seventeen large billiard tables and the other being
a coffee room, 150 ft long. There was also a large kitchen
and other offices. He had spent a large sum on decorations.
He said he had been 'for a period of seven years the proprietor of the extensive Coffee and Ice Rooms in Hungerford Market, where your petitioner held a licence for
Music without any complaint ever being made against
him'. 'The Arches', he went on, 'are now licensed as a
place kept for public refreshment, resort, and entertainment and in which place Spirits, Wines and other Liquors are
sold in accordance with licences duly obtained for such
sale, as well as Coffee, Chocolate, Ices, and other similar
refreshments'. He promised that the rooms would not be
used as a ballroom or casino but merely for the performance
of music. There would be no Sunday entertainment. His
petition was accompanied by a testimonial signed by
thirty-nine 'Inhabitants residing in the immediate Neighbourhood'. A report by the Justices of the Strand
Division declared that the grant of such a licence was 'not
only unnecessary but highly objectionable', but in spite of
this it was granted at the following Quarter Sessions of the
Peace.

In the rate-books of the period he is said to be carrying
on the business as Restaurant, Skating-Rink and Gym-
nasium. The largest arch (number 174), which goes right

back to what is now Hungerford Lane, soon began to take on
the recognised form of the early music-halls, a chairman
with the audience scattered around at tables. All the great
names of the period began to include an appearance here in
their rounds. The hall prospered and by 1875 the Arches
Music Hall is listed as one of the recognised music-halls of
London.

The place was familiarly known as 'Gatti's in the
Arches' as opposed to 'Gatti's in the Road.' Gatti died in
1878 and his widow Maria and their daughter Rosa
Corazza took over control in Villiers Street, followed by
his grandchildren G. and L. Corazza, still retaining the
Gatti name.

From about 1883, for some years, the hall became known
as the Hungerford Music-Hall, and as such was painted
by Sickert in 1888. In 1886 the arch was given a small gallery
on three sides and completely refurbished. Old familiar
names die hard in the public mind and eventually the
simple name of Gatti's Charing Cross Music-Hall was
adopted.

A description of the place in 1887 by the chief of the
London Fire Brigade, Eyre Massey Shaw (the 'Captain
Shaw' of *Iolanthe* fame) tells us of what he calls 'The
Hungerford Palace Music-Hall, near Charing Cross under-
ground station.' He says:

> Apparently it is well built, the walls are newly painted
> and decorated and the appointments are rich and new.
> All this goes to show that the proprietor is anxious to do
> his best for his patrons as far as lies in his power. But
> what is all this paint and plaster and gilding and uphol-
> stery worth when the building itself is little more than a
> rifle gallery? This hall holds over a thousand persons
> and there is but one entrance which leads into Villiers
> Street. The entrance at the very most is not more than
> six feet wide and it is the only means of exit from the hall.
> To reach the Stalls you turn out of a very small vestibule,
> down a flight of 21 stairs below the level of the street,
> where very narrow gangways divide the reserved stalls,
> the stalls and area. The long narrow hall is sub-divided by
> these narrow gangways.

Shaw is rather too generous in his estimate of the capacity,
as records show that when the hall was seated, after the
tables had been abolished, the auditorium held about 600.

The family eventually spread themselves and built a
restaurant and billiard saloon on the land in front of the
adjacent arches higher up Villiers Street. Later the Gate
Theatre, London's centre of the 'Experimental Theatre' in
the 1920s and 1930s was to find a home in part of these
premises until it was destroyed in the blitz. It remains
today only partially rehabilitated.

These enterprises flourished and in August 1890 the
Music-Hall itself at No. 174 added the next small arch
(No. 173) into its premises. It is these two arches which are
in use today as the Players' Theatre. By this date the five
arches between Hungerford Lane and the way through to
Craven Street were under the control of the Corazzas.

Gatti's Charing Cross Music-Hall, the name by which it
had now become known, continued successfully until the
rise of the more sumptuous temples of variety, in the early
years of the new century, and by 1903 it had closed and the
Gattis had left. Though several attempts were made to
reopen as a music-hall under new managers, in 1910
Nos. 173 and 174 became the home of the new-fangled
invention, the cinema, calling itself the Arena, and remaining open until 1923.

The premises were then used for boxing tournaments for a
short while, but remained mostly closed until it reopened as
the Forum Cinema in 1928 showing foreign films of
dubious reputation. With the coming of the war the
cinema closed, and it became an Auxiliary Fire Service
Depot, the arch also being used by E.N.S.A. to
store cinema equipment. It was in this state that a lease
of the premises was taken by Leonard Sachs and Jean
Anderson after the war and reopened as a new home
for the Players' Theatre and 'The Late Joys' in January
1946.

The name, the Players' Theatre, itself needs some
explanation, as it has belonged to two Club theatres and
been attached to several premises.

Firstly, a small studio theatre on the first floor of 6 New
Compton Street, Soho, opened in January 1927 as Play-
Room Six under the direction of Reginald Price and Hilda
Maude. In November 1929, on its removal to the ground
floor, its name was changed to the Players' Theatre, under
the direction of Dorita Curtis-Hayward. This organisation
moved, in April 1934, to premises in 43 King Street,
Covent Garden—the building which had housed Evans (late
Joy's) Song and Supper Rooms, the Victorian night-haunt,
and afterwards the National Sporting Club and called the
Kings Hall when let for theatrical performances. This
Players' Theatre and School of Acting, situated on the top
floor, did not long survive, and the premises became the
Eden Club.

In October 1936 the King Street premises were reopened
as a theatre club by Peter Ridgeway, calling itself the New
Players' Theatre. It was here, in December 1937, that
Harold Scott produced the first Victorian cabaret, which
was to become the germ of the entertainment which became
famous as Ridgeway's Late Joys. After the death of
Ridgeway in 1938, a mixture of plays and Victorian music-
hall continued to fill the programme until 1940. By then the

'New' had been dropped from the title, and it had come under the direction of Leonard Sachs. Owing to the blitz the club moved to premises in the basement of No. 30 Albermarle Street, where they remained until they acquired a lease of the two Villiers Street arches, reopening there on 14 January 1946.

Certain structural alterations were made and a completely new scheme of interior decoration carried out bringing the old music-hall back to life.

The policy of 'Late Joys' and occasional plays was continued as before. In 1949 the management passed to Don Gemmell, Reginald Woolley and Gervase Farjeon, and under their direction the theatre achieved world-wide fame, not only for its own particular style of entertainment but for its launching of Sandy Wilson's *The Boy Friend*. This 'musical comedy of the twenties' was first staged here in April 1953 and eventually transferred not only to the West End but was reproduced in all parts of the world. In April 1960 it was announced that Gervase Farjeon had relinquished his interest in the theatre. The annual Victorian Burlesque is also a part of London's Christmas entertainment. A full history of the Players' has been told in three books, *Late Joys at the Players' Theatre* (1943), and *Early Joys at the Players' Theatre* by Paul Sheridan (1952), and *Players' Joys* by Hal D. Stewart (1962) which was published to mark the jubilee of the 'Late Joys' on 6 December, 1962.

PART 4

Otherwise Engaged

Otherwise Engaged

INTRODUCTION

We have already noted that many of the suburban theatres and music-halls have been put to other uses. It now only remains to record the few buildings in the West End originally intended to house theatrical entertainment but which have later become otherwise engaged.

1 · The Carlton Theatre

Haymarket, S.W.1

Capacity: On opening as a theatre, 1150; as a cinema 1159

Opened 27 April 1927 with *Lady Luck*, a musical play (founded on *His Little Widows*) by Firth Shephard, music by H. B. Hedley and Jack Strachey, additional numbers by Rodgers and Hart. Produced by Felix Edwardes, under the management of Laddie Cliff and Edgar O'Brien.

*

The last newcomer to the theatres in the Haymarket, the Carlton, had only a short life with live entertainment.

Built at 62–65 Haymarket, on land which had been an old coaching stage, Anglesea Yard, later covered by shops and offices, it lies between Charles II Street and Norris Street, backing on to St Alban's Street.

Erected by a syndicate, the Carlton Theatre Company, it opened under the direction of Gilbert Miller. The theatre, designed by Frank T. Verity and S. Beverley, was the second to be built in London after the 1914–18 war; the Fortune was the first in 1924. *The Stage* says:

Italian and Spanish Renaissance details inspired the treatment of both the exterior and interior of the theatre. The exterior is a good pyramidical composition, with excellent spacing and rhythm of voids, giving a sense of solidarity. The difficult graduations from plain wall to enriched tympanums are dexterously maintained, the fillings of these being beautifully disposed as regards light and shade. The auditorium walls are of gold scrumble, the lower part being in golden brown oak, while the boxes are in cream and grey, picked out in dull pinks and bands of wedgwood blue and white.

Features of the building were the large stage, the two tiers, the royal circle and balcony being divided laterally by a cross aisle, the lower elevation of the line of sight, and the centring of all seats to the centre of the stage. The ceiling of the auditorium was interestingly constructed, each ceiling beam being a ventilator, and the treatment of the whole, in very pale colours, giving an effect of lace work.

A first production, *Lady Luck*, in which Laddie Cliff, Leslie Henson, Cyril Ritchard, Phyllis Monkman and Madge Elliott appeared, was a big success and ran for 324 performances. This was followed by a musical comedy drama, *The Yellow Mask*, by Edgar Wallace, then at the height of his fame as a writer of thrillers. It was an attempt to combine the sensationalism of melodrama with musical comedy, written with Wallace's usual speed. It did not remain long at the Carlton, transferring down the Haymarket to His Majesty's, and from there to the London Palladium, totalling 218 performances in all.

The next Carlton production was *Good News*, a musical comedy of American college life, with a mainly imported cast, remembered today by the song 'The best things in life are free' and 'The Varsity Drag'. After a revue *In Other Words* with George Robey at the end of 1928, the last theatrical production at the theatre was *Merry Merry*, with Peggy O'Neill and W. H. Berry, which opened in February 1929.

The 'talkie' boom had come and in the April it was announced that the theatre was to be 'wired for sound'. *Merry Merry* moved to the Lyceum and films took over. *The Perfect Alibi* was shown at three performances a day and twice on Sundays. The following year its original owners sold out to the Paramount Film Company and from then on it became a 'lost' theatre, though a partial return was made with a half-and-half programme, film and variety, in March 1960 when *The Anthony Newley Show* was presented twice daily with a film *Let's Get Married*, also starring Anthony Newley.

2 · The Dominion Theatre

Tottenham Court Road, W.1

Capacity: On opening as a theatre, 2800; as a cinema, 1712

Opened 3 October 1929 with *Follow Through*, a musical comedy by Laurence Schwab and B. G. de Sylva, music by de Sylva, Brown and Henderson. Produced by and under the management of Leslie Henson and Firth Shephard.

*

St Giles's Circus, the junction of Tottenham Court Road, Oxford Street, New Oxford Street, St Giles's High Street, and Charing Cross Road is an historic site. On the corner of Tottenham Court Road and New Oxford Street, Meux's Horse Shoe Brewery was established in 1809, covering an area between three and four acres. Before this another brewery had covered the ground as far back as 1764, which had been the site of St Giles's Leper Hospital, founded in 1101 by Matilda, Queen of Henry I. Next door to the brewery down the Tottenham Court Road stood a famous hostelry, the Horse Shoe Tavern, which in a rebuilt condition still remains.

Shortly after Henry Meux took possession of the brewery in 1809 began the construction of a vast vat to contain porter. This imposing container was 22 ft high, and held 3555 barrels of Meux's entire. In October 1814, this immense vat collapsed with a mighty roar and in a few moments the imprisoned porter had poured out and was playing havoc in the neighbourhood. Eight people lost their lives in what may be called a portery grave.

The brewery was pulled down in 1922 and for some years the site was vacant and was used by O'Brien's Fun Fair. In July 1925 the ground was levelled and screened round and opened as 'Luna Park' in aid of the Middlesex Hospital Reconstruction Fund. The main attraction was a large tent in which variety performances were given three times a day.

It was not until 1929 that the Dominion Theatre was built on part of the site, its frontage in Tottenham Court

Road and stretching round and behind the Horse Shoe to Great Russell Street on one side and to Bainbridge Street on the other. The new theatre under the direction of R. H. Gillespie was designed by William and T. R. Millburn, and built by Messrs Bovis. The façade of the theatre was carried out in Portland stone, the mode of decoration adopted throughout being that of the late French Renaissance. It is interesting to note that in an account of the new building *The Stage*, October 3, said: 'At first sight the interior of the house gives one the impression it was really meant for a super cinema. It is undoubtedly on the lines popularised by the modern picture palace. . . . It will be remembered that the last two West End houses, the Carlton and the Piccadilly, both opened with musical comedy, but are now playing pictures'. In the light of subsequent events this is an interestingly prophetic observation. The Piccadilly, built in 1928, went quickly over to the 'talkies' but had returned to the fold by 1930.

The vast Dominion Theatre proved quite unsuitable for stage presentations. Its opening production, a rather incomprehensible American golfing musical comedy, aroused a storm of disapproval from the very far distant upper regions on the opening night, despite its very distinguished cast which included Elsie Randolph, Ivy Tresmand, Ada May, Viola Compton and Leslie Henson. It only ran for 148 performances, and was followed by another musical, *Silver Wings*, and a variety season of two weeks with Maurice Chevalier. Then the inevitable 'talkies' took possession with a mixture of stage and screen presentations, beginning with *The Phantom of the Opera*, which had long awaited a London showing. A break was made for a pantomime *Aladdin* at Christmas 1930 and then back to films with *City Lights* in February 1931, Chaplin appearing in person on the first night to take his bow and speak at the end of his silent film in a 'talkie' era.

Once again in September a variety programme brought Jeannette Macdonald to London and in May 1932 Richard Tauber appeared in a revival of *The Land of Smiles*, but later that year the Dominion was taken over by the Gaumont British Picture Corporation becoming an ordinary cinema showing post-West End presentations.

The theatre was occasionally used for variety seasons in between films. Sophie Tucker and Judy Garland were among those seen. In 1958 Françoise Sagan's ballet *The Broken Date* was staged by the Ballet-Théâtre Français. Then it was occupied by the mammoth musical film version of *South Pacific* until autumn 1962. Similar films have followed in recent years. A return of live entertainment is promised in October 1974 with the production of *An Evening With Mr Ziegfeld—The Follies*.

3 · The Leicester Square Theatre

Leicester Square, W.C.2

Capacity: On opening 2000; Present capacity 1763

Opened 19 December 1930 with the film *Viennese Nights* by Hammerstein and Romberg and a stage Dance production including Balliol and Merton and the Victoria Girls.

*

The scheme to build a theatre on the north side of Leicester Square at the corner of St Martin's Street, backing on Orange Street, and having exits in Whitcomb Street, was prompted by Walter Gibbons, after his failure at the London Palladium, in association with Jack Buchanan. The actor was originally to give his name to the new theatre and arranged for a flat for himself to be built on the roof, which he occupied until it was bombed in the war.

Misfortune dogged the enterprise from the start. Certain land that was needed for backstage premises could not be acquired and other difficulties arose which were to lead to Gibbons's eventual bankruptcy. In the end it was decided to open the theatre as a cinema and Warner Brothers took the lease.

The theatre was designed by Andrew Mather and built by Gee, Walker and Slater Ltd. The exterior of the building was described as 'lightly classical with modern adjuncts in the form of framework to carry signs'. It is 'in white glazed terra-cotta with a steel and glass canopy, the façade consisting of tall fluted piers carrying a strong cornice with attic storey and pediment over. The most noticeable features are the tall, arched windows. At the top is an unwieldy and inartistic pediment, carrying on it the name of the house, supported by columns of Doric style'. The entrance hall of polished black marble was a notable feature. The interior was a free treatment of early Renaissance.

After a very short life the building was closed. A large number of structural alterations were carried out by

R.K.O., who became its new owners, under the supervision of Alistair MacDonald, and a complete new scheme of interior decoration was designed by Edward Carrick. A revolving stage was also installed.

It reopened in June 1931 with films. The following month Gracie Fields appeared for a week twice nightly, with a film as a prelude to the showing of her first talking picture *Sally in our Alley*. This opened on August 21, when the first 'Fifty-Fifty stage and screen programme' was presented. Besides the film, Jack Hulbert's song and dance show, *The R.K.O. Loud Speakers* was staged.

This style of programme continued for some time, but still more changes were to come. In March 1932 the name was changed to the Olympic but only till July, when it closed. The non-stop variety craze hit London. Daly's, the London Pavilion, the Prince of Wales', and the Duke of York's, were all to be involved in this phase of the theatre.

Under the management of Gordon Courtney, it returned to its original name, the Leicester Square, and opened its *Non-Stop Revels*, 'two till midnight, one shilling to five shillings, we pay the tax', on 8 August 1932. A nostalgic touch to the very modern bill was provided by Marie Kendall singing her famous song ('I'll Cling to You—Just like the Ivy'). Before a year had passed films had again taken possession of the theatre. This time it seemed to be permanently, though an announcement in 1943 then gave hope that it might return to its original purpose, but this promise was not fulfilled.

In April 1968 the cinema closed and the interior was completely rebuilt to the design of Mannering & Steele, re-opening in December.

4 · The London Hippodrome

The Talk of the Town

Hippodrome Corner, Cranbourn Street, W.C.2

Capacity: As a theatre, 1340

Opened 15 January 1900 with a programme of Circus and Variety. Under the management of Moss Empires, Ltd.

*

Built on a large island site on the Cranbourn Estate with its main entrance at the corner of Cranbourn Street and Charing Cross Road, bounded by Little Newport Street and Ryder's Court (now called Leicester Court), it comprises, beside the theatre, a public house, shops and offices and an entrance to Leicester Square underground station which crept in later beside its main entrance.

This theatre was originally built in order to carry out a long-cherished ambition of Edward Moss, founder of the Moss Empire Music-Hall Circuit, to give London a circus combined with elaborate stage spectacles. The architect was Frank Matcham and the building was erected during 1899. The decoration is Flemish Renaissance; the building was originally constructed with a circus arena and a large water-tank, the water for which was supplied from the Cran Bourne, which runs underneath the stage. The work of construction was carried out by Messrs Holliday and Greenwood, at a cost of £43,000.

Water shows that made history at the Hippodrome were *Siberia, The Bandits, Tally Ho! The Redskins* (in which 'a one-legged diver plunged into the seething waters below, from a height of 30 ft'). *The Earthquake, The Typhoon, The Avalanche* and *The North Pole* were also staged.

Lupino Lane made his first appearance here in *The Zuyder Zee*, and all but lost his life at one performance, being caught in the huge torrent of water and swept into the arena when the villain opened the flood-gates.

The famous artists who appeared on the Hippodrome

313

stage in variety are legion. They include Paul Cinquevalli, Chung Ling Soo, Max Darewski, Loie Fuller, Zena Dare, Happy Fanny Fields, Harry Fragson, Yvette Guilbert, Seymour Hicks, Clarice Mayne, Mrs Langtry, Ada Reeve, Mme Réjane and Irene Vanbrugh.

In 1909 the theatre was closed for reconstruction and the circus arena gave way to stalls. The variety policy remained unchanged, but circus vanished, to be replaced by operetta, opera, ballet, and later one-act plays, once these were allowed to be performed in the music-halls. In October 1909 Ludmilla Schollar and George Kiakscht from St Petersburg brought Russian Ballet to London and in the May of the following year English audiences saw Tchaikovsky's *Swan Lake* ballet for the first time, in a two-act version, with Olga Preobrajenskaja. Leoncavallo conducted his own opera *The Gipsies* in 1912 on the same bill as the American Ragtime Octette with Melville Gideon, which brought 'Ragtime' to London.

In December 1912 the first of the famous Albert de Courville revues *Hello Ragtime!* introduced London to the Joy Plank. After a short season of variety his second revue *Hello Tango!* followed. These were the great days of Ethel Levey, Shirley Kellogg and Teddie Gerrard. The war brought *Business as Usual* to the list. The names of the revues from then until 1925 give a guide to the history of the times: *Joyland, Flying Colours, Zig-Zag, Box o' Tricks, Joy-Bells, Jig-Saw, The Peep-Show, Round in Fifty, Brighter London, Leap Year,* and *Better Days,* in all eleven shows in ten years played twice daily, the staggering total of performances indicating their success. Every revue artist of the day was seen, from George Robey, Violet Loraine and Morris Harvey to Sophie Tucker, Paul Whiteman and his famous band.

The revue régime of de Courville was followed by an equally successful run of musical comedies, which lasted up to 1938. Some of the names will recall memories of popular hits of the period: *Mercenary Mary, Sunny, Hit the Deck, That's a Good Girl, Mr Cinders, Sons o' Guns, Stand Up and Sing, Mr Whittington, Yes, Madam, Please Teacher,* and *Hide and Seek.* Their stars included Jack Buchanan and Elsie Randolph, Binnie Hale and Bobby Howes, and Cicely Courtneidge, to name but a few.

A return to revue was made under the régime of George Black with *The Fleet's Lit Up, Black and Blue,* and *Black Velvet,* which was produced soon after the outbreak of war.

Musical comedy was again featured under this management with *The Lisbon Story,* and Ivor Novello's *Perchance to Dream* ran for 1022 performances from April 1945. In *Starlight Roof,* the next Robert Nesbitt revue, in 1947, little Julie Andrews made her bow to London.

The theatre was made into London's 'Folies Bergère' from 1949 to 1951, followed by a musical *Bet Your Life* with Arthur Askey, Julie Wilson and Sally Ann Howes. A strange mixture of plays, revues, musicals, ice shows and variety occupied the stage until 1958; the plays included *Anna Lucasta*, *The Desperate Hours*, and *The Caine Mutiny Court-Martial*.

The last production was the ill-fated *Dave King Show*, kept going during the star's illness by Benny Hill. The theatre then underwent drastic interior reconstruction to turn it into a combined restaurant and spectacular cabaret under the direction of Bernard Delfont, Robert Nesbitt and Charles Forte, the architect being George Pine. It reopened as *The Talk of the Town*, *Hippodrome Corner*, on 11 September 1958.

5 · The London Pavilion

Piccadilly Circus, W.1

Capacity: As a theatre, 1080; as a cinema 1180

Present Building opened as a music-hall 30 November 1885.
Under the management of Edwin Villiers.

Converted into a theatre and reopened 3 August 1918
with a revue *As You Were*. Under the management of C. B.
Cochran.

Interior completely reconstructed as a cinema; reopened
September 1934.

*

In Tichborne Street at the top of the Haymarket stood
the Black Horse, an old coaching inn. Over its stable yard
was built a hall which in about 1784 was used by Thomas
Weeks as an Exhibition Room. Later it became a room for
entertainments as the 'Salle Robin.' In 1859 the yard below
came under the management of Loibl and Sonnhammer
and became a cheap 'sing-song' saloon attached to the public
house. In 1861 this saloon was converted into a music-hall
called the London Pavilion which opened on February 23,
'the first music-hall de luxe' in the West End.

In 1874 Sonnhammer dissolved the partnership and
opened Scott's Restaurant in Coventry Street nearby. There
is an advertisement in *The Era Almanack* of that year
which reads: 'Original Entertainment rendered by Efficient
Artistes, and every novelty introduced. "A Voluminous
Programme," vide Public Press, Six American Bowling
Saloons.' In November 1876 Loibl bought the lease of the
Exhibition Room and began plans to enlarge the whole
premises making them all one, but he lost his lease to Edwin
Villiers in 1879.

Early in 1878 the Metropolitan Board of Works acquired
the building for proposed street improvements and paid
Loibl £109,300 for the property. It was at this hall that a
national sensation was made by the 'Great' MacDermott
with his immortal 'Jingo' song, sung for the first time on

an evening when the British political crisis over the Russo-Turkish War of 1877 was at its zenith. This hall was eventually demolished in 1885 when Piccadilly Circus was enlarged and Shaftesbury Avenue began to come into being. The closing date was 26 March 1885, and the demolition and rebuilding were executed in the short space of eight months. The second Pavilion, built by Edwin Villiers on the present triangular site was opened on 30 November 1885. Facing Piccadilly Circus it has Shaftesbury Avenue on one side and Great Windmill Street on the other. The exterior of this building remains to this day. It was designed by J. E. Saunders, the elevation by R. J. Worley, and built by Peto Brothers. Villiers paid a rent of £7000 per annum to the Metropolitan Board of Works. The Pavilion opened under the personal management of Edwin Swanborough. The new building had a ground floor resembling a Continental Café, which was occupied by marble tables, at the head of which sat the Chairman.

After the second Pavilion had been running for about a year it was taken over by the Syndicate Halls Company. They reconstructed it in 1886, abolished the tables, dispensed with the Chairman, and rearranged the ground floor with luxurious tip-up seats, which were an innovation in those days, as was the fact that they could be reserved. At the backs of the seats were little ledges with metal trellised edges for holding drinking glasses. In 1900 the whole of the interior was rebuilt by the Syndicate, who announced that they had 'found it necessary to cater for the growth of a public taste for art, elegance, and luxury of appointments'. The ground floor was raked, and the interior was decorated in the style of Louis XV, the scheme of decoration including a series of panel pictures by J. M. Boekbinder. As a result of this redecoration and reconstruction the Pavilion emerged once again as a pioneer of the even more palatial music-hall.

Swanborough was succeeded in management by Frank Glenister in 1897 and he remained until 1934, living in a flat over the building. Ceasing to be a music-hall in 1918, it was again remodelled and was reopened as a theatre under the management of C. B. Cochran. He had the façade lit with electric signs proclaiming it 'The Centre of the World.' This reopening inaugurated a new chapter—a series of spectacular revues which became world-famous and introduced many new artistes, authors and companies to London, and their story can be found in the numerous autobiographical and biographical books on C. B. Cochran.

After Cochran left the Pavilion and John Southern took control, it fell into line with the non-stop variety craze from 1932 until it closed.

In March 1934 it was announced that the London Pavilion was to be reconstructed as a cinema and that the

contract for the work of remodelling had been placed with
F. G. Minter, Ltd, by the United Artists' Film Corporation.
The plans were prepared by F. G. Chancellor and Frank
Matcham, and the cost was to be £50,000.

The last performance at the London Pavilion as a theatre
took place on Saturday, 7 April 1934, and the work of
demolition began on the following Monday. The interior
of the theatre was almost entirely rebuilt, the alterations
comprising the removal of the old boxes, the building of
two circles on modern lines, a widening of the auditorium
by the removal of the side promenades, the widening of
the stage by twelve feet, and the creation of a more spacious
entrance foyer. The work was completed in the very short
time of twelve weeks, and reopened as a cinema in September 1934. The whole building is due for demolition in
the controversial scheme for Piccadilly Circus.

6 · The Lyceum Theatre

(Theatre Royal, English Opera House, The Royal Lyceum Theatre)

Wellington Street, W.C.2

Capacity of present building when a theatre: 2814

Present Building opened 31 December 1904 as a music-hall with a variety bill (twice nightly). Under the management of Thomas Barrasford.

*

The Lyceum has been a topic of discussion for many reasons in recent years and much unnecessary sentimental talk of 'Irving and his theatre' has been heard; by rights the building should no longer exist, its life has been prolonged because of the last war, and it now holds a year-to-year reprieve from the G.L.C., but is a Listed building.

Despite its great name and inheritance, the present building apart from its frontage and back wall was built as a vast music-hall in 1904 by Thomas Barrasford to rival Oswald Stoll's Coliseum, then in course of construction, and which managed to open its doors only a week earlier than the new Lyceum.

The two halls vied for popularity neck and neck at the time of their birth. So much for the shade of Sir Henry Irving, who died in October 1905; he never entered the present building so far as can be traced. His theatre was closed in 1902 and destroyed in 1904.

The full story of all the theatre buildings on this historic site has been told by Austin Brereton in *The Lyceum and Henry Irving* (1903) and by A. E. Wilson in *The Lyceum*, published in 1952, and it is unnecessary to do more than give a brief survey of the main events in its life.

In 1771 the foundation stone was laid of a building in the Strand to be called the Lyceum on part of the gardens of Exeter House. It was opened on 11 May 1772 as a room for exhibitions, concerts and entertainments.

In the ensuing years it served many purposes until it was taken by Dr Samuel Arnold in 1794 and converted into a small theatre. He was unable to obtain a licence, Handy's Circus took possession, and for a time it became known as the New Circus. By 1799, however, it was calling itself the Lyceum Theatre, giving mixed entertainment. Madame Tussaud held her first London Waxwork show here in 1802.

Arnold evaded the licensing law and occasionally plays were performed. It was owing to destruction by fire of the Theatre Royal, Drury Lane, in 1809 that Arnold eventually obtained his long awaited licence and was able to open on June 26 as the Theatre Royal, Lyceum, housing the Drury Lane company.

When the company returned to their own rebuilt theatre in October 1812 Arnold retained his licence for the summer months.

In 1815 Arnold renamed his theatre the Theatre Royal, English Opera, almost completely rebuilding it the next year to the designs of Samuel Beazley, opening on 15 June 1816. This theatre remained in use, changing its name according to the season, from Theatre Royal to Opera House as occasion demanded, until 16 February 1830 when it was burnt to the ground. Thus ended the theatre at 254 Strand.

On 4 July 1834 the rebuilt theatre, with the now still remaining frontage in Wellington Street, was opened as the Royal Lyceum and English Opera House. This theatre, with minor alterations and many redecorations, remained in use until 1902 and became generally known as the Royal Lyceum Theatre.

The new theatre, again designed by Samuel Beazley and built in four months, was on a site slightly west of the first building, and facing the new street leading from Waterloo Bridge to Bow Street called Wellington Street. Arnold continued to run it successfully with opera, burletta and other entertainments, within the rules prescribed, until 1843 when the monopoly of the Patent Theatres was broken. Other managers beside Arnold tried seasons with varying success. Mr and Mrs Keeley were in command from 1843 until 1847 when Madame Vestris and Charles James Mathews took charge and a brilliant series of productions with Planché as the chief writer followed, until 1855, when Mathews went bankrupt. The extravagances of Vestris and her illness since 1854 had brought about an impossible state of affairs. Their famous management at the Olympic and Covent Garden, though an artistic success, had burdened them with debts and the crash came.

Once again the Lyceum was able to offer hospitality to a burnt-out company when in 1856 Covent Garden went up in flames. Seasons of opera were staged here until the new opera house was opened in 1858. In between playgoers saw Ristori and Charles Dillon (the West End actor, not to be

confused with William Charles Dillon, his East End name-
sake). Under Edmund Falconer's management Madame
Céleste acted here from 1858 until 1861; he was said to
have made £13,000 in this period. The Anglo-French actor
Charles Fechter brought romantic drama to the Lyceum
from 1863 to 1867, but after a curious régime under E. T.
Smith the theatre fell on evil days until 1871 when 'Colonel'
Hezekiah Bateman took it to exploit his daughters Kate,
Ellen, Isobel and Virginia. This turned out to be a momen-
tous landmark in theatrical history, as he engaged as his
leading man an actor called Henry Irving.

The story of how, in order to save the fortunes of the
enterprise, Bateman allowed Irving to produce a play in
which the actor had faith, called *The Bells*, and the outcome,
does not need retelling in these pages. It is to be found in
the many biographies of Irving which have been written.

After seven years under the Batemans, Irving took over
the management in 1878 with Ellen Terry as his leading lady.
From then until he resigned the theatre to a company in
1899 he was sole master of its destiny, and during this
time raised the status of the actor and gave Londoners a
series of memorable productions. He remained at the
Lyceum under the syndicate until 1902, appearing for
seasons between other productions which included *The
Only Way*, *Sherlock Holmes* and Frank Benson and his
company. Irving last trod the Lyceum boards as Shylock
on 19 July 1902, with Ellen Terry at his side. It was also the
end of their partnership and the theatre itself was doomed.
The L.C.C. demanded extensive alterations which the
syndicate, who had lost large sums on the non-Irving
seasons, were unable to carry out. The theatre remained
empty and up for sale. It was finally stripped of its glory in
March 1904 and razed to the ground except for the portico
and rear walls.

The new building, a music-hall, which arose on the site
was designed by Bertie Crewe and built by J. Parkinson,
who completed it in a short space of time ready to open on
31 December 1904 under the management of Tom
Barrasford.

The venture was not successful and lasted only
six months. The newly opened Coliseum attracted the
London audiences. A full-scale ballet, *Excelsior*, was
tried in September 1905 for a season but closure again
followed.

In March 1907 a new régime began under H. R. Smith
and Ernest Carpenter, presenting 'popular drama at popular
prices'. Their first venture was *Her Love against the World*,
followed by *The Midnight Wedding*, both by Walter
Howard. The seed of Lyceum melodrama had been sown.
The harvest was to be reaped later by the brothers Melville,
but before they enter on the scene, Smith and Carpenter

presented Matheson Lang in a long series of romantic
dramas, strangely enough including *Hamlet* and *Romeo
and Juliet*, produced to suit the particular tastes of their
public. Two pantomimes were staged during these years and
when Carpenter died in 1909 the brothers Walter and
Frederick Melville acquired complete control. They are said
to have bought the freehold for £240,000 and even so made
a considerable fortune from it during the thirty years they
were in possession.

The Melvilles continued the policy of melodrama, mostly
written by themselves, with such descriptive titles as *A
Girl's Cross Roads*, *The Girl who took the Wrong Turning*,
and *The Worst Woman in London*. An annual pantomime
also became a regular feature.

Despite quarrels between the brothers from time to time,
their policy succeeded until their style became outmoded.
Even then, up to the end, every new Lyceum play retained
in essence its melodramatic quality, as with the plays of
Edgar Wallace that were staged here. But the last ten
years of the theatre also saw such varied fare as Russian
Ballet and Opera, a revival of *Saint Joan*, and Reinhardt's
production of *The Miracle*.

Walter Melville died in 1937 and Frederick in 1938, leaving between them over £520,000. The future of the Lyceum
was then in doubt, and a sale was announced, for development of the site, with sundry adjacent properties, as shops
and offices.

The pantomime of 1938–9, *The Queen of Hearts*, was the
last at the theatre; in February its demolition was officially
announced by L. S. Marler and a syndicate. A transfer of a
revival of *Dracula*, followed the pantomime and finally six
performances of *Hamlet*, the John Gielgud production
which was to be taken to Elsinore, were given as a farewell
to the theatre, which finally closed on 1 July 1939.

Meanwhile, much to everyone's surprise, the development scheme was cancelled, as the L.C.C. wanted the land
to build a larger approach to Waterloo Bridge to provide
which the Gaiety Theatre at the Strand—Aldwych Corner
was also to go. It transpired that the L.C.C. had bought the
Lyceum in June, and on July 17 an auction sale stripped
the theatre of its fittings; the pickaxe was to follow. The
war intervened and the theatre remained a deserted shell
until, in 1945, the L.C.C., whose plans had completely
changed, advertised for offers to reopen the theatre. Donald
Wolfit tried to gain support to do this, but the authorities decided to let it as a dance hall to Mecca, Ltd, who
reopened after suitable alterations in the October on a
short-term but renewable lease, in which state it remains
to this day.

In defence of its actions the L.C.C. stated in 1952 that the
highest offer received for use as a theatre was £11,500, as

against the dance-hall offer of £20,000; but it would need £50,000 to restore it to theatrical use. How much more would this be today?

Live entertainment returned, for children, in December 1963, with an arena production of *Pinnoccio* and more recently Old Time Music Hall has been presented on certain evenings.

7 · The Playhouse

(The Avenue Theatre)

Northumberland Avenue, Charing Cross, W.C.2

FIRST THEATRE
Capacity: 1200

Opened 11 March 1882 as the Royal Avenue Theatre with a revival of *Madame Favart* an *opéra comique* by Offenbach, in an English version by H. B. Farnie. Produced by and under the management of M. Marius.

SECOND RECONSTRUCTED THEATRE
Capacity: 679

Opened 28 January 1907 as the Playhouse with a transfer of *Toddles*, a play from the French of Tristan Bernard and André Godferneaux, preceded by a one-act play *The Drums of Oudh* and an Interlude by Bernard Shaw. Produced by and under the management of Cyril Maude.

*

There is a story told that the original theatre was only built on this site because a speculator, Sefton Parry, believed that the South-Eastern Railway would have to acquire the ground, at a large profit to himself, for an extension scheme to Charing Cross Station. This however did not materialise and the building remains, almost tucked under the railway station, to this day. Sefton Parry specialised in this practice of theatre-building speculation. The first lessee was E. Burke.

The Illustrated London News, 4 March 1882 says that the theatre

is situated at the bottom of Northumberland Avenue, its front extending 160 ft. from Craven Street to the Thames Embankment. . . . The back of the theatre is close against the Charing Cross Railway Station. The elevation, of Portland stone, is in the French Renaissance style with some ornamental carving and with a number of

324

statues, including Shakespeare, between Comedy and Tragedy, over the principal entrance; the sculptor is Mr Plows of Brixton. The principal entrance to the dress circle and stalls is on the curve of the front; to the right of this, as you face the building, are the pit and gallery entrances on the Victoria Embankment; while to the left, in the direction of Craven Street are windows and a private entrance to the Prince of Wales's box, and the stage entrance is in Craven Street. The architects are Messrs Fowler and Hill the contractors were Kirk and Randall, of Woolwich. The internal decorations of French character, are in carton-pierre, by J. M. Boek-binder, their colour ivory and gold. Around the ceiling are medallion portraits of famous poets of all nations. The lighting is by a handsome glass chandelier in the middle of the house. The drapery, curtains and seats, are of red damask.

The opening production *Madame Favart* was the first of a long series of French comic operas given under several managements which filled the theatre until 1890. They included *Les Manteaux Noirs*, *Olivette*, *Laurette*, *Barbe Bleue*, *Nell Gwynne*, *The Old Guard*, and *Nadgy*. Florence St John and later Arthur Roberts were two of the names associated with these productions.

In 1890 the policy of the theatre changed and George Alexander made his first venture into management with *Dr Bill*. He remained here until he moved to St James's the following year, firmly established as an actor-manager. For a while the theatre did not find another success but Shaw's *Arms and the Man* burst upon an unsuspecting public in 1894 in a season given by Florence Farr and financed by Miss Horniman. The theatre was under the management of Charles Hawtrey from 1898 until 1900 and a run of 544 performances was achieved with *A Message from Mars*.

Early in the new century were seen Maugham's early play, *A Man of Honour*, and R. C. Carton's *Mr Hopkinson*, with James Welch. After this, in January 1905, Cyril Maude took over the management leaving the Haymarket Theatre where he had been established for some years.

He set about plans for the reconstruction of the theatre. The architect was again F. H. Fowler with Kirk and Randall as builders, and the work was almost completed when on 5 December 1905 part of Charing Cross Station collapsed onto the theatre. Six people were killed and twenty-six injured and the theatre badly damaged. Maude received compensation of £20,000 from the South-Eastern Railway. After some delay he began rebuilding the theatre, this time to the designs of Messrs Detmar Blow and Fernand Billerey; the builders were Patman and Fotheringham. Most of the original exterior was retained but a completely new interior was constructed: its decorations were suggested by Mortimer Menpes in a rich brown and gold. The new theatre was renamed the Playhouse and it eventually opened on 28 January 1907. Cyril Maude meantime had been carrying on at the Waldorf (Strand) Theatre. He remained at the Playhouse until 1915 presenting a long series of popular successes.

Frank Curzon then took the theatre, with Gladys Cooper as leading lady. She joined him in management in 1917, and from then until 1923 many successes were produced, *The Naughty Wife* (1918) and *Home and Beauty* (1919) among them. Later in 1927 Gladys Cooper was to return to the Playhouse as sole lessee. Meanwhile the long run of *White Cargo* filled the theatre for 821 performances from May 1924. The plays put on by Gladys Cooper, mainly with Gerald du Maurier, included *The Letter* (1927), *The Sacred Flame* (1929), *Cynara* (1930), *The Painted Veil* (1931), and many others up to 1933.

After Gladys Cooper, Leon M. Lion took command until 1935; from this time the theatre was called the Playhouse Theatre, a strange anomaly. The most notable success of this period was *Libel!* in 1934. During 1938 and 1939 Nancy Price ran her People's National Theatre here, but it seems that the theatre became rather 'off the map' for playgoers, one subsequent revue lasting only two nights. There followed a considerable period of closure until the theatre was reopened once again as the Playhouse by Claude Soman with a revival of *Home and Beauty* in November 1942.

For a time the theatre enjoyed success with *The House of Jeffeys* with Sybil Thorndike, a season by the Old Vic Company during which *Abraham Lincoln*, *The Russians*, and *Blow your own Trumpet*, an early play by Peter Ustinov, were produced. *Mr Bolfry* (1944) and *Lady from Edinburgh* (1945) followed. Evil days came again; revues, plays, ballet seasons, appeared all too quickly. *The Perfect Woman*, a farce, from November 1948 had 224 performances, and Agatha Christie's *Murder at the Vicarage* 127 performances from December 1949. After this there is nothing eventful to recall except that the theatre still retained its painted canvas Act Drop (the last in London) until it left the fold, becoming a BBC studio in 1951, the home of many broadcasts before a live audience.

8 · The Prince Charles Theatre

Leicester Place, W.C.2

Capacity: As a theatre 420

Opened 26 December 1962 with *Clap Hands*, the new revue from Canada directed by John Gray under the management of Bob Swash and Araby Lockhart by arrangement with Harold Fielding.

THE BUILDING

In 1958 Alfred Esdaile bought ground on the corner of Lisle Street and Leicester Place to develop as a block of offices including a small theatre in the basement. The foundation stone was laid by Flora Robson on 18 December 1961. The building, the first entirely new theatre in the West End since the Saville in 1931, was designed by Carl Fisher and Associates.

The entrance was put in Leicester Place so that it would be visible from Leicester Square; it was thus on the shortest frontage giving greater depth for the auditorium and stage, which were at street level.

Four mosaic sculptures have been incorporated into the design at the main entrance. They depict Harlequin, a clown, Nell Gwynn and a Fairy Queen, designed by the Hungarian sculptor G. Dereford. The ceiling is designed with five parabola sections and moulded beams.

There is not much heavy enrichment, but the side walls are based on Adam designs of flowing husks and ribbons. Below these panels the dado and panelling are made in specially hardened plaster, with simple mouldings.

The interior decoration of the auditorium has been carried out in fibrous plaster work by Claridges (Putney) Ltd.

The Theatre was built by Richard Costain (Construction) Limited.

THE PLAYS

It was announced during the building that Harold Fielding had taken a long-term lease of the theatre and it would be used for intimate entertainments, concerts and poetry readings. It was to be open at all times of the day and all days of the week. As Fielding and Esdaile say: 'Let us hope that the Prince Charles becomes the home of Theatre, the Arts and Music. May it also become, with its beautiful Leicester Room facilities, a home for those who want to see, hear and discuss the things which go to make up "Theatreland" and its allied arts.'

The opening production, *Clap Hands*, a Canadian revue had been presented successfully at the Lyric Theatre, Hammersmith in November and was transferred to inaugurate the theatre.

Early the following year the theatre was closed and 'renovated' for it was thought it was going to be converted into a cinema, but it was re-opened in April with a revue, *Looking for the Action*. Various attractions followed but the theatre was opened only spasmodically. The interior was completely re-decorated, the stage enlarged and a new bar was constructed, re-opening as 'Fielding's Music Hall' in February 1964. An attempt to transfer the 'Late Joys' and the atmosphere of the Players' Theatre Club was unsuccessful and in July 1965 Esdaile sold the premises for a cinema, and the interior was rebuilt in 1968–9, re-opening on 21 January as the Prince Charles Cinema.

9 · The Saville Theatre
(ABC 1 and ABC 2)
Shaftesbury Avenue, W.C.2

Capacity: **As a theatre 1200**

Opened 8 October 1931 with *For the Love of Mike*, 'a play with tunes', by H. F. Maltby, lyrics by Clifford Grey and Sonny Miller, music by Jack Waller and Joseph Tunbridge. Produced by H. F. Maltby and Campbell Gullan, under the management of Jack Waller.

THE BUILDING

At the upper end of Shaftesbury Avenue there remained many decaying slum properties, left over from the old St Giles' district, through which the Avenue had been cut in the 1880's.

A large island site was cleared, stretching from Stacey Street to St Giles' Place, with New Compton Street behind. A lease of this ground was acquired by A. E. Fournier, and a theatre built to the designs of Messrs T. P. Bennett and Sons, who were also responsible for the designs of the whole of the decoration, colour schemes and furnishing. The consulting architect was Bertie Crewe, and the builders were Messrs Gee, Walker and Slater.

A contemporary account says:

> The exterior of the house is of a most striking and unusual design. Of special interest is the main bas-relief frieze, depicting 'Drama through the Ages', modelled by Gilbert Bayes, the sculptor. Portions of this were exhibited at the Royal Academy 1930 and 1931, and the total length of this bas-relief is 129 feet. On this are representations of 'St Joan', 'Imperial Roman Triumphal Procession', 'Harlequinade', and 'War Plays', etc. Of arresting interest also are the pairs of plaques by the same sculptor, representing 'Art through the Ages'.

The Stage of 8 October 1931 goes on, after describing the seating in the stalls, circle and upper circle:

The stalls bar and saloon lounge adjoining, will please
the public, special care has been exercised in their equipment and decoration. The bar, which has mural paintings
by Mr A. R. Thompson, is 18 ft by 54 ft in front of the
counters, while the lounge, which is also decorated by
the same artist, is 42 ft by 40 ft. There is a sort of shopping
arcade in and about the lounge, as in the up-to-date
hotels, and it is quite big enough for tea dances or concerts. So comfortable, indeed, are the lounge and the
bar at the Saville, that it is to be feared that something
more than a warning bell will be necessary to clear them.

The new theatre opened on October 8, the day after the
Westminster Theatre (see No. 38). It was slightly damaged
in the 1941 blitz but was speedily repaired. When John
Clements took over the management in July 1955, a complete new scheme of interior decoration was designed by
Laurence Irving and a new mural by John Collins added
to the stalls bar.

THE PLAYS

The theatre opened on 8 October 1931, under the management of Jack Waller, with a musical play *For the Love of
Mike*, described as 'a play with tunes', by H. F. Maltby and
Clifford Grey, the 'tunes' being by Waller himself and
Joseph Tunbridge. This ran for 239 performances and was
succeeded in June 1932 by *Tell Her the Truth*, another play
with 'tunes', this time an adaptation of Frederick Isham's
Nothing But the Truth by R. P. Weston and Bert Lee
with music by Waller and Tunbridge, which ran for
234 performances. In March 1933 a musical fantasy on
Ambrose Applejohn's Adventure by the same authors and
composers began a run of 152 performances under the
title of *He Wanted Adventure*, all of which starred Bobby
Howes.
In 1934 came *Jill Darling!* a musical comedy by Marriott
Edgar and Desmond Carter with music by Vivian Ellis,
with Frances Day and Arthur Riscoe, which ran for 242
performances; and 1936 brought *Spread it Abroad*, a revue
by Herbert Farjeon with music by William Walker (209
performances), and *Over She Goes*, a 'musical tantivy' by
Stanley Lupino with music by Billy Mayerl (248 performances). In 1937 Beverley Nichols' revue *Floodlight*
and *It's in the Bag*, a musical show by Cecil Landeau with
music by Frank Rubens were produced and in the early
part of 1938 a revival of Aaron Hoffman's comedy
Welcome Stranger, with Harry Green in his original part
as played at the Lyric in 1921, and the *Follies of 1938*, an
ill-fated attempt to revive Pelissier's *Follies* in modern
form.
The Saville's first connection with more serious drama

came in November 1938 when Shaw's *Geneva* was presented. This was a satire on modern dictatorships and the League of Nations and ran for 237 performances. In pre-war 1939 Vernon Sylvaine's *Worth a Million* was here and then came J. B. Priestley's *Johnson over Jordan*, 'a modern morality play' as the author himself described it, transferred from the New Theatre.

Later in 1939 *Juggernaut* was presented, a play by Anthony Heckstall-Smith and E. P. Hare, which reached the Saville via a performance by the Repertory Players at the Aldwych Theatre in January 1939 and a try-out at Richmond.

The earlier years of the war were considerably brightened by the revue *Up and Doing* (1940), which continued a broken run after the theatre had been damaged by enemy action and repaired, in all it had 603 performances. Subsequent successes were *Fine and Dandy* (1942) and *Junior Miss* (1943), the former another successful revue and the latter an American comedy by Jerome Chodorov and Joseph Fields (from stories by Sally Benson), which ran 518 performances. The next success was *Big Boy* with Fred Emney and Richard Hearne, which scored 174 performances from September 1945. In 1946 the theatre came under the control of Bernard Delfont and *Here Come the Boys* with Jack Hulbert and Bobby Howes was presented in April. For the next few years the theatre had difficulty in achieving an established success until Cicely Courtneidge appeared in Ivor Novello and Alan Melville's *Gay's the Word* in February 1951. September 1952 saw the first night of an English musical hit *Love from Judy*, which ran for 594 performances. During 1954 and 1955 the theatre was under the direction of Patrick Ide and Hilda Scott, and the biggest success of this period was Cecil Landeau's revue *Cockles and Champagne*. In July 1955 John Clements entered into actor-management of the theatre and after opening with a new play, *The Shadow of Doubt*, he staged a notable season of revivals: *The Wild Duck*, *The Rivals*, *The Doctor's Dilemma*, *The Seagull* and *The Way of the World*. John Clements gave up the theatre in 1957 and control returned into the hands of the proprietors S.T.P. (Theatres) Ltd, who have since let it to various managements. Productions included *A Touch of the Sun* in January 1958, which transferred to the Princes to make room for *Expresso Bongo* in the April. The next production was *Valmouth*, the Ronald Firbank–Sandy Wilson musical from the Lyric, Hammersmith, in January 1959, followed by *Candide* in April and *The Edwardians* later the same year. 1960 saw the established success of Evelyn Laye in *The Amorous Prawn*, eventually to transfer to the Piccadilly Theatre.

In June 1961 it was announced that Bernard Delfont had purchased the freehold of the theatre and wanted to re-name

it The Gaiety; this threat was not carried out much to the
relief of theatre historians.

The lease changed hands several times and various re-
developments were proposed before it returned to Delfont's
hands in 1967.

The next two years saw constant change and only the
revue, *The Lord Chamberlain Regrets* (August 1961–
February 1962) and *Photo Finish*, the then new Ustinov
play (April–December 1962), have left any mark. *Semi-
Detached*, a modern comedy with Laurence Olivier, ran for
137 performances. *An Evening with Maurice Chevalier*
came next for a limited season, then *Pickwick*, a new
musical, opened on 4 July 1963 and played till February
1965, but short runs became the order of the day with visits
of the D'Oyly Carte Opera Company, Marcel Marceau and
various ballet companies. In December 1968 Danny La Rue
opened in *Queen Passionella and the Sleeping Beauty* and
brought success to the theatre. In July 1969 *The Resistible
Rise of Arturo Ui* was seen for a few months, to be
followed by a short-lived revival of *Anything Goes* and
the last play at this theatre was presented in December
1969, from the Yvonne Arnaud, Guildford, *Enemy*, by
Robin Maugham. After a short run the theatre closed and
the interior was completely reconstructed into two cinemas,
one above the other. ABC 1 and ABC 2 (seating 616 and
581 people) to the designs of William Ryder and Associates. The new cinemas opened on 22 December 1970.

Appendices

CHRONOLOGICAL LIST OF THE THEATRES OF LONDON

(Only the opening date, major reconstructions, etc., are noted; further details will be found in the text.)

The Seventeenth and Eighteenth Century

The Theatre Royal, Drury Lane

First Theatre, 1663–72.
Second Theatre, 1674–1791.
Reconstructed 1747, 1762, and by the Brothers Adam, 1775.
Third Theatre, 1794–1809.
Fourth Theatre, 1812–
  Portico added 1820.
  Colonnade added 1831.
  Auditorium reconstructed on many occasions, including 1822, 1841, 1851, 1871, 1873, 1894, 1901, 1908 (stage).
  Present auditorium (a complete reconstruction) 1922.

Her Majesty's Theatre

First Theatre opened as *The Queen's Theatre*, 1705–89, became later *The King's Theatre*.
Interior reconstructed 1778, 1782.
Second Theatre, 1791–1867, later became *Her Majesty's Theatre, Italian Opera House*.
Auditorium reconstructed 1796, 1799, and again when the exterior was remodelled 1816–18.
(A small theatre, *The Bijou*, was attached to this building, hired for concerts and other light entertainments.)
Third Theatre, 1869–92.
Fourth Theatre, 1897–
  Known as *His Majesty's Theatre*, 1902–52.

The Theatre Royal, Haymarket	First Theatre, *The Little Theatre in the Hay-Market*, 1720–1820, became *The Theatre Royal, Hay-Market*, 1766.
	Second Theatre, on an adjacent site, 1821–
	Interior reconstructed, 1843, 1872, 1880.
	Present interior, 1905.
The Royal Opera House	First Theatre, *Theatre Royal, Covent Garden*, 1732–1808.
	Reconstructed, 1784, 1792.
	Second Theatre, 1809–1856.
	Reconstructed as an Opera House, 1847.
	Present Opera House, 1858–
	Minor interior reconstruction 1863, 1899–1901.
	Dressing-room extension 1933.
	Amphitheatre reconstruction etc. 1964.
The Lyceum Theatre	First Building, *The Lyceum*, 1771–1830.
	Converted to a theatre, 1794.
	Reconstructed as *The Theatre Royal, English Opera*, 1816.
	Second Theatre, 1834–1903, became known as *The Royal Lyceum Theatre*.
	Present building with same façade opened as a Music Hall, 1904–
	Became a theatre, 1907–39.
	Reconstructed as a Dance Hall, 1945.

The Nineteenth Century

The Adelphi Theatre	First Theatre opened as *The Sans Pareil*, 1806–58. Became *The Adelphi*, 1819.
	Reconstructed, 1814, 1819, 1821, 1848.
	Second Theatre, 1858–1900.
	Third Theatre, opened as *The Century* (same façade with additions), 1901–29.
	Present Theatre, 1930–
The London Pavilion	First Music-Hall, 1861–85.
	Second Music-Hall, 1885–
	Reconstructed 1886 and 1918 (when it became a theatre).
	Interior completely reconstructed as a cinema, 1934.
The Players' Theatre	*The Arches* opened 1867–
	Became *The Hungerford* and *Gatti's Charing Cross Music*

Hall. Later a cinema, *The Arena*;
then *The Forum*.
Became *The Players'*. 1946.

The Vaudeville Theatre   1870–
Reconstructed with present façade,
1891.
Reconstructed   with   present
interior, 1926.

Royal Court Theatre   First Theatre opened as *The New
Chelsea*, 1870–87.
Became *The Belgravia* the same
year.
Reconstructed 1871 as *The Royal
Court*, and again in 1881.
Present theatre on new site 1888–
Reconstructed 1904, 1921, 1952
and 1964.
Rehearsal Room opened as *The
Theatre Upstairs*, 1971

The Criterion Theatre   1874–
Reconstructed 1883 and 1903.

The Savoy Theatre   First Theatre, 1881–1929.
Reconstructed, 1903.
Present theatre, 1929–

The Comedy Theatre   1881–
Reconstructed 1911, 1933 and 1955.

The Playhouse   Opened as *The Avenue*, 1882–
Reconstructed as *The Playhouse*
with completely new interior
1907.

The Prince of Wales'   First Theatre opened as *The Prince's*,
1884–1937.
Became *The Prince of Wales'*,
1887.
Present Theatre, 1937–
Proscenium etc. remodelled, 1963.

The Lyric Theatre   1888–
Reconstructed, 1933.

The Garrick Theatre   1889–

The Palace Theatre   Opened as *The Royal English Opera
House*, 1891–
Became the *Palace Theatre of
Varieties*, 1892 and *The Palace
Theatre*, 1911.
Amphitheatre reconstructed 1908.

The Duke of York's   Opened as *The Trafalgar Square*,
1892–
Became *The Trafalgar*, 1894, and
The Duke of York's, 1895.

Wyndham's Theatre   1899–

The Twentieth Century

The London Hippodrome 1900–
    Reconstructed as *The Talk of the Town*, 1958.

The Apollo Theatre   1901–

The New Theatre   1903–

The Coliseum   Opened as *The London Coliseum*, 1904–
    Became *The Coliseum*, 1931–

The Strand Theatre   Opened as *The Waldorf*, 1905–
    Became *The Strand*, 1909, *The Whitney*, 1911 and again *The Strand*, 1913.

The Aldwych Theatre   1905–

The Globe Theatre   Opened as *The Hicks*, 1906–
    Became *The Globe*, 1909.

The Queen's Theatre   1907–
    Reconstructed 1959.

The Victoria Palace   1911–
    On the site of *Moy's Music-Hall* c. 1840.
    Became *The Royal Standard Music-Hall*, 1863–1910.
    Reconstructed 1889.

The London Palladium   1910–
    On the site of *Hengler's Grand Circque*, 1871–1908.

The Princes Theatre   1911–
    Reconditioned 1962–63, reopened 1963 as *The Shaftesbury*.

The Regent Theatre   1911–
    Built as the Polytechnic Great Hall.
    Remodelled as the Polytechnic Theatre 1923.
    Again remodelled 1927.

The Ambassadors Theatre 1913–

The St Martin's Theatre   1916–

The Fortune Theatre   1924–

The Arts Theatre   1927–

The Carlton Theatre   1927–
    Became a cinema 1930.

The Piccadilly Theatre   1928–

The Dominion Theatre	1929– Became a cinema 1932.
The Duchess Theatre	1929–
The London Casino	Opened as *The Prince Edward Theatre*, 1930– Became *The London Casino*, 1936.
The Cambridge Theatre	1930–
The Phoenix Theatre	1930–
The Whitehall Theatre	1930–
The Leicester Square Theatre	1930– Opened as a cinema; reconstructed 1968.
The Windmill Theatre	1931– Formerly a cinema, the *Palais de Luxe*, opened 1910. Interior reconstructed 1964.
The Westminster Theatre	1931– Formerly a chapel; reconstructed as a cinema, *The St James' Picture Theatre*, 1924. Reconstructed with additions 1966.
The Saville Theatre	1931– Reconstructed as two cinemas 1969–70.
The Royalty Theatre	1960– On the site of *The London Opera House*, 1911–57. Became *The Stoll Picture Theatre*, 1917 and *The Stoll Theatre*, 1942.
The Prince Charles Theatre	1962– Reconstructed as a cinema 1968–9.
The May Fair Theatre	1963–
The New London Theatre	1973– On the site of the *Mogul Saloon*, 1847–1910. Renamed *The Middlesex Music Hall* by 1851. Reconstructed 1872 and 1891. Demolished 1910. Completely rebuilt and opened as *The New Middlesex Theatre of Varieties*, 1911. Reconstructed as *The Winter Garden Theatre*, 1919. Closed 1960. Demolished 1965.

THE OUTER RING

Sadler's Wells
Theatre, Finsbury

Sadler's Musick House, 1683–1765.
  Became a regular theatre 1753.
Second theatre, 1765–1928.
  Reconstructed many times with
    additions, notably in 1772, 1838
    and 1851.
Interior reconstructed 1879 and again
    in 1893 into a Music Hall.
Present Theatre 1931–

The Old Vic,
Waterloo Road

Opened as *The Royal Coburg
  Theatre*, 1818.
  Became *The Royal Victoria
    Theatre*, 1833.
  Minor reconstructions carried out at
    various times, principally in
    1871, 1880, 1927 and 1950.

Lyric Theatre,
Hammersmith

Opened as *The Lyric Hall*, 1888.
  Became *The Lyric Opera House*,
    1890. Final building 1895 (an
    almost complete reconstruction).
  Additions made 1899 and 1907.
  Became *The Lyric Theatre*, 1919,
    demolished 1972.

The Theatre Royal,
Stratford

1884–
  Reconstructed 1902.

Wimbledon Theatre   1910–

The Open Air   1933–
Theatre,
Regent's Park

The Mermaid,   1959–
Blackfriars

The Round House   1847–
  Reconstructed as a theatre 1969.

The Greenwich   1969–
Theatre

The Young Vic   1970–

The Shaw Theatre   1971–

LISTED THEATRES

Statutory List of Buildings of Special Architectural or Historical Interest—Grades I and II—issued by the Department of the Environment. There is no official definition of what these Grades entail, but generally Grade I are buildings of such great Architectural or Historic importance that no rebuilding or demolition can take place and Grade II are buildings of such great Architectural or Historic importance that no rebuilding or demolition can be undertaken without sufficient reason.

Grade I   Covent Garden, *The Royal Opera House*
                 Drury Lane, *The Theatre Royal*
                 Haymarket, *The Theatre Royal*

Grade II   *Albery Theatre*
                 Aldwych Theatre
                 Ambassadors Theatre
                 Apollo Theatre
                 Camden Theatre (not in use)
                 Coliseum
                 Comedy Theatre
                 Criterion Theatre
                 Duke of York's Theatre
                 Garrick Theatre
                 Golders Green Hippodrome (not in use)
                 Hackney Empire (not in use)
                 Her Majesty's Theatre
                 London Hippodrome ('Talk of the Town')
                 London Palladium
                 Lyceum Theatre
                 Lyric Theatre
                 Macdonald's (Hoxton Hall) (not in use)
                 Old Vic Theatre
                 Palace Theatre
                 Phoenix Theatre
                 Playhouse (BBC)
                 Queen's Theatre
                 Round House
                 Royal Court Theatre
                 St Martin's Theatre
                 Sadler's Wells Theatre
                 Savoy Theatre
                 Shaftesbury Theatre
                 Strand Theatre
                 Theatre Royal, Stratford East
                 Twentieth Century Theatre, Archer Street, Bayswater (not in use)
                 Vaudeville Theatre
                 Victoria Palace
                 Wilton's Music Hall, Whitechapel (not in use)
                 Wimbledon Theatre
                 Wyndham's Theatre

The Coronet Theatre (Gaumont Cinema) Notting Hill Gate is protected in a Conservation area by the Borough of Kensington and Chelsea.

THE ARCHITECTS OF
THE PRESENT THEATRES OF LONDON

(The numbers are those of the theatres in the main sections where
further details of interior decorators, etc., are to be found.)

The West End

1	*The Adelphi Theatre*	Ernest Schaufelberg
2	*The Albery Theatre*	W. G. R. Sprague
3	*The Aldwych Theatre*	W. G. R. Sprague
4	*The Ambassadors Theatre*	W. G. R. Sprague
5	*The Apollo Theatre*	Lewen Sharp
6	*The Cambridge Theatre*	Wimperis, Simpson and Guthrie
7	*The Coliseum*	Frank Matcham
8	*The Comedy Theatre*	Thomas Verity
		Redesigned interior (1955), Cecil Masey and Alester MacDonald
9	*Covent Garden, The Royal Opera House*	Sir Edward Barry
10	*The Criterion Theatre*	Thomas Verity
11	*Drury Lane, The Theatre Royal*	Exterior (1812), Benjamin Wyatt Interior (1922, reconstruction), F. Emblin-Walker and F. Edward Jones
12	*The Duchess Theatre*	Ewen Barr
13	*The Duke of York's Theatre*	Walter Emden
14	*The Fortune Theatre*	Ernest Schaufelberg
15	*The Garrick Theatre*	Walter Emden
16	*The Globe Theatre*	W. G. R. Sprague
17	*Haymarket, The Theatre Royal*	Exterior (1821), John Nash Interior (1904 reconstruction), C. Stanley Peach
18	*Her Majesty's Theatre*	C. J. Phipps
19	*The London Casino*	Edward A. Stone
20	*The London Palladium*	Frank Matcham
21	*The Lyric Theatre*	C. J. Phipps
22	*The May Fair Theatre*	George Beech
23	*The New London Theatre*	Exterior Paul Tortkovic Interior Michael Percival
24	*The Palace Theatre*	T. E. Collcutt and G. H. Holloway
25	*The Phoenix Theatre*	Sir Giles Gilbert Scott, Bertie Crewe and Cecil Masey
26	*The Piccadilly Theatre*	Bertie Crewe and Edward A. Stone
27	*The Prince of Wales' Theatre*	Robert Cromie

28	*The Queen's Theatre*	W. G. R. Sprague (1959 reconstruction), Westwood, Sons and Partners
29	*The Regent Theatre*	George A. Mitchell (as the Great Hall, Polytechnic) Reconstructed by F. J. Wills, 1927
30	*The Royal Court Theatre*	Walter Emden and W. R. Crewe (Partially redesigned interior, 1952), Robert Cromie
31	*The Royalty Theatre*	Lewis Solomon, Kaye and Partners
32	*The St Martin's Theatre*	W. G. R. Sprague
33	*The Savoy Theatre*	Frank A. Tugwell
34	*The Shaftesbury Theatre*	Bertie Crewe
35	*The Strand Theatre*	W. G. R. Sprague
36	*The Vaudeville Theatre*	Exterior (1891), C. J. Phipps Interior (1925 reconstruction), Robert Atkinson
37	*The Victoria Palace*	Frank Matcham
38	*The Westminster Theatre*	Arnold Dunbar-Smith (1966 alterations and extension), John and Sylvia Reid
39	*The Whitehall Theatre*	Edward A. Stone
40	*The Windmill Theatre*	Howard Jones (1965–6 reconstructed as Cinema and Casino) Anthony Wylson and Muray Waterston
41	*Wyndham's Theatre*	W. G. R. Sprague

The Outer Ring

1	*The Greenwich Theatre*	Brian Meeking
2	*The Lyric Theatre, Hammersmith*	Frank Matcham (demolished awaiting rebuilding)
3	*The Mermaid Theatre*	Elidir L. W. Davies
4	*The Old Vic*	Rudolph Cabanel Interior (1950 reconstructed), Douglas W. Rowntree
5	*The Open Air Theatre*	
6	*The Round House*	Robert Stephenson (1968 interior reconstructed as a theatre), Bickerdyke, Allen, Rich and Partners
7	*Sadler's Wells Theatre*	F. G. M. Chancellor (Redesigned proscenium 1959), Hope Bagenal
8	*The Shaw Theatre*	Elidir L. W. Davies
9	The Theatre Royal, Stratford	James George Buckle
10	*Wimbledon Theatre*	Cecil Masey and Roy Young
11	*The Young Vic*	William Howell

Club Theatres

1   *The Arts*   P. Morley Horder
2   *The Players*   ———

Otherwise Engaged

1   *The Carlton Theatre*   Frank T. Verity and Samuel Beverley
2   *The Dominion*   William and T. R. Milburn
    Theatre
3   *The Leicester*   Andrew Mather
    Square Theatre   Interior (1968 as a cinema), Mannering
                             and Steele
4   *The London*   Frank Matcham
    Hippodrome   Redesigned as The Talk of the Town
                             (1958), George Pine
5   *The London*   Exterior, E. J. Morley
    Pavilion   Interior (1934 as a cinema), F. G. M.
                             Chancellor with Frank Matcham
6   *The Lyceum Theatre*   Exterior (1834) Samuel Beazley
                             Interior (1904) Bertie Crewe
7   *The Playhouse*   Exterior (1882) Fowler and Hill
                             Interior (1907) Detmar Blow and
                             Fernand Billerey
8   *The Prince Charles*   Carl Fisher and Associates
    Theatre   Interior (1968–9 as a cinema), Carlo S.
                             Biskupek
9   *The Saville Theatre*   T. P. Bennett and Sons with Bertie
                             Crewe
                             Interior (1969–70 as a cinema),
                             William Ryder and Associates

ALPHABETICAL LIST OF ARCHITECTS

Allen—see Bickerdyke
Atkinson, Robert   *Vaudeville* (Interior)
Bagenal, Hope   *Sadler's Wells* (Reconstruction)
Barr, Ewen   *Duchess*
Barry, Sir Edward   *Covent Garden*
Beazley, Samuel   *Lyceum* (Exterior)
Beech, George   *May Fair*
Bennett, T. P. and Sons   *Saville* (as Theatre)
Beverley, Samuel   *Carlton*
Bickerdyke, Allen, Rich   *Round House* (Interior as
  and Partners   Theatre)
Billerey, Fernand—see Blow
Biskupek, Carlo S.   *Prince Charles* (Interior as
                               Cinema)
Blow and Fernand Billerey   *Playhouse* (Interior)
Buckle, James George   *Theatre Royal*, Stratford
Cabanel, Rudolph   *Old Vic*
Chancellor, F. G. M.   *Sadler's Wells, London Pavilion*
                               (Interior)
Collcutt, T. E.   *Palace*
Crewe, Bertie   *Phoenix, Piccadilly, Princes,
                               Saville, Lyceum* (Interior)
Crewe, W. R.   *Royal Court*
Cromie, Robert   *Prince of Wales', Royal Court*
                               (Reconstruction)

Davies, Elidir L. W.	*Mermaid, Shaw*
Dunbar-Smith, Arnold	*Westminster*
Emblin-Walker, J.	*Drury Lane* (Interior)
Emden, Walter	*Duke of York's, Garrick, Royal Court*
Fisher, Carl and Associates	*Prince Charles* (as Theatre)
Fowler and Hill	*Playhouse* (Exterior)
Gough, D. A.	*Hampstead Theatre Club*
Guthrie—see Wimperis	
Hill—see Fowler	
Holloway, G. H.	*Palace*
Horder, P. Morley	*Arts*
Howell, William	*Young Vic*
Jones, F. Edward	*Drury Lane* (Interior)
Jones, Howard	*Windmill*
Kaye—see Solomon	
MacDonald, Alester	*Comedy* (Reconstruction)
Mannering and Steele	*Leicester Square* (Cinema interior)
Masey, Cecil	*Comedy* (Reconstruction), *Phoenix*, Wimbledon
Matcham, Frank	*Coliseum, London Palladium, Victoria Palace, London Hippodrome, London Pavilion* (Interior), *Lyric*, Hammersmith
Mather, Andrew	*Leicester Square* (First Cinema)
Meeking, Brian	*Greenwich*
Millburn, William and T. R.	*Dominion*
Mitchell, George A.	*Regent* (as Polytechnic Great Hall)
Morley, E. J.	*London Pavilion* (Exterior)
Nash, John	*Haymarket* (Exterior)
Peach, C. Stanley	*Haymarket* (Interior)
Percival, Michael	*New London* (Interior)
Phipps, C. J.	*Her Majesty's, Lyric, Vaudeville* (Exterior)
Pine, George	*London Hippodrome* (Interior as Talk of the Town)
Reid, John and Sylvia	*Westminster* (Reconstruction)
Rich—see Bickerdyke	
Rowntree, Douglas W.	*Old Vic* (Reconstruction)
Ryder, William and Associates	*Saville* (Interior as two cinemas)
Schaufelberg, Ernest	*Adelphi, Fortune*
Scott, Sir Giles Gilbert	*Phoenix*
Sharp, Lewen	*Apollo*
Simpson—see Wimperis	
Solomon, Lewis Kaye and Partners	*Royalty*
Sprague, W. G. R.	*Aldwych, Ambassadors, Globe, New, Queen's, St Martin's, Strand, Wyndham's*
Steel—see Manning	
Stephenson, Robert	*Round House* (Exterior)
Stone, Edward A.	*London Casino, Piccadilly, Whitehall*

Tortkovic, Paul	*New London* (Exterior)
Tugwell, Frank A.	*Savoy*
Verity, Frank T.	*Carlton, Regent* (Exterior)
Verity, Thomas	*Comedy, Criterion*
Waterston, Muray—see Wylson	
Westwood, Sons and Partners	*Queen's* (Reconstruction)
Wills, F. J.	*Regent* (Reconstruction)
Wimperis, Simpson and Guthrie	*Cambridge*
Wyatt, Benjamin	*Drury Lane* (Exterior)
Wylson, Anthony and Muray Waterston	*Windmill* (as Cinema and Casino)
Young, Roy	*Wimbledon*